Working It Out

Working It Out

23 Women Writers, Artists, Scientists,
and Scholars Talk About Their Lives and Work

EDITED BY

Sara Ruddick and Pamela Daniels

With a foreword by Adrienne Rich

Pantheon Books

NEW YORK

Library of Congress Cataloging in Publication Data
Main entry under title:

Working It Out.

    CONTENTS: Hamod, K. K. Finding New Forms.—Lyndon, A. A. Juxtapositions.—Rorty, A. Dependency, Individuality, and Work. [etc.]
    1. Women artists—Biography. 2. Women authors—Biography. 3. Women scientists—Biography. 4. Women college teachers—Biography. I. Ruddick, Sara, 1935– II. Daniels, Pamela, 1937–

HQ1123.W64   301.41′2′0922   [B]   76-54624
ISBN 0-394-40936-1

Design by Kenneth Miyamoto

Manufactured in the United States of America

FIRST EDITION

Grateful acknowledgment is made to the following for permission to reprint previously published material:

Julian Bach Literary Agency, Inc.: Excerpts from "In Search of Our Mothers' Gardens" by Alice Walker. Copyright © 1974 by Alice Walker. First published in *Ms.* Magazine.

The Blacksmith Press: For "On Refusing Your Invitation to Come to Dinner" by Celia Gilbert. Copyright © 1976 by Celia Gilbert.

Chemical & Engineering News: Excerpt from letter from T. J. McGauley which appeared in December 7, 1970 issue of *Chemical & Engineering News*.

College English: Excerpt from "Women and the Literary Curriculum" by Elaine Showalter from *College English*, May 1971. Copyright by National Council of English.

Candida Donadio & Associates, Inc.: Excerpt from "No Important Woman Writer" by Hortense Calisher, which first appeared in *Mademoiselle*, February 1970. Copyright © 1970 by Hortense Calisher.

Susan Griffin: Excerpt from the transcript of a seminar on Lesbians and Literature at the Modern Language Association, San Francisco, December 1975, published in *Sinister Wisdom*, vol. 1, no. 2 (Fall 1976).

Harper & Row, Publishers, Inc.: Brief quotation from "The Munich Mannequins," Copyright © 1963, and "Stings," Copyright © 1965, by Sylvia Plath, from *Ariel* by Sylvia Plath, Copyright © 1965 by Ted Hughes.

Houghton Mifflin Company: Two lines from "Housewife" by Anne Sexton, from *All My Pretty Ones*. Copyright © 1961, 1962 by Anne Sexton.

The New York Times: Excerpt from an interview with Muhammad Ali, in June 29, 1975 issue of *The New York Times*. Copyright © 1975 by The New York Times Company.

Tillie Olsen: "One Out of Twelve: Women Who Are Writers in Our Century" by Tillie Olsen, from *College English*, October 1972. Copyright © 1972 by Tillie Olsen. In expanded form, this essay is to be included in *Silences*, a collection of Tillie Olsen's essays, to be published by Delta Books and Delacorte Press in 1977.

Oxford University Press: Brief excerpt from "God's Grandeur," from *Poems of Gerald Manley Hopkins*, 4th Ed., edited by W. H. Gardiner and H. H. MacKenzie.

The Real Paper: For "Birthday Poem" by Celia Gilbert, reprinted from the December 20, 1976 issue. Copyright © 1976 by Celia Gilbert.

Russell Volkening, Inc.: Excerpts from "Silences" by Tillie Olsen, which first appeared in *Harper's* Magazine, October 1965 issue. Copyright © 1965 by Tillie Olsen.

Scholastic Magazines, Inc.: Quote from Cartier-Bresson from *Images of Man*, Series 2, published by Scholastic Magazine, Inc., in cooperation with the International Fund for Concerned Photographers, Inc., pp. 76 and 82.

Small Moon, published by the Poetry Cooperative of Boston: For "Little Devil" by Celia Gilbert, reprinted from the February 1976 issue. Copyright © 1976 by Celia Gilbert.

Diana Trilling: Excerpt from a speech at a Radcliffe-sponsored seminar, "Women's Liberation, Myth or Reality," June 1971. © Diana Trilling. Originally published in the *Saturday Review*.

Naomi Weisstein: For a revised version of "How can a little girl like you teach a great big class of men? the Chairman Said: I was doing just fine until you asked me that question, I replied: Or Women/Scientists, Social Expectation, and Self-esteem," published by Les Femmes Publishing Company, Millbrae, California. Copyright © 1974 and 1976 by Naomi Weisstein. Earlier versions were presented at the University of Chicago, 1968, Yale University, February 1970, and at the June 1974 conference of the American Societies for Experimental Biology.

Wesleyan University Press: Brief quotation from "Falling" by James Dickey.

The Yale Review: For "Dependency, Individuality and Work" by Amelie Rorty. Copyright © 1971 by Yale University. The original version of this essay, entitled "Dependents: The Trials of Success," appeared in *The Yale Review*, 1971.

Susan Yankowitz: Excerpt from "Terminal" by Susan Yankowitz from *Three Works by the Open Theater*, edited by Karen Malpede, New York: Drama Book Specialists, 1974, p. 57.

Bess who has been fingering a fruit-jar lid—absently, heedlessly dropped it—aimlessly groping across the table, reclaims it again. Lightning in her brain. She releases, grabs, releases, grabs. I can do. Bang! I did that. I can do. I! A look of neanderthal concentration is on her face. That noise! In triumphant astounded joy she clashes the lid down. Bang, slam, whack. Release, grab, slam, bang, bang. Centuries of human drive work in her; human ecstasy of achievement, satisfaction deep and fundamental as sex: *I can do, I use my powers; I! I!*

Tillie Olsen
Yonnondio: From the Thirties
1935 (published 1974)

. . . modern women who, by force of youth, education, or temperament, are in some degree out of touch with the traditions of status received from the barbarian culture, and in whom there is, perhaps, an undue reversion to the impulse of self-expression and workmanship—these are touched with a sense of grievance too vivid to leave them at rest.

Thorstein Veblen
The Theory of the Leisure Class
1899

Contents

Acknowledgments

IN A COLLECTIVE EFFORT such as this one there are many to thank. We are grateful to all the friends and colleagues who contributed ideas, encouragement, and an attentive ear to this undertaking.

Linda Brownrigg originally conceived of a set of memoirs in which individual women would examine their graduate school experience and describe the difficulty of writing a dissertation that is both a meaningful piece of work and the fulfillment of a professional requirement. Her idea and the essays she engaged set this book in motion.

Evelyn Fox Keller was an active editorial participant in the project from the start; she secured contributors, read manuscripts, and offered sound counsel. Victoria Steinitz and Marilyn Young were there for us, with emotional and editorial support, whenever we needed them. Anne Lasoff proofread the manuscript and commented on each essay. Margaret Pennace and Carol Redford typed the essays and gently kept us in touch with the "reader's point of view." Barbara Plumb, Amy Huntoon, and Phyllis Benjamin at Pantheon have been enthusiastic and patient critics.

We want to thank our contributors, almost all of whom wrote for us before we could guarantee publication or recompense. In response to our request, they have written *personally* of their efforts to accomplish their work. We neither imposed nor expected a uniform ideological stand, feminist or otherwise. We are especially grateful to Tillie Olsen, who at the outset allowed us to use her name and her writing to clarify our ideals, and Adrienne Rich, who in response to our manuscript has written provocatively of the community of women as the enabling condition of our work. With this book we hope to have contributed to the community of women. We know that we have depended upon it.

Finally, there are those who live with us while we work. The self-reliance of our children, Hal and Lizza, and Andrew and Jonny, made our project possible. William Ruddick and Belden Daniels, accustomed to sharing domestic routine and parental responsibility with us, took over completely in hectic times so that we might see our work through, free from the practical cares and constraints of householding. Our families' pleasure in our achievement reminds us that success need not be fearsome, nor "work of one's own" a lonely pursuit.

S.R.
P.D.

October 1976

FOREWORD
Conditions for Work:
The Common World of Women

Thomas Victor

Adrienne Rich

. . . the common world is what we enter when we are born and what we leave behind when we die. It transcends our life-span into past and future alike; it was there before we came and will outlast our brief sojourn into it. It is what we have in common not only with those who live with us, but also with those who were here before and with those who will come after us. But such a common world can survive the coming and going of the generations only to the extent that it appears in public. It is the publicity of the public realm which can absorb and make shine through the centuries whatever men [sic] may want to save from the natural ruin of time.

—Hannah Arendt,
The Human Condition

I

WOMEN BOTH HAVE and have not had a common world. The mere sharing of oppression does not constitute a common world. Our thought and action, insofar as they have taken the form of difference, assertion, or rebellion, have repeatedly been obliterated, or subsumed under "human" history, which means the "publicity of the public realm" created and controlled by men. Our history is the history of a majority of the species, yet the struggles of women for a "human" status have been relegated to footnotes, to the sidelines. Above all, women's relationships with women have been denied or neglected as a force in history.[1]

The essays in this book are parts of a much larger work, which we are still struggling to possess: the long process of making visible the experience of women. The tentativeness, the anxiety, sometimes approaching paralysis, the confusions, described in many of these essays by intelligent, educated, "privileged" women, are themselves evidence of the damage that can be done to creative energy by the lack of a

---

[1] The historian Joan Kelly-Gadol suggests that a feminist view of history is not merely "compensatory history," a parallel to the accepted views of history as male. It means "to look at ages or movements of great social change in terms of their liberation or repression of woman's potential, their import for the advancement of her humanity as well as 'his.' The moment this is done—the moment one assumes that women are a part of humanity in the fullest sense—the period or set of events with which we deal takes on a wholly different character or meaning from the normally accepted one. Indeed, what emerges is a fairly regular pattern of relative loss of status for women in those periods of so-called progressive change." "The Social Relation of the Sexes: Methodological Implications of Women's History," SIGNS, vol. 1, no. 4 (summer, 1976).

sense of continuity, historical validation, community. Most women, it seems, have gone through their travails in a kind of spiritual isolation, alone both in the present and in ignorance of their place in any female tradition. The support of friends, of a women's group, may make survival possible; but it is not enough.

It is quite clear that the universities and the intellectual establishment intend to keep women's experience as far as possible invisible, and women's studies a barely subsidized, condescendingly tolerated ghetto. The majority of women who go through undergraduate and graduate school suffer an intellectual coercion of which they are not even consciously aware. In a world where language and naming are power, silence is oppression, is violence. Writing of the destruction of the civilization of Languedoc by the forces of the Church under Simon de Montfort, Simone Weil reminds us: "Nothing is more cruel to the past than the commonplace which asserts that spiritual values cannot be destroyed by force; on the strength of this belief, civilizations that have been destroyed by force of arms are denied the name of civilization; and there is no risk of our being refuted by the dead."[2]

For spiritual values and a creative tradition to continue unbroken we need concrete artifacts, the work of hands, written words to read, images to look at, a dialogue with brave and imaginative women who came before us. In the false names of love, motherhood, natural law —false because they have not been defined by us to whom they are applied—women in patriarchy have been withheld from building a common world, except in enclaves, or through coded messages.

> The protection and preservation of the world against natural processes are among the toils which need the monotonous performance of daily repeated chores. . . . In old tales and mythological stories it has often assumed the grandeur of heroic fights against overwhelming odds, as in the account of Hercules, whose cleansing of the Augean stables is among the twelve heroic "labors." A similar connotation of heroic deeds requiring great strength and courage and performed in a fighting spirit is manifest in the mediaeval use of the word: labor, *travail, arbeit*. However, the daily fight in which the human body is engaged to keep the world clean and prevent its decay bears little resemblance to heroic deeds; the endurance it needs to repair every day anew the waste of yesterday is not courage, and what makes the effort painful is not danger but its relentless repetition.[3]

---

[2] Simone Weil, *Selected Essays, 1934–1943*, trans. Richard Rees (New York: Oxford University Press, 1962), p. 43.

[3] Hannah Arendt, *The Human Condition* (Chicago: University of Chicago Press, 1958), p. 55.

Hannah Arendt does not call this "woman's work." Yet it is this activity of world-protection, world-preservation, world-repair—the million tiny stitches, the friction of the scrubbing brush, the scouring cloth, the iron across the shirt, the rubbing of cloth against itself to exorcise the stain, the renewal of the scorched pot, the rusted knife-blade, the invisible weaving of a frayed and threadbare family life, the cleaning up of soil and waste left behind by men and children—that we have been charged to do "for love," not merely unpaid, but un-acknowledged by the political philosophers. Women are not described as "working" when we create the essential conditions for the work of men; we are supposed to be acting out of love, instinct, or devotion to some higher cause than self.

Arendt tells us that the Greeks despised all labor of the body neces-sitated by biological needs. It was to spare themselves such labor that men kept slaves—not as a means to cheaper production. "Contempt for laboring, originally arising out of a passionate striving for freedom from necessity and a no less passionate impatience with every effort that left no trace, no monument, no great work worthy of remem-brance, spread with the increasing demands of *polis* life upon the time of the citizens [i.e., males] and its insistence on their abstention from all but political activities."[4]

And, in the aside of a footnote: "Women and slaves belonged and lived together . . . no woman, not even the wife of the household head, lived among her equals—other free women—so that rank depended much less on birth than on 'occupation' or function. . . ." According to the index, this footnote is the last reference to women, on page 73 of a volume of 325 pages on *The Human Condition*, written by a woman.

Every effort that left no trace . . . The efforts of women in labor, giving birth to stillborn children, children who must die of plague or by infanticide; the efforts of women to keep filth and decay at bay, children decently clothed, to produce the clean shirt in which the man walks out daily into the common world of men, the efforts to raise children against the attritions of racist and sexist schooling, drugs, sexual exploitation, the brutalization and killing of barely grown boys in war. There is still little but contempt and indifference for this kind of work, these efforts. (The phrase "wages for housework" has the power to shock today that the phrase "free love" possessed a century ago.)

---

[4] *Ibid.*, pp. 81–83.

II

There is a natural temptation to escape if we can, to close the door behind us on this despised realm which threatens to engulf all women, whether as mothers, or in marriage, or as the invisible, ill-paid sustainers of the professions and social institutions. There is a natural fear that if we do not enter the common world of men, as asexual beings or as "exceptional" women, do not enter it on its terms and obey its rules, we will be sucked back into the realm of servitude, whatever our temporary class status or privileges. This temptation and this fear compromise our powers, divert our energies, form a potent source of "blocks" and of acute anxiety about work.

For if, in trying to join the common world of men, the professions molded by a primarily masculine consciousness, we split ourselves off from the common life of women and deny our female heritage and identity in our work, we lose touch with our real powers and with the essential condition for all fully realized work: community.

Feminism begins but cannot end with the discovery by an individual of her self-consciousness as a woman. It is not, finally, even the recognition of her reasons for anger, or the decision to change her life, go back to school, leave a marriage (though in any individual life such decisions can be momentous and require great courage). Feminism means finally that we renounce our obedience to the fathers and recognize that the world they have described is not the whole world. Masculine ideologies are the creation of masculine subjectivity; they are neither objective, nor value-free, nor inclusively "human." Feminism implies that we recognize fully the inadequacy for us, the distortion, of male-created ideologies, and that we proceed to think, and act, out of that recognition.

In the common world of men, in the professions which the writers of these essays have come to grips with, it takes more than our *individual* talent and intelligence to think and act further. In denying the validity of women's experience, in pretending to stand for "the human," masculine subjectivity tries to force us to name our truths in an alien language, to dilute them; we are constantly told that the "real" problems, the ones worth working on, are those men have defined, that the problems we need to examine are trivial, unscholarly, nonexistent. We are urged to separate the "personal" (our entire exis-

tence as women) from the "scholarly" or "professional." Several of
the women who contribute to this book have described the outright
insults and intellectual sabotage they encountered as women in graduate school. But more insidious may be the sabotage which appears as
paternal encouragement, approval granted for internalizing a masculine subjectivity. As Tillie Olsen puts it in this book, "Not to be able to
come to one's own truth or not to use it in one's writing, even when
telling the truth having to 'tell it slant,' robs one of drive, of conviction, limits potential stature. . . ." Everywhere, women working in the
common world of men are denied that integrity of work and life which
can only be found in an emotional and intellectual connectedness with
ourselves and other women.

More and more, however, women are creating community, sharing
work, and discovering that in the sharing of work our relationships
with each other become larger and more serious. In organizing a
women's self-help clinic or law collective or a writing workshop, in
editing a magazine or creating a center for women's work like the
Women's Building in Los Angeles, in running a press that publishes
"lost" books by women or contemporary work that may be threatening or incomprehensible to male editors, in participating in a women's
prison project or a crisis center, we come to understand at first hand
not only our unmet needs but the resources we can draw on for meeting them even in the face of female poverty, the hostility of institutions, the lack of documentation of our shared past. Susan Griffin has
said that, for a feminist, writing may be solitary but thinking is collective. Any woman who has moved from the playing fields of male
discourse into the realm where women are developing our own descriptions of the world knows the extraordinary sense of shedding, as
it were, the encumbrance of someone else's baggage, of ceasing to
translate. It is not that thinking becomes easy, but that the difficulties
are intrinsic to the work itself rather than to the environment. In the
common world of men, the struggle to make female experience visible
at all—Will they take seriously a thesis on women? Will they let me
teach a course on women? Can I speak bluntly of female experience
without shattering the male egos around me, or being labeled hysterical, castrating?—such struggles assume the status of an intellectual
problem, and the real intellectual problems may not be probed at
all.

Working together as women, consciously creating our networks
even where patriarchal institutions are the ones in which we have to
survive, we can confront the problems of women's relationships, the

mothers we came from, the sisters with whom we were forced to divide the world, the daughters we love and fear. We can challenge and inspirit each other, throw light on one another's blind spots, stand by and give courage at the birth throes of one another's insights. I think of the poet H.D.'s account of the vision she had on the island of Corfu, in the *Tribute to Freud*:

> And there I sat and there is my friend Bryher who has brought me to Greece. I can turn now to her, though I do not budge an inch or break the sustained crystal-gazing at the wall before me. I say to Bryher, "There have been pictures here—I thought they were shadows at first, but they are light, not shadow. They are quite simple objects—but of course it's very strange. I can break away from them now, if I want— it's just a matter of concentrating—what do you think? Shall I stop? Shall I go on?" Bryher says without hesitation, "Go on."
> . . . I had known such extraordinarily gifted and charming people. They had made much of me or they had slighted me and yet neither praise nor neglect mattered in the face of the gravest issues—life, death. . . . And yet, so oddly, I knew that this experience, this writing-on-the-wall before me, could not be shared with anyone except the girl who stood so bravely there beside me. This girl had said without hesi-tation, "Go on." It was she really who had the detachment and integrity of the Pythoness of Delphi. But it was I, battered and dis-sociated . . . who was seeing the pictures, and who was reading the writing or granted the inner vision. Or perhaps, in some sense, we were "seeing" it together, for without her, admittedly, I could not have gone on.[5]

Even for those who would mistrust visionary experience, the episode is revealing as metaphor. The personal relationship helps create the conditions for work (out of her vision H.D. went on to create her great, late, long poems celebrating a matriarchal world and the quests of female heroes); no less does the fact of working together deepen and sustain a personal relationship. "If Chloe likes Olivia and they share a laboratory . . . this of itself will make their friendship more varied and lasting because it will be less personal."[6] By "like" I be-lieve Virginia Woolf (still, in that book, writing more cautiously than later in *Three Guineas*) also meant "love"; for "a laboratory" we can read "the creation of a common world."

Many women have known the figure of the male "mentor" who guides and protects his female student or colleague, tenderly opening doors for her into the common world of men. He seems willing to share his power, to conspire with her in stealing what Celia Gilbert

[5] H. D., *Tribute to Freud* (Oxford: Carcanet Press, 1971), pp. 50–54.
[6] Virginia Woolf, *A Room of One's Own* (London: Hogarth Press, 1929), p. 126.

names in this book "the sacred fire" of work. Yet what can he really bestow but the *illusion* of power, a power stolen, in any case, from the mass of women, over centuries, by men? He can teach her to name her experience in language that may allow her to live, work, perhaps succeed in the common world of men. But he has no key to the powers she might share with other women.

There is also the illusion that if you make your emotional and erotic life with women, it does not matter that your intellectual work is a collaboration with silence and lying about female experience. At a panel of lesbian writers at the Modern Language Association in San Francisco in December 1975, Susan Griffin[7] spoke of the damage we do to ourselves and our work in censoring our own truths:

> I feel that this whole idea of the Muse, of inspiration, is a kind of cop-out. There is something very fascinating going on with a writer's psyche when you are undergoing a silence, an inability to write. Each silence and each eruption into speech constitute a kind of struggle in the life of a writer. . . . The largest struggle around silence in my life has had to do with the fact that I am a woman and a lesbian. When I recognized my feelings as a woman, when I recognized my anger as a woman, suddenly my writing was transformed—suddenly I had a material, a subject-matter. . . . And then a few years later I found myself unhappy with my writing, unhappy with the way I expressed myself, unable to speak; I wrote in a poem, *Words do not come to my mouth anymore.* And I happened also . . . to be censoring the fact that I was a lesbian. I thought that I was doing this because of the issue of child custody, and that was and still is a serious issue. But I wasn't acknowledging how important it was to me, both as a writer and as a human being, to be able to . . . write about my feelings as a lesbian.
>
> In fact, I think that writers are always dealing with taboos of one sort or another; if they are not taboos general in society, you may just have a fear in your private life of perceiving some truth because of its implications, and that will stop you from writing. . . . But when we come to the taboo of lesbianism, this is one which is most loaded for everyone, even those who are not lesbians. Because the fact of love between women . . . is one which affects every event in this society, psychic and political and sociological. And for a writer, the most savage censor is oneself.

---

[7] Susan Griffin's works include: *Voices,* a play (Old Westbury, N.Y.: Feminist Press, 1973); "Rape: The All-American Crime," in Jo Freeman, ed., *Women: A Feminist Perspective* (Stanford, Calif.: Mayfield Publishing Co., 1975); *Like the Iris of an Eye,* poems (New York: Harper & Row, 1976); *The Sink,* short stories (San Lorenzo, Calif.: Shameless Hussy Press, 1974); *Letter: A Cycle of Poems* (Emeryville, Calif.: Effie's Press, 1974); and articles and lectures on motherhood and feminism, abortion, women, and the creative process.

The whole question of what it means or might mean to work as a lesbian might have occupied an entire essay in this book. Of past women whose thought and work have remained visible in history, an enormous number have been lesbians, yet because of the silence and denial that has enveloped lesbianism, we learn little from women's biographies about the relation of their work to their relationships with women or to the social taboos they lived among. One writer in this book mourns that "there was only one Alice B. Toklas." But in fact women's support to women *has* been there all along, lifetime or long-term comradeships. For many women, struggling for economic survival in the common world of men, these relationships have had to be dissimulated, at what cost to the work (let alone the relationships) we cannot begin to know. Every lesbian has been forced to walk past the distorting mirrors of homophobia before she could get down to the real problems of her work. Every lesbian artist knows that when she attempts to embody lesbian sexuality in her work she runs the risk of having it perceived pornographically, if it is not simply denied visibility. When a lesbian feels she may have to choose between writing or painting her truths and keeping her child, she is flung back on the most oppressive ground of maternal guilt in conflict with creative work. The question of economic survival, of keeping one's job, is terribly real, but the more terrible questions lie deeper where a woman is forced, or permits herself, to lead a censored life.

III

In thinking about the issues of women and work raised in this book, I turned to Hannah Arendt's *The Human Condition* to see how a major political philosopher of our time, a woman greatly respected in the intellectual establishment, had spoken to the theme. I found her essay illuminating, not so much for what it says, but for what it is. The issue of women as the laborers in reproduction, of women as workers in production, of the relationship of women's unpaid labor in the home to the separation between "private" and "public" spheres, of the woman's body as commodity—these questions were not raised for the first time in the 1960s and 1970s; they had already been documented in the 1950s when *The Human Condition* was being written. Arendt barely alludes, usually in a footnote, to Marx and Engels' engagement with this theme; and she writes as if the work of Olive Schreiner, Charlotte Perkins Gilman, Emma Goldman, Jane Addams, to name only a few writers, had never existed. The withholding of women from participation in the *vita activa*, the "common world," and the connection of this with reproductivity, is something from which she does not so much turn her eyes as stare straight through unseeing. This "great work" is thus a kind of failure for which masculine ideology has no name, precisely because in terms of that ideology it is successful, at the expense of truths the ideology considers irrelevant. To read such a book, by a woman of large spirit and great erudition, can be painful, because it embodies the tragedy of a female mind nourished on male ideologies. In fact, the loss is ours, because Arendt's desire to grasp deep moral issues is the kind of concern we need to build a common world which will amount to more than "life-styles." The power of male ideology to possess such a female mind, to disconnect it as it were from the female body which encloses it and which it encloses, is nowhere more striking than in Arendt's lofty and crippled book.

Women's minds cannot grow to full stature, or touch the real springs of our power to alter reality, on a diet of masculine ideology. This is not the same thing as saying that we can use nothing of these ideologies, or their methods, or that we need not understand them. But the common world of men cannot give us what we need, and parts of it are poisoning us. Miriam Schapiro, in this book, describes the process through which she begins to work: filling sheets of paper with smeared paint, images created "freely, mindlessly," going back to that place in childhood where she simply painted and was happy. To her husband, this appeared as "deprofessionalizing" herself. Yet the very concept of "professionalism," tainted as it is with the separation between personal life and work, with a win-or-lose mentality and the gauging of success by public honors and market prices, needs a thorough revaluation by women. Forty years back Virginia Woolf was asking:

> What is this "civilization" in which we find ourselves? What are these ceremonies and why should we take part in them? What are these professions and why should we make money out of them? Where in short is it leading, the procession of the sons of educated men?[8]

Her answer was that it is leading to war, to elitism, to exploitation and the greed for power; in our own time we can also add that it has clearly been leading to the ravagement of the nonhuman living world. Instead of the concept of "professionalism," we need, perhaps, a vision of work akin to that described by Simone Weil in her "Theoretical Picture of a Free Society":

[8] Virginia Woolf, *Three Guineas* (1938; paperback ed., New York: Harcourt Brace Jovanovich, Harbinger Books, 1966), p. 63.

A clear view of what is possible and what impossible, what is easy and what difficult, of the labors that separate the project from its accomplishment—this alone does away with insatiable desires and vain fears; from this and not from anything else proceed moderation and courage, virtues without which life is nothing but a disgraceful frenzy. Besides, the source of any kind of virtue lies in the shock produced by the human intelligence being brought up against a matter devoid of lenience and of falsity.[9]

If we conceive of feminism as more than a frivolous label, if we conceive of it as an ethics, a methodology, a more complex way of thinking about, thus more responsibly acting upon, the conditions of human life, we need a self-knowledge which can only develop through a steady, passionate attention to *all* female experience. I cannot imagine a feminist evolution leading to radical change in the private/political realm of gender that is not rooted in the conviction that all women's lives are important; that the lives of men cannot be understood by burying the lives of women; and that to make visible the full meaning of women's experience, to reinterpret knowledge in terms of that experience, is now the most important task of thinking.

If this is so, we cannot work alone. We had better face the fact that our hope of thinking at all, against the force of a maimed and maiming world-view, depends on seeking and giving our allegiance to a community of women co-workers. And beyond the exchange and criticism of work, we have to ask ourselves how we can make the conditions for work more possible, not just for ourselves but for each other. This is not a question of generosity. It is not generosity that makes women in community support and nourish each other. It is rather what Whitman called the "hunger for equals"—the desire for a context in which our own strivings will be amplified, quickened, lucidified, through those of our peers.

We also, of course, need community with our past. Women's art and thought and action will continue to be seen as deviant, its true meaning distorted or buried, as long as women's work can be dismissed as "exceptional," an interesting footnote to the major texts. Or, it will be encouraged for its timidities and punished for its daring. This is obvious to women who have tried to work along seriously feminist lines in the established professions. But even before the work exists, long before praise or attack, the very form it will assume, the courage on which it can draw, the sense of potential direction it may take, require—given the politics of our lives and of creation itself—more

---

[9] Simone Weil, *Oppression and Liberty*, trans. Arthur Wills and John Petrie (Amherst, Mass.: University of Massachusetts Press, 1973), p. 87.

than the gifts of the individual woman or her immediate contemporaries. We need access to the female past.

The problem, finally, is not that of who does housework and child care, whether or not one can find a life companion who will share in the sustenance and repair of daily life—crucial as these may be in the short run. It is a question of the community we are reaching for in our work and on which we can draw; whom we envision as our hearers, our co-creators, our challengers; who will urge us to take our work further, more seriously, than we had dared; on whose work we can build. Women *have* done these things for each other, sought each other in community, even if only in enclaves, often through correspondence, for centuries. Denied space in the universities, the scientific laboratories, the professions, we have devised our networks. We must not be tempted to trade the possibility of enlarging and strengthening those networks, and of extending them to more and more women, for the illusion of power and success as "exceptional" or "privileged" women in the professions.

Adrienne Rich

INTRODUCTION

WOMEN HAVE always worked. Throughout the world and down the years they have worked because they had to. All kinds of women everywhere have matter-of-factly taken on the necessary labor of survival and subsistence—childbearing, family caring, field tending, wage earning. There is nothing new in women working. What is new is that women in increasing numbers are *choosing* to work and that the work they are choosing to do is not justified solely by its contribution to the well-being of their families.

The choice of more and more women to earn an independent livelihood, pursue a career, or develop a work of their own is partly a result of technological and political changes: effective contraception, a longer life span, higher education, and most recently the revival of feminism. But the phenomenon of women actively, even urgently, claiming the right to do significant work is neither temporary nor superficial; it raises the even larger issue of the place of meaningful work in adult life for all of us, men as well as women.

When Freud was asked by some intrepid questioner what the healthy person should be able to do well, his deceptively simple answer was "to love and to work." Erik H. Erikson has extended and refined Freud's prescription in his formulation of intimacy and generativity as the two central developmental tasks of adulthood. We have always recognized women's work when it is expressed in the care of children or in domestic occupation, but for women as for men, generative activity includes creative, productive work in one's own right as well as on behalf of others, in the world as well as in the home. It includes the development of the capacity for effectiveness, responsibility—and the exercise of power. It refers to what one *does* with who one has thus far become—how one engages and expresses one's identity. The underlying question of this book is: *What is the place of chosen work in women's lives?*

These papers are a collection of autobiographic accounts by women of the place of our work in our lives, reflections on our particular efforts to define and pursue "work of our own" and to overcome the outer and inner obstacles to the legitimacy of such work. Yet these essays do not pertain to women alone. They are resonant with a human need to make a difference, to make one's mark in the world by producing with dignity something of use to others. The pride of Studs Terkel's stonemason and the ambition of the graduate student in physics are not so different as we have assumed. The accounts in this book are offered in the hope that at some time most women, most people, will be able to share both that pride and that ambition.

The women who have contributed to this book are writers, scholars, scientists, or artists. While each of us has made a commitment to some kind of autonomous creative work—to a "work of our own"—that work is not always identical with the jobs we hold. We are—or have been—mothers, political organizers, office workers, editors, nursery school teachers. Most of us teach in universities. The task of sustaining work of one's own, work not determined by financial needs, by parental or political obligations, or by participation in the paid labor force—indeed, sometimes at odds with these—provides special relevances and dilemmas for women. In a patriarchal world, female aspiration toward autonomous creative work is all too often dismissed, even denigrated, while women's initiative and competence outside the home are perceived as threatening anomalies. We ourselves have been fearful or reluctant to acknowledge our stake in our work, our pleasure in it. Our persistent inability to see ourselves as purposive workers is both cause and symptom of that "vivid grievance," that sense of stagnation and diffuse powerlessness, experienced by many women in our culture.

It goes without saying that artists, scientists, writers, and scholars are not the only ones who have committed themselves to autonomous creative work; however, in trying to clarify our own volatile relationship to our work as well as our sense of its developmental importance, we found it natural to turn to friends whose work resembled ours. Our project grew as projects do, more or less accidentally and spontaneously. The emphasis on intellectual and artistic work—unlike our original concern with *chosen work*—was not deliberate. We hope that women and men in all professions will make public the kind of reflection we have attempted here. In the meantime, we have decided to respect the fortuitous limitation of the works represented in these accounts, in the belief that variety of experience within a limited range of chosen work may be more illuminating than wide and obvious variation among many kinds of professions.

On the face of it, the work that we do—writing, research, the arts—seems especially conducive to combination with the responsibilities and roles that have traditionally occupied women. Unbound by the eight-hour day, the five-day week, most of us have been able to design a flexible structure for our work lives. Academic routine in particular releases those of us who teach from professional obligations during the summer, and throughout the year allows us to be at home during the domestic hours of the day. Those who work in the theater or in a laboratory or putting out a journal know a special variation of this work flexibility, in which scheduled obligations tend to come in spurts which, although completely disruptive of private life while they last, nonetheless alternate with recuperative periods for reflection, sociability, or family involvement.

Yet the freedom attending this flexible work structure is often illusory. Once committed to the work we have chosen, we often find that it becomes more time-consuming and unpredictably engrossing, more threatening to our private lives, than the formal obligations of our employment. The typical contributor to this book, moreover, has taken primary responsibility for raising two or more children, has a paid job, and has accepted an expanding number of professional, political, and social commitments. Within these circumstances she must constantly improvise a form for her work—which may feel more like a house of cards ever in need of repair than a dependable, comforting structure.

Furthermore, to the extent that much of our work is considered "feminine"—as many view teaching, or the arts, for example—or when our schedules seem to allow us a "woman's life," we are tempted to put ourselves down. Our work seems insufficiently hard or professional; if unpaid, it is somehow not serious—mere poetry. In the face of pervasive regard for the "masculine," as well as the careerism and sheer commercialism that continuously prejudice our judgments of human worth, we have had to learn to recognize and accept and respect the authenticity and purpose in our work.

To care about our work at all renders us unfeminine in the eyes of some. A few writers, notably two scientists and a sculptor who are engaged in work considered demonstrably masculine, remind us that at worst, our society tenaciously protects the division between "male" and "female" work, and that at best, we ourselves are not free of damaging sexual stereotypes. It is not surprising, then, that even in lives apparently permissive of chosen work, we hear of the difficulty of reconciling traditional duties with personal ambition, our need for concentration with domestic interference, and our wish to serve others with our standards of independent—even lonely—personal achievement.

For the most part, our kind of work requires that we work alone, often without deadlines or quotas or commissions to prod us. We have had to create for ourselves a livable—indeed, a workable—working day and work life. Many of us have become preoccupied with finding space and time to work, only to discover that, once alone, we turn anxiously away from the empty canvas, the blank page, the unphotographed scene. Some of us have written here of our fears—fear of success, exposure, or failure; fear of losing ourselves in our work or of sharing it; fear of beginning or of completing a piece of work. Others have insisted on the pleasure of work, and yet underscore the inordinate difficulty in letting their work be pleasurable. Still others remind us all that creative work often requires that we confront our "devil's thoughts," our ambivalent selves, and that we include the "dreamer," the "amateur," the "comedienne," in our most serious work.

Many women have discovered with surprise and happiness their need for colleagues, who have facilitated and enlarged the scope of their work and assuaged the loneliness; and in the struggle to create and sustain a positive tension between competition and cooperation, between criticism and support, they have confronted and resolved aggravated fantasies of winning and losing, success and failure, that autonomous creative work is heir to.

The writers in this book are women reporting from mid-life on the dilemmas and pleasures their work has afforded them. Almost all of us are near forty. Educated in the 1950s, at the height of the feminine mystique, we are a pivotal generation. The war in Vietnam, and political movements related to it, undermined the professional careerism of a few of us while giving others new occasions for activity and courage. We encountered the women's movement late, usually in our thirties. Our responses to it have varied. Some of us have welcomed new friendships with other women—we discovered that we were not alone in our ambition or ambivalence. Some of us have begun to question individual, hard-earned token achievement and to emphasize the struggles and rights of all women. Some of us have found that a new identification with and appreciation of women have transformed both the content and the aims of our work. Some of us have begun, or returned, to work—or renovated our private lives. All of us in one way or another have had to relearn our pasts. We have had to re-evaluate our purposes in working and re-review our commitments to our work and to those we love. Raised consciousness, whatever its ultimate value, has brought vulnerability and has invited risk. It has insisted on change.

Our stories are the evidence that significant changes can and do occur in adult lives—after we are supposed to be "grown up" and "settled down." Those of us near forty write as if the shape of our working lives is now fairly clear; yet the three women writing in their early fifties report considerable change in their forties. At the same time, our one younger (thirty-two-year-old) writer, describing her mother, now sixty-two, reminds us of the correspondence of our lives with those of women of all ages, many of whom were artists in the private spheres of home, garden, or neighborhood for want of a room or time of their own in which to produce more public works.

We who have contributed to this book are fortunate women in that whatever the variable economic circumstances of our childhoods or current lives, as a group we have had—or have been able to create for ourselves—the margin of freedom that chosen work requires. It takes discipline and even courage to create one's own work space and time; nonetheless, each of us is fortunate to know what it means to have a "room of one's own" and the ability to buy time to go into it.

In one way or another, many of these accounts acknowledge the disparity between the freedom represented by the rooms we call our own and the various restrictions, abuses, and oppressions in the world, sometimes even in the home just outside the door. Some of our writers tell of the insult and abuse they met with as they stepped outside that room to take their place in the world. For others, the conflict between work as organized by society and work as compelled by the heart is paramount. For a few, work and politics are inseparable. Politics— the attempt to redress social and economic inequities—is the work. And the work—a thesis, a radio program, a painting, a quilt, or a play—is politics. These writers address, on behalf of the rest of us, the haunting problem of privilege and the task of relating the work it allows to the lives of others.

In Doris Lessing's *Golden Notebook*, Anna asks: How can I write in a world in which so many are suffering? For many women, even to hear that question arouses guilt and inhibits the initiative to work. Many of us have asked similar questions of ourselves in moments of self-searching, and of others in moments of envy. No matter what the discomfort, women must ask these questions. We who have just begun to work with confidence and pleasure do not ignore those whose work provides them with little pleasure or purpose of any kind. It is only when most people can work with pride and pleasure that women, without guilt and yet without rejecting their history of service and care, can happily do their own work.

Although we are a distinct group of women by virtue of our age and the particular kinds of work we do, we hope our accounts will have relevance for other women in other circumstances. By describing our conflicts about work and our resistances to it, by relating not only instances of outrageous institutional discrimination but our own inner prejudices against ourselves, we may illuminate the generic aspects of any individual woman's ambivalence and confusion. Most important, in underscoring the self-discovery, the pleasure and the accomplishment that work has afforded us, we can also insist on the appropriateness of meaningful work in any life.

Because we are concerned with the value and purpose of work rather than with its ostensive reward, with discipline and commitment rather than with success, we did not particularly seek well-known women to write for this book. We did seek out women who had known self-consciousness, conflict and significant change in their work lives. We looked for women who wrote about, wrote for, identified with, women. Neither of these characteristics seems to augur well for conventional or visible success in a competitive, hierarchical male world.

Nevertheless, the women who contributed to this book have been successful in more than one sense of the word. Most hold the advanced degree appropriate to their work. Many have full-time positions with rank, tenure and salary appropriate to their age. Some have published books, won awards, edited a prestigious magazine, or served as college trustee. More than one might be called "famous." Contributors were not asked to stress their achievements although they were free to do so. Yet, even the unequivocally successful talk little of their "success." On the contrary. One eminent painter says, "I was tapped for the work I did . . . I was a 'token' woman in the male world. There was some slight satisfaction in that," and then proceeds to tell of years of self-doubt, hours of anxiety alone in her studio. Another woman whose *vita* would show a book, a university teaching award, numerous articles, conferences national and international, a guest editorship and jet-set lecturing, tells us, "I now feel free to do my own work. What has become difficult is determining exactly what that work should be." Still another, who begins with an account of a lecture she gave as one of a series of "distinguished scientists," does not dwell on that or on any other of her many successes; rather, she tells of an intensely painful formative experience, of years of defeat. Could it be that these women don't believe in success or in its trappings? Women have no history of success. We have not hoped to get it, are said to fear it; perhaps when it comes, we don't take it seriously. Then again, women have not been taught to keep the stiff upper lip, the face, the front; perhaps successful women are not afraid to reveal the confusions, timidities, and failures that are a part of all lives.

Whatever the reasons, we are pleased that success does not star in this book. There is already at least one good book about women and success and we hope that there will be more. But this book is not *about* success. It is about the conflicts and pleasures of work, about the place of purposeful, generative work in the adult years of women's lives. To be able to work with confidence and pleasure is not necessarily coincident and certainly not synonymous with public success and acclaim. It is possible to succeed at work that one despises and to take pleasure in work that does not result in tangible achievement or individual renown.

Though anon. may have been a woman, we have no wish to see women remain anonymous. Respect and recognition are necessary for self-esteem. At the same time, we do not wish to contribute to another American mystique. The mystique of success, which confounds and destroys the initiative of all too many of us—men as well as women— has intensified our struggles to find work of our own and to respect the work of others.

While putting this book together, we asked Tillie Olsen for permission to reprint her lecture, "One Out of Twelve: Women Who Are Writers in Our Century." Tillie Olsen differs from the rest of us writing here. Now in her sixties, she has belatedly won the recognition due her, and has a devoted following among women of all ages and especially among the young. Her success is anything but ambiguous, her life was anything but easy. In her writing, she has insisted on the difficulty, the necessity, the often unrecognized creativity, and the value of the work women have always done; at the same time, she emphasizes another value—that of autonomous, chosen work. Because of economic hardship, political commitment and family responsibilities, she had to postpone her writing again and again. She does not underestimate the constraints on most women's lives, the limits within which they must realize their aspirations. Yet she insists on the health of those aspirations, on women's *right* to be creative and to exercise power in their work.

It is difficult for most of us to maintain these several convictions simultaneously: to value women's work while trying to change women's lives; to portray the poignancy and wealth of family love while insisting on women's right to self-absorbing, demanding projects; to write and work for oneself while refusing to turn a deaf ear and blind eye to traditions of womanly service. In her writing, Tillie Olsen has integrated and imaginatively elaborated these convictions. For this reason, we conclude with her article as a concrete representation of the ideals of this book.

Sara Ruddick
Pamela Daniels

Working It Out

Finding New Forms

Isn't it better to find a new form, than cling with a perverse tenacity to the dried up and shrivelled husk?
—A Victorian feminist

Sue Scheid

Kay Keeshan Hamod

FOR THE PAST TWO YEARS, I have spent most of my time in two rooms in Oxford. The first is the upper reading room in the Bodleian Library, where I have devoured quantities of late-nineteenth-century novels and quantities of English candy—the former for the purpose of research in modern European intellectual history and the latter to lay the ghost of the strictly forbidden cigarette. My second room is in the semidetached house I share with my two children, a sixteen-year-old boy and an eleven-year-old girl. Here I wrap myself against the unheated English air, warm my fingers at the typewriter, and produce x number of golden pages amid the detritus of the dissertation-in-progress—the ashtray, the coffee cup, the precariously piled books, and the field of crumpled paper.

In the early hours of the morning, long after I have pronounced the nightly benediction on my children's sleep, and shortly after I have put away what I have written, it is often difficult to avoid pondering the way work shapes one's life. These interior monologues seem most insistent when I think of the dissertation chapter about the development of the women's movement in Victorian England, for the pioneer feminists saw work as one of the keys to women's freedom, and they had high hopes for what women would be able to accomplish for society once they entered the mainstream of active life beyond the home.

When the English women's movement began to take form in the 1850s and 1860s, women faced a number of formidable objective and subjective barriers to adult self-determination. Only one destiny—wifehood—was officially recognized. A girl's manners and expectations were shaped to that end, with the result that education, even for upper-class women, was appallingly inferior—a genteel dalliance with the intellect and the arts. Middle-class women neither received the practical training that would prepare them for wife- and motherhood, nor were they permitted to enter the universities and train for the higher professions. Therefore, if such a woman failed in the business of getting and keeping a husband, her options were narrow. She might remain in her family as the spinster aunt (sometimes as a kind of "upper servant"); she might work as a governess (an overcrowded and underpaid occupation); she might turn to literary activity if she had any talent (one of the reasons for the multitude of nineteenth-century women novelists and hack writers); or, if driven by economic need, she might take up labor "below her station," working as a seamstress or milliner at subsistence wages. (Working-class women, of course, had long worked in agriculture, factory, and mine, doing men's jobs at women's wages.)

Despite the difficulties of spinsterhood, some Victorian women chose to remain single, for marriage meant the loss of adulthood. As a wife, a woman was subject to her husband in every respect. She could not own property; she could not carry on any legal or commercial transaction (if she was hurt in an accident, for example, it was her husband who sued for and received compensation); and, if her parents had not protected her with a marriage settlement, her own income or earnings legally belonged to her husband (if she was deserted, her husband could return to claim anything she had managed to accumulate). The Victorian husband had the right to rule every aspect of family life and might literally imprison his wife in the home if he wished (a discipline not prevented by law until the 1890s). The children were legally his property; he determined their religion and schooling, and if the couple separated, he was awarded custody. Before 1839, the mother had not even had the legal right to see her children after a separation or divorce; with the 1839 reform, she gained visitation rights, but only if she had not been guilty of infidelity. Infidelity provided the husband with sufficient grounds for divorce, but not the wife—she was obliged to prove either desertion or cruelty, in addition to adultery. Even if she succeeded in obtaining a divorce, she faced a ruined reputation and the very real problem of maintaining herself, since her former husband was under no obligation to contribute to her support.

No doubt many Victorian men were dutiful and attentive, but the legal structure, together with the lack of options and exits for women, left husbands and fathers free to play the tyrant if they so desired. Of course, even tyrants take some risk; Victorian humor has it that the Arsenic Act was passed to make it more difficult for the housewife to dispatch the rat in her bedroom. However, the maintenance of masculine power was virtually assured by the fact that it was difficult for women to see their true social position. The objective barriers to their independence were matched by a subjective barrier—their acceptance of social definitions of feminine nature and role. In the 1850s and 1860s, women might still accept the age-old religious justifications for women's submission ("the Bible tells us so"), or they might become absorbed in a newer, more flattering reflection of themselves. In the modern mirror, woman appeared as "an angel," a creature of superior morality. She was sexually pure, as men could never bring themselves to be. As a mother, she was the never-failing source of self-sacrificial love; moreover, her motherly hand was extended to all in need—the unfortunate poor, as well as her overworked husband. Despite her Amazonian moral strength, she was also supposed to be delicate and passive, much in need of a man to protect and guide her and especially to keep her from the wicked world. She was too spiritual for commercial activity, too innocent for the franchise and politics, too delightfully spontaneous for intellectual discipline.

The angel symbolized a rich complex of needs—including men's desire to set moral (but not legal) limits to their dominance—but ultimately it served to control women by inhibiting them from making an objective analysis of their situation and by discouraging the kind of bold action required to overcome their disabilities. Under the brocade of false consciousness, the skeleton of social inferiority remained, but few women could understand what John Stuart Mill meant when he observed, "In the present day, power holds a smoother language and whomsoever it oppresses, always pretends to do so for their own good."

Was there a certain type of woman most likely to see through the facade? Not if "type" refers to categories of personal qualities, for all kinds of women—courageous and timid, ugly and beautiful, intelligent and stupid—cut themselves out to fit the angelic pattern. If, for example, they were temperamentally unsuited for passive delicacy, they often blamed themselves (angels are morally perfect; even at the cost of neurosis, they keep their tempers) rather than turning to examine the flaws in the social pattern itself. Quite often women actually fought hardest to preserve the status quo, taking alarm at any suggestion that they might have more to offer and more to expect. Margaret Oliphant, for instance, was an intelligent journalist who had struggled to support her three children after her husband's death. We might suppose she would have appreciated Mill's *Subjection of Women,* but, in fact, her review exalts the angelic homebody and reverberates with the fear that women would only prove themselves inferior if they were allowed freedom.

It was not always easy even for the pioneer feminists to confront stereotypes of feminity. However, women like Elizabeth and Millicent Garrett, Bessie R. Parkes, Barbara Leigh Smith, and Josephine Butler shared a certain vantage point from which it was possible to see alternatives. None of them had been brought up to fit the role assigned to women of their status. Although they came from affluent families, a life of leisure seemed to them merely "the privilege of going mad in white satin." They felt the lack of congruity between their high social standing and their low feminine status. Why were they considered barely capable of directing themselves when their masculine counterparts were expected to direct the nation? In their families, they had absorbed the advanced Liberal position and become familiar with the various reform movements that had preoccupied progressives in the first half of the century. Thus, they had what others lacked—a theoretical framework for understanding not only their own nonconformity, but many of the problems of women throughout society. If other dominated groups had sought and secured self-determination, then it could not be "unnatural" for women also to strive for the right to fulfill social duties, find satisfaction in employment, represent their interests in Parliament, and compete equally with men for material, moral, and social well-being.

In the formative period of English feminism, the right to work was considered fundamental to self-determination. One of the first organizations of the women's movement was the Association for the Promotion of the Employment of Women, founded in 1858 to enlighten the public and to serve as an employment agency. In the next year, the same feminists began to publish *The English Woman's Journal,* a periodical that was even printed by women (the Victoria Press). The theme of women, work, and independence dominated this periodical throughout its existence. Writers compared the English situation with that in other countries and pointed out that "the angel" was neither ubiquitous nor eternal. They urged society to provide better education for all women and to remove the constraints that prevented them from engaging in skilled labor, clerical work, and the professions. They highlighted abuses of women workers and reported the difficulties faced by women who were suddenly thrown on their own resources by the death or financial failure of husbands. The correspondence column, "Open Council," was filled with letters from readers who had gained their first opportunity to express the work problems of women (such as those of the deserted wife, who had to work in order to live, but who was fired whenever it was discovered she was married).

In the process of debating these issues, *The English Woman's Journal* clarified two aspects of spinsterhood that had never been boldly acknowledged. First of all, the feminists pointed out that not all Englishwomen would be able to marry even if this were their fondest wish. Partly because of male emigration, there was an enormous surplus of women at this time (the ratio was as high as seven to four). Under such circumstances, it was unrealistic to insist on marriage as woman's only true destiny; it would be far better to admit the problem and make it possible for unmarried women to find themselves (and social respectability) in work. Second, it was not true that every woman wanted to marry. Some were ready to explore new territory and show what women could do without men's protection and guidance. Inspired by a desire to render social service, many were convinced that women could make a real contribution to the entire society if their energies and abilities were freed and activated. Why should such "spinsters" be the butt of jokes and the victims of social discrimination? No one was attacking marriage and the family, endorsing sexual freedom, or imagining utopias. It was simply more realistic to admit that some women would never fit the stereotypes, and that any woman, married or single, might find it necessary to earn her own living. The consciousness that she could, would give her a feeling of independence, a thing not to be despised in any walk of life.

Of course, all of this seemed dangerously revolutionary to some nervous gentlemen. Feminists always had to put up with various misconstructions, aspersions on their characters, veiled threats, and dire warnings. They were told, for example, that their children would be "injured before their birth by the undue activity of brain which weakens their mother's physical powers," and thus they would be born feeble or "die in her arms, quenching out her courage in the bitterest waves of personal suffering." (This is my favorite Dire Warning, since I recall the day when my reading of *War and Peace* was interrupted by labor pains. My son was healthy and squalling, but I must admit that my courage was quenched in the Russian Lit. exam a week later.)

What really brought the feminists' enemies to the point of hysteria was that women began to show signs of developing an independent social philosophy, a phenomenon ironically related to those angelic expectations. Because it had always been thought proper for women to extend their "fundamental altruism" in charitable activities, feminine ambitions had been channeled in this direction. When the feminists took up the theme of social service, they not only broadened the goals; they asked a number of disturbing questions. How was it, for example, that middle-class women were told they were too delicate to work while working-class women had always labored alongside their men? Wasn't it hypocritical to show such concern for middle-class children and at the same time work the sons and daughters of the laboring classes to within an inch of their lives?

In the last half of the century, women (especially the unmarried daughters of the middle class) not only continued their traditional charitable involvement, but took part in a number of other projects meant to benefit the lower classes—education of pauper children; cooperative workshops; instruction of working-class women in child care, sanitation, and skills; management of housing projects; and day-care for the children of women workers. These young ladies had previously been sheltered from the rough-and-tumble of life; moreover, no one had taught them to rationalize suffering as a necessary part of economic progress. They were shocked at the depths of Victorian poverty, appalled that girls were forced into prostitution in order to survive, caught up in sympathy for children who would never receive the promised gift of equal opportunity, and inspired by the independence of many working-class women who coped successfully with problems their "betters" had not known existed.

When these middle-class women turned to social reform, they often denounced their brothers for hypocrisy and demanded that reality be brought in line with ideals. They were not radical, but they were a threat to the status quo, for they had the gift of drawing attention to naked emperors. This was especially apparent in the 1870s and 1880s, when a remarkable woman, Josephine Butler, spoke out clearly against exploitation and class bias; organized a coalition of feminists, working-class men and women, Salvation Army people, and Quakers to protest the legalization of prostitution; and, with the help of a muckraking newspaperman and a former prostitute, managed to blow the lid off international traffic in girls as young as eleven. When even conservative women began to issue condemnations of prostitution and the system of sweated labor, it seemed as if women were preparing a moral crusade that would bring society into conformity with a set of "feminine" ideals. It is a nice irony that some gentlemen reacted with angelphobia: women were *too* moral (among other things, women were beginning to call for a single sexual standard, claiming that men should live up to the standards of purity set for women); women didn't understand the necessity for struggle and force; and their protectiveness would eventually lead to the grandmotherly state—that is, socialism.

Actually, these gentlemen were overreacting, for the women's movement so far remained true to its own origins—Liberal in viewpoint. As so often happens in social life, the very theory that had afforded feminists an insight into women's problems eventually came to block a more comprehensive understanding. Feminists were sincere in their social reform efforts, and they were often able to extend a helping hand across class lines; but the movement as a whole failed to realize the difference between middle- and working-class needs and attitudes. The "right to work" did not necessarily make sense to a working-class woman who was spending her life in a factory because her father or husband could not make enough to support the family. The feminists' tenet of free competition collided with the working-class position on unionization and limitation of hours on the job; the feminists' insistence that women needed no special favors made it difficult to recognize how vulnerable working women were in some situations, especially if they were mothers. For these reasons (and for others, having to do with differences in life-styles), few working-class women were drawn to feminism.

By 1900, the feminist debate about social reform and the nature of women's work was overshadowed by the apparent sine qua non of further progress—suffrage. Efforts to secure the vote preoccupied the attention of both constitutional suffragists and militant suffragettes throughout the Edwardian period, and when the franchise was at last secured after World War I, feminism fell into quiescence.

Not until the 1960s did feminist debates again claim public attention. We might say that this second phase began at the apex of the first, for nearly all the major goals of the nineteenth-century women's movement have been achieved—even equal pay and equal employment opportunity are within sight. Our conditions, therefore, are much improved over those of Victorian feminists. Nonetheless, I think we have much to gain by studying women's history, for certain things do not change so very much in the course of one hundred years. Though the content of their statements may differ from ours, we still recognize certain stock characters by their relationship to the movement—the moderates and radicals within, the women who write books criticizing women's liberation, the males who scoff, the males who smile sweetly, and the men who are willing to change themselves as well as help us change. In several different ways, we still have the problem of "seeing through" a number of social stereotypes.

In the formative period of contemporary feminism, we have been much concerned with understanding our emotions and exploring patterns of personal relationship. This has been both necessary and illuminating; however, I think we may be in danger of missing some important insights that are obtainable from a different position. We might approach this position by asking whether feminism seeks progress for all women, or just for those who "feel as we do." Have we progressed further than Victorian feminists in building bridges between middle- and working-class women? To this question some might reply: "We spoke, but they didn't listen." In that case, I would remind them of the Victorian feminists, who saw much, *but not* all, and I would ask again: "Yes, but did you speak to *their* problems?"

The answer to this question will inevitably be complex, for social life is full of contradictions and dizzying dialectics. I recall attending a conference on women's work organized by people who were well aware that women work at all kinds of jobs and in all kinds of social environments; therefore, they issued just as many invitations to unions as to universities. Women from the latter came in hundreds, and from the former—in a dozen. Perhaps we can begin to understand some of the reasons for this if I relate one incident from the same conference.

We were viewing a consciousness-raising film which portrayed the process of feminine socialization from childhood, through adolescence, to young adulthood. At one point, one of the heroines was shown accepting a job in a beauty shop, whereupon the film-makers let us know what they thought of the commercial and sexual meaning of false eyelashes, permanents, wigs, and 1,001 lotions and lipsticks. This, of course, seemed a perfectly understandable comment, quite routine for the women's liberation movement. However, the woman to my left (a factory worker from Chicago) was quite agitated. She turned to me and whispered, "They don't understand how many of us go into beauty work just *because* we want to be independent. We can have a shop at home—be our own boss, be there when the kids come home from school, and keep ourselves together if the old man cuts out."

She was expressing the distance between the viewpoints of those whom Americans refer to as white collar and blue collar workers. This distance cannot simply be wished away, for each viewpoint has been developed over a long period of time, in response to different forms of education (in both the narrow and broad senses of "education"), different options in life, and ultimately, different ways of making a living. Therefore, if feminism is to speak for all women, it will be necessary to listen to all women. Both groups of working women have been isolated from each other; we need honest interchanges and a good deal of mutual re-thinking if we are ever to approach a comprehensive understanding of issues germane to us all.

A friend of mine works in a laundry; her father is a foreman in a steel mill who has had to work long and hard to get to his position. One day she hailed me on the street, and over a cup of coffee she told me in no uncertain terms of her disgust for the young leftists who had dropped into the laundry to discuss wages and unionization. "Long-haired, hippie, pot-smoking brats!" she said. "They come straight from babyhood to the university, their fathers pay all the bills, and they sit around all day reading big words—and then they have the nerve to come and try to *manage* us. Ha! They never worked a day in their lives!" To this, I answered many things, mostly about not judging books by covers and about the possibility of important messages being delivered by messengers one doesn't like. However, she waved me away impatiently. "What's the use," she said. "You eggheads never understand. After all, did *you* ever work—I mean, really work?"

It is difficult to explain—to anyone—how staring into space, rummaging through note cards, and spinning out words is work. I understood what she meant, for I have been a carhop, a waitress, a bakery clerk, a typist, an Addressograph operator, an encyclopedia sales-person, and a preschool teacher, as well as a university teaching assistant and Ph.D. candidate. I have also had sixteen years of experi-ence as a mother. If someone asks me, "What are you?", I am not being facetious if I answer, "I am a sort of bridge." Perhaps I can best clarify this by presenting an account of the rivers I have crossed. In doing so, I will be treating myself as I did the Victorian feminists earlier; I am not interested in personal qualities, but in the back-ground and life experience that produce certain opportunities for insight.

The journey begins, as usual, with my parents—one an attorney and the other a teacher. Both were exceptionally able to hand on their experience, their enthusiasms, and their intellectual curiosity. How-ever, they were also "bridge-builders." Firmly committed to the ideal of equality, they did not see a chasm between those who worked with their heads and those who worked with their hands (or between intel-lectuality and action). "Oh, for goodness sake," my mother used to say, "life is not only in books! Put that down, go outside and look at the world!" My father said, "You will be narrow-minded if you don't work."

So—I worked. First as a carhop, then as a waitress in what we might politely call a small café. These jobs, of course, are not in the cellar of American society, but they were, and are, very poorly paid. Since they require no training, they are often the temporary resort of the drifting poor I would come to know better some years later. Waitresses tend to be treated as servants; some people seem to store up their hostility just for the occasion. However, one must have tips in order to make a living wage, and in my small café, it was not sufficient to be polite and efficient. I suppose what bothered me most were the sexual connotations of service and tipping, especially since I was young and innocent, unprepared to deal with ribald jokes and leers. I once brought myself to discuss this with *Lou,* the dishwasher (an ample woman with wispy gray hair), and *Iva,* one of my fellow waitresses (a flash of long green fingernails and wavy red hair). Lou agreed with me completely, but then Lou had hated men ever since Charlie ran off and left her washing dishes. We knew she was washing Charlie out with the cups and saucers, because she was always mourn-fully singing her own version of liberation: "Git yore c-o-l-d feet outa my bed . . ." Iva, on the other hand, thought I was silly, for she loved to flirt, and did it in a beautifully stylish way, with lots of self-confidence and tongue-in-cheek. It was her art form, and nobody took it seriously since she was very much in love with her husband. Iva told long romantic tales of her past loves and hopes; Lou gave her a side-long glance and sang louder.

After this, I went to college—and worked for half-days, first as a bakery clerk (a placid, low-paid job with some sweet fringe benefits) and later as a typist. A typist, of course, has a higher status than a waitress or clerk and is usually better-paid; she must have some training and skill. We part-time typists were at the bottom of the secretarial hierarchy. We spent our days at isolated tables, turning out page after page, stencil after stencil, sometimes in languages we couldn't read. I hated this job bitterly. I had no interest in what I was doing, no control over assignments or conditions, and practically no association with other human beings except at coffee break. This seemed the epitome of alienation—until the next year, when I was promoted to the Addressograph machine. (The Addresssograph operator is the one who puts your name on junk mail, and the machine is like a giant typewriter, except that one types on metal plates instead of paper.) For four hours a day and eight on Saturday I sat in a tiny room (alone), working a machine that sounded like a convict's cup across jail bars. This experience resembled work on an assembly line in a factory; it was very difficult, if not impossible, to imagine any purpose to endless repetition and stressful noise. By coffee break, I was feeling so dehumanized I would have welcomed a shout from a foul-mouthed truck driver. When I complained to *Andrea,* a full-time typist, she sighed and said, "Yes, I just set my life aside when I come to work." She was a dainty, quiet woman who longed to return to being "just a housewife" and to spend her days knitting tiny sweaters, but, for the moment, she spent most of her waking hours in "suspended life" in order to support her dental-student husband. It was more disturbing to think about *Doris,* a middle-aged unmarried woman who always seemed to wear gray and to look somewhere beyond you. If Doris didn't find life at work, was she likely to find it in the boarding house where she had her single room?

As for me, I was attached to my Addressograph by economic necessity. In my junior year at the university, I had married another student, and by my senior year, we were expecting a baby (much to our surprise, I might add). The company I worked for had a rule that women must stop work when they were five months pregnant, but since we needed the money, I plodded on self-consciously until a week before my son was born. Shortly after this event was announced in the births column of the local newspaper, I received a call from the female personnel director, who (sarcastically) fired me for infraction of the rules.

Both my husband and I finished our undergraduate degrees, and he wanted to proceed to graduate school. However, since we had no money, he decided to spend the year running a tavern belonging to his father. That year was a revelation to me; we lived in the inner-city neighborhood of a grimy, industrial urban area, and I saw for the first time what it was like for people to have no options whatsoever, to be entirely preoccupied with survival. (For example, whether your children would eat or not eat during the next week might depend on your ingenuity in getting hold of your husband's paycheck, if he had one, before it went down in drink. Or, if you wanted to forget you were in hell, you might yourself need booze or drugs; in this case, survival might depend on how many clients you could bring to your room.) At the time, I was as innocent of the depths of poverty as the Victorian women I have described. Understanding things as an outsider, with a different set of values and expectations and even a different sort of language, I was yet an insider, for we were there as residents, not kindhearted or bureaucratic emissaries from the upper world. (Under such circumstances, one quickly comes to understand certain things— for instance, the attitude of the police toward those who have no status or strings to pull.) Brought up in an egalitarian family, I was also innocent of certain stereotypes and anxieties. This meant that I understood, but did not share, the prejudices of the small enclave of better-off neighbors. Struggling to maintain self-respect and a sense of order in their lives, they found scapegoats, for they had no other way of analyzing the situation. They were in terror of losing what little inner and outer control they had over their lives, or slipping into the vortex of brutality and violence which always seemed a single step away. Indeed, it was very hard to avoid the sense of drowning; it was like a nightmare in which you are trapped below the earth, unable to find a way out and sure that what you hear is not a rescue party, but the rushing water which will soon sweep over your head.

My friend *Florence,* who worked nights as a cocktail waitress, fought hard against the city, for she and her husband were desperately anxious to escape from family circumstances that threatened to pull them under. Florence was at this time very young, pretty, and openhearted, the kind of person who takes in every stray dog or cat and shares the little she has with those who have less. At one point, she took in a stray baby and brought it up as her own daughter. From her, I learned about the charity of the poor to the poor, and I discovered that human beings sometimes sing in their chains. However, I also learned that it is sentimental to expect the human spirit to overcome the engulfing urban corruption. Eventually, Florence went down. I think her daughters deserve something better than pity.

Living under the earth gave me a different yardstick for measuring the liberation of women. I have been impatient, and sometimes angry, with the comfortable wives I came to know after my husband finished his master's degree and began teaching. I am sorry that they themselves suffer from psychological imprisonment, but I cannot deny my own awareness that they are wasting freedoms other women will never touch. I remember feeling that I had slipped through the looking glass when I saw two of my new neighbors standing nose to nose arguing whether a rock was on Mrs. A's or Mrs. B's side of the property line. Under the earth, people don't worry about such lines, because they don't have property.

In the "suburban period" of our lives, we were still paying the bills we had accumulated; thus, I needed to work, but I hated to be away from home, as we now had a small daughter as well as a school-age son. I solved the problem by establishing a preschool in our home and began what was to be eight years of teaching three-, four-, and five-year-olds. Like the beautician's shop at home, this seemed a "natural" solution, for preschool teaching is considered a feminine job, an extension of the motherly role. One hopes that in the future it will also be thought of as an extension of the fatherly role. With this in mind, I hired male as well as female assistant teachers. The social status of the preschool teacher is low; she is commonly thought to be at the very basement of the educational hierarchy of elementary, secondary, college, and university teaching. However, I discovered a disparity between this assigned status and the teachers' own perception of their worth. Self-respect was enhanced by a certain freedom of action deriving from the fact that theories of early childhood education are still in flux and no cut-and-dried curriculum has been established. I have met and liked many preschool teachers, who enjoyed the work very much, even though it can be emotionally and physically exhausting (and poorly paid).

During these years, I worked in my private preschool, in Head Start, and in a cooperative. Each of these situations differed from the others, but in all of them, the children taught me as much as I taught them. Children at this age are explorers, discovering for themselves what adults have long since taken for granted. They test themselves and the environment, perfect their skills, try on new language and social roles—and in the process, they learn about and from each other. It is hard work learning what it means to be a human being, and there are times when children struggle *mano a mano* with the adults who are there to guide them. But many preschool teachers have the rare capacity to cheer a faltering step as much as a joyous leap; they are able to recognize the needs and abilities of all kinds of children—the brilliant, the brain-damaged, the creative, the physically handicapped, those who withdraw into fantasy and those who rip about like wild winds.

Unlike the elementary teacher, the preschool teacher is usually in close contact with the parents of her pupils—which means, still, mostly the mothers. In eight years of teaching, I came to know about five hundred mothers, the majority of whom were middle-class women with some college education. In general, these women were personable, talented, and intelligent, and they were devoted to their children. They taught me much about motherhood, but they also bewildered me, for I had never before realized the damage done by certain stereotypes of motherhood. These women were, first of all, made insecure by popular Freudianism—the tendency to trace radical personality disorders to inadequate mothering (not, one notices, inadequate fathering). Because they had assumed too much responsibility for their children's happiness, they were often burdened by unwarranted anxiety and guilt. Occasionally, they were unable to face the fact that their children had real difficulties, for this was to admit failure as mothers. But more often, they exaggerated problems and worried about things that were normal for certain ages and temperaments. I am convinced that most of these women were doing all that is humanly possible for their children; in some cases, they were sacrificing themselves heroically.

If we recall the Victorian definitions of feminine nature, perhaps we can see that these mothers were still under the shadow of the angel; moreover, they were expecting themselves to be sophisticated in their altruism (that is, to read psychology in order to learn how to love). Unfortunately, too many mothers still push and prod themselves in order to get into the social pattern; they are critical of *themselves* rather than skeptical about social expectations. This is why I would like women to look outward, to understand that there is always more on heaven and earth than is known by contemporary experts.

Perhaps we might begin by admitting that motherhood is work, first of all, *hard* work. It is not "natural" to get up at 3:00 A.M. to tend to a shrieking child; it requires considerable self-discipline. Second, we should point out the models of work which are *not* suitable for motherhood. I often felt that mothers were offering up their children in the same spirit that one submits a paper to a professor or a project to a boss—hoping that "the work" will receive an "A" or be put in the top basket. Needing tangible evidence of their children's—and their—success, mothers often pushed their children to be competitive, thereby unknowingly intensifying a quality that in itself calls for a critical reappraisal. More sensitive mothers often thought of their children as works of art and of themselves as artists, molding a beautiful character as a thing-in-itself. But human clay is different; does not lie still. One does not work with children as one does with words and things.

Perhaps I can clarify what I mean by describing *Kate,* a friend of mine who is married to an attorney and has two small boys. Although she is highly educated and has had several years of experience in what is commonly viewed as a man's profession, she has given it up "for the sake of the children." Consequently, she brings all her superior intelligence and enormous energy to the task of the "artist-mother"—arranging children in beautiful patterns of human behavior. I admire her ideals and I admire Kate, but I think she is dead wrong. It is too much to ask such a woman to live solely in the four walls of her home—and, furthermore, to keep herself from recognizing she is bored. It is also too much to expect two small boys to stand constantly in the gale of their mother's strong personality. As chance would have it, one of these children is temperamentally her antithesis. She worries constantly about his "daydreaming," and then, because she is a thoughtful woman, she worries about her worrying about his daydreaming. Most of all, she fears (with good reason) that the tensions between them will become guerrilla warfare when he is an adolescent. Kate, who is ten times more energetic than most of us, is a "woman of action," a leader and organizer who should be exercising her skills among adults. I don't mean that she's not cut out to be a mother; there always have been excellent mothers among active, managing women, but perhaps in the past they found fulfillment scouring a huge house, milking the cows, teaching Sunday school, nursing the neighborhood, and raising thirteen upright sons and daughters.

As things are now, it would be better if we could openly ask ourselves whether we are qualified to work as full- or part-time mothers, or whether we actually find the job distasteful. Mothering as "labor" requires someone who can tolerate disruption and handle messy things and situations. Mothering as a "profession" requires that one know a good deal about human behavior (the behavior of thirty-year-old women as well as that of five-year-old children) and that one have the ability both to give discipline and receive suggestions. Like teachers, nurses, ministers, marriage counselors, social workers, and psychologists, mothers must be able to tolerate and understand a certain kind of human interaction. Those they deal with have minds and desires of their own; sometimes they will respond, sometimes not. Eventually, if the mother has done her job well, they will walk away smiling. (And how many other workers are required to aspire to their own redundancy at the early age of forty-five?) To look at mothering this way is not to deny the reality of parental devotion, but to hope for the enlightenment of love; it takes a kind of distancing and self-discipline to avoid overindulging or overmanaging one's children. If a mother wants to identify with and possess her creation, she ought to have "brain-children" as well as real human babies. ("I love scholarly work," says one friend, "because you *force* it into shape. It's not like sitting around for nine months waiting for something to happen to you.")

At the present time, those of us who try to combine the motherly career with other work (either out of need or by choice) often find ourselves running impossibly fast while our heels are nipped by guilt. ("Yes, I think I do remember Mother. Isn't she the one who is always too busy?") However, I think we should resist the guilt, keep on cutting new patterns for ourselves, and make these patterns visible to others.

As a preschool teacher for nearly a decade, I enjoyed the children and will never regret the experience, but I always considered it an interim job. Actually, for two of those years I taught preschool in the daytime and went to school at night in order to obtain a master's degree in Humanities. I remained in preschool because of my family's needs; my husband had returned to the university to work on his Ph.D. and it was necessary to augment his teaching assistantship. (We can criticize these arrangements as the product of male chauvinism, but only if we also ask why it is impossible to support a family on a teaching assistantship. During all the years I was running impossibly fast, so was he—for example, holding a night job as well as teaching. If I was serving him, whom was he serving?)

During my last year as a preschool teacher, I was becoming increasingly anxious to get on with certain intellectual projects, and I felt the tensions of spending every social occasion discussing tantrums and toilet training when I wanted to talk politics. This is a good example of the way the social role conceals an individual's full personality. I found it surprising that a few weeks after I had begun to study history, I was suddenly thought capable of expressing an intelligent opinion on international relations, political tensions, multinational corporations, etc., etc. No one, of course, thought I was capable of discussing hyperactive children or Piaget's theories. Only my calling card—"graduate student in history"—had changed; I had not. Finally, when I was in my early thirties, I was able to begin work on a Ph.D., to finish the course work, and pass the comprehensives. Unfortunately, my marriage disintegrated during these years (for reasons not related to graduate school). Therefore, as I sit here in my room in Oxford, I am a rather elderly graduate student, divorced, with two children to support, and wondering how on earth to get the money together for the year I need to finish my thesis.

I am listening tonight to bells that have rung for hundreds of years at Oxford. I can't help wondering why it is so difficult for us to learn from our history. This is not to say that one should "obey the teachings of history" or that I espouse cyclic theories; on the contrary, what we can learn by comparing today and yesterday is that social life changes, sometimes for the better. Most of us *do* have more freedom and opportunity than Victorian women had. I doubt very much if progress would have been made unless some women had been capable of protesting, setting goals, and attempting to achieve them. This is the lesson we can learn from the Victorian experience: human beings are not free to design life just as they would wish it, *but they are not powerless either.*

Contemporary feminists have done much to puncture stereotypes, to encourage the rethinking of sex roles and relationships, to work for change in the education of girls, and to open up the question of women's work by insisting on equal pay and equal opportunity. I applaud their accomplishments, but I am also reminded of the unknown Victorian woman who left this note in the margins of *The English Woman's Journal:* "We shall have to ask for more than this." At present, we insist that a woman be treated "just the same as a man." Are we sure we want to be treated as most men are in our society? Or do both sexes deserve something better? We assume that we solve the problem by making women equal competitors. Will those who push their way to the top really have a clearer view from there?

A "clearer view" means that we see the connection between Kate, the worried mother and potential organizer; Kay, the student and worried mother; Lou, the dishwasher who sang bitterly of liberation; Iva, the waitress who made her own romance; Andrea, the typist who dreamt of babies; Doris, who spent her life in a straight-backed chair —and Florence, who was on a slab in the morgue before she was thirty. Feminism does not yet speak for all women, and will not do so until it is able to push for radical solution to the problems that make it difficult for many to survive, much less to think about self-fulfillment.

If we are to begin to understand the social and economic obstacles to women's liberation, women from all levels of American society must see through their stereotypes of each other and speak clearly of what they know. We must avoid the tendency to slip into private worlds and to imagine individuals in isolation from the larger patterns of social relations. Because we need to know not only how the other feels but also what she does, I think it is most productive to focus on the question of women and their work. By clarifying our experiences as workers, I think we will be able to offer some insights for anyone who doubts the emperor's glorious raiment. Women, perhaps, are in an optimal position to discuss the division of labor, once they learn to interpret their kinds of work to each other. My friend from the laundry must explain that the phrase "because you never worked a day in your life" really means "because you were never trapped by economic need into a lifetime job which gave you no personal satisfaction." Similarly, I must be able to communicate my expectations: that work be socially valuable, as well as personally rewarding; that work advance the process of self-discovery, revealing what we are capable of doing and making; and that it should leave us with a sense of integrity rather than shattering us physically and emotionally. When we discuss job satisfaction and question the present organization of labor, we may be surprised to discover our subtle resistance to certain dominant attitudes. Many of us have worked in a stop-and-go rhythm, learned to understand mothering and other work, handled a range of problems practically simultaneously. This multiple activity has its difficulties, but it also makes the dominant pattern seem ridiculous. Doesn't it seem that people are being cut to fit jobs rather than the other way around?

We may also become skeptical about the dichotomization of home and work. I am impatient with those who glorify motherhood in the language of the greeting card and yet would never consider rewarding mothering as one of the fundamental forms of work in any society. I am equally impatient with a certain feminist tendency to speak of mothering as a mere mode of imprisonment, something we would never find ourselves doing if not seduced by a clever enemy. It is possible to design comprehensive solutions that take into account the very different quality of these choices on three levels of American society: "under the earth," the choice may be between children's health and mother's health; for the factory worker, it may be between children's opportunity (college, for example) and mother's desire to be a homemaker; and, in suburbia, it may be between a notion of children's perfect happiness and mother's desire to do something for and by herself.

Under changed circumstances, mothering might gain the *social* support and recognition it deserves. With adequate medical care, for instance, fewer women would arrive in the delivery room without ever having seen the doctor. We might proceed to the consideration of maternity benefits so that those who usually work outside the home could afford to remain home for a certain length of time; of a livable mother's salary instead of grudging "welfare"; of extensive day-care centers for preschoolers and supervised recreation for school-aged children (publicly financed but run cooperatively by the parents); of programs of further education, cultural enrichment, and employment training; of socially productive work for those who have completed their mothering; and of reform of work patterns that prevent fathers from participating in parenting. With some practice, we might even stop viewing our children as personal possessions and realize that adults are mutually responsible for the next generation . . . Of course, none of this will happen as long as we are unable to channel our national wealth for the good of both present and future generations.

If women begin by gaining insight into their work both in and out of the home, I think they will be surprised to discover just how much they contribute to society. Then, perhaps, they will help each other answer a reasonable question: *"Are women able to find themselves in the social forms they help to perpetuate?"*

POSTSCRIPT, IOWA CITY, 1976

Two years have passed since I left Oxford. I have another room, another desk—and a dissertation almost ready for the typist. This "brain-child" of mine is not as beautiful as I would have wished (still overweight, still suffering from acne), but at least it stands on its feet, looks you in the eye, and speaks clearly.

In front of my desk is a blank wall, washed puritan white to protect the scholarly mind against distraction, but on the other side of the room, the windows look out on the Iowa landscape, sepia-toned in late winter. To the right, beyond a fringe of trees, is the stubble of a soybean field; to the left, the meandering Iowa River and a hill of wind-bent oaks. My children and I know this countryside well, for we go together to pick morel mushrooms and wild strawberries in the spring; blackberries, plums, and rum cherries in the summer; tart apples and hickory nuts in the autumn.

We live in a pastoral setting—but Iowa City is also a surprisingly cosmopolitan university town in a liberal state, and thus quite different from the stereotype of "middle America." These windows of mine are not in an American Gothic farmhouse, but on the sixth floor of a huge apartment complex; most of our neighbors are students, artists, and professionals from all over the world. When my children and I walk through these fields and woods, we may see Huck Finn, struggling to land a golden carp—but we are just as likely to see the African painter, catching the violent summer sun on his canvas.

In this city, nearly all of my women friends are involved in some kind of collective action: in the Black, Chicano, or Native American movements; in a broad spectrum of feminist programs; in trade unionism; in the cooperative movement; or in the various parties and organizations of the left. I am teaching Comparative Women's History in the further education program at the University of Iowa; my students are mothers, factory workers, secretaries—women who know what it is to juggle several sets of responsibilities.

Thus the majority of the women I know here have made an exhilarating and frightening leap into the "middle of things" and are swimming through crosscurrents without any certainty that they will reach the other side. After a lifetime of golden spoons, my friend *Eve* has exchanged a law career for the low-paid and often frustrating work of a union organizer. After a lifetime of working to support her children, my friend *Ruth,* a brilliant woman in her sixties, has finally entered the college classrooms she long regarded "from the outside, like a kid with her nose pressed against the glass of an expensive shop."

During the past two years, I've seen many women surmount their feelings of isolation and doubt, and I've also seen them reach out to others across the barriers of educational background, race, age, and personal circumstances. Such experiences have confirmed my belief that women have a significant role to play in "finding new forms" for our society. As a historian, I remember how often women have been defeated, but I also recall how often they returned to the middle of things. In Josephine Butler's speeches, presented a century ago, I recognize the weariness ("I am, as many of my fellow workers are also, a good deal tired and worn out . . ."), and I also recognize—and reaffirm—the stubborn hope:

> Let us cast away our unworthy narrowness . . . and look
> boldly forth towards the dawning day.

TRANSITIONS

To Laura at eleven

1

I see that sometime in the night
Frightened by your Protean dreams,
You have renounced your baby anarchism,
And fled in terror from your revolutionary body.

Awkward at my morning door,
Arms folded across your tiny breasts,
Citing patterns and procedures,
You denounce me to the governors:
"This one is not like other mothers!"

2

Against this knock upon the door,
I have prepared a scribbled self-defense;

I plead guilty and not guilty.

Your mother's often gone,
Even when she scolds you;

What she cooks sometimes
Tastes bitter as history;

She wears books on her fingers
Instead of rings.

3

Once upon a time like yours
I learned to think of thinking
As the joyful arc of the highest swing.
I was greedy, throwing tantrums for ideas.

Once upon a time like mine,
Before I knew your name,
I thought that you and I
Would chase elusive thoughts on prairie winds,
Or stroll together in some winter clarity.

4

But now, neither yours nor mine,
Time is set by hands I cannot push alone,
And both of us are set to ordeal trials.

Some cannot walk through fire unburned,
Some cannot swim when weighted down with lead.

In daytime, I consider how to breathe,
Pace myself; a too-quick burst of speed,
A glance aside,
And I shall fall.

Must run
At night across a stubble field
May not wear shoes,
Must carry weights across my shoulders,
And continue to be reasonable.

5

Having perceived my strange
long-distance run,

You may become
A passionate mover of Time

Or, a passionate baker
Of chocolate cakes.

6

Eleven years ago, I filled myself
Complete with mother's greed,
And then I gave you to yourself;
Whispered we would learn together.

This is the painful part of growing:
Compassion for the child not yet its own.

This is the painful part of growing:
Compassion for the mother
secret from you.

Kay Keeshan Hamod

Juxtapositions
alice atkinson lyndon

WHEN I THINK BACK about becoming a sculptor, I find myself paraphrasing Pound: I had over-prepared the event, that much was *essential*. What inner compulsion creates a fascination with objects, to the extent that even words, when I consider them for very long, lose their sound references and actual meanings and begin to assume shapes in my mind—vivid—contingent, always asymmetrical? I find that I *must* bring these shapes to three-dimensional fruition. As well as the images that lodge in my memory: early delight in the backs of closets, secret rooms hidden in bushes, and beckoning spaces behind windows passed in the street. Night dreams of levitation, serene skimming over houses and people.

I imagine my own body moving through space, jumping, kicking, propelling and rearranging itself to assume the spaces that a sculpture occupies or will occupy. For this reason, movement images from film impress me deeply: the skater in *Carnal Knowledge,* now dressed in that gorgeous silk sheath Dominique Sanda wore in the dance sequence in *The Conformist,* endlessly gliding as Scott Joplin plays the languid "Solace" and a ragtime waltz, "Bethena." Form without symmetry, flawless syncopation.

An absolute fear of flying, coupled with love of the objects that planes and wings *are,* results in an intense desire to fabricate aedicular spaces cantilevering everywhere. I'm talking about making sculpture —enclosing, connecting, extending form and space—maneuvers that not only demand their own spaces, but also imply other places that I enter in fantasy, rooms with great serviceable wings propelling them through the air. These "smaller" aggressive forms compel my imagination to explore and inhabit; and as I work, I am able, physically, to project my body into the spaces with which I come in contact.

These fascinations didn't become formidable until I was twenty-two, when, stimulated by an art history course on Romanesque sculpture, I started sculpting in France. At first, the experience was no more than it was meant to be—an attempt to understand the technique of stone carving first hand. Although the work was arduous and the exercises often seemed arbitrary, soon the process of handling the stone and giving it new form became mentally and physically extremely satisfying and serious.

Returning to the United States in 1958, primed to concentrate in medieval sculpture and architecture, I entered graduate school in art history at Berkeley. I began a course in clay modeling, but then switched to one in welding technique—I shared space in a small studio, where I spent hours brazing and soldering light-gauge metal. The switch is important because it clarified in a concrete decision my "instinctive" sense of sculpture. For me, it was important—even necessary—to construct sculpture additively from a core, which is what you do when you weld, rather than to subtract from the material at hand by chipping away at it from the outside, which is the essence of stone carving.

The kinds of structures I began to envision and eventually to make were related to abstract expressionism (the paintings of Franz Kline, perhaps). They would later be parodies of pieces of furniture: common coffee tables and love seats, and, more importantly, flying machines. I equipped one coffee table with its own plumbing, clumps of hinged pipes underneath that could be rearranged or redirected on impulse. Another piece, *Hog Shaver's Chariot,* was a three-sided life-size box with wings and wheels, handles, a grill for peering out at the world, and, on the interior, a pair of large chrome lips.

In the spring of 1960, still working on my master's degree, I was also pregnant, and left school for one semester. When my baby was born in the summer, I had neither income nor employment. I was offered instead two fellowships. One was a Woodrow Wilson grant to finish my thesis at Berkeley; the other was an invitation to study medieval Danish architecture for a year at the Danish Royal Academy of Fine Arts in Copenhagen. I wanted a change from my life in Berkeley, so I went off to Denmark with my infant son. I worked diligently on my architectural history project for several months. Continuous exposure to stocky Danish Romanesque buildings, and

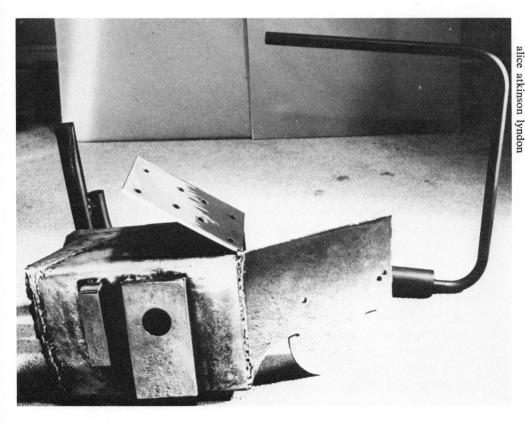

American Mailbox #10, chrome-plated steel

particularly my impressions of the form and layout of the five towers of my favorite church, Kallundborg, produced dramatic sculptural juxtapositions in my mind, and the urge to make sculpture surfaced forcefully.

I tried to return the balance of my stipend to the Danish Ministry of Education so that I would not feel morally obligated to finish my project. The Ministry was quite perplexed; probably I should have kept the money. At any rate, I rented a basement room, bought lots of plaster, and began making large amorphous plaster pieces. To support myself, I started working for a tile-setter and mason. I can't forget the expression on the face of the Danish woman whose bathroom floor I was relaying when she learned that I had had about thirty minutes' experience in tile-setting. When I discovered my employer had no intention of paying me, I stopped taking my turn stirring our tub of concrete, accepted a bicycle offered up in exchange for my efforts, and with it found another (paying) job in a newspaper plant, counting and crediting returned newspapers and periodicals.

I had planned to remain in Denmark, but I was undeniably over-educated for the jobs I managed to find, and, more critically, my eighteen-month-old baby suffered one respiratory infection after another in an interminable northern winter. So we made our way to the south of France; while there I received an offer of a teaching assistantship at Berkeley in an architectural history course in the art department, and I took it.

During the year of that assistantship (1962–1963), I transferred my own work to the studio department in order to concentrate on sculpture. The studio department at Berkeley had established its own foundry for metal casting. While women students were not then permitted to handle the furnaces or the crucibles of molten metal, and while this may have been a form of prejudice about the capabilities of women, I think it is important to say that I personally never experienced other forms of sexist prejudice in that department. We all made our own molds, rammed up the molds before the pouring, and cleaned the pieces afterward.

I received my master's degree in sculpture in June 1963, was hired by the School of Architecture to take charge of their slide collection, and married an architect. I was totally involved in three-dimensional forms—him!, architecture, and sculpture. I had done several small bronze pieces my last year in the studio department, but was becoming increasingly fascinated by aluminum because of its lighter weight —a moderately large piece might weigh as little as fifteen or twenty pounds—a distinct advantage in the business of forming and carting large pieces of sculpture.

For lightweight flexibility, cardboard isn't bad either, as I discovered in the fall of 1964, surrounded by packing boxes and a new baby daughter, born two weeks after we moved to Oregon (the new location of my husband's work). First makeshift, then almost serious, these cardboard constructions began to fill our entire living space. The one I liked best, *Mother Machine,* I had cast in bronze—the first piece for which I hadn't done most of the casting preparation myself.

With another sculptor, I found a welding shop in Eugene, run by a congenial, sympathetic man whose main job was reinforcing saw teeth. During the time we worked in his shop, our proprietor started making sculpture himself. A truck-repair garage next door had bins of rejected parts and scrap metal that were superb. It was here in his workshop that those parodies of furniture and the grounded flying boxes took form. Hovering in my mind during those Oregon years were the image of Baudelaire's Albatross, with its *"grandes ailes blanches,"* and that exclamation from Gerard Manley Hopkins, "and with ah! bright wings."[1]

Working in Oregon seemed easy, even natural. This had a lot to do with supportive working conditions (all too easily taken for granted). For example, steel and aluminum companies didn't seem to find it odd that a woman would come around looking for factory material. Furthermore, they made deliveries to studios and gave charge accounts, so that if pressed, I could make a telephone order. There was inexpensive studio space readily available in vacant auto-body shops and welding shops, and many people were fascinated by the sculpture itself. There were three or four young women close by to help me in caring for my children. In 1966, I had three gallery shows. Two were joint shows with another sculptor—the first for small work in January and the second for larger pieces in May—followed in November by a one-woman show of the larger pieces in another gallery and city. Six weeks later my second daughter was born, in January 1967. I thought I *could* do *everything*! In the spring, we moved once again, to Massachusetts; pride goeth before a reassessment.

Perhaps all these supportive conditions, one of which was and is my husband, misled me there for a while. I confused the Oregon work-oasis with the real world. Not only had my sculpture taken form and made sense there, it felt right. Work "feels right" when conditions and

[1] Gerard Manley Hopkins, "God's Grandeur," *Poems of Gerard Manley Hopkins* (New York: Oxford University Press, 1970).

people are supportive, when it is self-generated. Too often, as women, we find that our work must be tailored to fit situations that are, conceptually and actually, generated by men. We may "fail" not because we are incompetent or lack initiative, but because in authoritarian, man-made work situations a female may easily be dominated, discouraged, or ignored.

Unfortunately, I remember too many such situations. At one point I was accepted into architecture school, but was scared off by the pressure of an older male architect, who convincingly portrayed a noncareer after school because of prejudice against women in this field. The prejudice was undoubtedly real enough, but I am disgusted with myself that I listened and was swayed. Or: My major professor in graduate school classified me as "excellent ideas, but no follow-through" because I wanted to work on the results of my research in Denmark rather than on his pet project. Or, again: A male faculty member advised an undergraduate student of mine, unsure whether to go into art history or painting, "Oh, you don't want to be a woman artist. They are nasty and bitchy."

Another cover memory: I received notice of my scholarship to study in Denmark while my newborn son and I were visiting my parents, who were supportive of me during a trying time. Filled with glee and pride, I showed the notice of award to my father. He quickly read it and dropped it on the floor with the remark, "Now that you are a mother, you must care for your child properly, and none of this nonsense." Fearing that he might interfere bodily with my going to New York to catch my designated ship (and I have no idea whether my fear was justified or not), I became rather devious, flew "home" to California from Indiana, and then took a train back to New York to get my ship—all this with my six-week-old son.

The Danish liaison office seemed skeptical too about the compatibility of motherhood and scholarship; they asked me to leave the baby somewhere and proceed to Denmark. I couldn't imagine "leaving the baby somewhere," and, in fact, I was able to obtain loving part-time child care from a young Danish wife, and eventually a quasi-dormitory living situation with a built-in infant nursery where my son and I could be together in surroundings extremely conductive to studying and working.

I felt no conflict between my sex and my work when I was a student in Europe, either in France or in Denmark. I think that in France this was probably a result not so much of liberal attitudes about sex roles, but of the political power assumed by students then. They were an important group in the society. Both in France and in Denmark, many women worked, and in Denmark there was an excellent system of child-care centers for working mothers. Here in the United States, difficulties arise not just from prejudices about working women, but particularly from our (puritan?) resistance to the idea of working *mothers* and insistence that there is only one kind of child care, and that kind is maternal.

As they have evolved, my work choices have meant for me a certain alienation from "standard" feminine roles, but I haven't discarded those roles like so much scrap metal. This sometimes produces inevitable feelings of distress about job combinations, and I don't necessarily mean jobs with financial remuneration. I rely on my husband's support and "collaboration." He sees me as a person whose work choices do not include certain societally indicated "female tasks," and yet because we have a family, we have constantly to examine what the nature of family commitment must or can be when both parents choose their work. I have managed, not by subtracting

Orville's Sunny Chair, cast bronze

one or the other role task, but by juxtaposing choices in an additive way. The nature of these juxtapositions became clearer to me when we moved to Massachusetts. Although my family remained supportive, events and conditions did not, and the difficulty of combining roles seemed much clearer and much greater than it had on the West Coast.

When I arrived in Cambridge-Boston and went to get a charge-deliver at a local aluminum supplier, I was laughed out. *No such thing! To an individual???* Only a tedious cash-and-carry could be arranged, and I don't like driving. A few months later, I failed to get a fellowship for which I had applied to a feminist institution. I was convinced from the interview that it was mainly the large size of my pieces and the very act of welding that put them off. The questions "Fire?" and "Large?" came up entirely too many times for their comfort, or mine. I came away with the feeling that even in this institution, which intended to support women with family commitments in pursuing their work, certain jobs were deemed more appropriate, more "supportable" than others. Jobs perhaps of a more delicate nature like scholarly research, poetry, photography; or less delicate but more familiar, such as the practice of medicine.

These incidents loomed large in my mind—in part, no doubt, aggravated by the disorientation of our move east. Rightly or wrongly, they created an unsympathetic image of the Boston area as a literary-intellectual rather than an aesthetic-intellectual place, where my large asymmetrical pieces would be dismissed or go unremarked in a pre-Alan Lelchuk polite literary society. At that point my wings were really dragging the ground. One of my friends has indeed suggested that my large sculptures reflect the scale and the open ambience of the West, and that my current interest in photography may be in some sense an accommodation to a tighter urban environment. My camera I can carry with me.

It is true that my work is, physically, a demanding process. Many people don't expect a woman to do this kind of heavy work. Once, for example, I spent an entire year struggling to make an inner image three-dimensional by combining steel and aluminum, one under a great tension in relation to the other. Under this tension, the lighter, more flexible aluminum became incredibly strong. I was "slapped" many times by the metal flipping out of its clamps; or, when securely bolted down, it pulled heavy steel frames over and out of place. I finally abandoned the project, because in order to assure the stability of the flaglike aluminum banners, I would have had to change the design in such a way that my image of the supple flag would have been lost.

Whatever the practical or ideological obstacles, an architectonic scale is important to me. The proportions of the piece I'm working on must imply a large, open space even if the piece itself is medium or small in size. I have tried to work very small and am always frustrated by being "all thumbs" when attempting to work in miniature—as, for example, when I have to submit models of large-scale works for competitions or for the fabricators of my large exterior sculpture.

I admit that some men seem to have much greater physical strength in their work than some women have. When I look at Mark di Suvero's giant sculptures, I am overwhelmed by the presence of an enormous physical energy that I can't seem to muster. Yet I would also cite the formidable presence of Louise Nevelson's large black sculpture, *Transparent Horizon*, recently installed at MIT by this magnificent seventy-six-year-old woman, aided, of course, by machines and workmen. It is extremely important to learn not only to envision and obtain, but also to *direct,* whatever aid—physical, mental, or technological—is available.

This is a critical idea to convey to women studying sculpture. Most of my students at Wellesley College are definitely afraid of the physi-

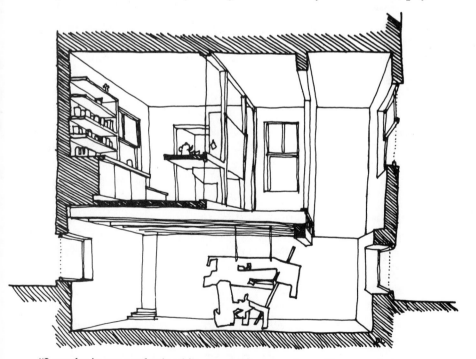

"I can be in my work pit while my children use the walkway cooking space above" (drawing by Donlyn Lyndon)

cal aspects of trying to make sculpture, and if I have read them right, they are somewhat afraid of looking at contemporary sculpture as well. At first, I attributed this diffidence to class distinctions—more or less affluent middle-class girls resisting the manual-training aspects of making sculpture—but it may very simply be lack of experience. I was the first person hired to teach sculpture in studio classes in the art department at Wellesley, and in the past the department's art history courses did not emphasize modern and contemporary sculpture.

During my first year at Wellesley, there was a show in the art department gallery of the work of women artists in New England. I had the only large piece in the show, a cast bronze and steel sculpture called *Orville's Sunny Chair*—two connecting high narrow spaces with extending winglike sections beside a smaller horizontal box, both "dwelling places" moving along on wheels.

A student, in a review, described the sculpture as aggressive and masculine. Later I cornered the student critic, who happened to be in one of my classes, and asked her if she understood much about sculpture or had ever really looked at sculpture. She replied negatively to both questions, and further confessed that the adjectives "masculine" and "aggressive" had nothing at all to do with the piece in question, but rather with my behavior as she perceived it through grapevine anecdotes—that is, that I welded (*masculine*) and that I had lifted a car bumper (*aggressive*). I assure you that the bumper to which she referred was not attached to a car. At home, my son helped me to see the humor in all this with a fantastic image of me jumping into a convenient campus phone booth and emerging as Super Teacher in my bumper-lifting costume.

But if I have taught these girls anything, or if my work says anything, it has to be (as a friend put it) that "massive is not masculine." I want them to know that the ability to use tools and to solve problems physically does not maim a woman or necessarily inhibit her relationships with others, women or men. The risk-taking that this ability entails offers students the satisfactions of problems well-initiated and excitingly solved. I have been startled to discover that the prejudices, anxieties, and misunderstandings about my kind of work that one might expect to find in the attitudes of men also lurk in feminist consciousnesses and in institutions designed to support women's emergence in an active work world.

My personal work world depends very much upon the kind of work space available to me. Studio space was hard to come by and outrageously expensive in Cambridge or Boston. I had "inherited" one reasonable and desirable space from another artist, but it was located in a funny pocket of the city without AC current, so I couldn't use my power tools and electric welder there without a costly generator. Also, I needed a space which I could use at night without having to drive. (Because of a retinal degeneration I cannot see at night.) So we decided to purchase an older house in the Boston area with enough light and space for my work.

A home studio, although not an ideal situation—being there physically generates the idea of availability and the plain fact of lots of interruptions—had to be an acceptable alternative. There is no telephone in the studio space proper, but I rarely answer a telephone anyway. It is a crude invasion of privacy. (How can someone, without my permission, because of the plethora of electronic means available, arbitrarily plunge into my work and time and place?) I temporarily used the dining room for lighter-weight work such as drawing and stitching vinyl bags for use in sculptural combinations, and eventually I created another workroom on our top floor opposite a new darkroom. There, removed from the rest of the household, I can work on drawings, prints, and photographs. But, the basement of the house had to be the major studio space for larger (heavier) pieces; here, materials could be bought in from the back through a door on grade, and a concrete floor and stone walls are safer if one is going to be welding.

The basement, however, was, and still is, dark and damp. The rear section had a raised wooden floor and tubs; once the laundry room, it was less damp by far, but still quite dark. My architect husband and I decided to tear out two thirds of the kitchen floor (above the old laundry room) as well as a porch on one side of the house so that the studio space would be lit on three sides and from a double-story window on one of these sides.

The remaining third of what used to be the kitchen became a walkway-galley with storage cupboards and the usual kitchen machines along a linear path. By means of these spatial arrangements, I hoped, with my family's help, to combine domestic and professional "works" rather than having to choose one and completely phase out the other. More "phasing out" than I anticipated has occurred in the last two years, however, as I no longer cook very much, and then only in the simplest fashion. My children and husband all take turns and jobs are traded. My husband and I cook some, my kids cook a lot, a regular house guest cooks, and we often go out to eat.

I can be in my work pit while my children use the walkway cooking space above. I can give advice from below, but it is usually not necessary, as they all have learned to cook rather well. Raising the children to be this independent involved a period when they were allowed to "find and prepare" regardless of the disorder they created. The detritus from a two-year-old's getting her own chocolate ice cream from the freezer would drive some people berserk; now the children are sometimes orderly, and even clean up afterward.

I want to emphasize that I am not unwilling to perform tasks that are generally considered feminine, but I am unwilling to sustain what becomes for me in the instance of cooking a particular kind of work overload. I work with my own, or with students' formal juxtapositions all day long; especially since I began teaching sculpture as well as doing it, I find that when I get home from work I am depleted of the creative energy it takes to "arrange" foods to make a meal. For me, food combinations such as walnuts on broccoli—like additive sculpture—involve presentations of objects in terms of their color, shape, and spatial arrangement. English muffins with peanut butter, and Bosc pears and a fat glass of dark beer surrounded by massed yellow

Pembroke Gateway, 1975, painted steel and brass

candles and purple anemones are simple, but somehow beautiful. If I feel many times that I cannot make such a presentation, this is not a matter of feminist protest but the result of "shape-juxtaposition fatigue."

In 1973, during a four-month work period in San Francisco, I began to photograph mechanical service apparatus on top of buildings in the city because I was excited by their sculptural qualities. Gradually I became fascinated by the spatial descriptions that I was able to obtain in the photographs themselves. I could experiment with the relationships of windows and pipes to buildings; persons to rooms, walls, and openings; and do so without breaking my back. Because of the physical endurance required in making sculptural pieces, it is more difficult to make the rapid changes one envisions in the mind's eye, and to see, in fact, how the spaces and their occupying forms will relate to each other after the change. The photographic process permits an immediacy and directness which allows yet another kind of exhaustive investigation. In an hour, with Polaroid film, I can make twenty to thirty juxtapositions of a corner to a wall, column, or window, or see ten ways in which the curve of my daughter's face relates to the curve of a column. Photography allows me thousands of associative and visual overlappings immensely poignant in themselves and also suggestive and directive for my next piece of sculpture.

At present, I am working on the problems of combining transparent positive film material with opaque materials such as metal and paper, so that the sculptural boundaries are extended. This extension, through photographs, gives me what I can only describe as a mysterious occupation of territories. The spatial complexities that engage me in those territories are the same ones that overwhelm me when I hear the sounds of a cello; they are the miradors brought to mind by the thinner sounds of a guitar, and the exquisite spatial areas between shoulder blades and in camera hardware, and all these borne on "thin human wings spread out . . . the air beast-crooning to her . . ."[2]

alice atkinson lyndon

[2] James Dickey, "Falling," *Poems, 1957-1967* (Middletown, Conn.: Wesleyan University Press, 1967).

Dependency, Individuality, and Work

Amelie Oksenberg Rorty

Diana Michener

This essay was originally delivered in 1969, as a lecture at the University of Pittsburgh; it was then submitted to *The Yale Review* and subsequently revised for publication there in 1971. I have somewhat rewritten the essay for this book, but have kept it in the impersonal mode in which it was first written. It grew out of my personal experiences and observations, however, and the reader is surely entitled to know where it comes from.

I was born in Belgium of Polish parents. They are interesting people, free spirits but fiercely close parents. My father descended from a long line of rabbis and diamond cutters. Though he had been picked by his family to go into diamond cutting, he set for himself the life of a free-wheeling intellectual who tried to live out the ideas of the philosophers he admired: Rousseau, Jefferson, the late Tolstoi. He occasionally traded in diamonds, but because he despised that profession, he exercised it as little as possible—only enough to finance his various philosophic experiments. Though she viewed my father's enterprises with a cool and ironic eye, my mother went along with them. A linguist who sometimes fell into canning beans and making summer dresses out of grain sacks, she introduced steadiness and composure into what otherwise might have been chaos. Farsighted, my parents left Europe just before the war. Descended from families that had for centuries been urban, they bought a run-down farm in the Blue Ridge Mountains of Virginia and rehabilitated it by hand, on their own.

Though I remember Belgium (gray, cold, empty, dull), I spent most of my childhood on an isolated American farm; the nearest neighbors had never seen foreigners before, let alone Jewish foreigners trying to live an eighteenth-century life. The folk of the Virginia mountains were a reserved, proud, kindly, Christian, wholly mysterious people. I have, ever since, been strongly and usually disastrously drawn to such people. Though I have never succeeded in understanding them (nor have they usually been able to make much sense of me), I cherish them and long for their company and for the serenity I imagine them to possess. My primary sense of life is the alien child's wonder: "What could the grownup *goyim* be thinking and feeling?" Considering how strange the world is, this is probably not a bad question to be asking, though it leads to a certain loneliness. My younger brother, who grew up as an American, has a wholly different outlook on life; he is in the middle of it, an active participant.

School? It was awful. I went to college as soon as I could. The University of Chicago accepted students by examination, so I went off at fifteen. In those days, an undergraduate education at the University of Chicago sent one to philosophy. I developed a passion for it, an addiction. I could hardly ask someone the time of day without turning the inquiry into a deep philosophical consideration of the difference between Time and Eternity. Fortunately or unfortunately, we were all like that at the U of C, so I was not lacking for good, intimate friends. Most of us became philosophers, thereby saving the rest of the world a lot of trouble. Many of us married philosophers. I too married another Chicago philosopher when we were graduate students at Yale, both of us still infants and *idiots savants*, each self- and universe-centered with not much else in between.

Marriage? I found it a very lonely business, lonelier than not being married. Now that I am no longer married, I have the right to call a few friends to come over to pass the evening away; then, I had to ask for permission, which was often not granted because of Work. Her husband is often the last person to whom a young woman with standard graduate student miseries can turn for help. The men, most of them proud and insecure, are struggling with similar problems; a wife's insecurity is an intolerable added burden. On the other side, I was, as I expect many women are, just plain afraid of my husband, too anxious for his good opinion, too sensitive to his dark moods. As a young man, my husband was a person of high and austere ideals, rather rigid, very reserved, a brilliant philosopher. He was dedicated to the greater glory of God through philosophy, and to developing his self-respect. He was not inclined to notice that I was uneasy and frightened; and even with good will, he had little experience that would have enabled him to help me deal with my difficulties. Now that he thinks less of philosophy and, as he should, more of himself, he is, I hope, enjoying life more.

Jobs. The minute I first walked into the classroom, right after I left Yale, I found I adored teaching. The show-off ham had a captive audience and a respectable excuse. I could tell myself I was opening student minds to alternative universes, introducing them to Critical Thought, when what I was really doing was enjoying myself.

More jobs, always within commuting distance of my husband's jobs.

(I taught at Wheaton, Rutgers, Barnard, Haverford.) I did the commuting and the housekeeping and whatnot. Whatnot included a certain amount of writing, but less than I would have liked. And certainly not as good or as responsible. (No *Sitzfleisch*.) We decided to have a child. Since I was so enamored of the joys of teaching, I continued to do that full-time. We had a son, a superb fellow, now fifteen, whose wise and wry tact I admire. How he has managed to put up with the hard times both his parents have given him is not altogether clear to me.

For one reason and another and mostly for no reason at all, I decided in 1971 to take a two-year research fellowship at King's College, Cambridge. Since my husband didn't hold with this idea, it meant a divorce. So I took a divorce too. Ever since then, I have been teaching and scribbling and more or less continuing life as usual, enjoying above all sitting in front of the fireplace with friends pondering the strangeness of the world.

This account of myself suggests that the events of my life form a story. My parents were like this, so I became such and such; I went to the U. of C., so the inevitable happened; I married this sort of man, so my life took a certain course. But this sort of narrative gives an autobiography more shape than I believe it really has. It locates the directions and turns of a seemingly continuous movement. In truth, the real agents of my life have been, as I believe they are in every life, Time and Chance. Most of the events that were formative were coincidences. It was pure chance that I heard about the University of Chicago's early admissions program; pure chance that having decided to do graduate work in philosophy at Yale, I should meet an old Chicago classmate there. Everything crucial might easily have been wholly different. The good things that have happened to me—and there have been many—seem to have been largely a matter of good fortune. I am less convinced that the damaging things might have gone otherwise. I do not have the sense of having been at the center of my life, directing its course; I am not even aware of having been there at all, living it all out. Nor do I seem to myself to be the Outcome of All That Has Happened. I recognize only a certain continuity of style, the style of a solemn owl hoping to grow up to be a womanly Charlie Chaplin, but not quite able to manage the juggling with the careless air that it requires.

THE FIRST AMERICAN public act was a declaration of independence. We projected self-determination by an act of separation and war; and now we measure our success in achieving independence by our capacity to secure the respect, if not effect the domination, of others. Autonomy is measured by productivity and creativity of a rugged and tangible sort. It is the quantifiable aspects of power on which we focus —more, and bigger, and stronger—and it is the impact on others that seems to count most. Everything in our society today preserves and reinforces that original purpose. Our schools are organized to promote self-reliance, to encourage the initiative of children in setting their own projects and completing them resourcefully. Children are admired for autonomy, and gain their self-respect through self-reliance. Literature is judged for its power and impact, and intellectuals, wishing to be forceful, judge themselves by their effects on others.

Even the more cooperative and craftsmanlike virtues of laboring for a common end—the sorts of virtues that require a commitment to a shared purpose, and a willingness to adapt one's gifts to the general needs of the community, to set aside or ignore the will to leadership— even these gifts are fundamentally judged by the capacity to stand by, independently, to contribute individual resourcefulness. Individual creativity and originality come first; the secondary cooperative virtues are their shadow, and are modeled after them: for it is still the stamp of individuality that we admire.

Of course independence and its connection with manifest power is a myth; and in our clearest moments we know it to be so. Nevertheless by this myth we are all judged, judge one another and ourselves. We put ourselves on trial; we try one another, we are trials to one another. With judgment comes self-contempt and hatred. We do have countervailing myths, myths that draw us in other directions of cooperation and reliance. But having them doesn't liberate; it only adds conflict to contempt.

By these standards of self-defining lives, most women must judge their own lives failures. From the most trivial to the most profound ways, the lives of women are not self-determined, but find their shape and substance, their tempo and content, determined by the lives of their fathers, their husbands, and their children. Trivially, we take our names from our fathers and our husbands. More importantly, we live where the work of our husbands takes us, we move in the social and intellectual circles formed by their lives; our time and employment are determined largely by the demands and achievements of our men. Of course we can negotiate these matters; but that indirection reinstates and reinforces dependence. It makes us coy or demanding, for by and large we negotiate on the basis of affection rather than cooperation. If all of our expectations were otherwise, if we were judged by quite different models, the messages of dependence might not be so debilitating. But the myths and the expectations are what they are, and the judgments follow upon them.

The lives of most men are hardly autonomous or self-determined either. But the terrible irony is that our dependence, instead of bringing us closer together as common victims of our myth, only ends by separating us further. Not even the most senior corporation executive can determine his own work or his own life-style. But he does have one relative advantage—an advantage he has won at his own cost; even at his most powerless, he determines the social realities of his family. The most helpless Nevada croupier can say, "Okay, we're not making it here, we'll pull up stakes and go elsewhere." And the family goes. Of course this very fact is a millstone around his neck. Precisely what empowers him, in relation to his family, is also what leads to mutual resentment. Women resent their dependence; men resent the crippling dependence of their families, their expectations and demands, their passive resentment. The cycle of power by control breeds a cycle of hatred, defeat, and self-contempt.

Women's traditional roles—maintaining comfortable households and raising children, as they are now defined—must be self-defeating failures. The reasons for this come primarily from the realities of our economy. Every household art is now advertised as effortless, every good is sold as a time- and work-saver, every gadget made to be used by pressing a button. The message is that every idiot can do it; it seems to follow that anyone who spends her life doing it must be an idiot. Tasks that were once formidable achievements, that once involved the exercise of ingenuity, are no longer represented in that way. Of course women who run households know better, but their claims, matched against all advertising, sound like nagging complaints. Women provide the necessities, and in our society, the necessities are the very least of what we expect. Those who provide them, therefore, gain the very least of our respect.

Our interest in mobility actually dominates our family allegiances or affections. We rarely know the families of our friends; we often hide our own. How then can any woman judge her worth by raising a family when she knows that every self-respecting child must get out of the shooting range of family life as soon as possible? In the American middle class, woman's tasks are the solitary ones of nagging, socializing, of promoting dead and unfulfillable ideals, of giving empty praise. Performed in isolation in the suburbs, these are hateful and debilitating tasks because they cannot be performed well.

In fact, the education of children is far too important a matter to be left to mothers alone; they are no more intrinsically suited to the exacting demands of that task than any other arbitrarily designated group of people might be. Raising children is the task of the whole of society. If tragedies and dramas of family life have taught us nothing else, they have taught us that in corrupt societies the capacity to raise children lovingly, with wisdom and patience, is not very widespread; women are no more likely to be endowed with it, as a class, than men. The exercise of that capacity, when it exists, cannot be exacted from one person in a family. For the greater part of the history of mankind, child raising was not exclusively in the hands of mothers or even of women; it was a job for the extended family, and extended neighborhood. It is only relatively recently, in industrial and urban societies, that child rearing has been thought to be the job of mothers of nuclear families. We are now just beginning to realize how devastating it can be for children to be intimately exposed only to one person during their early formative experiences.

This form of family life cannot help but be damaging to children. Independently of the psychological inroads made by their sensing the resentment of their frustrated mothers, there is the damage done by the inconsistency between the theory and the practice of democratic rule. How can we expect to develop independent, self-reliant, *democratic* traits, when children see that one member of the family has her whole life centered on performing intimate and personal services for the others? The middle class is in the shadowy area halfway between a servant society and a society of genuinely autonomous individuals. We have not outgrown a servant society; we've just rebaptized "cook," "governess," "maid" and called her "mother." That technology has made these duties easier to perform doesn't affect the location of responsibility. Dependence on an unacknowledged and essentially unrewarded servant is not conducive to democratic respect for others.

Defeated by their failures, middle-class women often turn to the arts, to self-expression, hoping to find there not only release but also real development. But no amount of gardening, weaving, and modern dance, not even becoming part-time students and part-time community organizers, will help unless society actually values these activities, needs them and honors them. If turning to self-expression is regarded primarily as therapeutic, the hidden message is always self-destructive. Self-expression presupposes a self; it cannot be used, magically, to acquire one without reinforcing the message of debility and disability. It is only when the activities of self-expression—whether they be low or high culture, whether they be playful or utterly serious—are regarded by the society as important that the exercise of such activities can carry importance. That means they cannot fundamentally be private acts; that is just tolerated onanism. Self-expression will bring self-respect only if it expresses the fundamental conflicts, the basic problems of society, if it holds a mirror up to the whole society for clearer vision rather than a private mirror for a private anguish.

The arts, almost without exception, portray the lives of men and women in disastrous ways. In novels, male protagonists regard their dependence on their women as a sign of their own debility, to be corrected by a certain amount of aggression toward women. If they could, they would free themselves of their mothers, their wives, their daughters. Even in moments of desire and tenderness, even in moments of community, protagonists in novels wish to be freed of what seems emotional and sexual bondage. It is in trouble and need rather than in common friendship that men turn to women. Of course that must lead to the deepest ambivalence, to resentments and to the dialectic of independence and domination. Women reading about themselves in this light must feel a distance from themselves; not recognizing themselves, they feel shame and loss. For, like the heroes of novels, we come to expect earth-motherly and impossible graces from ourselves; the merely human, the merely finite, represents failure. And having failed, we consider ourselves despicable. No wonder men want to be freed of us, since they have made us represent all their unfulfilled, and perhaps unfulfillable, desires. Of course, the heroes of novels represent impossible ideals for men too; and men as well as women condemn themselves by their heroes. But the range of achievable psychological types in male characters is much wider. There are very few Wives of Bath in fiction, and even the Wife of Bath is an earth goddess in lusty dress, a hard act to follow.

But the worst indignity is the place that women have in the economy. Our primary social function is that of sparking the economy by being consumers. In the first place, we are the spenders of what we have generally not ourselves earned. And that puts us in potential conflict with the men who earn what we must spend. What is worse is that most consumer goods—whether they are sold to men or to women—convey a message of personal worthlessness. Goods are sold to men as bearing a message of power, with the false promise that owning them enhances, or at least expresses, stature and achievement. They are large and mechanized; they move fast, far, and hard, and they are often potentially destructive. The implication is, tragically enough, that a man's identify is enhanced by something that is not fundamentally within his own person. This is indeed quite a different

conception of power from that conveyed by the ability to grow cauli-
flowers or make gargoyles out of mud, or by being stoical and humorous in times of stress. The objects that convey status can only be
bought and operated. They are external to a person, do not spring
from his character but attach themselves to him. And in the end he
becomes dependent upon them; he is their inept servant. And the
same is true, even more powerfully, for women./The ornaments we
buy to adorn ourselves or our houses, to display ourselves, are sold to
us on the grounds that having them will magnetize attention; we are
told that by possessing them we shall become more attractive. But the
hidden message is that we are only genuine persons if we can magnetize others; in *ourselves* we barely exist./Our essential unornamented
selves in an unornamented environment are not good enough; without
the products we buy, the suggestion is, we are nothing, essentially
nonpersons.

The dispossession of our bodies goes further. Aggressive consump-
tion debases the great grace of discovering oneself through being
loved into the poverty of feeling whole only when one is possessed, as
if loving were not the appreciation, but the appropriation, of another.
The poetics and politics of this subject have already been exploited, so
I want, instead, to focus on the practical medical consequences of
women's dispossession of their bodies. Women are discouraged from
becoming surgeons or airplane pilots on the grounds that periodic
dysmenorrhea affects judgment and performance. This is done without
extended studies of the irregular malfunction of the male glandular
system, and without any concerted attempts to stabilize or relieve the
side effects of the menstrual cycle.

The allocation of funds for research in pharmaceutical companies
is—as are all decisions about the distribution of scarce resources—a
complex political matter, sensitive to fashion, publicity, economic
pressure. Of course a certain percentage of funds is always allocated
to research on contraception and on what are regarded as female
ailments. But women, like the poor, are underrepresented when the
crucial issues determining percentages and priorities are decided in
the executive councils. As long as pharmaceutical companies can
market their products without scandalous loss of life, the sorts of
dangers and discomforts that can mar a person's work will receive
little attention. Nor is it immediately clear how women can form the
sort of noisy lobby that would make it worth the difference in cost for
the companies to undertake concerted and intensive research.

The lives of the women who are in the entourage of academic and professional men—lawyers, doctors, and the like—carry extra hazards. For while the wife of a postman or a grocer can respect the social value and understand the personal satisfactions of her husband's work, she knows that she could do it too and knows pretty much how she could do it. It is not like being married to a priest or being the nurse of a great surgeon; there is nothing sacred involved. But the women who surround scholars, scientists, and politicians are in the service of men who feel entitled to demand sacrifice from their women without embarrassment. They are not doing it in their own name, but in the name of something that is supposed to transcend them all. Which means that the women don't even have a right to their grievances, which are presumed to prove their lack of seriousness, to be signs of faithlessness, even of frivolity. Who are they to want to define their own lives and leisure, their tempos and occupation, against the demands of such service? And even if an intellectual drives himself, it is at least his choice and, in the end, his achievement. What the women get out of that, if they are lucky, is a grateful note in the preface commending them for their patience and thanking them for their encouragement. There is nothing lower than being the servant of the servant of the sacred; in that world, even any stirring of self-definition is guilt-ridden, shameful.

The wives of intellectuals and professional men are often as highly trained as their husbands, often as intent on their work and scholarly projects. But what typically happens is that, at a time when both are just starting to work, the man gets a better job offer than the woman; the woman follows him and takes her chances on finding something within the vicinity. There is rarely anything to match his working conditions, his stimulation; she is lucky if she finds anything at all. The common pattern is for her to languish at home, trying to work on her book or finish her thesis, all the while blaming herself for making little progress. At first her husband is sympathetic, but he loses sympathy fairly quickly. After all, she has, at this stage, more time than he; if she can't work, it is perhaps because she really isn't interested or, as it turns out after all, has less to say. Neither of them recognizes that intellectual productivity requires a special environment. Academic men often discover, on sabbatical leaves, that the time spent in isolation, just outside Oxford in a little village, is less productive than the time when they are also carrying on their teaching duties. Very often they become miserable and despair of their own capacities. The truth is that, for most people, the regular companionship of colleagues working in roughly the same area is not only a support but a virtual necessity. Even what seems like solitary work is often social in nature; one has to take the last paragraph down the hall and try it out on someone, one has to try to explain a thesis to a skeptical seminar. It is there, and not in the totally solitary environment, that work gets done. Not realizing this, a young couple may decide that the wife who can't seem to write in solitude, without a job, was not really cut out to be a scholar after all. They begin the round of children. After that, the frustrations and the despair really set in, because the woman was probably just as much of an intellectual as her husband, and simply didn't realize that an intellectual needs the sustaining life of colleagues, companionable sparring partners. So the woman who has turned her back on what she thought was her life, and turned her full attention to something she had originally thought would only be a part of her life, is a woman who is defeated and bitter. She will resent her husband's successes, and blame herself. Eventually her husband will accept her account of the situation and alienate himself, finding his real life in his work or his colleagues or the young graduate students, women who are still interesting and not yet embittered. Everyone has here made a terribly damaging mistake resulting in a tragic waste of talent and, in the end, of affection as well.

If the wives of intellectuals and professionals are thus held in a self-denigrating bondage, without even the right to grievances, then women who are themselves professionals or intellectuals are held in triple bondage. Everything around us tells us that intellectual life is a full-time job: our colleagues are entirely given over to the details of their work. It demands more, often, than even the most stouthearted and devoted man can give. Not all of it, to be sure, is directly connected with scholarship or teaching or medical service. There is a great deal of detailed and distracting administrative work, too; but all the work flows in the same direction, and it is all done in camaraderie, with the cooperation and help of like-minded colleagues. In all this, independence, originality, and above all productivity are the marks of worth. Productivity in research and charisma in the public sphere of one's profession are indeed the criteria of success. And those are absorbing occupations. Professional women have been told that they must take on the roles of wife and mother as well, if they are to be fully developed human beings. And they are told, too, that such occupations, unlike those of husbands and fathers, are—or should be—fully absorbing as well, though less esteem is attached to them because their productivity is less visible. So what then are intellectual women to do? Half-time and halfhearted scholarship is regarded as contemptible; half-time and halfhearted womanliness is regarded as contemptible. And either alone is said to be only half human.

Women can, perhaps, take satisfaction that, as earth mothers and intellectuals, they can lead richer lives than their colleagues, but when shall they find the time for such reflections? Of course many women do manage it—if they are rich, or have helpful relatives, or have superhuman energy, ingenuity, patience and humor, and the mind and heart of thirty saints and geniuses, not to mention the constitution of a healthy horse in its prime. And even then, there is a terrible cost. For such women must become immensely efficient, and efficiency—cost accounting—involves a character loss. It saps originality and creativity. Women who must juggle the demands of many different sorts of lives, tend to become efficient, and so become competent rather than profoundly original scholars. This is no mean feat; it is the daily stuff of scholarship, and most men would be glad to do the sort of competent, productive, time-scheduled work that women intellectuals can do even when their attention is fractured by multiple responsibilities.

But there is something else. Even the most solidly competent men —those who do not aspire to originality or profundity—have that sweet freedom, the freedom of time and movement, that schedule-juggling women do not have. We all need time for sheer musing, for reading novels, playing music, wandering about the rivers. And this is precisely what efficient scholarly women do not have; we become harried, impatient, harsh, less in touch with the wilderness in the world and in ourselves. We cannot respect our eccentricities, cannot honor them to see where they may lead us. We are very good at getting around set limits, at ordering the spaces and necessities around us, but every direction of our lives closes off the possibility of our being able to *refuse to see* those limits. And that is where real originality must be—in really not knowing what to think next and in not caring whether there is a pattern to which the thought will conform.

Moreover, the attention spans of intellectual women who have also accepted traditional roles are fractured by the million emergencies that are the substance of domestic life; even when they can schedule working time, the stray reminder to buy bread on the way home has a way of cropping up as one tries to write a good book on the history of the apostolic succession. Men have stray thoughts too—the napes and ankles of their secretaries distract them, as do plans for an academic coup. But some distractions are draining and some are energizing; some take strength and others give strength. The draining ones nag us, demand something from us; the sustaining ones are those of appreciation, delight, and power. Heavily scheduled women have little time for the sheer contemplative delight that, in ways we do not yet understand, gives life to thought, gives it form and perhaps originality. Of course decent self-respecting professional men can and do take on all sorts of domestic responsibility; but it is always their choice to do so, an act of generosity on their part, and it contributes to self-esteem. In the traditional division of labor, the women are assigned daily, nagging responsibilities for jobs that are never done. There is no rest from them or esteem attached to them.

As competent professionals, women who accept traditional family roles will also tend to be harried and pressed, with little time for sheer companionability. And because none of us really values astringent temperamental traits, the shadow of self-contempt or perhaps even simple animal dislike for ourselves hangs over us. It hangs over all parts of our lives, because with all our harried efficiency we also believe that half-time attention is full-time betrayal. It is important for us to realize that these are not fundamentally the problems of females, but the problems of pressured and divided persons.

Many young academic women marry someone in their own field whose gifts and presence of mind make their company winning. Often such young men are quite unsure of themselves, and their wives must cope with their depressions, their obsessive doubts about their work and status. Academic women and their husbands frequently come to a division of temperament as well as a division of labor in their marriages. The men represent standards of precision and dedication to work; they insist on accuracy and testily correct their wives. The women take on the humane side; they take on the responsibility to provide emotional support and the warmth of friendship. This kind of total division of emotional roles is of course harmful to both; each secretly resents the fact that the other already fills the place where growth lies.

Professional academic women often conclude early on that their husbands outrank them in gifts. And indeed the husbands, for familiar social as well as individual reasons, generally do advance faster and further than the wives. Increasingly self-deprecating, the women frequently become either timid or strident about voicing their views, and remain acutely uncomfortable with either "accommodation" to their increasing sense of inequality with their husbands.

Women frequently must find jobs within commuting distance of their husbands' often more prestigious work places. Even when women are well qualified for the jobs they fill, their positions are ambiguous. They partly owe, or may feel they owe, their jobs to their husbands' good connections and prestige. When the husbands travel in exalted professional circles, the wives come along, benefitting personally, professionally, and socially from the company their husbands keep.

Eventually the husband achieves tenure. His place in the world assured, his growing reputation in his field giving him a sense of his powers, he can now spread himself; he is ready to take walks on Sunday, to explore Greece. But whereas once his wife would have cherished his company, delighted in his wanting to spend time with her enjoying some of life's pleasures, she has come, by this time, to see him through distant eyes. His anxiety and ambition have taken their toll on her regard for him. She cannot see him as do his new friends, charmed by the great professor's (new-found) delight in bird watching and concocting hollandaise sauce. She remembers the times when she couldn't get him to keep the spaghetti from boiling over or go to the movies on Saturday night (let alone to stop fidgeting in embarrassment whenever her outspoken theories seemed foolish or inaccurate); these memories now stand in the way of her pleasure in his company. The husband in turn has come to view his wife as a negative and resentful figure. No one likes being regarded with a cool and critical eye, especially when one has at long last come into one's own professionally. With a mixture of guilt and a perfectly natural wish to be adored, the husband also retreats and becomes detached.

If the sadness and strain caused by these difficulties lead a couple to separate, the chances are that the wife will suffer far more as a former-wife-and-colleague than she did as a wife or than she would have had she never traveled on her husband's passport in his professional circles. Friends and colleagues of "the couple" are now less available to the separated wife than new-formed acquaintances. Former friends and colleagues, believing a choice must be made, choose the husband. After all, it is usually the husband whom they see at meetings and the mailbox, whose life is contiguous with theirs. Without any malice or forethought, the lines of continuity and connection with the wife are broken.

Seeing herself as she believes others see her, the separated wife, like the unmarried woman, is apt to sense herself strange and a stranger. Socially insecure, dependent on the good will of those who can no longer give it wholeheartedly, a woman in these circumstances is too dispirited to work well. Sensing that she has come to be perceived as a resident alien, she may become embittered and withdrawn. There are of course other sources of productive energy than those that are sustained by a feeling of communal participation and regard: anger, outrage, a sense of injustice, raw competitiveness, absorption in important work. But for good or ill, and for reasons we do not fully understand, few women are very good at the ruthless concentration of energies that satisfying and satisfactory achievement calls for. When the perfection of the work threatens the perfecting of our lives, we almost automatically, though often unwillingly, gravitate to what will sustain the life.

Unfortunately, the courage and the spirit it takes to do our work with conviction and élan depends on the kind of communal support that women lack, whatever their domestic condition may be. However, it is only by placing ourselves in actual working situations with men that we will find such support. Only if women and men work together, can we come to rely on one another, and thus to perceive one another as complex persons. We need to place ourselves in situations of mutual *reliance* rather than in relations that polarize dependence and independence. Relations of dependency are zero-sum games; one member's gain means the other's loss. As one member grows, the other languishes. The story of dependence is told by Henry James in *The Sacred Fount* and by William Blake in "The Mental Traveller." Relations of reliance are not zero-sum games; both gain by the contributions of the other, at the cost of neither.

One can perhaps imagine a world in which the specialists temperamentally bent on competitive success happen coincidentally to be male. Perhaps, in this world, females might also happen to be non-competitive people who want to develop a variety of traits in themselves and who find genuine satisfaction and fulfillment of personality in the service of their families. Certainly men have tried to tell us, and to tell themselves, that ours is such a world; a world in which a good father achieves integrity by developing his individuality and contributing *his* talents to the community, while a good mother must find professional and personal meaning in the very process of setting the individuality of her desires aside for the good of the family. We may speculate whether such a world would be a better one than ours, with fewer conflicts and happier people. But it is a matter of observation, and not of speculation, that even if this were an ideal world, it certainly is not our world. Divisions of temperament do not coincide with sexual differentiation. Of course social organization and social practices—every avenue of culture and ritual—can reward this bifurcation, can force it where it does not exist naturally. And, for a while, such heavy pruning may benefit a species, although it takes a heavy toll on individuals who are forced to go against their grain. But pretending that the results of pruning are the designs of nature is another matter.

It is not beyond our ingenuity to sketch constructive plans to overcome the crude bifurcations that now obsess us: between men and women, independent individuals and dependent servitors, competitive specialists and amateurs. The talents we need, and therefore the temperaments we can respect, are far more widely distributed across sexual, ethnic, and class lines than has been thought.

Many people would prefer to have part-time jobs, so that they can devote more time to making dry-stone fences, writing haiku, raising children, or speculating about the minerals on Mars. It is possible that the balance between specialists and nonspecialists, between competitive and musing types, is such that the goods we now prize (specialized medical care, for example) will not be endangered because no one would, without social pressure, choose specialized work and the intensified life that goes with it. In all probability, however, promoting a fuller range of temperament and ability requires far-reaching social and economic changes.

It is just such changes, and our assumptions about the directions they should take, that we ought to be exploring. We need a profound and revisionary analysis of our social and economic priorities and the distribution of labor and esteem that these priorities demand. It is in such common tasks of social planning that men and women must work in mutual reliance. In a practical way, we must, with simplicity, clarity, and matter-of-fact determination, place ourselves in positions where our lives and works match our temperaments and capacities. This requires more than redefining patterns of child-rearing responsibility. The reform of the family is only a small part of the larger task of redefining the grounds for mutual esteem. We must give up the myths of success, power, and independence; revise our conceptions of human worth. I reflect with some bitterness and irony that, even in trying to think clearly about the situations of women, it is independence and liberation that I emphasize.

I don't believe that we are now in any position to know whether women's problems in finding and doing their work—at their most profound level—are primarily sexual or primarily socioeconomic. Whatever the case, I am not sanguine about the prospects of improving our conditions within our lifetime. Even if we were clear about how to reform our conceptions of self-respecting lives, to change our criteria for mutual esteem means to overcome forces of resistance and inertia so powerful as to undo the lives of transitional generations.

However splendid the achievements of those who commit themselves to searching out better social forms, their revolutionary stance exacts a heavy price in the impoverishment and isolation that usually characterize lives lived cross-grain to the temper of the times. The mechanisms of social vindictiveness against social explorers—as women are today in the United States—are as vicious as they were in the nineteenth century; that these forces are less visible only makes them more powerful.

Be that as it may, this is a period in which we explore new and ancient forms of social life. We have much to hope for and much to lose. Many of us have willingly accepted the ancient Chinese curse, "May you live in interesting times," not because we hope for joy, but because there is no reasonable, acceptable alternative.

Amélie Rorty

Birth of the Amateur
Pamela Daniels

alice atkinson lyndon

It is calm and peaceful in the delivery room. I am lying on the
delivery table. In very slow motion, my obstetrician, who is
V. I. Lenin (the familiar face of Bolshevik poster art), is benevo-
lently nodding toward me and delivering the baby from my navel.

I WAS ALMOST twenty-six when I dreamt this dream in the spring of
1963. A Ph.D. candidate and tutor in political science at Harvard, I
had passed my generals in January. Uncertain about a thesis topic, I

had contracted to join the interdisciplinary staff of teaching fellows in Erik Erikson's undergraduate course on "The Human Life Cycle" in September.

I gave birth to my first child in May. Lenin was not my obstetrician and babies are not born from the navel—I knew that much. But I was like a newborn myself in the inner world of my own psyche, an innocent on the "royal road." I found the dream charming, even funny, but for a long time I could no more fathom the benign incongruity of its imagery than I could dispel its sense of imminence.

I read *The Interpretation of Dreams* for the first time that summer, in which Freud demonstrates that dreams are filaments leading back into the past and down into the dark places of the unconscious— symbolic fulfillments of the most powerful fantasies and archaic ambitions of childhood. The regressive tug of the dream was, and is, clear enough: down and back to the classic oedipal wish of the little girl and to the chaste complacency of the childhood conception of how babies are born. Yet the dream not only evoked the past, it intimated the future. To paraphrase Dylan, "Something's being born here, but you don't know what it is, do you, Mrs. Jones?"

I have come to interpret this "delivery dream" as a metaphor for generativity[1] conflict. The dream is about the conflict between dutiful dependence in work versus a self-generated sense of responsibility for what I do. It is about being a daughter and the importance of fathers to me versus being a mother and making a connection with my own mother. It is about the overlap between work and love. It is about the

---

[1] Erik H. Erikson's concept of the identity crisis is well known. It has captured the imaginations of youth, clinicians, and the general public. Less familiar is his conception of the psychosocial crises of adulthood. Moving beyond identity, Erikson has elaborated Freud's prescription for adult vitality—to love and to work—in the adult stages of Intimacy versus Isolation and Generativity versus Stagnation (*Identity: Youth and Crisis* [New York: W. W. Norton, 1968]). I want to spell out my sense of Erikson's concept of generativity because it is a timely idea, because it has illumined my sense of work that is worth doing, and because it has provided the theoretical frame for the work I now do—research in the psychology of adult development.

Generativity refers to what people *do* with who they have become—to the extension, elaboration, and revision of individual identity in patterns of love and work and care. The heart of generativity in Erikson's definition is "the concern for establishing and guiding the next generation." This caring concern for the next generation includes, but is not restricted to, parenthood; it refers to any and all activity included in what the Hindus call the "maintenance of the world."

In principle, the idea of generativity moves beyond this culture's traditional division of labor based on sex-role stereotypes. That is, *for both sexes*, generativity refers to both procreation and production, to the capacity for nurturance and for achievement, to a sense of personal accomplishment as well as support for the accomplishments of others. Implicit in the concept of generativity is the developmental prescription of activity, of continuing growth and change in order to remain alive in one's work and love.

tension between professional identity and a more elemental self-definition. Working through the dream puzzle has been symbolic of the slow-motion process of self-discovery and self-acceptance that has enabled me to begin to stand on my own, to love myself enough to define and pursue work I would love to do—to recognize the amateur dimension of generative adult work. It has helped me to clarify and begin to resolve fundamental confusion in my head about what women can create, produce, and generate.

To begin with in the dream, lying on the delivery table, I am both a special kind of patient and a passive participant in the proceedings. And indeed, there was a passive, insensible quality about my graduate apprenticeship. Academic political science was the culmination of a series of "choices" determined for me by others and by the fact that I did well in school. A firstborn daughter, I was bright and unquestioning, a very good girl. To please my father (and over the years, the gifted and encouraging teachers, men and sometimes women, who were like him) was purpose enough.

Psychoanalysis has given us the concept of the cover memory—that is, a memory that not only stands out vividly in the mind but also functions as a magnet in the unconscious, "standing for" a cluster of related and similar incidents, wishes, and feelings. A dominant cover memory from my childhood is the small momentous rhetorical ritual my father and I often performed in company. "When your Daddy tells you to do something, what do you do?" he would ask, and my response was "Do it." No father was more proud, no daughter more obedient.

But fathers don't stay with us for life. Not even for very long. As my parents turned to care for my brother, who was born when I was two and a half, I recreated them, their standards and expectations, in the form of a constant companion, a sober little boy of about four whom I called Gudge.[2] He was my secret mentor. He set the pace, called the shots, knew right from wrong, took me across the street, kept me a prudent distance from that baby brother. Whatever Gudge told me to do, I did. He could count on me, I could count on him. We were inseparable.

Confident of his tenure in my inner world, Gudge was eventually replaced in my everyday life by neighborhood friends and schoolmates. In school, I turned out to be a very good student—because I followed instructions brilliantly and did my homework thoroughly. I aimed to please and did. I won the spelling bee, the Latin prize, the

---

[2] Just learning to talk, I pronounced the initial letter "j" hard as in "gut" rather than soft as in "judge."

Phi Beta Kappa key, the Woodrow Wilson fellowship. All without reflection or inner consent. I went from kindergarten to graduate school without asking why. Ambitious for me, my parents, especially my father, wanted me to be a foreign service officer (or a college president); so I majored in political science. Yet as I moved up, grade by grade, achievement by achievement, no one consulted me, least of all me. Until 1963, I had been a devotedly willing and at the same time involuntary participant in my own career development.

Although my marriage straight out of college ruled out the foreign service, it took me to India, where I began to study the history of the struggle for independence. Marriage did not change my mind about work. On the contrary, it effectively quelled ambivalence; I was spared anxiety about whether outright ambition would compromise my "femininity," which in the cultural currency of the fifties meant marriageability. I never came to look upon my work as "filler"—as something a woman does while waiting for the right man. I was lucky; without suspense, I married the person with whom I still choose to share my life. Neither of us intended that I drop my work or exchange my safeguarded, seemingly independent ambitions for wife-and-motherhood. It was not a point of ideology in those inter-feminist years; we were as matter-of-fact as we were naive. Confidently determined not to reduce the scale of my life, I planned simply to incorporate these new roles into it.

So far, so good. But by now I had a thesis to produce. For the first time in my life I paused in my work: Could I deliver the goods? And, more to the point: What were the goods anyway? An acquaintance at work, no novice at dream interpretation, when I related the delivery dream to her, commented wryly, "That's hopeful. Most women dream of their intellectual product as shit." Still dependent upon fatherly advocates (and the fraternal Gudge) to set the standard, unaccustomed to find or expect support in the work sphere from other women, I was not susceptible to the indirect feminist encouragement in her interpretation. Like "most women," I judged myself and my work harshly. Moreover, I was unconvinced that the "baby" in the dream was a Ph.D. thesis or any other intellectual product. Deep down and dimly, I sensed that there was a good deal going on in the delivery room of that dream—by way of drawing out hidden aspirations and purposes—that I, under cover of graduate work and mindless pursuit of achievement, was avoiding.

The doubt and hesitation cropping up in 1963 were by no means all that conscious. Although I had once seriously considered transferring to the History Department because I found the abstraction and quantification in political science uncongenial, my reservations were intellectual; they did not go to the heart of the matter. I undertook my orals with neither more nor less anxiety than others approaching that hurdle. True, I was putting off thesis planning, but this seemed acceptable, given the new claims on both work and love energies of teaching The Human Life Cycle and caring at home for a brand new one, my son's.

Although I now see the conservative, subtly constraining correspondence between the tendency of male faculty to view bright women as favorite daughters and my own still paramount identity of deferential, dutiful daughter, the point here is that I was not treated unfairly, nor was it suggested that women and political science were incompatible. The Government Department in the early sixties included a few women graduate students and (untenured) women faculty, some of whom have gone on to successful, even eminent careers as political scientists. Susanne Rudolph, an early mentor,[3] appreciating my restlessness in political science, assured me that I could very well do history and study biography within the structure provided by the Government Department, and she provided the means to do so, an independent study course in which we pieced together the history of Indian nationalism through the first-person writings of its leaders. Moreover, when she left Harvard she introduced me to the person through whom my life and work would take an unexpected turn.

This brings me face to face, in a roundabout way, with Lenin and his incongruous presence on the obstetrical service. To be sure, he had proposed violence as the midwife of the revolution, but the dream tempo suggests that the "revolution," whatever its undisclosed nature, would take place in slow motion—with patience, not violence. Lenin, in the dream, clearly stands for the lifelong primacy in my inner world

---

[3] Daniel Levinson and his co-workers at Yale have emphasized the critical importance of the presence or absence of mentors in the career development of men. (See *The Seasons of a Man's Life* [New York: Alfred A. Knopf, 1977].) According to Levinson's findings, the ideal mentor is not an awesomely senior patron, *guru*, or parent figure, but rather an experienced, somewhat older co-worker who, not only by example—a mentor is more than a role model—but through regular professional contact and direct encouragement, criticism, and support of work-in-progress, introduces a younger person to a specific work world and "shows the way." The currency of a developmentally significant mentor relationship is not deference and distance but a sort of "dailiness" and the ever more equal give-and-take that generates colleagueship—such that the younger person learns what he or she needs to learn to work alone, choose new colleagues, and eventually become a mentor to others.

Given the sociology of the professions, most women do not benefit from this kind of tutelage and support in their work. By and large, women still must make it on their own, and part of the price of success is a well-defended isolation.

of the figure of the "good father" bestowing benevolent praise and wishing me well—indeed, the best. And also perhaps the unconscious wish for a more radical one.

Moreover, condensing things as dreams do, Lenin symbolically represents political science, the profession in which I was apprenticing. Father of the Bolshevik revolution, political activist, translator of Marxist economics into day-to-day actuality, advocate of working women, Lenin is a symbol of patriarchal power, revolutionary activity—and the liberation of women.

An obstetrician he was not. And indeed, when pregnant, I had steered clear of the host of prominent patriarchs in the Boston obstetrical establishment and deliberately chosen a fraternal young doctor with a new practice who I hoped would have the time and the inclination to answer my questions fully and lend me his books—in short, to teach as well as deliver. As the dream suggests, in its admixture of political science with the primal act of childbirth, I intellectualized childbirth as I did all things sensual, inner, and mysterious. It was an academic assignment, part of the feminine curriculum; I wanted to prepare well, learn the facts, stay in control of the situation, and pass the test at the end.

Yet the dream setting was a delivery room, not an examination hall; the dream event suggested not more of the familiar tests and judges, but the birth of something new—the possibility of stepping out of repetitive cycles of dependency by turning inward at the center of being, as symbolized in the umbilical connection.

A dream is a clever masque. Who was behind this oddly sanguine Lenin, this revolutionary in obstetrical disguise, this hopeful, helpful special delivery man? The free associations that unmask dream figures travel their own mental pathways. Much later than the occurrence of the dream itself, my "dream work" went like this: Lenin . . . revolution-as-violence, revolution-as-benevolence . . . obstetrician/midwife . . . too formidable, too androgynous to be my real obstetrician . . . some other obstetrical authority then? . . . Eastman, the author of the guidebook for expectant mothers I had used . . . Lenin, Leningrad, the east . . . the man from the east. The associations stopped with the definitive click of recognition. For by the time of the dream I had met another formidable man from the east (Vienna) who fundamentally wished women well. An innovator in another modern revolutionary tradition, psychoanalysis. A clinical, rather than a political activist. I am referring of course to Erikson.

Eight months pregnant, I had first met Erikson, just back from India, in the spring of 1963 in an interview for the job of section leader in his undergraduate course. Although we discussed India and our mutual interest in Gandhi, mainly we compared notes on the psychological implications of moving into the next generation. I was not dismissed to the nursery on account of being pregnant, but invited to review his work, to read Freud's early clinical writings over the summer, and to join the staff of his course in the fall. Far from disqualifying me, motherhood somehow enhanced my qualifications to teach in that course.

I worked with Erikson for more than seven years, teaching sections in The Human Life Cycle, participating in his faculty seminar, doing historical research for the book that became *Gandhi's Truth*, and editing some of his other writings. His role in my work life, however, is not so easy to summarize or to isolate from the impact of our relationship on my life as a whole. He was part teacher, part father figure, part collaborator, part friend—and from time to time the amalgam changed.

Erikson was both more and less than a professional mentor. Our association benefited my work in several ways. First, my unorthodox apprenticeship in clinical thinking and psycho-biographic method converted my intellectual interests from political history to life history. Second, working as his editorial collaborator, I developed skill, experience, and a reputation as a good editor who knew the literature of developmental psychology; competence in this professional support role brought me a series of editorial jobs that help pay the bills during the years of personal homework essential to defining work of my own. Third, the years of section work in The Human Life Cycle created close ties with an entire generation of students, some of whom, now thirty years old, have become my "sample" in a longitudinal field study of adult lives.

While I do not dismiss these contributions to my work, Erikson's influence was crucial in a more personal sphere and in less tangible ways. I didn't need a career mentor in 1963 so much as authoritative permission to step back from a premature professional commitment and take some affirmative action on the inner ground of my own psyche. Erikson's sanguine concepts and his judicious presence combined to give both psychological permission and intellectual legitimacy to the inner revolution augured in the delivery dream.

Although deeply repressed pathogenic memories call for systematic clinical treatment, it doesn't require a formal psychoanalysis for the unconscious transference of certain childhood patterns onto adult relationships to become conscious and potentially liberating. My intense positive transference to Erikson "worked" without conventional psychoanalytic intervention on his part; the dutiful daughter identity was perfected and played out. It may seem improbable that I would outgrow the dependency—the "clinch"—of daughterhood in a relationship that so intensified it; however, when transference works, it works that way. Moreover, Erikson took me seriously in adult roles; he engaged me as a co-worker, admired me as a mother, eventually became my friend. Matter-of-factly trusting that I could become someone new, he did not intrude on that process, but provided me with a "margin of freedom" to look inward—if *I* chose to do so. The ground was thus prepared for the homework of the ensuing years. For what was being born in the dream delivery room was neither offspring nor career but some primary connection with myself, an inner life, a sensual core, a recessed dimension I have come to call the *amateur*.

> Pursue, keep up with, circle round and round
> your life as a dog does his master's chaise
>   Do what you love.
> Know your own bone; gnaw at it,
> bury it, unearth it, and gnaw it [still].[4]
>   —Thoreau

The dream intimated a slow delivery; between the faint quickening of insight and the ability to comprehend and act upon it there was a long gestation and an acute work crisis. Outwardly, I continued to perform in the goodgirl/superwoman mode to which I/we/they were accustomed. I knew no other. I finished the first semester in Erikson's course—which took grit, as the differences between psychoanalytic inquiry and political science inquiry perceptibly began to hit home. I managed to outline a thesis on a militant Indian nationalist. I wived and mothered, weaned my son, and become pregnant again—an unconscious effort to obtain the career recess I couldn't admit I needed. My second child was due on Thanksgiving, 1964; I took a year out from Erikson's course, returned in the fall of 1965, and taught not one but two sections. In 1966, I became the head section leader and course administrator. I continued to work with Erikson on Gandhi. I continued to postpone serious thesis work.

I was invited to give a course of my own in Indian history in the

---

[4] Letter to H. G. O. Blake, March 27, 1848, in *The Correspondence of Henry David Thoreau*, Walter Harding and Carl Bode, eds. (New York: New York University Press, 1958), p. 216.

winter of 1968 at a nearby college. I accepted enthusiastically and spent the fall of 1967 in solid hours preparing syllabus and lectures, work I enjoyed. I designed a terrific course. But when the time came actually to teach it, suddenly, at the last minute, I found I couldn't. I couldn't face that class on my own authority. More than that, symbolically, I was not prepared to step out from under the protective cover of identification with the "good father" and confront the dilemma of obedience and autonomy.

I experienced this crisis then as breakdown and failure in the work sphere. I have since come to see it as an abrupt shifting of gears—as something more intricate and radical than a refusal to take the next logical step up the career ladder, although it was that too. Nor was it simply a conscious fear of failure, or an unconscious avoidance of success—although these may have been in it. I celebrate this crisis as I do birthdays, because it marks the first crack in trusty but useless old armor, the end of a resistance I didn't know I had, and the beginning of "getting it together" from the inside out rather than the other way around.

On the surface, it seemed I had merely been overwhelmed by the logistics of teaching that course—winter weather, commuting in a 1954 Ford, the necessity of more regular child care arrangements. Some said I'd taken on too much. Perhaps they were right; yet I felt no grievance on this score. My planning was meticulous, and furthermore, logistics had never immobilized me before (or since). I had successfully organized my life and staunchly juggled all the roles that came my way. Indeed, I jealously viewed the multiplicity of roles as the guarantor and guardian of vitality, as insurance against a one-dimensional, housebound life.

I have asked myself whether I was "really" guilty about being a part-time mother. Although Belden had always encouraged and supported my work—"whatever I wanted to work out"—only in the aftermath of what became for both of us a crisis in our relationship to each other as well as to our work and to our children did he become serious in a daily way about fatherhood. In early 1968, parenting in our household by and large meant mothercare; the three days a week I wasn't home the boys had baby-sitters. Was this crisis just a spasm of the guilt painfully familiar to all mothers who "also work"? This may have been part of it, but I wasn't convinced. In fact, my version of the conflict was the reverse: I held back from identifying with the mother in myself, guiltily surmising that to do so would betray my "career"—the obligations to compete and achieve, to live up to my education, to be my father's reward.

Ironically, by the winter of 1968, child care had actually become simpler. Our sons, five and three and a half years old, now spent weekday mornings in a good nursery school close to home and were getting more and better attention than ever. I fully expected to experience a liberation of maternal conscience and an expansive sense of progress in the work sphere, not the screech of inner brakes. Yet, once children are in school, although daily life is easier, in a psychological sense one's work may become more difficult and problematic. As long as I had had to do the juggling act, there was no time to examine commitment, refine aspiration—or confront ambivalence.

I believe it is important to say that this crisis, however painful, was circumscribed. As women must, in my daily life I had to "keep on keeping on." In householding, with my children, with all but a few friends, I functioned as usual. I did not stop working; nor did I change my mind about the importance of achievement to my self-esteem. But it took a conspicuous failure—as it often does in persons who relentlessly drive themselves in high gear so as to sustain the enthusiasm, self-confidence, and denial of inner conflict upon which their identity is premised—to tell me what I otherwise refused to recognize, not only that the career track I was on was the wrong track[5] but that I had some serious unresolved "work problems."

I am not unmindful of the economics of my retreat from the prescribed career track. As one friend reminded me, I could *afford* not to teach that course. Yes and no. The course I didn't teach was a one-shot proposition, the pay less than a thousand dollars; given the hours of preparation, the money would have covered child-care expenses, with a little left over. I had contracted to give the course because I was confident of the material and because a course of my own was "the next step." I did not do it for the money. Like many other middle-class women of my generation, I had never made the connection between work and earning power—fathers and husbands earned the livelihood. The classic adolescent female work experience, baby-sitting, provided me with spending money while I lived in my father's household. As a married woman, the monetary rewards of my work, such as they were, were also "extra" rather than essential. Teaching fellowships paid the baby-sitters and nursery school tuition; editorial fees were our spending money: with one check we bought the dining room table, with another a new typewriter. Deep down, I didn't connect

---

[5] As it became clear to me that political science had allowed a kind of mindless pursuit of achievement, and as "pure" academic ambition was superseded by doubts and by a clinical perspective—although my professional future would be the more uncertain—I quietly let the thesis die.

work and money, and in this sense I was not a professional. Nor did I work for the sake of the work itself; I didn't connect work and love, and in this sense I was not an amateur either.

My failure of will in 1968 took me by surprise; however, the pressures had been building up for five years. The defenses that had allowed me to function in the dutiful-daughter role, even to star in it, had crumbled, and I became exquisitely vulnerable to the conflicts against which they had defended. I was forced to own up to my lifelong inability to distinguish, psychologically, between satisfaction and perfection, between critics and judges, between work and performance. When it came to the critical performance test, the conscientious academic dissolved, and I was left standing there, unable to face that class.

Finally, it seems clear to me now that superwoman too was played out, exposed for who she was: a good Girl Scout accumulating merit badges. The lurch to a halt on the academic career track was the sequel to the delivery dream. It became impossible, at the age of thirty, to resist any longer the task of giving form to the unbidden shadowy insights of the last years. I had begun to suspect that, for me, if motherhood was less than an identity, it was nonetheless more than a role, and that the confining, immobilizing curtailment of life's possibilities that I had associated with the "inside world" of motherhood and household was, unforeseen, threatening from the opposite direction.

Before I would be able to move on and make my work my own—to approach it as self-expression rather than as command performance—it was necessary to shift gears and "come home." To become an *amateur—one who loves:* herself, others, her work. Literally, homecoming meant reclaiming a full and playful sexuality—becoming less of a "wife" and more myself. It also meant engaging my sons in a different way, more directly, responsively, and serendipitously—becoming less of a "mother" and more myself. My family helped. They made me laugh, made me listen; they made me reckon.

In the work sphere, homework has meant coming to terms with the amateur in myself. By amateur I do not mean the popular definition of one who works as a pastime, or in an unskilled, halfhearted way. I mean amateur in the ancient sense of "devotee"[6]—someone who does what (s)he loves and loves what (s)he does.

Do what you love. I came upon these words days after the delivery dream. Do what you love . . . Pursue your life . . . Know your own

[6] See Joan Erikson, *Saint Francis and His Four Ladies* (New York: W. W. Norton, 1970), p. 12.

bone. Sensing an "answer" to the dream in the Concord radical's unspeakable suggestion, still I was unable to make the connection; I filed the quotation away, with the dream itself, in a notebook I keep of passages, poems, photographs, and dreams. For someone like me, who trusted only one prescription for initiative, "Do what your father tells you to do," and who "made sure" by appointing a guardian Gudge, the words were heresy. Do what you love? How can you do that and do what you ought? Becoming an amateur in work means turning passive into active: getting beyond the oughts of others in order to transform conscientious schoolgirl competence into the pleasure and autonomy that characterize generative work.

"Doing what you love" means knowing yourself well enough to be able to answer the question, "What would you love to do?" and loving yourself enough to ask it. The years after the work crisis of 1968 were fundamentally, if not primarily, taken up with the homework of self-pursuit—the process of ferreting out the "independent feminine" confined within the Daughter, the Girl Scout, Superwoman. The means were several. I became increasingly deliberate, even fervent, sometimes obsessive, in my introspection; I worked on my dreams, alone and with other friendly dreamers; and I kept a journal as a means of accounting for the changes, of thinking out loud about motherhood, and especially as a means of making room for my mother in my inner world and restoring our severed connection.

For almost thirty years, my convictions about what counted, and who, had depended on men. I knew I was my father's daughter; yet, "we think back through our mothers if we are women," Virginia Woolf reminds us in *A Room of One's Own*.[7] What about my mother?

Despite conventional appearances and my success in the role of the good girl, I have always seen myself as a maverick, as unconventional, an outsider—the adolescent army daughter on the edge of her successive social worlds; the worldly yet naive freshman who arrived on the Wellesley campus, sight unseen, from Turkey; the woman graduate student in the early sixties; the mother in the park-and-playground matriarchy who "also worked." But "maverick" not only suggests the odd independent, apart from the group; its essential meaning, of course, is "the motherless one." I looked it up one day (in the dictionary my mother had given me on my eleventh birthday) and replayed the deadlock dream I had had over and over again during my first pregnancy:

[7] Virginia Woolf, *A Room of One's Own* (New York: Harcourt Brace Jovanovich, 1929), p. 79.

> Standing by a wall telephone, its receiver attached by a long curly
> cord, I am calling my mother to tell her my baby's name, but
> I can't remember her phone number, and when I remember her
> phone number, I can't remember the baby's name. We are
> disconnected.

My mother, who died suddenly three years before I became a
mother myself, was almost thirty when she married, thirty-one when I
was born. Even as she cut a dashing public figure in the depression
years with her teaching job and her roadster—the epitome of security
and freedom—privately she envisioned herself in the negative identity of a spinster schoolteacher. She didn't think a man would choose
her to be his wife and the mother of his children; when that dream
came true, she unconditionally and with grateful relief exchanged her
lonely independence for his love and company and the anticipation of
a family.

My mother and I were friends in a mutually guarded way; we were
never deeply intimate. The loss is irretrievable. I think now that the
distance we kept between us, and the reserve, were rooted not so much
in our predictable, if ever so indirect, rivalry as in an ambivalent comprehension of our sex—what to make of being a woman—an uncer-
tainty we had in common but shyly never confided in each other.

What to make of being a woman? Even as I repaired our connection—culling my mother's memory in family talks, reading what
she might have read when I was born (accounts of Amelia Earhart on
the one hand, the *Ladies' Home Journal* on the other), searching our
correspondence from the years I spent away from home, courting her
image in snapshot albums—I was baffled. From what I could gather,
she didn't have the answers any more than I did. Maybe Anne Sexton
was right when, speaking for prefeminist women in a patriarchal
world, she wrote, "A woman *is* her mother. That's the main thing."[8]

In the early seventies, as I returned to my mother and found an
enigma there, I also turned to other women, particularly to a young
feminist and former student of mine who was writing about her struggles to "place" her new motherhood in a feminist life. Reading her
Motherhood Journal[9] led me to begin to "research" my own motherhood, to become conscious of it in a new way. Her admission of
ambivalence freed me to acknowledge my own and permitted me to
admit not only the place of motherhood in the constellation of my

---

[8] "Housewife," *All My Pretty Ones* (Boston: Houghton Mifflin, 1961, 1962).
[9] Alice Abarbanel, "Redefining Motherhood," *The Future of the Family*, ed.
Louise Kapp Howe (New York: Simon & Schuster, 1972).

inner world, but its legitimacy—its centrality—in my everyday life.
Gathering in my notes and reflections, I found myself identifying with
my friend Alice—*even where our values and choices differed*. This
resonance and sense of solidarity with her, and, for the first time in my
life, potentially with women in general, constituted my feminist initiation.

These feelings of implicit collaboration in the experience of
motherhood may seem an unlikely focus for a conversion to feminism,
given the careerist thrust of the women's movement. But for me, it
happened that way. By this, I don't mean that motherhood made me a
feminist. Far from it. When I became a mother, I was still disconnected from the mothering I had known, staunchly holding out
against the woman in myself. I was a graduate student trying to make
it in a male world on their terms; men were the standard, women the
deviation. Our independence was not what it seemed, for our orientation was male. In those years, in the sphere of work, women were
generally not in touch with one another except as competitors. We
were furtive friends, skittish colleagues.

Only looking back, do I recognize the vague uneasiness that I was in
some way profoundly at odds with myself. I now suspect that this
unconsciously contributed to my wish to become pregnant. Pregnancy
is manifestly female; like feminism, pregnancy can be a means of
consolidating one's sexual identity. In 1962, feminism was not an
option. Pregnancy was. And I "chose" it. It was through the recon-
sideration of all this, ten years later, that I finally cut through a lifetime of male orientation and dependence and for the first time
identified wholeheartedly with my sex.

The psychoanalytic process of looking inward to give depth to
consciousness and the feminist experience of moving outward toward
other women to "raise" it continue side by side. Both have been, and
still are, for me, necessary to independence and initiative in work.
Although insight still quickens a sense of vulnerability as well as ex-
hilaration, I no longer have to deal with this irony in isolation, but
turn more often for support to like-minded friends.

My work has changed, as well as my sense of responsibility for it. I
have begun to define and engage in the long-term work I want to
do—clinical field research in the psychology of adult development.
Professional support work as an editor has gradually evolved into
more mutual writing partnerships and into the kind of active editorial
enterprise represented in midwifing this book.

What we do matters. With whom we do it may matter as much, or
even more. Money and a room of one's own, Virginia Woolf pre-

scribed for women who would write fiction. *Deadlines* and *colleagues,* a friendly sponsor said to me, for those who would embark upon research, see it through, and write it up; and she has provided me with both.

The old work problems of judgment and performance remain. Work on others' behalf is, as it always has been for me, free of conflict, and I do it well. When I sit down to write a sentence of my own, however, whenever I try to think "rough draft," Gudge invariably turns up to cramp my style with "End Product." Recently, as I approached a deadline in a writing collaboration with a new colleague, the familiar anxieties surfaced in a whoosh—procrastination in the face of the impossible inner standard, the grind of perfectionist gears, the performance panic. "This is impossible," I said, ready to give up before I had begun. "No, it isn't," my co-worker replied calmly. "I don't care if it's nonsense, give me three pages in an hour. In *any* form." There was something companionable about the way she said it—partly a dare, partly an invitation. The difference between a colleague and a superego, it occurred to me, is that a colleague accepts a first draft, *expects* a first draft. Colleagues are competitive, cooperative, supportive, and human; a superego is no substitute. Although Gudge is still with me, unlike before, he comes and goes. I can look him in the eye, and when I do, I recognize him for who he is—ever more the standard-bearer than the playmate or mentor.

On a recent field trip to California, in a conversation with a friend about the fragility of initiative in women and its compromising effect on the female experience of generativity, I found myself describing Gudge—how he still intrudes in my work whenever it is self-generated and ambitious, whenever it is "my own." My friend, a clinician, mused, "Your Gudge is too serious. Liven him up a little. Draw a picture of him doing something human like tying his shoe." Before I had a chance to try his idea, it generated a dream that suggests some progress in the humanization, even the feminization, of Gudge:

> I am sitting in a deep, round black-canvas easy chair with my college roommate and a little girl, both of whom are visiting me. There is plenty of room in the chair for the three of us. In a "daring, inviting" gesture, I get up to play a new record I want them to hear.

A dream often prompts its own mode of interpretation. This one seemed to invite a consideration of the "inner household" intimately and comfortably accommodated in the lap of my psyche. If the little girl is me-as-a-child, my father's daughter and Gudge's ward, then my college roommate—a conscientious, upright person who is now a member of the clergy—is an exquisitely appropriate unconscious choice to sit in as the unprecedentedly feminine Gudge.

There I am, on my own, away from home and family, the guest of others for a month, doing work about which I care enormously. And the dream casts me as host, my childhood and my conscience not as proprietors but as guests in my inner world. The dream is a reminder that we cannot altogether deny old identities (and their guardians), but must "take care" of them in new ways. In the authoritative and playful act of getting up to put on some new music for them, I take my distance from my childhood and my conscience. "The important thing is," my dream confidante said: "Were they listening?"

Yes, they were.

Pamela Daniels

On Work

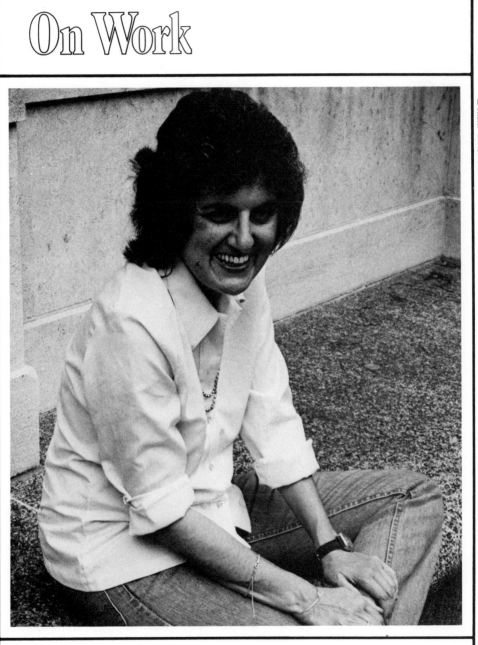

Catharine R. Stimpson

I AM A MEMBER of an elite. My grandparents were not. I am single. My grandparents were not. What, then, unites us, besides skin, genes, and blood? Devotion to a theory and practice of work. Their work has helped to generate mine.

My father's father, as a boy in the 1880s, herded cattle in Dakota. Later, he dug graves, waited on tables, and cleaned furnaces to earn his way through medical school. My mother's mother got up every morning at four o'clock to do the baking for the little restaurant she and my grandfather ran next to the train station in Nashua, Iowa. Work was, for them, the cause of survival; the effect of necessity. Whether they were happy or not was irrelevant. Success was a guarantee—of sorts—against disaster.

However, my grandparents were not raw materialists. They wanted to give their children more than they had gotten from their parents; to be active links in the chain of being upwardly mobile. By 1905, for example, my mother's parents had saved enough money to move West. There, they figured, they might do well enough to send their children to college. My maternal grandfather had graduated from high school; my grandmother had not. Doing well also meant working with skill and character. Rewards might be gained at the price of mercy toward oneself, but never at the price of justice and legality.

Even after they had found some security, even after they could tell stories to grandchildren who wore Stride-Rite shoes and braces, anxiety guarded them. If one worked well, one would sever the harsh past from the less dangerous present; the present from an even less dangerous and more generous future. But if things went wrong or if one did not work well—or worse, if one refused to work at all—the present would collapse back into the past, and the future would disappear. "Shirt sleeves to shirt sleeves in four generations" was a choral refrain of the adults in my childhood. Several families in town exemplified the maxim. Once, they had made it. Then, because of sloth or lack of purpose or lazy, spoiled children, they had lost it: the accumulated money, local prestige, ability to pay cash, the chance to take vacations.

This ideology of work and the need to fulfill it dominate me still. Even before I saw my first Blake engraving, my picture of myself as a worker was that of an angel: wings and body of fire; shooting toward

My thanks to Kim Townsend for his comments on these paragraphs.

heaven, at once desperate and choreographed; longing to leave the hereness of the base world behind and go into orbit in welcoming space. Yet, my experience of work, the psychology of living out the calendar it organizes, is not that of my grandparents or parents.

For of course, they are there, a pressure from the past. If I fail—a fear that haunts me as chronic illness does the flesh—I will have failed them. Unable to redeem their sacrifices, I will have denied the gift of their denials, of their sweat and discipline. I will have abandoned them, and in the harsh, clear dialectic of conditional love, they will have the right to abandon me.

Despite such apprehensions, I expect to like what I do. Pleasure is one of the privileges of professionalism. I do like most of what I do, very much. At the end of a good lecture, or of the draft of an essay or story, I may feel a rush not altogether remote from ecstasy. I say, "It worked." One reason I can have fun in my teaching job is that it offers some protection against financial catastrophe through social security, medical insurance, a pension plan. Because of this, I am partially dependent upon an institution. However, I am not dependent upon a person. To lose the autonomy and freedom that supporting myself underwrites would be a spiritual catastrophe.

Supporting myself also underwrites my refusal to marry and have children, my cheerful social isolation. I am the second of seven surviving children, the first of five girls. Making my brother's bed, washing my siblings' diapers, helped to convince me that the sanctity of domestic love could never sufficiently compensate for the rigors of domestic service. One can have stability in love without ordinary homeyness.

Some people suspect my declarations of independence. "Evasion of maturity," they mutter. "Unnatural behavior." Because I believe in the unconscious, I will hypothetically admit that I may want a child; that such a desire may jostle with my superego in hidden psychic regions, to emerge sublimated as affection for nephews, nieces, and the children of my friends. However, the taste of self-deception is familiar. The seeming absence of that combination of marshmallow and metal when I talk about my single life and why I like it, about the personal wisdom of my rejection of roles of wife and mother, assures me that I am being genuine.

I am part of a modern historical pattern. A number of women have found a traditional female role and serious work outside of the home incompatible. So did one of my mother's sisters, a chemist, who never married. So did my father's sister, a rollicking woman who married only after she had lots of jobs, including a position with the Red Cross during World War II and in a European refugee camp afterward. The

ability to recognize a set to which one belongs is helpful for self-understanding, but the decisions through which I joined that set were made before I knew there was one.

The family member who most consistently sustained me was my mother. Though she burdened me with some of her fantasies and expectations about my future, she also freed me from a debilitating pressure to accept the dictates of femininity as usual. She urged me to have a more intellectually gratifying life than she felt that she had had. I need not imitate her life, she said, as long as I did something that was both respectable and excellent. If she encouraged me, my father did not discourage me. Indeed, he paid the bills for the ambiguously supportive and straightforwardly expensive women's college I attended.

Those of us who reject both the idea of failure and the conventional criteria of feminine success must construct our own tests of triumph. I am now trying to articulate a new set of standards which will be of fresh vitality and worth. To do so, I am pulling apart a sticky conflation of fame and success that I have made; trying to attend more strictly to things for their own sake, rather than to things for the sake of fame and success; and withdrawing from an overexacting submission to two other tests of worth I once used.

The first asked me to score as perfectly as possible at public trials such as an IQ test. They publicly measured me both against an absolute standard and against other people. The second demanded that I win as much praise and as many expressions of esteem as possible. Because such qualitative statements of esteem can be elusive, even enigmatic, victory in the second test was much more demanding than in the first.

Such examinations were exhausting. They also bred ambivalence about other people. Significant human applause metered my sense of the worth of my work. However, if that work was to win that applause, I had to better most humans. Another self-image, less hot and glamorous than that of the orbiting angel, was to stand alone on a plain—rivals vanquished, vanished, banished. At once in thrall to and at odds with others, I wanted to achieve a version of ascribed status.

Whatever the tests of success, no matter who or what the agencies of judgment may be, I am most genial and relaxed when working well. During my middle twenties, back in America after two happy years of study in Europe on a Fulbright, I was empty of both animating purpose and a job that might execute and symbolize it. The need for them was too strong to permit me to go to hell with a big splash. My dissipations were reasonably trivial, demeaning rather than tragic. My jobs were menial. During one, a secretarial position in a reform campaign, I forgot my name was "Catharine" and began to believe that I had been rebaptized as "girl." If I learned things I needed to know, my curriculum specialized more in the tacky than in the extreme. During this "lost period," I had megalomaniac fantasies about the future. At the very least, I would be a senator before I was forty. My most arrogant dreams of work were as sweetly lurid as some nineteenth-century American landscape painting. They burst forth when my guilty sense of having betrayed my promise—the assurance to past and present generations that I had a talent the future would recognize —was at its most rapacious.

The lost period incorporated the first two or three years of Columbia Graduate School. I entered there to prepare for work that might carry with it both significance and freedom. My emergence from this period marked the end of some necessary growing up, some exploration of possibilities of not being "good." It also coincided with the growth of the New Feminism. In 1966, when I was thirty, I went to my first feminist meeting, a chapter of NOW, in a church basement near Columbia. By then I was also teaching freshman English at Barnard College. The women's movement has fertilized my consciousness and morality; without it I would still have worked ambitiously. I have an appetite for autonomy, self-expression, recognition, and for change. However, the women's movement has given me dignified hopes, ideas, and a community. If my grandparents and parents worked for their blood family, I work, in part, for my political relatives.

Feminism also places me in a paradoxical position. Beyond its call for sexual equality is a legitimate skepticism of such "male values" as the love of power, endorsement of competitive zeal, and an equation of worth with worldly deeds. Still, I want my share of power; I have my share of competitiveness; I go after my share of worldly deeds. I work as a middle-class man might. I have repudiated woman's subordination and her constricted role in the home, but not the well-meaning professional's role in the world. A serious worry is that I, though an active feminist, may be phallocentric; that I may be more in love with power, victory, and the craving ego than I need to be in order to work autonomously, creatively, energetically.

This anxiety, that a discrepancy exists between my politics and my personality, is but one of several sources of psychic insomnia. Much of my life is spent in public performance: teaching, speaking, publishing. The gap between the performance and the self-doubt of the performer sometimes seems unmanageable. I like reassurance, but I hesitate to confess dependency on it. No amount of inoculation against self-pity has fully immunized me against its sickly charm. I get lonely.

One accepts such minor crises of belief and of the emotions as one does weeds. In my middle years, I think I have been fortunate. I wonder if I ought not to rearrange my occupations—perhaps to write more and to teach less. A legacy of mobility is restlessness. I often remember my mother's mother, the wonderful security of her unconditional tenderness. A world without her resilience and capacity for love would be terrible, unacceptable, but, in brief, I am glad that I am not, and will not, be her. However, I regret that as I received and achieved much of what she wanted for her family—my education, for example—I also received and achieved what my politics have ultimately taught me to suspect: that membership, albeit marginal, in an elite.

The Anomaly of
a Woman in Physics
Evelyn Fox Keller

Diana Michener

A COUPLE OF MONTHS AGO I was invited to give a series of lectures at a major university as one of a "series of distinguished guest lecturers" on mathematical aspects of biology. Having just finished teaching a course on women at my own college, I somehow felt obliged to violate the implicit protocol and address the anomalous fact of my being an apparently successful woman scientist. Though I had experienced similar vague impulses before, for a variety of reasons arising from a mix of anger, confusion, and timidity, it had never seemed to me either appropriate or possible to yield to such an impulse. Now, however, it seemed decidedly inappropriate, somewhat dishonest, and perhaps even politically unconscionable to deliver five lectures on my work without once making reference to the multitude of contradictions and conflicts I had experienced in arriving at the professional position presumed on this occasion. Therefore, in a gesture that felt wonderfully bold and unprofessional, I devoted the last lecture to a discussion of the various reasons for the relative absence of women in science, particularly in the higher ranks. The talk formed itself—with an ease, clarity, and lack of rancor that amazed me. I felt an enormous sense of personal triumph. Somehow, in the transformation of what had always appeared to me an essentially personal problem into a political problem, my anger had become depersonalized, even defused, and a remarkable sense of clarity emerged. It suggested to me that I might, now, be able to write about my own rather painful and chaotic history as a woman in science.

Origins are difficult to determine and obscure in their relation to final consequences. Suffice it to say that in my senior year of college I decided I would be a scientist. After several years of essentially undirected intellectual ambition, I majored in physics partly for the sake of discipline and partly out of the absence of any clear sense of vocation; and in my last year I fell in love with theoretical physics.

I invoke the romantic image not as a metaphor, but as an authentic, literal description of my experience. I fell in love, simultaneously and inextricably, with my professors, with a discipline of pure, precise, definitive thought, and with what I conceived of as its ambitions. I fell in love with the life of the mind. I also fell in love, I might add, with the image of myself striving and succeeding in an area where women had rarely ventured. It was a heady experience. In my adviser's fanta-

sies, I was to rise, unhampered, right to the top. In my private fantasies, I was to be heralded all the way.

It was 1957. Politics conspired with our fantasies. Graduate
schools, newly wealthy with National Science Foundation money,
competed vigorously for promising students, and a promising female
student was a phenomenon sufficiently unique to engage the interest
and curiosity of recruiters from Stanford to Harvard. Only Cal Tech
and Princeton were closed to me—they were not yet admitting women
—and I felt buoyant enough to challenge them. I particularly wanted
to go to Cal Tech to study with Richard Feynman—a guru of theoretical physics—on whose work I had done my senior thesis. In lieu of
my being accepted at Cal Tech, an influential friend of mine volunteered to offer Feynman a university chair at MIT, where I
would be admitted. Heady indeed.

Even then I was aware that the extreme intoxication of that time
was transitory—that it had primarily to do with feeling "on the brink."
Everything that excited me lay ahead. I had fantasies of graduate
school and becoming a physicist; what awaited me, I thought, was the
fulfillment of those fantasies. Even the idea of "doing physics" was
fantasylike. I could form no clear picture of myself in that role, had
no clear idea of what it involved. My conception of a community of
scholars had the airiness of a dream. I was intoxicated by a vision that
existed primarily in my head.

Well, Feynman was not interested in leaving Cal Tech, and so I
went to Harvard. More accurately, I was pressured, and eventually
persuaded, by both a would-be mentor at Harvard and my adviser, to
go to Harvard. At Harvard I was promised the moon and the sun—I
could do anything I wanted. Why I was given this extraordinary sales
pitch seems, in retrospect, all but inexplicable. At the time, it seemed
quite natural. I dwell on the headiness of this period in order to convey the severity of the blow that graduate school at Harvard actually
was.

The story of my graduate school experience is a difficult one to tell.
It is difficult in part because it is a story of behavior so crude and so
extreme as to seem implausible.

Moreover, it is difficult to tell because it is painful. In the past, the
telling of this story always left me so badly shaken, feeling so exposed,
that I became reluctant to tell it. Many years have passed, and I might
well bury those painful recollections. I do not because they represent a
piece of reality—an ongoing reality that affects others, particularly
women. Even though my experiences may have been unique—no one

else will share exactly these experiences—the motives underlying the behavior I am going to describe are, I believe, much more prevalent than one might think, and detectable in fact in behavior much less extreme.

I tell the story now, therefore, because it may somehow be useful to others. I *can* tell the story now because it no longer leaves me feeling quite so exposed. Let me try to explain this sense of exposure.

Once, several months into my first year in graduate school, a post-doctoral student in an unusual gesture of friendliness offered me a ride home from a seminar and asked how I was doing. Moved by his gesture, I started to tell him. As I verged on tears, I noticed the look of acute discomfort on his face. Somehow, I had committed a serious indiscretion. It was as if I had publicly disrobed. Whatever I said, then and always after, it somehow seemed I had said too much. Some of this feeling remains with me even now as I write this article. It is a consequence of the assumption in the minds of others that what I am describing must have been a very personal, private experience—that is, that it was produced somehow by forces within myself. It was not. Although I clearly participated in and necessarily contributed to these events, they were *essentially* external in origin. That vital recognition has taken a long time. With it, my shame began to dissolve, to be replaced by a sense of personal rage and, finally, a transformation of that rage into something less personal—something akin to a political conscience.

That transformation, crucial in permitting me to write this, has not, however, entirely removed the pain from the process of recollecting a story that retains for me considerable horror. If I falter at this point, it is because I realize that in order for this story to be meaningful, even credible, to others, I must tell it objectively—I must somehow remove myself from the pain of which I write. The actual events were complex. Many strands weave in and out. I will describe them, one by one, as simply and as fairly as I can.

My first day at Harvard I was informed, by the very man who had urged me to come, that my expectations were unrealistic. For example, I could not take the course with Schwinger (Harvard's answer to Feynman) that had lured me to Harvard, and I ought not concern myself with the foundations of quantum mechanics (the only thing that did concern me) because, very simply, I was not, could not be, good enough. Surely my ambition was based on delusion—it referred to a pinnacle only the very few, and certainly not I, could achieve. Brandeis, I was told bluntly, was not Harvard, and although my training there might have earned me a place at Harvard, distinction at

Brandeis had no meaning here. Both I and they had better assume I knew nothing. Hence I ought to start at the beginning. The students they really worried about, I was informed, were those who were so ignorant and naive that they could not apprehend the supreme difficulty of success at Harvard.

These remarks were notable for their blatant class bias and arrogance, as well as for their insistent definition of me on the basis of that bias—a gratuitous dismissal of my own account that I experienced recurrently throughout graduate school. The professor's remarks were all the more remarkable in that I had expressed exactly the same intentions in our conversation the previous spring and had then been encouraged. What could account for this extraordinary reversal? There had been no intervening assessment of my qualifications. Perhaps it can be explained simply by the fact that the earlier response was one of someone in the position of selling Harvard, while now it seemed there was an obligation to defend her. (It is ironic that universities should be associated with the feminine gender.) Nor was it coincidental, I suspect, that this man was shortly to assign to one of the senior graduate students (male, of course) the task of teaching me how to dress.[1]

Thus began two years of almost unmitigated provocation, insult, and denial. Lacking any adequate framework—political or psychological—for comprehending what was happening to me, I could only respond with personal rage: I felt increasingly provoked, insulted, and denied. Where political rage would have been constructive, personal rage served only to increase my vulnerability. Having come to Harvard expecting to be petted and fussed over (as I had been before) and expecting, most of all, validation and approval, I was entirely unprepared for the treatment I received. I could neither account for nor respond appropriately to the enormous discrepancy between what I expected and what I found. I had so successfully internalized the cultural identification between male and intellect that I was totally dependent on my (male) teachers for affirmation—a dependency made treacherous by the chronic confusion of sexuality and intellect in relationships between male teachers and female students. In seeking intellectual affirmation, I sought male affirmation, and thereby became exquisitely vulnerable to the male aggression surrounding me.

I had in fact been warned about the extreme alienation of the first year as a graduate student at Harvard, but both my vanity and my

---

[1] My attire, I should perhaps say, was respectable. It consisted mainly of skirts and sweaters, selected casually, with what might have been called a bohemian edge. I wore little or no makeup.

naiveté permitted me to ignore these warnings. I was confident that things would be different for me. That confidence did not last long. Coming from everywhere, from students and faculty alike, were three messages. First, physics at Harvard was the most difficult enterprise in the world; second, I could not possibly understand the things I thought I understood; and third, my lack of fear was proof of my ignorance. At first, I adopted a wait-and-see attitude and agreed to take the conventional curriculum, though I privately resolved to audit Schwinger's course. Doing so, as it turned out, seemed such an act of bravado that, daily, all eyes turned on me as I entered the class and, daily, I was asked by half a dozen people with amusement if I still thought I understood. Mysteriously, my regular courses seemed manageable, even easy, and as I became increasingly nervous about my failure to fear properly, I spent more and more evenings at the movies. In time, the frequent and widespread iteration of the message that I could not understand what I thought I understood began to take its toll. As part of a general retreat, I stopped attending Schwinger's course. I had begun to lose all sense of what I did or did not understand, there and elsewhere. That I did well in my exams at the end of the semester seemed to make no difference whatever.

Meanwhile, it was clear that I was becoming the subject—or object —of a good deal of attention in the Physics Department. My seriousness, intensity, and ambition seemed to cause my elders considerable amusement, and a certain amount of curiosity as well. I was watched constantly, and occasionally addressed. Sometimes I was queried about my peculiar ambition to be a theoretical physicist—didn't I know that no woman at Harvard had ever so succeeded (at least not in becoming a *pure* theoretical physicist)? When would I too despair, fail, or go elsewhere (the equivalent of failing)? The possibility that I might succeed seemed to be a source of titillation; I was leered at by some, invited now and then to a faculty party by others. The open and unbelievably rude laughter with which I was often received at such events was only one of many indications that I was on display—for purposes I could either not perceive or not believe. My fantasy was turning into nightmare.

In lieu of support I began to long for anonymity, but the anomaly of my position had made it so public that there was no hiding. My real world began to resemble a paranoid delusion. Many people in Cambridge knew who I was and speculated about me. None of them offered friendship. Once, feeling particularly lonely on a Saturday night, I went for a walk by the Charles River. I was sitting on a bench, deep in thought, when a young man, a stranger, appeared out of the

dark, sat down, and began to recite a detailed knowledge of me—
what I was doing, who my friends were, where I had come from, and
other particulars. Finishing his recitation, he got up and walked away.
When real events so take on the qualities of delusion, it becomes
difficult indeed to expect the credulity of others. Yet I remained
frighteningly sane and had no difficulty in recognizing the reality—
only in understanding it.

It is sometimes hard to separate affront to oneself as a person from
affront to one's sensibilities. Not only do they tend to generate the
same response—one feels simply affronted—but it is also possible (as
I believe was true here) that the motives for both affronts are not
unrelated. I went to graduate school with a vision of theoretical
physics as a vehicle for the deepest inquiry into nature—a vision perhaps best personified, in recent times, by Einstein. The use of
mathematics to further one's understanding of the nature of space,
time, and matter represented a pinnacle of human endeavor. I went to
graduate school to learn about foundations. I was taught, instead, how
to do physics. In place of wisdom, I was offered skills. Furthermore,
this substitution was made with moralistic fervor. It was wrong, fool-
hardy, indeed foolish, to squander precious time asking why. Proper
humility was to bend to the grindstone and learn techniques. Contemporary physics, under the sway of operationalism, had, it seemed,
dispensed with the tradition of Einstein—almost, indeed, with Einstein himself. General relativity, the most intellectually ambitious
venture of the century, seemed then (wrongly) a dead subject. Philosophical considerations of any sort in the physical sciences were at an
all-time low. Instead, techniques designed to calculate nth-order cor-
rections to a theory grievously flawed at its base were the order of the
day.

Physics had become a major industry. Huge investments poured
into experiments, the results of which needed subsequently to be
matched by theoretical calculations. Paralleling the influx of money
was an influx of manpower. They couldn't all be creative innovators.
The Baconian vision of an army of scientific foot soldiers was imminent; and Harvard physicists, whatever they were doing, were, by
definition, the best—they were the generals. The status of the elite had
to be protected even though the very conception of elite was uncertain. While there was general agreement about what the student rank
and file should (or rather, should not) be doing, the generals seemed
considerably confused about what they should be doing. The work of
Harvard's most distinguished theoretician conveyed a sense of grand
sweep. While he was roundly faulted and criticized for the abstract

formality of his approach, his status as the best went unchallenged. Even among the elite, then, there was a lack of clarity about the nature and rules of progress and excellence, and a certain amount of scrambling. Somehow the notion of different but equally valid postures did not seem tenable—the preoccupation with ranking was over-riding.

My naiveté and idealism were perfect targets. Not only did I not know my place in the scheme of things as a woman, but by a curious coincidence, I was apparently equally ingenuous concerning my place as a thinker. I needed to be humbled. Though I writhed over the banality of the assignments I was given, I did them, acknowledging that I needed in any case to learn the skills. I made frequent arithmetic errors—reflecting a tension that endures within me even today between the expansiveness of conception and the precision of execution, my personal variation perhaps of the more general polar tension in physics as a whole. When my papers were returned with the accuracy of the conception ignored and the arithmetic errors streaked with red—as if with a vengeance—I wondered whether I was studying physics or plumbing. Who has not experienced such a wrenching conflict between idealism and reality? Yet my fellow students seemed oddly untroubled. From the nature of their responses when I tried to press them for deeper understanding of the subject, I thought perhaps I had come from Mars. Why, they wondered, did I want to know? That they were evidently content with the operational success of the formulas mystified me. Even more mystifying was the absence of any appearance of the humility of demeanor that one would expect to accompany the acceptance of more limited goals. I didn't fully understand then that in addition to the techniques of physics, they were also studying the techniques of arrogance. This peculiar inversion in the meaning of humility was simply part of the process of learning how to be a physicist. It was intrinsic to the professionalization, and what I might even call the masculinization, of an intellectual discipline.

To some extent the things I describe here are in the nature of the academic subculture. They reflect the perversion of academic style—familiar in universities everywhere—a perversion that has become more extensive as graduate schools have tended to become increasingly preoccupied with professional training. My experiences resemble those of many graduate students—male and female alike. What I experienced as a rather brutal assault on my intellectual interests and abilities was I think no accident, but rather the inevitable result of the pervasive attempt of a profession to make itself more powerful by weeding out those sensibilities, emotional and intellectual, that it considers inappropriate. Not unrelated is a similar attempt to maintain the standards and image of a discipline by discouraging the participation of women—a strategy experienced and recounted by many other women. Viewed in this way, it is perhaps not surprising that the assault would be most blatant in a subject as successful as contemporary physics, and in a school as prestigious as Harvard.

Perhaps the most curious, undoubtedly the most painful, part of my experience was the total isolation in which I found myself. In retrospect, I am certain that there must have been like-minded souls somewhere who shared at least some of my disappointments. But if there were, I did not know them. In part, I attribute this to the general atmosphere of fear that permeated the graduate student body. One did not voice misgivings because they were invariably interpreted to mean that one must not be doing well.[2] The primary goal was to survive, and, better yet, to *appear* to be surviving, even prospering. So few complaints were heard from anyone. Furthermore, determined not to expose the slightest shred of ignorance, few students were willing to discuss their work with any but (possibly) their closest friends. I was, clearly, a serious threat to my fellow students' conception of physics as not only a male stronghold but a male *retreat,* and so I was least likely to be sought out as a colleague. I must admit that my own arrogance and ambition did little to allay their anxieties or temper their resistances. To make matters even worse, I shared with my fellow classmates the idea that a social or sexual relationship could only exist between male and female students if the man was "better" or "smarter" than the woman—or at the very least, comparable. Since both my self-definition and my performance labeled me as a superior student, the field of sociability and companionship was considerably narrowed.

There was one quite small group of students whom I did view as like-minded and longed to be part of. They too were concerned with foundations; they too wanted to know why. One of them (the only one in my class) had in fact become a close friend during my first semester. Though he preached to me about the necessity of humility, the importance of learning through the tips of one's fingers, the virtue of precision—he also listened with some sympathy. Formerly a Harvard undergraduate, he explained to me the workings of Harvard and I explained to him how to do the problems. With his assistance, I acquired the patience to carry out the calculations. We worked together, talked together, frequently ate together. Unfortunately, as the

[2] Indeed, most people then and later assumed I had done badly—particularly after hearing my story. Any claims I made to the contrary met with disbelief.

relationship threatened to become more intimate, it also became more difficult—in ways that are all too familiar—until, finally, he decided that he could no longer afford the risk of a close association with me. Out of sympathy for his feelings, I respected his request that I steer clear of him and his friends—with the consequence that I was, thereafter, totally alone. The extent of my isolation was almost as difficult for *me* to believe as for those to whom I've attempted to describe it since. Only once, years later in a conversation with another woman physicist, did I find any recognition. She called it the "sea of seats": you walk into a classroom early, and the classroom fills up, leaving a sea of empty seats around you.

Were there no other women students? There were two, who shared neither my ambition, my conception of physics, nor my interests. For these reasons, I am ashamed to say, I had no interest in them. I am even more ashamed to admit that out of my desire to be taken seriously as a physicist I was eager to avoid identification with other women students who I felt could not be taken seriously. Like most women with so-called male aspirations, I had very little sense of sisterhood.

Why did I stay? The Harvard Physics Department is not the world. Surely my tenacity appears as the least comprehensible component of my situation. At the very least, I had an extraordinary tolerance for pain. Indeed, one of my lifelong failings has been my inability to know when to give up. The very passion of my investment ruled out alternatives.

I had, however, made some effort to leave. At the very beginning, a deep sense of panic led me to ask to be taken back at Brandeis. Partly out of disbelief, partly out of the conviction that success at Harvard was an invaluable career asset, not to be abandoned, I was refused, and persuaded to continue. Although I had the vivid perception that rather than succeed I would be undone by Harvard, I submitted to the convention that others know better; I agreed to suspend judgment and to persevere through this stinging "initiation rite." In part, then, I believed that I was undergoing some sort of trial that would terminate when I had proven myself, certainly by the time I completed my orals. I need be stoic only for one year. Unfortunately, that hope turned out to be futile. The courses were not hard, never became hard in spite of the warnings, and I generally got A's. But so did many other students. Exams in fact were extremely easy.

When I turned in particularly good work, it was suspected, indeed sometimes assumed, that I had plagiarized it. On one such occasion, I had written a paper the thesis of which had provoked much argument and contention in the department. This I learned, by chance, several weeks after the debate was well underway. In an effort to resolve the paradox created by my results, I went to see the professor for whom I had written the paper. After an interesting discussion, which incidentally resolved the difficulty, I was asked, innocently and kindly, from what article(s) I had copied my argument.

The oral exams, which I had viewed as a forbidding milestone, proved to be a debacle. My committee chairman simply failed to appear. The result was that I was examined by an impromptu committee of experimentalists on mathematical physics. Months later, I was offered the following explanation: "Oh, Evelyn, I guess I owe you an apology. You see, I had just taken two sleeping pills and overslept." The exam was at 2:00 P.M. Nevertheless, I passed. Finally, I could begin serious work. I chose as a thesis adviser the sanest and kindliest member of the department. I knocked on his door daily for a month, only to be told to come back another time. Finally I gained admittance, to be advised that I'd better go home and learn to calculate.

My second year was even more harrowing than the first. I had few courses and a great deal of time that I could not use without guidance. I had no community of scholars. Completing the orals had not served in any way to alleviate my isolation. I was more alone than ever. The community outside the physics department, at least that part to which I had access, offered neither solace nor support. The late fifties were the peak of what might be called home-brewed psychoanalysis. I was unhappy, single, and stubbornly pursuing an obviously male discipline. What was wrong with me? In one way or another, this question was put to me at virtually every party I attended. I was becoming quite desperate with loneliness. And as I became increasingly lonely I am sure I became increasingly defensive, making it even more difficult for those who might have been sympathetic to me or my plight to approach me to commiserate. Such support might have made a big difference. As it was, I had neither colleagues nor lovers, and not very many friends. The few friends I did have viewed my situation as totally alien. They gave sympathy out of love, though without belief. And I wept because I had no friend whose ambition I could identify with. Was there no woman who was doing, had done, what I was trying to do? I knew of none. My position was becoming increasingly untenable.

Had I been married, would I have fared differently? I came to believe not only that marriage offered the only support possible, but even more, that my failure to marry was somehow the root of all my difficulties. But, it seemed, my career choice, and my attitude toward

it, discouraged all suitors. Where was the way out? Ideally, I had
thought they would come together—physics and love. But they
seemed to cancel each other out. My most frequent fantasy was that I
would return to the Physics Department one day, victoriously, a
physicist with a baby in my arms. My impoverished imagination could
conceive of no better vindication. Even my fantasies conformed to
stereotype.

What had happened to my dreams? Although I had, shortly after
my orals, arranged to transfer out of Harvard at the end of the second
year, when that time came, my hopes and plans (not to speak of
momentum) were too thoroughly shattered for me to consider going
elsewhere. After two years of virtually continuous denial of my perceptions, my values, and my ambitions—an experience that might
then have been described as brainwashing, and ought now be called
schizophrenogenic—my demoralization was complete. Feeling pushed
to the wall, I decided, midyear, to give up physics and return to a
world I realized must still exist, somewhere outside. Though I remained officially enrolled in graduate school in order to collect my
monthly stipend, my commitment to physics was over. Even before I
stopped attending classes formally, this change of heart was visible
enough to trigger a remarkable change in my fellow students, who
became, overnight, friendly and sympathetic. Clearly, I was no longer
a threat. Ironically, at the end of my second year, during which I had
done virtually no work and attended few classes, I still got A's. I
include this as a comment on the grading system at Harvard.

I recognize that this account reads in so many ways like that of a
bad marriage—the passionate intensity of the initial commitment, the
fantasies on which such a commitment (in part) is based, the exclusiv-
ity of the attachment, the apparent disappearance of alternative
options, the unwillingness and inability to let go, and finally, the inclination to blame oneself for all difficulties. Although I can now tell
this story as a series of concrete, objective events that involved and
affected me, at the time I eventually came to accept the prevalent view
that what happened to me at Harvard simply manifested my own
confusion, failure, neurosis—in short that *I* had somehow "made" it
happen. The implications of such internalization were—as they always are—very serious.

Now I had to ask *how* I had "made" it happen—what in me required purging? It seemed that my very ambition and seriousness were
at fault, and that these qualities—qualities I had always admired in
others—had to be given up. Giving up physics, then, seemed to mean
giving up parts of me so central to my sense of myself that a meaning-

ful extrication was next to impossible. I stayed on at Harvard, allowing myself to be convinced once again that I must finish my degree, and sought a dissertation project outside the Physics Department.

After drifting for a year, I took advantage of an opportunity to do a thesis in molecular biology while still nominally remaining in the Physics Department. That this rather unusual course was permitted indicated at least a recognition, on the part of the then chairman, of some of the difficulties I faced in physics. Molecular biology was a field in which I could find respect, and even more important, congeniality. I completed my degree, came to New York to teach (physics!), married, bore children, and ultimately began to work in theoretical biology, where I could make use of my training and talents. This proved to be a rewarding professional area that sustained me for a number of critical years. If my work now begins to take me outside this professional sphere, into more political and philosophical concerns, this reflects the growing confidence and freedom I have felt in recent years.

Inner conflict, however, was not to disappear with a shift in scientific specialization. While it is true that I was never again to suffer the same acute—perhaps bizarre—discomfort that I did as a graduate student in physics, much of the underlying conflict was to surface in other forms as I assumed the more conventional roles of wife, mother, and teacher. The fundamental conflict—between my sense of myself as a woman and my identity as a scientist—could only be resolved by transcending all stereotypical definitions of self and success. This took a long time, a personal analysis, and the women's movement. It meant establishing a personal identity secure enough to allow me to begin to liberate myself from everyone's labels—including my own. The tension between "woman" and "scientist" is not now so much a source of personal struggle as a profound concern.

After many years, I have carved out a professional identity very different from the one I had originally envisioned, but one that I cherish dearly. It is, in many important ways, extraprofessional. It has led me to teach in a small liberal arts college that grants me the leeway to pursue my interests on my own terms and to combine the teaching I have come to love with those interests, and that respects me for doing so. It has meant acquiring the courage to seek both the motives and rewards for my intellectual efforts more within myself. Which is not to say that I no longer need affirmation from others; but I find that I am now willing to seek and accept support from different sources—from friends rather than from institutions, from a community defined by common interests rather than by status.

As I finished writing this essay, I came across an issue of the annals of the *New York Academy of Sciences* (March 15, 1973) devoted to "Successful Women in the Sciences." The volume included brief auto-biographical accounts of a dozen or so women, two of whom were trained in physics and one in mathematics. Because material of this kind is almost nonexistent, these first-person reports are an important contribution "to the literature." I read them avidly. More than avidly, for the remarks of these women, in their directness and honesty, represent virtually the only instance of professional circumstances with which to compare my own experience.

It may be difficult for those removed from the mores of the scientific community to understand the enormous reticence with which anyone, especially a woman, would make public his or her personal impressions and experiences, particularly if they reflect negatively on the community. To do so is not only considered unprofessional, it jeopardizes one's professional image of disinterest and objectivity. Women, who must work so hard to establish that image, are not likely to take such risks. Furthermore, our membership in this community has inculcated in us the strict habit of minimizing any differences due to our sex. I wish therefore to congratulate women in the mainstreams of science who demonstrate such courage.

Their stories, however, are very different from mine. Although a few of these women describe discrete experiences similar to some of mine, they were generally able to transcend their isolation and discomfort, and in their perseverance and success, to vindicate their sex. I am in awe of such fortitude. In their stories I am confirmed in my sense that with more inner strength I would have responded very differently to the experiences I've recorded here. The difficulty, however, with success stories is that they tend to obscure the impact of oppression, while focusing on individual strengths. It used to be said by most of the successful women that women have no complaint precisely because it has been demonstrated that with sufficient determination, anything can be accomplished. If the women's movement has achieved anything, it has taught us the folly of such a view. If I was demolished by my graduate school experiences, it was primarily because I failed to define myself as a rebel against norms in which society has heavily invested. In the late fifties, "rebel" was not a meaningful word. Conflicts and obstacles were seen to be internal. My insistence on maintaining a romantic image of myself in physics, on holding to the view that I would be rewarded and blessed for doing what others had failed to do, presupposed a sense of myself as special, and therefore left me particularly vulnerable. An awareness of the political and social realities might have saved me from persisting in a search for affirmation where it could not and would not be given. Such a political consciousness would have been a source of great strength. I hope that the political awareness generated by the women's movement can and will support young women who today attempt to challenge the dogma, still very much alive, that certain kinds of thought are the prerogative of men.

Evelyn Fox Keller

In Search of
Our Mothers' Gardens
Alice Walker

I

*I described her own nature and temperament. Told how they needed
a larger life for their expression. . . . I pointed out that in lieu of proper
channels, her emotions had overflowed into paths that dissipated them.
I talked beautifully I thought, about an art that would be born, an art
that would open the way for women the likes of her. I asked her to
hope, and build up an inner life against the coming of that day. . . . I
sang, with a strange quiver in my voice, a promise song.*
— "Avey," Jean Toomer, *Cane*

THE POET SPEAKING to a prostitute who falls asleep while he's talking—

When the poet Jean Toomer walked through the South in the early twenties, he discovered a curious thing: Black women whose spirituality was so intense, so deep, so *unconscious,* that they were themselves unaware of the richness they held. They stumbled blindly through their lives: creatures so abused and mutilated in body, so dimmed and confused by pain, that they considered themselves unworthy even of hope. In the selfless abstractions their bodies became to the men who used them, they became more than "sexual objects," more even than mere women: they became Saints. Instead of being perceived as whole persons, their bodies became shrines: what was thought to be their minds became temples suitable for worship. These crazy "Saints" stared out at the world, wildly, like lunatics—or quietly, like suicides; and the "God" that was in their gaze was as mute as a great stone.

Who were these "Saints"? These crazy, loony, pitiful women?

Some of them, without a doubt, were our mothers and grandmothers.

In the still heat of the post-Reconstruction South, this is how they seemed to Jean Toomer: exquisite butterflies trapped in an evil honey, toiling away their lives in an era, a century, that did not acknowledge them, except as "the *mule* of the world." They dreamed dreams that no one knew—not even themselves, in any coherent fashion—and saw visions no one could understand. They wandered or sat about the countryside crooning lullabies to ghosts, and drawing the mother of Christ in charcoal on courthouse walls.

They forced their minds to desert their bodies and their striving spirits sought to rise, like frail whirlwinds from the hard red clay. And when those frail whirlwinds fell, in scattered particles, upon the ground, no one mourned. Instead, men lit candles to celebrate the emptiness that remained, as people do who enter a beautiful but vacant space to resurrect a God.

Our mothers and grandmothers, some of them: moving to music not yet written. And they waited.

They waited for a day when the unknown thing that was in them would be made known; but guessed, somehow in their darkness, that on the day of their revelation they would be long dead. Therefore to

Toomer they walked, and even ran, in slow motion. For they were going nowhere immediate, and the future was not yet within their grasp. And men took our mothers and grandmothers, "but got no pleasure from it." So complex was their passion and their calm.

To Toomer, they lay vacant and fallow as autumn fields, with harvest time never in sight: and he saw them enter loveless marriages, without joy; and become prostitutes, without resistance; and become mothers of children without fulfillment.

For these grandmothers and mothers of ours were not "Saints," but Artists; driven to a numb and bleeding madness by the springs of creativity in them for which there was no release. They were Creators, who lived lives of spiritual waste, because they were so rich in spirituality—which is the basis of Art—that the strain of enduring their unused and unwanted talent drove them insane. Throwing away this spirituality was their pathetic attempt to lighten the soul to a weight their work-worn, sexually abused bodies could bear.

What did it mean for a Black woman to be an artist in our grandmothers' time? In our great-grandmothers' day? It is a question with an answer cruel enough to stop the blood.

Did you have a genius of a great-great-grandmother who died under some ignorant and depraved white overseer's lash? Or was she required to bake biscuits for a lazy backwater tramp, when she cried out in her soul to paint watercolors of sunsets, or the rain falling on the green and peaceful pasturelands? Or was her body broken and forced to bear children (who were more often than not sold away from her)—eight, ten, fifteen, twenty children—when her one joy was the thought of modeling heroic figures of Rebellion, in stone or clay?

How was the creativity of the Black woman kept alive, year after year and century after century, when for most of the years Black people have been in America, it was a punishable crime for a Black person to read or write? And the freedom to paint, to sculpt, to expand the mind with action, did not exist. Consider, if you can bear to imagine it, what might have been the result if singing, too, had been forbidden by law. Listen to the voices of Bessie Smith, Billie Holiday, Nina Simone, Roberta Flack, and Aretha Franklin, among others, and imagine those voices muzzled for life. Then you may begin to comprehend the lives of our "crazy," "Sainted" mothers and grandmothers. The agony of the lives of women who might have been Poets, Novelists, Essayists, and Short Story Writers (over a period of centuries), who died with their real gifts stifled within them.

And, if this were the end of the story, we would have cause to cry out in my paraphrasec of Okot p'Bitek's great poem:

O, my clanswomen
Let us all cry together!
Come,
Let us mourn the death of our mother,
The death of a Queen
The ash that was produced
By a great fire!
O this homestead is utterly dead
Close the gates
With *lacari* thorns,
For our mother
The creator of the Stool is lost!
And all the young women
Have perished in the wilderness![1]

But this is not the end of the story, for all the young women—our mothers and grandmothers, *ourselves*—have not perished in the wilderness. And if we ask ourselves why, and search for and find the answer, we will know beyond all efforts to erase it from our minds, just exactly who, and of what, we Black American women are.

One example, perhaps the most pathetic, most misunderstood one, can provide a backdrop for our mothers' work: Phillis Wheatley, a slave in the 1700s.

Virginia Woolf, in her book, *A Room of One's Own,* wrote that in order for a woman to write fiction she must have two things, certainly: a room of her own (with key and lock) and enough money to support herself.

What then are we to make of Phillis Wheatley, a slave, who owned not even herself? This sickly, frail, Black girl who required a servant of her own at times—her health was so precarious—and who, had she been white, would have been easily considered the intellectual superior of all the women and most of the men in the society of her day.

Virginia Woolf wrote further, speaking of course not of our Phillis, that "any woman born with a great gift in the sixteenth century [insert *eighteenth century,* insert *Black woman,* insert *born or made a slave*] would certainly have gone crazed, shot herself, or ended her days in some lonely cottage outside the village, half witch, half wizard [insert *Saint*], feared and mocked at. For it needs little skill and psychology to be sure that a highly gifted girl who had tried to use her gift for poetry would have been so thwarted and hindered by contrary instincts [add *chains, guns, the lash, the ownership of one's body by someone else, submission to an alien religion*], that she must have lost her health and sanity to a certainty."

[1] Okot p'Bitek, *Song of Lawino: An Africa Lament* (Nairobi: East African Publishing House, 1966).

The key words, as they relate to Phillis, are "contrary instincts." For when we read the poetry of Phillis Wheatley—as when we read the novels of Nella Larsen or the oddly false-sounding autobiography of that freest of all Black women writers, Zora Hurston—evidence of "contrary instincts" is everywhere. Her loyalties were completely divided, as was, without question, her mind.

But how could this be otherwise? Captured at seven, a slave of wealthy, doting whites who instilled in her the "savagery" of the Africa they "rescued" her from . . . one wonders if she was even able to remember her homeland as she had known it, or as it really was.

Yet, because she did try to use her gift for poetry in a world that made her a slave, she was "so thwarted and hindered by . . . contrary instincts that she . . . lost her health. . . ." In the last years of her brief life, burdened not only with the need to express her gift but also with a penniless, friendless "freedom" and several small children for whom she was forced to do strenuous work to feed, she lost her health, certainly. Suffering from malnutrition and neglect and who knows what mental agonies, Phillis Wheatley died.

So torn by "contrary instincts" was Black, kidnapped, enslaved Phillis that her description of "the Goddess"—as she poetically called the Liberty she did not have—is ironically, cruelly humorous. And, in fact, has held Phillis up to ridicule for more than a century. It is usually read prior to hanging Phillis's memory as that of a fool. She wrote:

> The Goddess comes, she moves divinely fair,
> Olive and laurel binds her *golden* hair:
> Wherever shines this native of the skies,
> Unnumber'd charms and recent graces rise.
> [Emphasis mine]

It is obvious that Phillis, the slave, combed the "Goddess's" hair every morning; prior, perhaps, to bringing in the milk, or fixing her mistress's lunch. She took her imagery from the one thing she saw elevated above all others.

With the benefit of hindsight we ask, "How could she?"

But at last, Phillis, we understand. No more snickering when your stiff, struggling, ambivalent lines are forced on us. We know now that you were not an idiot nor a traitor; only a sickly little Black girl, snatched from your home and country and made a slave; a woman who still struggled to sing the song that was your gift, although in a land of barbarians who praised you for your bewildered tongue. It is not so much what you sang, as that you kept alive, in so many of our ancestors, *the notion of song.*

II

Black women are called, in the folklore that so aptly identifies one's status in society, "the *mule* of the world," because we have been handed the burdens that everyone else—*everyone* else—refused to carry. We have also been called "Matriarchs," "Superwomen," and "Mean and Evil Bitches." Not to mention "Castraters" and "Sapphire's Mama." When we have pleaded for understanding, our character has been distorted; when we have asked for simple caring, we have been handed empty inspirational appellations, then stuck in the farthest corner. When we have asked for love, we have been given children. In short, even our plainer gifts, our labors of fidelity and love, have been knocked down our throats. To be an Artist and a Black woman, even today, lowers our status in many respects, rather than raises it: and yet, Artists we will be.

Therefore we must fearlessly pull out of ourselves and look at and identify with our lives the living creativity some of our great-grandmothers were not allowed to know. I stress *some* of them because it is well known that the majority of our great-grandmothers knew, even without "knowing" it, the reality of their spirituality, even if they didn't recognize it beyond what happened in the singing at church—and they never had any intention of giving it up.

How they did it: those millions of Black women who were not Phillis Wheatley, or Lucy Terry or Frances Harper or Zora Hurston or Nella Larsen or Bessie Smith—nor Elizabeth Catlett, nor Katherine Dunham, either—brings me to the title of this essay, "In Search of Our Mothers' Gardens," which is a personal account that is yet shared, in its theme and its meaning, by all of us. I found, while thinking about the far-reaching world of the creative Black woman, that often the truest answer to a question that really matters can be found very close. So I was not surprised when my own mother popped into my mind.

In the late 1920s my mother ran away from home to marry my father. Marriage, if not running away, was expected of seventeen-year-old girls. By the time she was twenty, she had two children and was pregnant with a third. Five children later, I was born. And this is how I came to know my mother: she seemed a large, soft, loving-eyed woman who was rarely impatient in our home. Her quick, violent temper was on view only a few times a year, when she battled with the white landlord who had the misfortune to suggest to her that her children did not need to go to school.

Alice Walker

Minnie Lou Walker

    She made all the clothes we wore, even my brothers' overalls. She made all the towels and sheets we used. She spent the summers canning vegetables and fruits. She spent the winter evenings making quilts enough to cover all our beds.

    During the "working" day, she labored beside—not behind—my father in the fields. Her day began before sunup, and did not end until late at night. There was never a moment for her to sit down, undisturbed, to unravel her own private thoughts; never a time free from interruption—by work or the noisy inquiries of her many children. And yet, it is to my mother—and all our mothers who were not famous—that I went in search of the secret of what has fed that muzzled and often mutilated, but vibrant, creative spirit that the Black woman has inherited, and that pops out in wild and unlikely places to this day.

But when, you will ask, did my overworked mother have time to know or care about feeding the creative spirit?

The answer is so simple that many of us have spent years discovering it. We have constantly looked high, when we should have looked high—and low.

For example: in the Smithsonian Institution in Washington, D.C., there hangs a quilt unlike any other in the world. In fanciful, inspired, and yet simple and identifiable figures, it portrays the story of the Crucifixion. It is considered rare, beyond price. Though it follows no known pattern of quiltmaking, and though it is made of bits and pieces of worthless rags, it is obviously the work of a person of powerful imagination and deep spiritual feeling. Below this quilt I saw a note that says it was made by "an anonymous Black woman in Alabama, a hundred years ago."

If we could locate this "anonymous" Black woman from Alabama, she would turn out to be one of our grandmothers—an artist who left her mark in the only materials she could afford, and in the only medium her position in society allowed her to use.

As Virginia Woolf wrote further, in *A Room of One's Own:*

"Yet genius of a sort must have existed among women as it must have existed among the working class. [Change this to *slaves* and *the wives and daughters of sharecroppers*.] Now and again an Emily Brontë or a Robert Burns [change this to *a Zora Hurston or a Richard Wright*] blazes out and proves its presence. But certainly it never got itself on to paper. When, however, one reads of a witch being ducked, of a woman possessed by devils [or *Sainthood*], of a wise woman selling herbs [our rootworkers], or even a very remarkable man who had a mother, then I think we are on the track of a lost novelist, a suppressed poet, of some mute and inglorious Jane Austen. . . . Indeed, I would venture to guess that Anon, who wrote so many poems without singing them, was often a woman . . ."

And so our mothers and grandmothers have, more often than not anonymously, handed on the creative spark, the seed of the flower they themselves never hoped to see: or like a sealed letter they could not plainly read.

And so it is, certainly, with my own mother. Unlike Ma Rainey's songs, which retained their creator's name even while blasting forth from Bessie Smith's mouth, no song or poem will bear my mother's name. Yet so many of the stories that I write, that we all write, are my mother's stories. Only recently did I fully realize this: that through years of listening to my mother's stories of her life, I have absorbed not only the stories themselves, but something of the manner in which she spoke, something of the urgency that involves the knowledge that her stories—like her life—must be recorded. It is probably for this reason that so much of what I have written is about characters whose counterparts in real life are so much older than I am.

But the telling of these stories, which came from my mother's lips as naturally as breathing, was not the only way my mother showed herself as an artist. For stories, too, were subject to being distracted, to dying without conclusion. Dinners must be started, and cotton must be gathered before the big rains. The artist that was and is my mother showed itself to me only after many years. This is what I finally noticed:

Like Mem, a character in *The Third Life of Grange Copeland,* my mother adorned with flowers whatever shabby house we were forced to live in. And not just your typical straggly country stand of zinnias, either. She planted ambitious gardens—and still does—with over fifty different varieties of plants that bloom profusely from early March until late November. Before she left home for the fields, she watered her flowers, chopped up the grass, and laid out new beds. When she returned from the fields she might divide clumps of bulbs, dig a cold pit, uproot and replant roses, or prune branches from her taller bushes or trees—until night came and it was too dark to see.

Whatever she planted grew as if by magic, and her fame as a grower of flowers spread over three counties. Because of her creativity with her flowers, even my memories of poverty are seen through a screen of blooms—sunflowers, petunias, roses, dahlias, forsythia, spirea, delphiniums, verbena . . . and on and on.

And I remember people coming to my mother's yard to be given cuttings from her flowers; I hear again the praise showered on her because whatever rocky soil she landed on, she turned into a garden. A garden so brilliant with colors, so original in its design, so magnificent with life and creativity, that to this day people drive by our house in Georgia—perfect strangers and imperfect strangers—and ask to stand or walk among my mother's art.

I notice that it is only when my mother is working in her flowers that she is radiant, almost to the point of being invisible—except as Creator: hand and eye. She is involved in work her soul must have. Ordering the universe in the image of her personal conception of Beauty.

Her face, as she prepares the Art that is her gift, is a legacy of respect she leaves to me, for all that illuminates and cherishes life. She had handed down respect for the possibilities—and the will to grasp them.

For her, so hindered and intruded upon in so many ways, being an artist has still been a daily part of her life. This ability to hold on, even in very simple ways, is work Black women have done for a very long time.

This poem is not enough, but it is something, for the woman who literally covered the holes in our walls with sunflowers:

> They were women then
> My mama's generation
> Husky of voice—Stout of
> Step
> With fists as well as
> Hands
> How they battered down
> Doors
> And ironed
> Starched white
> Shirts
> How they led
> Armies
> Headragged Generals
> Across mined
> Fields
> Booby-trapped
> Ditches
> To discover books
> Desks
> A place for us
> How they knew what we
> *Must* know
> Without knowing a page
> Of it
> Themselves.

Guided by my heritage of a love of beauty and a respect for strength—in search of my mother's garden, I found my own.

And perhaps in Africa over two hundred years ago, there was just such a mother; perhaps she painted vivid and daring decorations in oranges and yellows and greens on the walls of her hut; perhaps she sang—in a voice like Roberta Flack's—*sweetly* over the compounds of her village; perhaps she wove the most stunning mats or told the most ingenious stories of all the village story-tellers. Perhaps she was herself a poet—though only her daughter's name is signed to the poems that we know.

Perhaps Phillis Wheatley's mother was also an artist.

Perhaps in more than Phillis Wheatley's biological life is her mother's signature made clear.

Alice Walker

May Stevens

My Work and My
Working-Class Father

ALTHOUGH MY MOTHER never earned a penny after she married, I always knew I would earn my living. I don't know how I knew it. It was probably the result of growing up in New England in a working-class family. I remember my father saying I should marry someone with a college education (something he did not have), someone *like me*. It would have been unthinkable for him to suggest, or for me to envision, marrying for money—or even that "it's just as easy to marry a rich man as a poor one." The Presbyterian Scottish shipbuilders I grew up among just didn't think that way. Hard work, clean living, and saved money were the way. No shortcuts.

From art school on I knew I would be an artist; that meant that I would continue to paint. How that related to earning a living I did not know. In art school, trying to plan my life, I came to the conclusion that this society would not pay me for doing the things I liked to do (painting, writing poetry). I never expected to be paid for giving the best of myself, only for performing tasks in flawed institutions, using my talents and moral values minimally, if at all. I remember discussing these things with a clever boyfriend who had come to the same conclusions about society as I had, except that he proposed to join it, succeed within it on its own terms, while I, the idealist, wanted no part of it, wanted only to be left alone to make my paintings and my poems—after a day's work in the office or shop. Money and power were no concerns of mine. I do not think my attitude had to do only with being a woman (no woman ever thought she could change the world, said Simone de Beauvoir); it also had to do with class, with the examples of my father, who was a pipe fitter in the shipyard (but who owned his own house), and our friends and relatives, none of whom was in business or the professions.

My mother and father never doubted my ability to take care of myself. I had been a loved and trusted child. I was a successful and much-admired student. I was not in the habit of asking for help. The realm of art and ideas, a mystery to my parents, was respected, but not basic. I would build my life on these things, but I would take care of the practical side of living, too.

I went to art school blindly, obliviously, stubbornly, taking only courses in fine arts, having no idea where it would all lead. I avoided all commercial art courses and all teacher education courses although I had never met an artist who didn't teach. And I had never met—or even heard of—a woman who was an artist. (Rosa Bonheur, whose *Horse Fair* hung over our living room sofa, on the flowered wallpaper, had been dead a long time.)

The very righteousness and propriety of my Scottish neighbors that gave me strength and purpose also sent me to art school instead of a regular college. I was afraid of being an old maid—which I equated with being a teacher. If I went to a regular college, I felt I would inevitably end up being a teacher and unmarried, as New England schoolteachers had always been and, for the most part, still were. My scholastic ability coupled with shyness had frightened off most boys. I was deeply embarrassed to be caught reading a book on a Saturday night instead of playing the dating game. Art school would save me, substituting bohemianism for the prim academic life. I chose to confound "their" predictions, make my life riskier, more open. The pressures to succeed as a "girl" weighed heavy upon me; it took me a long time to realize that the problem was not to find someone who wanted to marry me but to find someone I could give myself to wholeheartedly.

So I faced my future armed only with the conviction that I would always paint and that I would earn my own living. Beyond that I had no plans, no ideas, almost no fears. I chose, at every turning, to do the thing I wanted to do, and watched and waited.

After I graduated from art school I illustrated a textbook, which I enjoyed, and then took a demeaning job doing layouts for ads in a local newspaper. I wanted to follow my friends to New York, but stayed in my parents' house for a year because they begged me to. When I got a telegram from my closest art-school friend telling me there was an empty room in her building, I packed my things and left home for good.

I arrived in New York full of a sense of adventure. I enrolled in night classes at the Art Students League and got a nine-to-five job selling gifts in Hammacher Schlemmer. Five nights a week I painted. And I waited for my life to unfold.

The first night I walked into the Art Students League I asked the class monitor to assign me a locker. He was wearing an army shirt, spoke with an unplaceable European accent, and seemed not at all a youth but a man. He was twenty-eight, had served three years in the American army, and had lost his family to native anti-Semites in Eastern Europe. He was beginning seriously to study art. His paintings were always gray. In June we married and in September we sailed for Paris to study art—and live—on the GI bill. Pregnant, I quit the

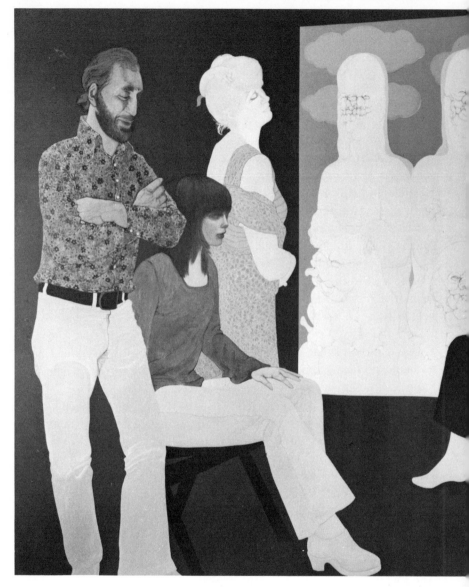

Artist's Studio (After Courbet), 1974, acrylic (Collection Robert H.
Orchard, St. Louis, Missouri)

Académie Julian and for three years lived in the suburbs of Paris
painting and raising our son.

It was miserably hard. The houses were cold and damp; I developed
arthritis. No woman friend was there to advise or comfort me. I was
alone with my child and Dr. Spock. My husband shared all my pains,
but he was away all day at school. When he brought his professor
home to dinner, M. Sabouraud looked at all the canvases I was pour-

ing my loneliness into and said: "Not honest. Too strong for a woman."

My husband and I joined a cooperative gallery run by American students on the left bank of the Seine. I showed my work there and tasted acclaim. Nothing sold. Why should it? I was doing what I wanted to do. But in the columns of the Paris dailies and weeklies my work was reviewed with favor: "May Stevens, young painter, come to

Paris to perfect herself . . ."; ". . . this art, in its gentle melancholy, does not lack nerves . . ."; and, these pictures "testify to the authentic emotion of the artist before the world that she feels called upon to reveal to us . . ." The only criticism was directed at one painting that referred to a political trial of seven black men in Virginia. The critic of the Paris edition of the *New York Herald Tribune* said it was a fine painting, but it suffered because of its title: *Martinsville Seven.*

Returning to New York in 1951, I took those courses I had refused to take before. Now I could be a teacher. I passed the exams

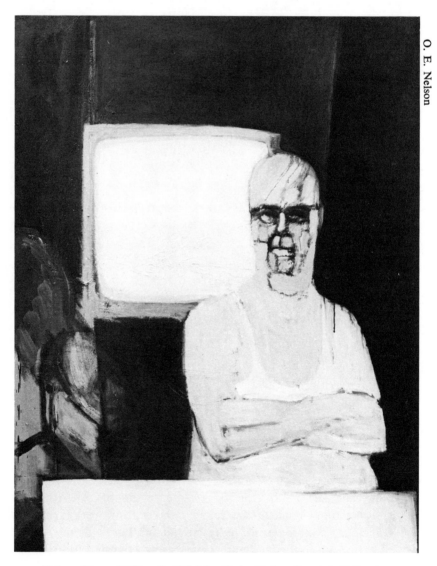

O. E. Nelson

Prime Time, 1967, oil (Wichita State University Art Collection, Wichita, Kansas)

and began to teach in the New York City high schools when they were first being called "the blackboard jungle." I came home from school every day and went to bed. It took a year for me to find my bearings, to lose my fear. I began to love teaching. I continued to paint and exhibit. Five years later, I asked for a leave of absence without pay because I was having difficulty completing work for a scheduled exhibition. The leave was refused and I quit my job, al-

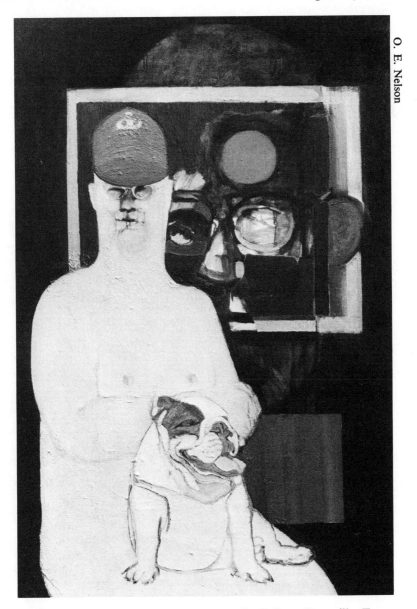

O. E. Nelson

Big Daddy, 1967–68, oil (Collection Dulin Gallery, Knoxville, Tennessee)

though I was by that time teaching at the prestigious High School of Music and Art. Friends told me I could have pretended to have lower-back pain (an untraceable ailment) or pleaded nervous exhaustion and been permitted to take a medical leave. But I would not do that. I had been hired to teach in that special school because I was an exhibiting artist. I had dragged paintings in for my first interview and showed catalogs and reviews to prove my standing as an artist. My friends warned me I was giving up a secure job and losing pension rights and accumulated benefits. Governing my life by such petty securities frightened me more than losing my job. I managed to find part-time college teaching fairly soon.

Our lives were organized around work. Both R. and I taught, painted, and took care of our small son. There were never any rugs on the floor or curtains on the windows. Our lives were stripped for work. The living room was our studio, the bedroom our son's room. We slept on a daybed in the living room/studio. We went to the movies in shifts. It was a life of very hard work, but it was focused. It seemed to me rich, all-involving, the only way to live. We had no hobbies.

Big Daddy Paper Doll, 1971, acrylic on canvas (Collection Brooklyn Museum, New York)

In my work I used my son as subject. A boy holding the root ball of a young tree, or playing on white sand with a coral-colored crab under a dark blue sky. A boy with a huge, black, white-horned bull; the goose boy; boys with kites—these were the themes that came from my daily life. My life and art revolved around my son.

Later, when he was older, I, still teaching, still tied to the house, became emotionally involved with the civil rights movement. I followed daily the bus burnings in Alabama and read every word I could find. Out of this came a series of paintings called *Freedom Riders,* mostly black and white, full of images of pain. I was locked into a suburban apartment and a teaching job, but I lived mentally in the South. When Malcolm X was killed, I went to see him laid out in Harlem. I made drawings and etchings of that dead figure, of that dead head.

We lived in Queens near a housing development for people connected with the United Nations. We spent evening after evening discussing politics with Asians, Africans, Europeans. The anti-American theme was continuous and pervasive. I, too, had high moral sensibili-

ties and despised neo-colonialism, capitalism, imperialism, racism, anti-Semitism, etc., etc., but as each such evening wore on I began to feel more and more depressed. I would be the only American in the room and it began to smother me, all this anti-Americanism. I wanted to cry out, "There are good things here, too. Look at me—I'm an American. I'm not like that." I became suspicious of their smugness.

I decided I had to accept myself as an American. I had to stop envying Europe, old culture, great subtlety, refined manners. I would be direct and plain; I would be brash as opposed to their discretion. I had to be myself and that had to be worthwhile. I told myself that something which is itself has value.

I began to paint my own family background. I painted out of love for those lower-middle-class Americans I came from and out of a great anger for what had happened to them and what they were letting happen, making happen, in the South and in Vietnam. When I started on this theme, my European-born husband told me there was no merit in the idea. I asked him not to come into my studio anymore until invited.

I had two recent photographs—one of my father, one of my mother. They were snapshots, terrible to see, revealing of what life had done to these people I loved, and of what they had done to each other. The photograph of my mother was too terrible for me to deal with. I started to paint my father.

My mother, when I was growing up, did not sew, did not cook well, and did not keep a beautiful house. She had been forced to leave elementary school when her father died. She had no social graces and no talents. She only loved me and my brother without question. When my brother died at sixteen and I left home, the long disorientation consumed her and she was committed to a state mental hospital.

Sexism and classism, male authority and poverty-and-ignorance were the forces that crippled my mother; the agent in most direct contact with her was, of course, my father. But the equation cannot be written as two equal forces of sex and class focusing their oppressive powers through one man onto my mother. Poverty (class) ground her down from the beginning (when it took a bright child out of school to make her a mother's helper to the rich folk on the hill) and used male dominance to do it (her brother was kept in school) and religion to sanctify the arrangement and squelch her own desire. She was taught to be good. She was a good student. She was always good—until she painted the kitchen red in the middle of the night and screamed at the passing cars.

My father was helpless to deal with his hopeless, useless wife. He grew to hate her, so as not to pity her and feel the full pain. She was fat. She didn't know how to dress, nor how to talk. We couldn't bring anyone home; my mother might embarrass us. My father put his hat on his head and drove away in his car. We (I, my brother, my mother) didn't know where he was going, how long he would stay, if he was coming back.

My father's politics were aligned with those of management. He joined the company union and talked against commies, Jews, niggers, etc. He had his own scale of racial acceptability, with the English, Scots, and Germans at the top. The Irish Catholics (my mother's ethnic background) were above the Mediterranean peoples but linked to them by common traits: religion, expressiveness, fondness for alcohol, and sexual promiscuity.

These ideas made me almost physically ill—as it does now to write them down. But I liked my father. I waited up for him to come home from work at 11:00 P.M. when he worked the afternoon shift. I often walked him to the shipyard gate, which was ten minutes away from our house. We laughed and talked and teased. He said I had a face like that of a kid being sassy to a cop. When I began to paint this man, I touched home base.

In my studio I sweated out this past; my colors changed, the forms changed. I left subdued color, soft edges, veils of misty tone for bright, hard colors and clear, sharp edges. The portrait of my father, under-shirted, before a blank TV screen turned eventually into a symbol of American complicity in the war in Southeast Asia. I named the figure *Big Daddy*. It became, through painting after painting, a monster (smiling, congenial) of my own making and finally had little to do with the man it was based on. It passed out of the specific and became an abstract vehicle for my anger. As I marched in anti-war parades I worked out in my head new images of the complacency, the obtuse-ness, the incredible thick-skinned "niceness" of clean, well-fed Americans. I saw them in contrast to the tiny dark-skinned people they towered over at six o'clock every day on the news.

In spite of our parallel careers, I had always felt I was taken less seriously as an artist than R. Now, as a political artist (which I had been intermittently before), I faced another discrimination. As Lucy Lippard has written: "In a post Duchampian and Warholian day when *all* materials and activities and subjects are automatically accepted as art-worthy, overt politics remains virtually the only tabu."[1] Words like cartoon, caricature, and propaganda were thrown at me. I

[1] Lucy Lippard, *From the Center* (New York: E. P. Dutton, 1976).

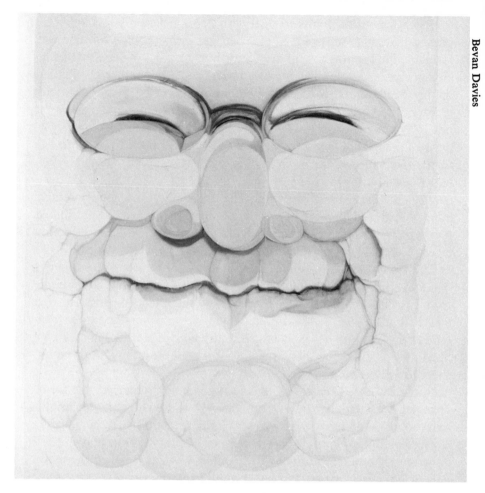

Bevan Davies

"It smiles and sucks you in." *Head*, 1973, oil (Courtesy of the Lerner-Heller Gallery, New York)

found using political themes was like waving a red flag; it infuriated the defenders of art's purity. It was hard to make my work seen through the dust and smoke cast up around it. It was hard to make it understood that this art was at the same time political and highly personal, that the two terms are not contradictory—or that they are contradictory the way life is, the way my feelings about my family are.

When the women's movement came along, I realized how strongly anti-patriarchal were these fat male figures that bulged on my canvases. The figure in *Head* shows his face spread across a six-foot square in fleshy pinks and lavenders. It is soft, as difficult to pin down as a cloud or steam. But pervasive, all-encompassing. It smiles and sucks you in; it is seductively beautiful in tone and texture. That head is like a total environment, one that is next to impossible to escape from. I think of all the cities along the networks of highways and all the buildings and libraries in those cities, all, all designed and built by men./And all the books in all those libraries, with the philosophies and the theories, the poems and the paintings, the religions and the sciences, all written, all designed by men. And I feel that I am hammering against the air.

Work for me has meant establishing my identity and my freedom in the face of pressures of many kinds/The roles of wife and mother and working woman (teacher) have eaten away at my energy and courage./I have had to fight to get my work seen and understood. The comparison with my painter-husband and his work, and the competition that inevitably exists even in the most loving relationship, have chipped at my strength. The art-world necessities of modishness and historical determinism in style, as well as the sexism of art history and art criticism, have had to be analyzed and combatted. Every one of these issues distracts and takes time from the real battle—that painful, private battle in which each artist works out her/his way to the most honest and authentic statement. I see a real similarity between that struggle and the way a woman (and any other oppressed person) creates herself through trusting her own needs and desires and working to achieve them. I have not had a psychological difficulty getting down to work, but rather the problem of finding my true work within my chosen field, of finding the task that only I could do—which is the artist's task.

A major thrust of contemporary women artists' work has been autobiographical. This is true in my case and in many others': Pat Lasch does her ancestors, Audrey Flack her jewels, Alice Neel her granddaughter Olivia and her daughter-in-law Nancy. In addition to the *Big Daddy* series based on my family, my father and his ethnocentrism, I have gone back to writing poems, perhaps to say some of the things the paintings could not say. In the past few years I have written many poems about my mother, whose aborted life is for me the clearest argument for the liberation of women. And one or two for my father, who was, after all, my father and loved me, without understanding. When he died I wrote this poem, which, contradicting somewhat the image from the paintings of Big Daddy, makes the picture of him more complete, more real:

LETTERS FROM HOME

MY FATHER TIED PACKAGES WITH WHITE WAXED STRING IN A SMALL
TIGHT NET KNOTTED AT EVERY INTERSECTION SO THAT YOU WERE
SURPRISED WHEN BEING CUT OPEN THE STRING CASE DID NOT STAND
ALONE.   THEY BORE ME PRESENTS THOSE BOXES CAUGHT IN STRING
CANNED GOODS TO PARIS FEAST FOR POOR STUDENTS ELECTRIC
BLANKETS WITH ENERGY GONE PILLED WOOL PENCILS SAYING
BETHLEHEM STEEL COTTON DUCK STOLEN FROM HIS PLACE OF WORK
FOR ME TO PAINT ON   BOXES OF JELLO CONDENSED MILK. AND
ONCE HE ARRIVED IN QUEENS IN THE DEAD OF NIGHT WITH AN OLD
WASHING MACHINE WITH WRINGER ON TOP.   HE HAD A NEW ONE.

WHEN I ARRIVED IN A NEW PLACE THERE WAS A LETTER WAITING
ARRIVED TWO DAYS BEFORE.   DEAR MAY   THE WEATHER IS COOL
RAINY.   WENT TO LODGE LAST NIGHT DAMN CAT WON'T LET ME
WRITE WHAT DO YOU WANT FOR XMAS LET ME KNOW HAD A COOKOUT
ON THE FOURTH ADDIE CAME AND MAUDE AND BERT CORN HOT DOGS
WATERMELON THEN THEY WENT SWIMMING FOR CRISSAKES WHY DON'T
YOU CURL YOUR HAIR LOOK LIKE SOMETHING   YOU LOOK LIKE SOMETHING
THE CAT DRAGGED IN WHY DO YOU WEAR BLACK ALL THE TIME WHAT
ARE YOU A WOP   YOU KNOW YOU CAN BECOME AN AMERICAN BUT YOU
HAVE TO BE BORN A YANKEE YOU ONLY LIVE ONCE.   YOU'RE DEAD A
LONG TIME   CHEER UP   LOVE RALPH

DEAR DADDY THIS IS A LETTER I SEND TO YOU WHERE YOU ARE NOW
DEAD A LONG TIME SINCE AUGUST AND NO LETTERS COME.

May Stevens

Joann Green
At Work on
Tales of Chelm

A few scenes from one of the acts, sometime after the first act and before the last one

(SUBTITLED) any act can be the last one

IN SCHOOL

Scene 1

On the playground of an elementary school. Sounds of swings creaking, children leaping, squealing, improvising. Buses lumbering through the surrounding city. On the stone slab of a porch attached to the school building "Cinderella" is in rehearsal. CHUBBETTE is directing. Moppets are giggling unrulily.

CHUBBETTE: Take your time. Slower. Why are you laughing? Look at her. Take your time. Hold her foot while you put the shoe on.

MOPPETS: (giggle giggle)

CHUBBETTE: I mean her leg. Hold it like something important. Now put the shoe on. It fits. She is your love.

MOPPETS: (giggle giggle)

CHUBBETTE: O.K. Cinderella, the shoe fits. Feel it on your foot. Take your time. O.K. Prince. Say your line.

PRINCE: It is you. I will marry you, and give you half my kingdom.

CHUBBETTE: You should look at her when you talk to her. O.K. Cinderella. Say your line.

CINDERELLA: It is me. Thank you. I'll take half the kingdom, but I would like to travel a bit before I decide if I wish to settle down with you.

The school bell rings.
The sounds of the swings, the squeals, the giggling, and the traffic fade. The moppets march off the porch and into the school. CHUBBETTE joins the line, but she takes her time.

Scene 2

Musical introduction. "Summertime (and the livin' is easy)." It is a recording.
Curtain opens to reveal the painted backdrop of a rooming house.
CHUBBETTE enters. She acknowledges the victrola. She bows. On one hand CHUBBETTE holds a tray on which several bowls of steaming oatmeal are balanced. On her other hand is a soft stack of pillows. She is fifteen.

CHUBBETTE clears her throat and begins to juggle. She juggles the tray and the oatmeal and the pillows. As she juggles, CHUBBETTE notices a sign being lowered from the flies.

POCONO PLAYHOUSE—ONE MILE

CHUBBETTE sidles to and from the sign. She juggles more fiercely, her eyes on the sign.
Eventually, CHUBBETTE flings pillows, oatmeal, and tray into the audience and twirls toward the sign.
CHUBBETTE picks up the sign, which becomes a broom, with which she sweeps up the stage in a dance of ecstasy, her pointed toes barely touching the spilled oatmeal on the floor.

Scene 3

This scene is preceded by a very boring scene of exposition. Talk talk talk. College students are discussing the madness of CHUBBETTE for holding a playwriting contest among them, and for actually deciding to direct the winner's play.

This is a dream scene.

CHUBBETTE appears, slightly mad, slightly conscious of it. It is unclear for whom she is playing the part of someone who appears slightly mad, but it is clear that both for herself and for those who view her there is delight and relief in the irresponsibility of her madness.
The dream continues for a long time, reappears throughout the play, and often forms itself during other events, interrupting, interfering, luring, challenging, and lovely.

The dream:
On a stage are two persons of definite, but indeterminate, sex. At each turn of a head, at the merest gesture, at every inflection of their alien language, a light focuses and refocuses. With each shift of focus the rhythm of their movement alters, and with each inconstancy the patterns of their relationship become apparent. Compassion and connection, indifference and dissolution. All is clear, instant by delicately perceptible instant. Off the stage sits JOANN. She is in the dream, yet she is able to see herself, to see herself seeing, to see herself seeing herself. Time stops. Time warps.
JOANN knows, and is aware that she knows, that in this space, there is neither yesterday nor tomorrow. All things human are possible. In this passion there is trust.

This dream must in no way appear to be the ramblings of an imagination gone mad.

If there is applause at any time, the scene is, temporarily, over. The dream continues. The two on stage are totally aware of each other. Their awareness makes JOANN's stomach jump.

JOANN is clearly in love, with her own imagination.

The author wishes to thank S. Jane Murphy Smith for inspiring this dream with her play *Lucifer*.

Scene 4

Collage.

OLDER MAN: Nuclear physics. It's the wave of the future. The science prize you won in high school.

OLDER WOMAN: It's as easy to love a rich man as a poor one.

TOGETHER: Theater?
              You'll outgrow it.
              To be an actress, you have to be beautiful.

JOANN (whispers):   Director. (She opens an umbrella.)
As the scene continues, JOANN opens umbrella after umbrella against the shower of clichés. JOANN repeats "Director," distinctly, calmly, stubbornly, as she stands, thoroughly protected, thoroughly paralyzed, by the weight of all those umbrellas.

OLDER MAN (in his wisdom):   Wishing will not make it so.

JOANN: Director. (She opens an umbrella.)

OLDER WOMAN: Not even a little bit of lipstick?

JOANN: (Opens an umbrella.)

AT HOME

Scene 1

It is a dreary scene. The author wishes at this moment to emerge through time and advise the audience to partake of a cool collation, or to perform a natural ablution, during this scene. The author acknowledges that she never really enjoyed this scene, and wishes to announce that it was actually the producers' wish that she include it. The author wishes to state that she has nothing against such scenes in general, or in principle. She wishes to refrain from moralizing, and to abandon the obligations of realism. In addition, and in sincerity, the author wishes to state, on a program note perhaps, that she has no regrets. (hello, Shoshanna, hello, Jonas)

The scene takes place inside a MAN's pant cuff.
It is a rather pleasant place to lounge about, but a rather difficult place to get out of.
Awkward, but well pressed.
A kind, but monotonous, voice filters through the herringbone.

MAN'S VOICE: why don't you do some thing go to the thea ter the way you used to you used to en joy go ing to the thea ter vo lun teer at a litt le thea ter re mem ber how you en joyed thea ter

ANOTHER VOICE: No. I don't remember.

MAN'S VOICE: you used to tell me all a bout the thea ter re mem ber

ANOTHER VOICE: No. I don't remember.

MAN'S VOICE: find your self some thing to do

("Oh, but I do.
I go from the kitchen to the bathroom
From the bathroom to the bedroom
From the bedroom to the living room.")[1]
And so the scene continues. Day after day. Time is the stage manager. It is a painfully predictable scene, which the author would like to spell out, but she does not remember.

[1] Susan Yankowitz, *Terminal*, in *Three Works by the Open Theater*, Karen Malpede, ed. (New York: Drama Book Specialists, 1974), p. 57.

Scene 2

There is now a large mirror inside the cuff.
A not-so-small baby crawls in front of it. The mirror must be so large
that the not-so-small baby crawls in front of it no matter where the not-
so-small baby crawls. It is important that the baby does what it does.
This is not artifact, and, anyway, it is impossible to direct children.
JOANN is reclining in the cuff. Her lethargy has achieved a pallor that
matches the shade of the cuff quite nicely.

The baby crawls in front of the mirror. Eventually, the baby sees herself in the mirror. (The director has no need for concern here. It happens.) The not-so-small baby makes faces at herself in the mirror, and
watches her faces changing. She watches her own smiles, squints, and
frowns, and is fascinated with the forms of her own feelings.

The light reflected from the mirror focuses and splays out again as the
child turns her head or tilts her hand. The light from the mirror glows
in faintly remembered patterns on the walls of the cuff. The patterns of
an old dream intrude on the scene, interrupt, fade, fuss, and fidget
about the child playing and JOANN reclining.

JOANN watches the child and watches the light, and makes no connection save in her increasing sensitivity to the awkwardness of her own
reclining.

Scene 3

JONAS is five years old. His eyes are green, like his mother's (the author's). An incredibly beautiful child.

His mother is in the room, somewhere. It is of no importance. The
mother can be represented as a HEART/EAR.
If there is any sound at all, it is only the little-boy sound. A slow tap-
ping against the side of a bed, perhaps, or a fingernail scratching a
headboard. Perhaps the only sound is the sound of a little boy's
blinking.
There is no light source. The little boy is intimately, totally, endearingly
visible, vulnerable, true.

JONAS (says):

> I
> knew
> who
> I
> was
> but
> then
> I
> forgot

The words suffuse the air as breath.

There is no fade-out.

The words, the little boy, the heart/ear, and the green eyes remain forever, and forever, and forever.

SCENE: THE TURNING   (subtitled)   The Returning

The scene smells of chlorine. Everyone in it is green and overweight. The heads of the women are thrust forward by the tug of a grotesque brooch that pends from their necks. The hands of the men are pocketed, ersatz erections. It is 86 degrees. A soft breeze carries the scent of chlorine from nose to nose. There is no dialogue. Only sighs, sighs, and more sighs. Occasionally someone sniffs, discreetly.

Nothing ever happens.

The people purchase unnecessary baubles, pretend to perfect contract bridge and coronary artery disease, eat, discreetly, pee, discreetly, and die, but that they do somewhere else, and it is never mentioned.

Nothing happens.

No one says anything.

Just out of sight someone white is blowing off someone yellow's head, someone black is cleaning someone white's toilet, five white females are hoisting each other's consciousnesses, six red males are desperately trying to recall a dance they never knew, somewhere bombs are falling, somewhere black is beautiful, somewhere women are people, somewhere someone speaks.

But none of that is in this scene.

Here everyone is green. Here everyone sighs.

JOANN's voice bubbles up from the chlorine:
> All fantasy is innocent
> (gurgle gurgle)
> All true theater is about the loss of innocence
> (gurgle gurgle)
> Metaphor transcends experience
> (gurgle gurgle)
> I am lonely (gurgle) for my passion (gurgle)
> Theater (gurgle)

JOANN flails about through the chlorine, now drowning, now saving herself, now swimming, now sinking.

A heavy head turns and sighs obesely. JOANN floats in a wedge of time, calm, warm, at once connected with and detached from the green and heavy head. The head droops ever so slightly, and the moment closes. The scene ends with a sigh, a gurgle, and a swift kick in the pants.

AT THE THEATER

Scene 1

The Cast:
Blond Young Man, chewing gum and contorting his wrists.
Black Young Man, balancing on his elbows.
Tall Young Man, whistling "God Bless America."
Young Woman, clutching a knee to her chin.

The Crew:
Musician, talking into the agitator of a washing machine.
Director, seated in the middle of a mass of paper, babbling.

The scene:
Confusion and disintegration. Reams of paper, notes, scripts are everywhere. No one seems to pay attention to anyone. Each individual is passionately in charge, clutching, coddling, crumpling, eating paper. The Director always has more paper.

The props:
A torn sheet, a bowl of water, an apple.

Improvisation:
(   )

In spurts, without definable logic, the paper world finds its order. The sheet becomes a horse's mane, a sail, a handkerchief. The apple stays an apple. The Musician drinks the water. The cast becomes a confederation of individuals. A community of purpose informs the space and time.

Time is defenseless against a lifetime, or a moment, on the stage.

The actor is a shaman; the image is his ritual.

Listen.
You can recognize a song you have never heard before.
A song that sings with you.

Scene 2

Click of a slide projector, flash of a photograph.

Scraps of paper litter the stage lightly.

Midnight, and a few of the company and friends are together, seeing the pictures.

Click, flash.

Among those watching, Sara H. is dying of cancer.

Click, flash. One play is no more. Another play is to be.
The photographs remain.

Sara is disappearing. The cancer remains, and grows.

The play took hold of time. Time took hold of Sara.

Click, flash.

Scraps of applause litter the universe.

The photographs take hold of time.
Sara's empty hands are twenty-five years old.

Sara, next to your life, the theater is such a minor miracle.

Scene 3

OLDER WOMAN alone. Alone. Alone. She is very clean. There is much very clean furniture around her. A very clean bathtub tilts precariously over her. On either side of her is a pile of news clippings. The OLDER WOMAN holds a large dust rag. It is very clean. The WOMAN is dusting the clippings. Perhaps she is smiling.

Scene 4

This scene is played in front of a curtain. There is no podium. JOANN appears simple, but tasteful; assured, but not aloof; warm, but not enslaved by emotion; intelligent, but not pedantic; attractive, but not seductive; mature, but not aged; perfect, but with touches of imperfection so that the audience can identify with her; womanly, but not feminine; honest, but not demanding; passionate, but not sinful; good, but not holier-than-thou; compassionate, but not victimized; accomplished, but not overbearing; superior, but reachable; wise, but willing to learn; vulnerable, but not about to be destroyed; loving and independent, despite the need for love.

Notwithstanding the difficulty of establishing this image, the author continues to search for it.

JOANN (says):   These are the plays I have directed, these are the actors I have worked with, these are the persons who have worked with me.

(and she lists them, adding personal comments throughout, the shock of one, the delight of another, references to awards in tones of humble pride)

not forgetting Shoshanna and Jonas

not forgetting Sara H.

remembering the remarkable closeness which is a rehearsal

remembering the audience which so soothes and so completes

thinking of the earth/time which so alters when re-seen after having been envisioned in two hours on the stage wondering, do we see our time differently because of this play or that play, do we, have I helped, Sara, please, say yes.

time away from Jonas and Shoshanna

trying trying o so hard not to judge myself
for creating, with a company,
for sharing, with an audience,
in the middle of everything, a few moments of blithering joy.

Sara Ruddick

A Work of One's Own

MY RECENT INTEREST in work and women's complicated relation to it grew out of two experiences. The first was an experience of worklessness. I was twenty-six years old, and had completed four years of graduate school, when I followed my husband to his job intending to write a dissertation. I had no children. My husband was interested in my work and supportive of any time or effort it took. He and I easily shared the few jobs involved in maintaining ourselves in our small apartment. In short, I had no excuse for a work paralysis so complete that for some months I was unable to read or talk about anything relating to my thesis, let alone to write about it. Although I recovered in some months from the worst of this paralysis and eventually wrote the thesis, I suffered for many years afterward from serious inhibitions, halfheartedness, and vacillation in my work—the legacy, in a milder form, of paralysis.

Two features of this experience astonished me. First, I was completely surprised by and unprepared for the pain of worklessness—a pain that pervaded my life despite the fact that I was married to a man I loved and respected and who loved and respected me, a pain that recurred in periods of worklessness despite the fact that I soon had children whose presence was a joy and delight to me. Secondly, I found that I knew nothing about myself, about my own history as a worker. I had learned to think of life as a matter of personal relations, to think about myself as a daughter, wife, friend, and lover. I knew more about myself as a mother, more about babies even before I ever had children, than I knew about myself as a worker. This was partly because I was a woman; in my generation, women's work histories were so buried in our love histories as to be barely visible. It was partly because neither I nor the young professionals around me had been thinking about the meaning, the uses, the "good" of our work. These were the *early* sixties, years of affluence, professionalism, and privacy. Cleverness, clarity, subtlety, taste were our virtues, professional success its own reward.

The second critical experience grew out of my efforts to avoid repeating the first. Two years ago I was granted a notoriously mixed blessing—a leave from my teaching duties. So long as I taught, I had both work and a place in which to do it. The unstructured time a leave offered, free not only from obligation but also from community, was threatening. I wanted to write, but could I? Although I had something to say to people who seemed to be listening, the very idea of so much time made me pen-tied. The isolation and paralysis of the thesis years returned to haunt my night thoughts, whatever daytime reasons might reveal. Following my natural bent, I looked for *books* about work, work problems, the meaning of work. I was disappointed. I found numerous books about *jobs,* how to get them, who had them, who lost them. I learned more about the suffering and boredom most men and women experience in jobs that allow them little autonomy or dignity, let alone the leisure and support "work problems" presume. But I found next to nothing about the development of the capacity to work alone—to begin, sustain, and complete a piece of writing, for example. I wanted to know "how to do it" and why I couldn't. Despairing of books, I turned to people, to friends whose work—writing, teaching, thinking, making—resembled mine. I found that many people had been puzzled about their work or, for a time, unable to work. We began to talk and out of that talk this book was born.

I will try to trace the steps that led first to my inability to work and then, later and gradually, to a recovery of a sense of myself as a worker. I hope that my story will be sufficiently familiar to be useful to others. Although I have never voluntarily stopped working, it is only recently that I have had work I can do with confidence in its worth and my competence, and that I can count on being *able* to work most days, ordinary days, when there are no classes to prepare or deadlines to meet. At long last I have been *learning* to work. By that I mean that there is in my daily life a satisfactory predominance of activity over passivity, of reality over fantasy, of creation over conception. It continues to astonish me that this simple human ability to work brings so much additional pleasure, order, solace, and meaning to my life.

A "Life Plan" makes sense of early hopes and provides attainable goals that seem worthwhile when achieved. The Woman's Life Plan did this for me. The Plan is simple: to marry well, to bear and raise children who thrive, to accept age and one's children's children. Ancillary activities, varieties of pleasure and service, complement the basic goals. The Plan is embedded in particular plans, particular strategies and fantasies, bequeathed by individual families in different social classes.

In Midwestern, middle-class America, where I grew up, the Plan was so widely endorsed by peers and adults alike that I had no need to articulate it, only to live it. My earliest play included my future family; my earliest accomplishments would, I thought, be put to their use.

Later, by example, precept, chapel sermon, and friendly gossip I was taught the Plan's lessons. When in fact I did marry and have children as planned, I experienced the pleasures and sense of well-being I had been led to expect. The Plan has worked well for me, though it hasn't for others. I neither defend nor criticize it. I simply underline its existence.

Growing up, I was taught and accepted the myth of sexual division —the myth that the world, and especially the world's work, is divided by sex. Since I was trained by the Woman's Life Plan and looked forward to achieving its goals, I should have looked forward to a woman's work. But from early adolescence I was puzzled. What does a woman *do* when living out the Plan? I could see that women mothered, kept house, "entertained," cared for elderly family members, and contributed to various community projects. When these activities are done well, and they were in my family, they take time; they require discipline and numerous practical and moral strengths. I could see that time was being used up; I could not see how time was used— controlled and ordered by plans. Since I was given to fantasy, it was crucial for me to live *in* time, to make sense of the day's hours. I always respected women's work but it did not present sufficiently clear-cut tasks or long-range objectives to satisfy my fundamental need to live purposively.

Furthermore, from an early age I felt unsuited for women's work. I had no practical bent, and contrary to popular opinion, practical incompetence is no virtue in women who deal with much of practical life. I was not socially adept, had no interest in cooking or sewing, hated to shop, lacked any aesthetic sense of domestic as opposed to natural beauties, felt ill at ease around young children, had no knack for dressing well. I was, in short, unpromising as a woman's apprentice. My mother and her friends were tolerant of my eccentricities, so I suffered little from my inability.

Indeed, no one close to me, certainly neither of my parents, ever suggested that I would have to choose between a "woman's life" and a work of my own. For as I grew up I was subject to another middle-class myth—the myth of "opportunity and vocation." Both sexes, all classes, so the myth ran, have a right to work of their own, which, with effort and talent, they will discover and develop. Year after year our teachers tested us, boys and girls alike, in the hope that our "interests" would be revealed, and in turn our "vocation." Neither mothering nor householding was considered a vocation, although everyone knew that successful girls were supposed to find their primary work "at home."

When I was young, there seemed to me to be only one kind of truly desirable work. Respectable work was professional, the worker essentially self-employed and therefore independent. Such work required training, earned status and money, but was free from the taint of commercialism. It was interesting, of use to others, performed outside the house. It took up most of one's days, earned the right to service at home and respect in the community. The work was far too absorbing, far too public, to be compatible with the Woman's Life Plan. Indeed, the person doing the work usually depended on someone else's living the woman's life and providing him with support.

Although the self-employed professional was almost always a privileged white male, this work ideal was as inappropriate for most middle-class white boys as it was for their sisters. Most professionals only appeared to be self-employed, much professional work was of dubious use to others, and commercialism was an aspect of the culture, not of the trades. Moreover, to become a professional one had to have the kind of intelligence rewarded in classrooms, consistent financial support, understanding parents, and lots of luck all along the way. In late adolescence, boys and girls alike had to make their peace with an ideal of work that was rarely realized. Although both sexes might suffer from the cruel and foolish ideal of professionalism, girls had a special burden. Intelligence, luck, support, and understanding could not save them from the radical conflict between their sexual identity and this work ideal.

I rejected "women's work," but I rarely considered "men's" work—professional work. Although I imagined future families, I had no comparable fantasy career. When I was already nearly adolescent, I was greatly taken with *Sally Wins Her Wings*—the story of a pilot who, though glamorously attractive, rejects immediate love for the disciplines and adventures of flying. About the same time I cut out advertisements for writers' schools, realizing, I suppose, that any wings I might acquire would be far less challenging to hearth and home than those of the braver Sally. From grade school on I wrote— stories, then poems, then essays—and took my writing fairly seriously.

My ambition to write did not seem to me more valuable—or different in kind—from my other ambitions: to ride well, to be elected to the student government, to read *all* "the great books." It was my teachers who judged that my writing and academic projects were serious enough to be considered "work." My interest in writing and studying had been spontaneous, unself-conscious. My "work," from the outset, was in danger of becoming a self-conscious identity. Recognition came too early, was too closely connected to performance, sometimes even to graded performance. I learned to depend on approval, to seek and to manipulate it by nonintellectual means. When I got approval, I could not be confident what the approval was for. My own confusion was encouraged and compounded by the ambivalence of the approvers, especially male approvers. I learned that, however I won it, the approval was not reliable. My intellectual activity was frequently praised for its weakness, as I was praised for being not only an intellectual but a woman as well. It was clear that to get the big apple, to be both intellectual and woman, meant being not too much, not too obviously, not too insistently the intellectual.

So long as the future seemed distant, however, I was encouraged to play at having work. Such playing at work has consequences. Years later, when it was deemed natural, even praiseworthy, to give up any independent work or ambition and withdraw to the "woman's life," I had experienced too often and too intensely the pleasures of work. I believe that worklessness is painful to most women who have been given educations like mine. If worklessness was especially painful for me, it is probably because I was, by virtue of my parents' hard work and good will, especially blessed. In a life of unearned good fortune, two blessings stand out.

First, in those years of adolescence when social pressures are strongest to commit oneself prematurely to the Woman's Life Plan, I was sent to a boarding school run for girls and in their interests. There was a head*master* to remind us of patriarchical life, but the dean and almost all the teachers were male-less women—some "spinsters," some divorced, some widowed, some young and potentially marriageable. Their male-less condition seemed so normal then that I didn't distinguish among reasons for being in it. In this school, teachers clearly acknowledged that we all wanted to achieve and to be rewarded. In this school, I developed loves I later learned are shared by many young girls—loves for Plato, Spinoza, Shakespeare, poetry, and "nature."

Later, after two years of college I was blessed with a second fortunate experience of work. My parents, despite considerable misgivings, sent me for a summer to a Shakespeare Institute in England. There I worked and played, loved a fellow student and Shakespeare's Beatrice, enjoyed travel and the theatrical performances that were part of our curriculum. My papers, whether on Macbeth's imagination or on Isabel's lack of mercy, seemed to me important and engrossing. I felt as if I were learning to live as well as to read. Although in awe of Shakespeare, I never wondered whether I had something to say. Unafraid of my loves, I had no work problem. Finding pleasure and emotional significance in my work, I had no difficulty in submitting to its demands. With such happiness, the Woman's Life Plan took care of itself.

However, that summer now appears as an interlude in the midst of a college experience that was eroding my sense of myself as a worker. I had been self-confident in my work only so long as the sexual demands of adult life were a matter of the distant future. At Vassar the shadow of adulthood fell across even my sunniest, most naive ambitions. Whereas college was the schoolgirl's sufficient future, once in college we were encouraged to confront our expected, real futures, namely marriage and motherhood. Although Vassar was still a women's college and had then a woman president, it was permeated by the myth of the sexual division of work, hence of adult life. The myth was expressed in Freudian language that could not have been popular in a conservative girls' school but was in a liberal women's college. It was tacitly assumed in the domestic life-style—and, in some instances, in the explicit sexism—of an increasingly male faculty. It was expressed in the self-doubt and self-deception of the younger women faculty, who suffered from it most.

My reaction to the change from school to college was defensive. I denied the existence and ignored the practice of the sexual division of work. I was attracted by Mannheim's *Ideology and Utopia,* which spoke of a class above classes, made up of intellectuals free from political and economic determination. If intellectuals constituted a classless class, they might also be a sexless class. Comforted by this fantasy, I talked as if my future projects were independent of the Woman's Life Plan. In denying profound if conventional desires for a man and children, I was simply driving the desires underground. Since I didn't recognize their existence, I couldn't begin to deal with these "womanly" desires in a realistic way, couldn't begin to assess their conflict with other anomalous, sexless desires and ambitions.

Even as I denied conventional desires, I protected them by doing work that did not require self-knowledge or personal commitment. This was especially evident in my study of philosophy. Like many young students, I came to philosophy from religion. I found in metaphysics a tougher, more resilient attempt to make sense of the Big Questions. From my earliest encounters with it, I was also attracted to philosophy because it was witty, critical, even frankly aggressive. I was thought gullible and often chided for my seriousness. In return, I felt besieged by confused and sentimental ideals. Philosophy provided a weapon to use against my own romanticism and others' unwelcome expectations. Moreover, the mere *doing* of philosophy provided unambiguous pleasures of insight, mental exercise, sustained argument. At the same time, philosophy was hard, it was work. It was sufficiently tough, sufficiently respectable, sufficiently male to be the basis of a career.

Yet, I had then, and to a large extent still have, an observer's relation to philosophy. Spectatorship came naturally in a subject where most of the participants, teachers and writers, were men. As a spectator I found it possible to develop the skills that would enable me to enjoy and profit from the sport without feeling it odd that I had nothing to contribute to the game myself. Moreover, the aggressiveness I enjoyed from the sidelines was not something I could happily display. However eager I was to win arguments with roommates or friends in small groups, I was unable, publicly, to behave in a way I had been taught was both morally and sexually undesirable.

In the past years, as women have learned to talk to each other, our many fears—fear of success, fear of commitment, fear of pleasure, fear of exposure, fear of the "feminine," and, more consciously, fear of failure—have become depressingly familiar. The hidden patterns of my choices twenty years ago now seem all too clear. At first, in college, I had thought of myself as a critic, perhaps even a "creative" writer. Significantly, it was a woman who took my mind seriously and urged me to consider the training and responsibilities of criticism. Yet I did not continue my studies in literature. I stopped writing stories after a short story was well received. I stopped writing poems after two of my poems were published. I stopped studying literature after my happiest, most successful summer. I recognized even then that success somehow, mysteriously, made the work dangerous. Success in work which I viewed as feminine and which felt naturally mine would have forced me to risk failure, to know myself and confront my desires. I retreated to spectatorship.

For many years, unable to commit myself to a career in philosophy, I believed that my work troubles came from choosing the wrong subject. But this explanation underestimates both the public conditions and the private motive of my choice. In the academic world of the late fifties, almost any subject would have permitted the spectatorship that feeds on apolitical privacy, almost any subject would have required (for success) a competitive and committed professionalism incompatible with the Woman's Life Plan. Had the Shakespeare summer been followed by studies in New Criticism at an ambitious graduate school, my love of literature would have been trivialized and sorely tested. By the same token, in recent years, as I have learned to do philosophy with others and to some purpose, philosophy itself has allowed active, caring engagement.

In moving toward philosophy and away from literature, I was expressing in a specific way, a deep and general commitment to security, passivity, and spectatorship. An almost all-male department that taught a subject I considered "hard" and "rigorous" gave me the place and the space to live out that commitment, while pretending to myself and others that I had chosen some work of my own. In our discussions today of work and its problems, many of us talk in terms of a dual existence. We see through two lenses, travel on two rails, live in two spheres—one of work, the other of love. I used to think that I needed to find a work life to run parallel to my love life. Now I believe that I needed to recover the inseparability of work and love common among children, natural to me as a schoolgirl. It is said that women are unable to compartmentalize their lives. Superficially this is true of me; I cannot work when the people I love are unhappy or when I am unhappy with them At a deeper level, I long insisted on a division between work and love, an insistence born out of many fears: that work can destroy love as it takes you from home, first your parents' and then your own; that work can hurt and be hurtful; that work is not after all classless and sexless, but reveals as it expresses its own sexual and political origins. In college I learned to avoid work done out of love. My intellectual life became increasingly critical, detached, and dispensable. If I self-deceptively denied my desires for the conventional loves of a man and children, I refused even to recognize the loves that work demands in its own name: love for oneself, love for the ideas and creations of others, love for the people one works with, love for the knowledge, change, and beauty that work alone can achieve.

In the spirit of the decade, I treated my move toward philosophy as a Significant Choice bestowing a preprofessional Identity. College over, I found it easy to act on the Identity, to take the next step and enter graduate school. I had come to depend on the companionship an academic community provides and I looked forward to an urban life of some excitement within a familiar structure. I was not disappointed. My years at Harvard were happy ones, but that happiness had little to do with my work. Partly because it was a low period for the Harvard Philosophy Department, partly because I was overeducated and undercommitted, I rarely attended classes during my first two years. When I try to recall my intellectual life, let alone my classroom life, I draw a near blank. My mind as well as my heart was elsewhere. I met and fell in love with the man I later married, a graduate student in philosophy. The promises of the Woman's Life Plan were about to be realized. Happy in the love the Plan anticipated, vicariously delighting in the work I would marry, I could overlook the fact that I was unsuited for woman's work and was otherwise workless.

I continued to act, even at some level to believe, as if I had work of my own. I expected to teach philosophy as a part-time supplement to the Woman's Life, but I was completely innocent of the realities of professional life and of the place of graduate school in that life. I lived my academic life as if it had no consequences. During three of my four years at Harvard I taught, and learned that I could teach easily and with pleasure. Yet I never took the simplest steps to get to know or to impress those people who could have helped me get the jobs that would have enabled me to continue teaching. The last two years I attended interesting seminars as an "auditor" who rarely spoke. It is significant that the seminar that excited me most was a seminar on the philosophy of logic. Admittedly, the issues of that seminar were central to philosophy, yet there is no part of philosophy in which I would be less able to make a contribution. It not only left me untroubled; it seemed completely fitting that I should be excited about an inquiry in which I was incapable of engaging, except as an appreciative spectator. In short, I still acted as if I were futureless, and my innocence was allowed and confirmed by the prevailing political optimism and sanguine sexism of those long-distant years.

To my surprise, when I followed my husband to *his* job and found myself in a male world without work of my own, I clung to a hollow and inappropriate sense of myself as a professional philosopher. Although I had scorned the closed-mindedness, the careerism, the conservatism of my fellow students, I myself was burdened for years by a timid professionalism. Harvard's training, and the identity it allowed, had become intimately, unconsciously connected with lessons of respectability I had learned as a child and consciously repudiated as an adolescent. Even now, I can surprise myself, wondering whether a question is "really" philosophical, whether I should ask questions I haven't been trained to answer. Now, however, timid respectability appears clearly as the burden it is. As a young graduate student in my husband's world, I clung to a professional identity partly *because* I lacked the interests, the colleagueship, the public philosophic life that would have made that identity viable.

When my husband began looking for a job, both of us found it natural (though neither of us insisted) that his career come first. We hoped he would get a job in a community with several colleges, but the best offer came from Dartmouth. Neither of us even considered my staying in Cambridge, continuing to teach, and sharing the man-

ageable commute. The partial separation would have benefitted us
financially and intellectually, but these were the early sixties and no
one was doing that. Mainly because I was neither engrossed in nor
committed to any work of my own, we lacked the imagination to cut a
pattern suited to us. Foolishly, we counted upon jobs in the neighborhood, or upon some private and unprecedented creativity of mine. But
there were no jobs, and Dartmouth undermined whatever intellectual
initiative I had had.

Dartmouth was then a male college with a handful of women teachers, some of whom later told me of their suffering. The faculty was at
best committed to patriarchal domesticity, at worst frankly and insult-
ingly chauvinistic. The place of women in a community where women
had no place was openly debated. Many of the women were quietly
desperate as they attempted to make a life for themselves amidst children, housework, and an extremely limited social world that honored
without markedly exhibiting male intelligence. It was at Dartmouth
that I learned the distinction, now familiar, between people and wives.
Wives were patronized while their lives were exalted, were almost
always treated with contempt—albeit flirtatious contempt, were
praised for their failure to be ambitious rather than encouraged to
achieve. The wives, in turn, meeting for gossip and baby showers,
spoke of their husbands as if they were overgrown, slightly pathetic
children—spoiled, pettily tyrannical, too squeamish to change a
diaper, too incompetent to cook a dinner. It was thought virtuous to
placate these husbands while appearing demure. I've no doubt that
individual men and women, when alone, treated each other with
concern and respect. Publicly, however, male contempt was met with
the now familiar resentful superiority of the oppressed toward their
masters.

Although I was repeatedly invited to leave the wives, to join the
people, I was unable to be myself in either group. Although I sometimes expressed the desire to be "just a wife," I never felt easy with the
women around me. However I pretended otherwise, I couldn't really
respect them. I was not at that time conscious of the forced, limited
options the sexist division of work presents. I feel considerably
ashamed of my lack of respect for those whose work was unappreciated and exploited, whose lives were much more difficult and less
fortunate than mine, and who treated me with generosity and kind-
ness.

I was unable to join the "people"—who were also the men—
because I didn't really belong among them. Although I was asked to
participate in an introductory course and was invited to philosophy

discussions, and although people asked respectfully about my work, I felt these were token gestures. I was still my husband's wife. My special status was doubly noxious. On the one hand, it was easy to feel an intruder, a fraud, a charity guest. On the other hand, because I had special or no status, I felt challenged to prove my right to be in those very places where I was so uncomfortably placeless. It was as if I were continually seeking invitations to parties at which I would be miserable and turning down invitations offered in good faith only to feel excluded if they were not offered again.

Demoralized and confused, alien both in the professional world I clung to and the woman's world I found myself in, I tried to do a piece of work: to write a dissertation. My husband not only supported my work; he insisted on it. Threatened not by my work but by the aggrieved anger of my worklessness, he seemed indifferent to the problems of competition, domestic neglect, and self-absorption that his friends, the community, and I myself expected in any marriage in which The Wife Had Work of Her Own. He urged me to write now and "sip sherry in the bath later"—making work appear simultaneously a duty, a right, and an illicit pleasure.

I never stopped, never was allowed to stop, *wanting* to work. Had I put my books and papers away, I don't know what would have happened. As it was, my severest work paralysis lasted only the school year. During the summer, in a more congenial environment, I managed to do some work. By January, eighteen months after we had arrived at Dartmouth, I began to set about my thesis in earnest, and finished it a year later. I worked alone. Too unsure of myself to share my work, I was capable only of defensive polemical debates that tried the patience of others and certainly served me badly. Although Wittgenstein's writings, the subject of my thesis, lend themselves better than most philosophy to tentative, subtle, uncompetitive exploration, in public I could treat them only as so many theses tacked to somebody's door.

We stayed at Dartmouth four years. My husband recognized my need to get out sooner than I had the courage to express it. He had some reason for leaving and made up others, but he left principally on my account and looked for a job in a city where we both could be happy. He had a grant, then a visiting appointment, finally a permanent post which enabled me to live first in Boston and for the last eight years in New York. Four years should be a short time. Yet, despite its brevity, I was quite demoralized by the Dartmouth experience and quite unable to understand the demoralization. I left Dartmouth with a small son and a credential, a Ph.D. I had lived the Woman's Life according to plan and received its blessings. The work I had developed outside that plan, and the credentials I had earned, gave me an identity that felt lifeless and alien. I didn't consider applying for a full-time teaching post. Instead, I had a second child and a number of part-time jobs that left me essentially unconnected to the academic world. Although I was encouraged to revise parts of my thesis for publication, my efforts to do so seemed disconnected from anything else in my life. I gave up revising the thesis, but continued to look for "something to say"—a subject.

Voluntary efforts came to little. Unfinished papers littered my desk. I was happy to return to them for a few hours a day, happier still to leave them for my "real" work. Occassionally, the rewards and labors of raising small children allowed me to forget the pleasures of writing and systematic thinking. Often, however, I remembered them and missed them sorely.

I have recently recovered the ability to work. To trace the steps of that recovery I must backtrack a bit. Eighteen months after an incapacitating work paralysis I began and soon finished a dissertation. What had allowed me to work again?

The answer, however troubling its implications, is clear. I began to organize my thesis almost the day I learned that I was pregnant. I outlined it in the early months of pregnancy, wrote it in the last months. I worked long hours, then lounged in the bath, not with sherry but with Guttmacher, then Spock. At home with a new baby, I revised, then defended the thesis. Later, while pregnant with my second child, I took a part-time job in a publishing house, an experiment which allowed me to test and reject an alternative to academic work. In my daughter's infancy I returned to my desk—for a few hours on good days. There, for the first time in a decade, I developed non-philosophical intellectual interests (in anthropology and psychology) which brought new life to my philosophical work.

The conjunction of work and maternity is puzzling. Why should new parenthood, which subtracts enormously from the time available for work, nonetheless make work more likely? Other women have reported similar puzzling conjunctions. One obvious explanation is that with conventional feminine desires obviously satisfied, the fear of success in "unfeminine" work is less acute. Another is that pregnancies and childbirth constitute success. Moreover, for me infant care was, in itself, inspiriting work which bred a general self-confidence. Pregnancy and motherhood enabled me to feel, and therefore to be, more *intellectually* competent on no grounds other than my proven capacity to do the work that women have always done.

For every woman whose independent work feeds on the pleasures of maternity, there must be several others for whom motherhood spells the end of earlier aspirations. Freedom from financial worries, early experiences of work pleasure and the value my husband placed on my work made my case a special one. Nonetheless, my sudden and all-too-explicable reprieve from work paralysis confused me. Only recently have I been able to accept the fact that strength came from such a common and womanly experience. Yet I learned one lesson immediately and forever: my work problems were not what they appeared to be, but masked some deeper, unrecognizable conflicts. Before my pregnancy I seemed to suffer from numerous, separable disabilities. I was unable to begin to read or to write on the blank page. Then again I couldn't stop reading; I felt that I was never prepared. Sometimes I couldn't construct an outline, other times I couldn't fill out a beautifully constructed outline with a single sentence. On and on the problems went. Yet the insurmountable difficulties disappeared—almost literally, overnight. The hard work of writing remained. Sometimes it was exhausting, sometimes tedious, sometimes discouraging; but writing is all of that.

Beneficial as motherhood was for me, it did not enable me to work more than fitfully and halfheartedly once the thesis was completed. For that, I needed a community and a subject. The most obvious source of community was the academic world. For various reasons, that world seemed alien and distant—as my father's law office had seemed to me as a child. It was a male world, and philosophy was my husband's subject. I was looking for a place of my own. Moreover, these were the war years. It was difficult to identify with a professional identity. Guilty, angry, and impotent, I saw too clearly the evils of academic institutions but was temporarily blind to their virtues and strengths.

On the other hand, I liked to teach, knew I taught well, and was trained for no other work. Despite considerable guilt and anxiety, I allowed myself to make use of my husband's money in order to take only part-time jobs free from departmental responsibilities and commitment to professional philosophy. For some time, I kept one eye on an imaginary *curriculum vitae* and pretended to myself and others that I would soon seek a more responsible post. Yet when the time came and a position was available, I turned the other way.

Ill-paid and without status, these part-time jobs have nevertheless been essential to my recovery of my working self. Almost always in the immediate neighborhood of my home, they have allowed me a flexibility that seemed essential when the children were younger, desirable even now that they are of school age. Moreover, even scattered teaching, unconnected to programs or departments, provided a welcome check on my fantasies of self-importance, my assumption that my ideas were as clear to others as they were to me. With others I discovered that I would never succeed or fail so grandly as, alone in my study, I might hope or fear.

For the past four years I have taught in two programs, whose governing purpose is to provide pleasure and knowledge for instructor and student alike. In circumstances of freedom and respect, I have found my teaching not only a medium for presenting my work, but real work in its own right. I have come to care for my students' lives and minds—a love, if one might call it that, which I had been taught to avoid. Among students, I am neither a guru nor a chum. Keeping the distance I find natural, I have developed a genuine working relationship with those I teach, a relationship that gives me an enormous pleasure I am just beginning to admit and to appreciate. Among these students and my colleagues I have learned to talk with and in front of others; to disagree with little tension or aggression; to listen without fear that I will have nothing to say in return.

Even within these programs, however, I continued to search for a subject, not realizing for some time that I did not so much have to find a professional niche as to relinquish the ideal of professionalism. The slow—and, in retrospect, comically painful—process of deprofessionalization had many episodes. For example, I wrote an unprofessional, widely read paper on sex; I studied and taught Greek philosophy, even learning some Greek for the purpose, knowing that I was not and never would be qualified to "do something" with it; I sought an opportunity to teach women, many of them "housewives," and found that I not only respected them but identified with them more easily and closely than with any other students.

Perhaps the most important episode in this deprofessionalization began with a break from all things great and serious. One winter about three years ago, I decided to give myself occasional holidays in the New York Public Library after a week's work. I went there to read Virginia Woolf's unpublished diaries; then in the evenings I began to reread her novels. This reading was completely divorced from public ambitions or expectations. Insofar as I brought problems to my reading, they were personal—connected with my sense of aging and death, with an interest in women and feminism, with my earliest love for my mother and fears for her death. Indeed, I was more than a little in love with Virginia Woolf herself.

At some point I began to turn this personal enterprise into something more public. I talked to others working on Woolf, read a paper on Woolf and *her* mother at a conference devoted to Woolf's work, lectured on her feminism, published an article, imagined a book on which I am now "working." As my private holidays were transformed into public work, I had to deal with work "problems" that became amazingly clear when freed from institutional or professional disguise.

For example, when pleasure turned into work, I became vaguely uneasy with work's pleasures. I realized the source of my dis-ease one afternoon while reading Leslie Stephen's touching letters to his wife. I was amply protected from the charge of frivolity by an array of serious reasons for reading this correspondence, for spending my time so pleasurably on a weekday afternoon. My defenses held up as long as the letters yielded some insight into "Victorian family structure" or "Woolf's early masculine identifications." I felt virtuous when the letters were painful to read—when, for example, Stephens wrote about his daily struggles with a schizophrenic daughter from a previous marriage. I was especially content when I could take notes. But I was undone when I came to Stephens's quaint description of a Harvard football game, replete with cheerleaders. Told with the detachment of a visitor foreign to both sport and America, the tale was charming, delightfully amusing—and completely without general implications for understanding life, love, and death. I couldn't read on. With a great show of purposefulness, I packed up my notebooks and went home. It was only on the bus downtown that I realized my folly and reflected on the toll such folly must have extracted over the years. No wonder I so feared work, if work was pleasure's enemy.

Pleasure was not my only problem. Reading Virginia Woolf was emotionally engrossing, psychologically challenging, a "personal" confrontation. Yet I had until now used my work to escape and protect myself from the complexities of "real" life. Then again, I had become dependent on a professional identity, however ill-fitting. Reading fiction did not seem sufficiently tough, sufficiently "male" to be professional. And if it were professional, I was completely untrained. Finally, I had come to this reading with private concerns. Unexpectedly I found that Virginia Woolf had a profound and comprehensive political vision of the connections between patriarchy, violence, tyranny, and economic oppression. And that political vision was inextricably entwined with epistemological and metaphysical insights, with the impulse to philosophize evident throughout her fiction. Virginia Woolf's *politics* began to shape and inspire my "real," officially sanctioned philosophical work. And that "real" work, done in my classes as well as at my desk, fed into and was fed by my study of Woolf. In reading *Three Guineas* and then rereading *To The Light-*

house, I felt as if I were learning to think and feel in new ways. For the first time in years my mind was truly alive, truly mine. With an urgency which overcame self-consciousness, I sought out other readers who loved and were learning from Woolf. I needed to share the results of my work with colleagues who would share their work with me.

My playful holiday had become heady, serious business. It was the Shakespeare summer all over again—suspiciously adolescent and romantic for a middle-aged mother. I was, in fact, being given a second chance to learn the lessons of that college summer, to unlearn the divisions that had burdened my life—divisions between work and pleasure, male and female, professional and amateur, political and personal, all aspects of the damaging separation of work from love. I could not simply reject such divisions, deep-rooted in my past and my culture. I could only try to decrease their power so as to increase my own. To do so I had to give up the deepest aspect of the division between work and love, which was at the heart of my work problems: the division between A Woman's Life and independent, demanding, autonomous work.

The division between a Woman's Life and autonomous work has a practical aspect. It is by no means easy to fulfill the duties and experience the pleasures of family life when absorbed by demanding work. Nor is it easy, in the midst of a busy private life and extensive teaching, to be disciplined and committed to work not required by a job. For me, however, the practical aspects of the division between private and public, woman and work, masked unrealistic ancient beliefs. A good woman should not want work of her own; the wish for such work betrays "neurosis" or, worse still, "narcissism." Above all, one should be healthy and good.

In recent years these ancient beliefs have surfaced. Their power dispelled, even to speak of them courts boredom. Yet it was not so long ago that I furtively turned the pages of *The Feminine Mystique* in a back corner of a Dartmouth bookstore. Then, when to my delight I had a daughter, I began to read feminist literature openly. As she grew, my daughter's strength and independence inspired and frightened me. I had to welcome, even to imitate it. Reading was no longer enough. Since entering graduate school, my colleagues and friends had been men. Now I began to need, and to say I needed, women friends.

I cannot overestimate the strength of this need. During important transitional years I depended on the daily companionship of a new-found friend as well as constant telephone contact and frequent visits from school and college friends. Recently, since I have had more colleagues of both sexes, and since I have worked more confidently, I have become less intensely dependent on individual women. Yet I still must find my own divided identity—as a woman and a worker— reflected and confirmed in the lives, loves, and ambitions of other women.

As I gradually came to work on my own, the divided identity became less divisive. My idea of a Woman's Life, a woman's home, has changed profoundly. My husband was something of a feminist before I was anything of one. But good will is not enough. We had to *learn* what it meant to share parenting and family life. We had always shared tasks, (though not so equally as we do now); we have only recently shared responsibility. I will not rehash familiar issues here, but simply will repeat what others have often asserted: so long as the social conditions of motherhood are inimical to self-respect, the desire to mother will be threatening. So long as profound desires are threatening and therefore disavowed, experience is impoverished. In my case, so long as that impoverishment continued, I could not have the self-love necessary for work of my own. Nor could I, without the self-respect of shared responsibility in my intimate, private life, gain the self-respect necessary for me to act with some freedom in the public world.

It was, of course, largely a cultural phenomenon—the movement of women—that enabled me to achieve a new self-respect at home, made me confident and clear about my need for the friendship of women, enabled me to read Virginia Woolf in a new, politically relevant way, and provided like-minded readers for me to talk to. That movement also transformed my sense of women's aspirations. It is difficult now to remember how activating it was less than ten years ago to hear it proclaimed that women, like men, wished to create a way of living that suited not only our personal hopes but also our more impersonal ambitions. No person close to me had ever tried to persuade me that my interests should be, if not identical with, at least subordinate to, those of my husband and children. No one had identified my aspirations with selfishness. But the identification was tacitly assumed by those around me and energetically imposed by the media catering to a "mass" always assumed to be somebody else. I had carried an invisible, almost amorphous weight, the weight of guilt and apology for interests and ambitions that should have been a source of pride. When that weight was lifted, I felt almost literally lighter, certainly more energetic, more concentrated.

Stirred to self-knowledge and action by the courage and honesty of feminists, I gradually became able to say that I *wanted* to work and had been unable to work effectively. In the transformation from work-less discontent to relative satisfaction in work, perhaps the most important step was simply to acknowledge that I had ambitions I couldn't fulfill. A simple acknowledgment, surely. But years of defensiveness and ambivalence, supported, even lauded, by those who liked female "intellectuals" to be "women" too had taken their toll. I could begin to work only when real failure, whatever the shame, became more desirable than the sentimental, illusory success an "interesting woman" was offered by the feminine mystique.

I wanted to work. But between the desire and the act fell shadows too numerous to mention. What to do? I turned, as I had learned to do, to other women. We put together this book. I wrote, and rewrote, this essay. I dug up that buried history of myself as a girl working, as a woman working. And it seems to me that miraculously, finally, in the midst of this collective, non-professional, serious, womanly project, I look up and realize that I am able to work.

Sara Ruddick

Catching the Sun

Diana Michener

I HAVE A VILLAGE inside me. It's a noisy place. The laundress nags about the pile of dirty laundry, the cook wants the groceries, the mother reminds me of the children's school performances, the housekeeper shakes her finger at the messy rooms, the friend suggests a cozy lunch, the secretary coughs nervously at the stack of bills, the lover chirps over the frivolity of a new dress, and the village chronicler

hounds me about the projects I promised to photograph. I answer that
I'll have time for each of them, but I tend to lie to my villagers—I
don't always have time. Usually, it's the chronicler who has to be the
most patient.

I think the reason I am constantly flirting with personal anarchy is
that everything in my life overlaps. I move from one activity to another without any definite boundaries. Every part of what I am or
trying to be is lived within my house. My darkroom is between the
laundry and the kitchen, my shooting studio is in a corner of my
bedroom, and I find it difficult to shed my house and family and enter
into the privacy of my work. I have tried going out of my house,
walking around the block a few times, and re-entering only as a
"photographer." It works sometimes, but not always.

"Weightless like shadows of trees"

The hardest time is the morning. I wake up feeling vacant, weight-less like shadows of trees; everything appears incomprehensible, floating in a dense body of water. I try to let the litany of the village take over—I hear my two daughters (ah yes, I'm a mother) and I feel my husband next to me (yes, I'm committed to a shared life) and then my arms and legs gain weight, I am being glued back together, I can get up. I am thankful for my children; they pull me directly into the day. There are the hugs and the good-mornings, the breakfasts and the definitions—I'll be home at three-fifteen, I have a flute lesson, are you going out tonight? And there is the flurry of their setting off—the arguing and the laughing, or both, but always an abundant, eager movement out into the street. I am glad for them; they have brushed off the night. After their departure, I prepare for the next flurry—my husband. We have breakfast together. It's often a disconcerting ritual.

I keep myself quiet. I smile a lot. I concentrate on the minute exchanges of daily schedules. I want him to leave quickly; I don't want him to ask me any questions about my photographic work; I am afraid he will block my view. If he gets too close, I may become all pliable and dependent and say, "Don't leave me. I'm jealous of you, your office and community of people. I want to go somewhere too; I don't want to work alone today. Take me with you, I'll be a good girl, please . . ."

I don't want to be that little girl anymore—soft and expectant, dreaming of fairy tales and playmates. And, besides, I have made my choice. Still, stepping up to that first morning embrace of work is intimidating. Everyone else has been signaled away to a socially approved destination, and I am left to make up my own. I feel the panic of wandering in the empty hall. It's that ghastly female stuff in me— the seduced-and-abandoned conditioning—that leaves me slightly frazzled, and makes me wish my lover, my husband, would take over

"I'm afraid he will block my view"

"The empty hall"

the burden of choice for me. Even worse is that sometimes I am pushed back into the territory of my childhood, and become for a moment the little girl who used to sit shivering in her nightgown in the dark on the stairs listening to the grown-up voices below and wishing terribly to be discovered and hugged, to be included. Often after my husband's last kiss, as the door closes, that child darts through me. The only way to get rid of her is to recite my daily chant: Pick up your camera, click the shutter, trust yourself in the process of your own work, don't clutter your head with other things . . . there are no judges. This is what I tell myself as I slither through the laundry pile and dishes and, like an alligator lumbering up onto the riverbank to catch the sun, pull myself into my work.

I have always taken pictures the way people keep journals and diaries. It's a way of ordering my reactions to the world, of placing my ideas and feelings in a concrete form outside myself, of breaking my isolation. I didn't think about what I would *do* with photography when I first began four years ago.

I was married at twenty-one, and had a daughter a year afterward. It was a close connection—my daughter and my B.A. from Barnard College; they came a month apart. Two years later I had another daughter. I loved being a mother. The earth was doing its bragging in me, and suddenly everything changed, I no longer felt like an orphan. They made me belong. My first husband and I were separated when the children were three and five years old. The three of us built a strong family unit. My daughters were my connection to life at its most magical and primitive level. I needed them as much as if not more than they needed me. We lived together and shared our growing up. When they went to school, I also returned. Thinking I wanted a master's degree in education, I enrolled at Bank Street College. In a video tape workshop, I became fascinated by the nature of film. I stopped wanting a master's degree and dropped out of school. A few months later, I underwent a back operation and was forced to drop out of everything. The doctor advised three months to recover, so with my daughters I rented a house in the country and spent the summer there, recuperating. Long walks were part of my therapy. I could only walk very slowly, and I remarked to a friend that the world looked totally bizarre—not the same place at all—when observed at this speed. He suggested I borrow his camera, then showed me how to develop film and later how to print. I remember my introduction; he brought his enlarger into my kitchen, we waited until it was dark, and then put black cloth over the windows. It all seemed fabulously mysterious—the black night, film in an enlarger, trays with chemicals, and out of it all an image on a piece of paper. I was awed and the wonder stayed with me. It grew into excitement as I began to understand the exacting discipline of the photographic process.

Back in New York I took private lessons from a photographer, and then started to experiment myself. There was so much to learn—cameras, lenses, the properties of film, exposure techniques, chemicals, printing methods. Then, too, there was the magic; film has its own strange means of keeping the subject objective in a way that a painting never can. I had studied painting, drawing, and sculpture in art school when I was younger, but I'd never liked the marks my hand made—somehow they were too personal. With photography it was possible to remain out of the picture, to become absorbed only, I thought, in the presentation of an image—frozen in time and space, something real and yet unreal, impervious to tactile manipulation. As I became more and more engrossed—reading Edward Weston's *Daybooks*, looking at the intricacies of shadow and light around me, searching for the invisible through the visible—I experienced the first strong pull away from my house and children.

I wanted to talk to other photographers. In the spring of 1973, I enrolled in a workshop run by Ansel Adams in Yosemite, California. It was exhilarating; for ten days I did nothing but live photography— talking, working, learning. There was one terrifying moment. In one of the workshops, we were asked to show our previous work. As one by one the other students stepped up and displayed their pictures, I felt increasingly isolated. My pictures had nothing to do with theirs. Their images all seemed to belong together; they were instantly recog-

nizable as good examples of traditional photographic subjects—snow on rocks, people caught in the flux of everyday life—and they provoked immediate, lively discussions. The pictures I had brought—my best ones, I thought—included studies of my seven-year-old daughter's torso, a vacant sofa with the imprint of two people's bodies left on the cushions, a half-open door leading to a deserted kitchen, a man's shirt hanging on a doorknob to dry in the sun, a bunch of flowers wrapped in white tissue paper, buildings seen through a dirty window, and a woman in a Victorian lace dress straddling a chair. I hoped that time would run out, that I could escape with my pictures unshown. It didn't. When finally I had to put my pictures up in front of the class, there was silence. A student said to the instructor, "I don't understand them. Could you tell us what they are?" People giggled. The instructor was kind, but lame. Without much conviction, he muttered that I obviously worked in an intensely personal way with my own private symbols, and then suggested that I learn the zone system (an exposure method) to improve the quality of my prints. But I hadn't been trying to create a private symbolism; I had just been photographing what interested me. I felt baffled and alone, but, in the end, determined at least to improve my technique.

Back in New York, I worked hard—to the point of exhaustion. Washing prints in the kitchen sink while trying to cook dinner and listen to homework recitations before going out in the evening made me frantic. I felt constantly hungry but couldn't eat. Compulsively I over-stocked the refrigerator, but kept dreaming it was empty. I bought photographic books, but had little time to read them. I prowled the house in the middle of the night, desperate for a few extra hours.

Finally I made a decision: I would demand four entire summer weeks to myself. The children went to their father, and I rented an empty farmhouse on a remote bay in Prince Edward Island. It sounded idyllic—no telephone, running water, or electricity, just a hand pump and a wood stove—and absolutely peaceful. A whole month without interruptions, a time to photograph without other responsibilities; a time for me.

During the drive to Prince Edward Island, one image kept recurring: as a child, I would wake up on my birthday certain that downstairs in the living room, behind every chair and sofa, was a surprise party. As I turned into the last dirt road—two tire tracks divided by tall weeds—I saw the peaceful bay in the distance. I speeded up; my Grandma Moses house must be around the bend. Suddenly I slowed down; I must have taken a wrong turn. All around me were ugly signs of desolation—rusty tin cans, unraveled chicken wire, pieces of abandoned farm equipment, seatless chairs, a broken-down black-leather horse buggy. My haven was a dilapidated farmhouse with peeling paint, several broken windows, and a half-collapsed chimney. Inside there was no surprise party. The place smelled sickeningly of mice, nails poked up through the floorboards, and the five rooms were virtually unfurnished. After unloading the car—suitcase, camera equipment, sleeping bag, and food—I wanted to lie down, even though it was early afternoon. In one of the deserted rooms, I found an old iron bed. I unrolled my sleeping bag on it, put on a long cotton nightgown, and crawled inside.

For three nights and two days, I lay there, stumbling out of bed only to relieve myself in the bushes by the front door. I kept some cookies and Granola on the floor by the bed and nibbled them from time to time. I lived in a strange world of dozing, neither asleep nor awake, way past caring. I looked blankly at the knots in the wood on the ceiling, and listened to the birds singing outside and the patter of scampering and scratching above my head.

On the third morning, I woke up laughing. The laughter shook me. It filled the bedroom with outrageous echoes that seemed louder than their original source. The reverberations became stronger, increasing in volume until I felt I wasn't making the noise but was trapped inside it. It was frightening and brutal. It seemed to rebuke me: "You are useless, a mother who can't even get out of bed without her children calling, needing, wanting her." I pulled the sleeping bag over my head to shut out the sound. I lay still, grateful for the silence. I knew I could lie there for days and that no one would come to rescue me. Then a new laughter came, chasing the old one away and all the self-pity too. Suddenly, everything struck me as terribly funny—the rumpled sleeping bag, the pathetic scraps of food, my fetal position. I continued to laugh. I had never laughed so freely, so affectionately at myself, and it felt good. As I swung my legs out of the sleeping bag and felt the floor beneath my feet, it seemed as though I were getting up by myself for the first time since I was a child. I stretched. I found my camera, placed it on the tripod, set the self-timer and re-enacted my getting up. It was my first self-portrait.

The next day and the days that followed had a definite pattern to them. I always awoke at about five-thirty and did photographic studies in the dawn light—of spider webs, the grasses along the shore, an old wagon wheel—anything in the landscape that provoked a feeling of discovery. Afterward I swam, and then ate a leisurely breakfast on the doorstep in the sun. I studied until noon, reading photographic books

and thinking about experiments I wanted to do. The middle of the day
was languid. Usually I took long walks without my camera, ferreting
out places I wanted to photograph. Sometimes I picked wild rasp-
berries and blueberries, dug mussels at the shore, or went into town
for supplies. In the moist late-afternoon light I took pictures again.
When evening came, I had a long wallowing swim, read on the beach,
wrote in my journal, and waited for the sunset. Then I drifted home,
lit the stove, and curled around the kerosene lantern, a novel, and
food. Day after day, I feasted on moments.

After I returned to New York, I was absorbed for weeks in my
Prince Edward Island pictures. I felt strong from the days spent alone.
Even the demands of the children and home didn't threaten me. I still
trusted my own direction. One night came the challenge I didn't want
voiced. At dinner, the man I loved berated me for not showing him
any of my photographs. Stunned, I pulled out the pictures and the
journal of my experiences at the farm. "They're beautiful," he said;
"both the words and the images. You should get them published." I
thought he was just trying to woo and flatter me, and I smiled and
said, "Oh well, maybe." But later he brought it up again, and I let him
help me shape the material into a photographic essay. Eventually, a
selection from it was published in *Ms.* magazine.

Seeing it in print, on newsstands, was exciting in a surprisingly
impersonal way. I had exposed myself, but it didn't feel like my former nakedness. My work was out there in a place all its own; it had
survived me. Still I felt nervous when friends talked about it. I found it
hard to hear their words. They challenged one of my oldest fears—
what to do next. I didn't know. Somehow the contact with the world
had disoriented me. I didn't feel like a "real" photographer, and I
wanted to be told the steps I should take—like an aspiring knight—to
become one. During this period I married the man who had been
prodding me. At his instigation, I was introduced to a woman
photographer whom I greatly admired. Hoping she would direct my
course, I showed her my pictures. She said the one thing I was most
afraid to hear. "I can see *you* in all these photographs. You have your
own style. All you need to do is keep developing it, keep taking pictures." Inside I felt a cry, the cry of a premature baby. I wasn't safe
any longer. I was visible.

After that, I rarely showed my pictures to anyone, even to my
husband. At times, I was totally unable to click the shutter. Instead, I
would stand in front of something I wanted to photograph and say to
myself, "That's an uninteresting picture; you're crazy to want to take
it." Then I would walk away, only to return the next day and do the

same thing. I started to have fantasies about working for a newspaper or magazine. There, I would be told by others what to do. The *me* would be taken out of my pictures. But I was both too timid and too wild with frustration to pursue this fantasy. At other moments I thought I needed a professional studio outside my house. I lost days looking for one, knowing all the time it was a foolish pursuit I couldn't afford. Finally, after months of playing these charades with myself, I decided to expand the darkroom in my house. Until then, my darkroom had been a cramped closet without a decent sink—or ventilation; after printing for hours I would have terrible headaches. It was a makeshift place; it didn't call attention to itself and it allowed me to hide from everyone—especially myself. I knew I had to force myself to build a better work place. It took me three months to do it. I spent hours searching for proper sinks, only to decide they all cost too much

"A friend"

money—and then spent the money on Christmas presents for my husband and children. I said I didn't want to ruin the architectural integrity of the house. I said a lot of things. In the end, though, it was
built. While the carpenter hammered away, I pretended it wasn't
happening. At night, I imagined it was occurring invisibly. I made
mistakes in planning the room—mistakes of detail I'd never make
when arranging a bowl of flowers or cooking a big meal.

"Peering into windows"

I have started to work again; it's slow, but I'm feeling a new enthusiasm. I'm energized again by going walking with my camera, and I'm able to click the shutter. I've started to take more portraits. I like the collaborative aspect of it; the sitter has to cooperate, if only by acknowledging my presence. I agree with Cartier-Bresson, who has said: "The most difficult thing for me is a portrait . . . It's a question mark you put on somebody. Trying to say 'Who is it?' . . . And you have to try and put your camera between the skin of a person and his shirt—which is not a very easy thing." I am exhausted afterward—it's an intense, brief love affair—and I am fearful of developing my film, afraid it will be blank. But I now know the luxury of commitment. Photography brings into focus, literally, the hunger and thirst I feel toward life; it allows me to grab hold, press in on an image and reclaim it from the fluidity of my own vision and emotions. The intensity of the act makes me feel alive.[1]

I used to feel ashamed that I was not a participator, only an observer—the next-door neighbor, always peering into windows—but I am beginning to trust my waiting and watching, and to think of my tiptoeing as an active step. I am learning to outtalk the frightened little creature who shadows me—the one who says, "Be careful, don't make a fool of yourself, everyone is going to laugh," the one who is gleefully waiting for me to fall down. Now I stick my tongue out at her and say, "Look, I can dare to fall down, and look, I can get up, and look, I'm not too hurt to try again." I have to be bratty with her or she will taunt me at the wrong moments. Once I get into my work, she can't find me. Nor can anyone else. It's intoxicating in there—and a bit dangerous. Will anyone be there when I come out? Will I be able to reconnect? But my villagers are always waiting, and when I have stopped working, I am better at listening to them, even glad—no matter how noisy their demands—that they are there.

Diana Michener

---

[1] The Cartier-Bresson quote is from the pamphlet *Images of Man*, Series #2. Published by Scholastic Magazine, Inc., in cooperation with the International Fund for Concerned Photographers, Inc., 1973, p. 76.

Learning to Work
Virginia Valian

IN THIS PAPER I describe a particular work problem, its symptoms and my cure for it. The problem is a luxury. It can only surface if one has been relatively well-educated and if the work in question intrinsically allows for self-development and self-fulfillment. In general, then, only a small minority of people—those who are doing, or preparing to do, work they care about—can have the problem. The problem consists of being unable to work, not because of external pressures such as lack of time, but because of internal problems, which can be exacerbated or disguised by external pressures.

I discuss work problems from a personal point of view; however, two small incidents, both of which occurred more than six years ago, will illustrate why I came to think that work problems have more than personal significance.

Incident I: I was talking to a friend, a novelist, who had a work problem which he thought stemmed from living in an oppressive society. How could he write novels when the government was killing people in Vietnam? I couldn't believe that was the source of his work problem, because I knew it wasn't the source of mine, even though I was spending almost all of my time in anti-war politics. I was sure that even if the revolution happened the next day, and a politically perfect society immediately came into being, I would still have a work problem; so would he, and so would lots of other people. In fact, more people than ever before would have a work problem, because now *everybody* would have the same freedom from want and autonomy in work that only a few had before the revolution. I thought it was important to work for political equality, but that it was also important to understand the psychology of work.

Incident II: At a feminist meeting on the subject of women and socialism, a woman was discussing a waitress at a local restaurant. She described the waitress as completely dedicated to her job and to pleasing her employer, a perfectionist who worked long, hard hours for insufficient pay, without complaint. Then she said, "That's just the kind of person we need to work for socialism after the revolution." I was appalled. Was this waitress to be a slave her entire life? I hoped that her life would change after the revolution, that she would work because she wanted to and not because she was driven by a puritan ethic. Nor did I want to view people only as workers for socialism; I wanted people to get something out of society as well as contribute to it.

The questions raised by these incidents are complex. I don't have answers to them. The more I talked to people about work, however, the more it seemed that everyone had crazy, often punitive, attitudes toward it. The combination of political discussions of work and my own severe work problem led to my search for a personal solution, which I will describe in the following pages.

I had had a work problem all my life, but I didn't know it until college. The symptoms in college were straightforward. I never studied, I seldom went to class; yet I defined myself as a future psychologist and had no questions about the desirability of doing meaningful intellectual work for the rest of my life. I did so poorly in college that I did not apply to any graduate schools; I was not interested in going to any school that would accept me. To test my seriousness of purpose, I enrolled instead as a special student at a good school in Boston. I reached a nadir; of the three courses I registered for, I dropped two and failed the third. I drew a blank whenever I considered my future. At that point, a kind friend intervened. She helped me get a job as a technician and urged me to begin psychoanalysis, which I did six months later.

Two years after finishing college I felt ready to begin graduate study at a school that would accept me; the school was suggested by the same kind friend. Analysis had made, and continued to make, a difference. I attended classes, I studied periodically, I applied for and got a fellowship that assured me of support for three years. I ran experiments. On the other hand, I often spent days in which I did nothing but read novels and sleep. I wrote my papers only at the last minute, and I never once worked an intellectual problem through to its conclusion. I did enough to get by.

By the summer of 1969, I was twenty-seven years old, involved in the anti-war movement, and living in Cambridge in a $140/month apartment with the man I still live with (a philosopher without a work problem). I had finished analysis the previous year, and had just finished the research for my thesis. It was time to write it. By the end of the year, however, I was spending all my time doing political work or sleeping, and no time working on my thesis. In January 1970 I resumed therapy (for eight months) because my future suddenly seemed as empty as it had before I had begun analysis. I knew that as things stood I could not write my thesis, and if I didn't write my thesis and get my degree, I didn't know what else I would do.

During those eight months it became clear to me that I did not want to become a full-time political person, because it was too limiting. I wanted to live an integrated life that included doing intellectual work, having close relationships, being politically active, and developing other interests such as playing the piano. But that integrated life couldn't happen unless I got rid of my work problem. A few days before my last therapy session I began thinking about how to get rid of it.

THE PROGRAM. Masters and Johnson's book, *Human Sexual Inadequacy,* gave me the key. In it, Masters and Johnson stressed that sexuality is a natural physiological process, with orgasm as a natural end point. They were concerned with the internal roadblocks that prevented full sexual enjoyment; their clients, for example, consistently reported that they felt like observers rather than participants in their own sexuality, that they were always thinking of the hoped-for end point instead of enjoying the activity for itself. Together with constant discussion sessions, therapy took the form of breaking the sexual act down into its components and asking clients to begin by just touching each other, with no expectations or demands. The process was then slowly reassembled, with couples moving on to the next component only after they were comfortable with the preceding one.

It occurred to me that mental work is like sex in certain respects, although at first it seemed a bizarre comparison. The most important aspect of the analogy was the idea that work was natural. I had always thought of work as something I had to make myself do, something I didn't intrinsically enjoy. The analogy suggested that I was getting in my own way, that I was preventing myself from enjoying myself. It wasn't that I had to learn somehow to force myself to work, but rather to remove the roadblocks in the way of enjoyment.

I continued the analogy and decided I needed a similar form of therapy. I needed to break the process down, starting at the least threatening level, slowly building up and assembling the whole, and discussing how I felt and what I was learning as I was doing it. The program thus had something in common with behavioral modification techniques, but it was also different in a crucial way. The common feature was starting with a small, imaginable, doable piece of behavior and working up; the crucial difference was the absence in my program of any idea of punishment or reward. In my system, the intrinsic pleasure I now believed was obtainable through work would be reward enough; an external reward would imply that work was not rewarding in and of itself. The same was true for punishment: it was punishment enough not to work. An external punishment would imply that the work itself was not enjoyable, that I needed punishment to force me to work.

I decided that I wanted to work every day, because I wanted to experience that constancy of working that I had always denied myself, and because I thought that once I had my work problem under control I would want to work every day, even if only for a short time, and I wanted to approach the ideal state as nearly as possible at the very beginning. I also knew that if I were going to work every day, it had to be in small amounts or I would never manage it.

First I had to decide whether to work a set amount of time every day, or to work until I had completed a set amount of work every day. I chose time. A page can take an entire day to write, or only ten minutes, depending on how difficult it is. I knew that sitting at my desk concentrating and working for a whole day was beyond me. With a set amount of time I would know that I could stop, and exactly when the time would be up. That knowledge helped make it easier to start. Others with work problems have described to me the images they associate with working. They all have in common the theme of relinquishing control of oneself: of being a slave, or going into a tomb, being buried alive, being shut off from the world. The anxiety about working is reduced when the time period is fixed.

After opting for quantity of time rather than quantity of work, I needed a figure. I talked about it with J, the man I live with, and he suggested three hours. Three hours! The very thought gave me an anxiety attack. How about two hours? Two hours! The very thought . . . One hour? More reasonable, but still not possible. Half an hour? Getting closer but still too much. Fifteen minutes? Fifteen minutes. Fifteen minutes. Now there was a figure I could imagine. A nice solid amount of time, an amount of time I knew I could live through every day.

Of course, people laugh when I say fifteen minutes. What can you accomplish in fifteen minutes? Well, more than you would think. Fifteen minutes with no interruptions, no pencil sharpening, no trips to the bathroom, no trips to the kitchen, no telephone calls; fifteen minutes of solid work can be very profitable. I didn't plan to stay at fifteen minutes for the rest of my life, but it seemed like a good place to start.

In my first fifteen minutes I confronted my thesis. I figured out what different types of work were immediately involved in finishing it: 1) a linguistic analysis of a speech corpus; 2) background reading for an introduction; 3) writing the introduction; and 4) writing a methods section. I assessed how great a block I had against each of these activities, and decided to start by spending fifteen minutes analyzing the corpus (low anxiety) and fifteen minutes either doing background reading or writing the methods section (high anxiety). By day number two I was going to be working half an hour—fifteen minutes on one thing, fifteen minutes on another. Soon I moved up to a total of forty-five minutes—fifteen minutes analyzing, fifteen reading, and fifteen writing the methods section. The moments of extreme anxiety were still to come. They appeared when I had done enough background reading to begin writing the introduction. I then realized that even fifteen minutes was out of the question, for by this time I knew just how long fifteen minutes was. So I scaled it down to five minutes.

I still remember that first five minutes. I didn't do it until the evening. I announced to J that I was going to begin my five minutes. I sat down and set the timer for five minutes. I think it was such a momentous event because it was a commitment. It wasn't this particular five minutes, but all the future ones that this one represented. I worked steadily, though with difficulty and anxiety; I knew, however, that I could last out five minutes of difficulty and anxiety, so I continued. At last the bell went off and I collapsed. I went into the bedroom and threw myself on the bed, breathing hard and feeling my heart race. It was really a big deal. After that evening it wasn't such a big deal, and I gradually worked my way up to fifteen minutes.

RULES AND RATIONALES OF THE PROGRAM. The first rule was that the fifteen-minute period had to be spent solely in working. My feeling of accomplishment depended on having a chunk of time that I did not fritter away in any way. I also had to learn that losing myself in my work was not dangerous. Most important, I noticed that I tended to stop working the minute I hit a difficult problem. Working in fifteen-minute chunks meant that occasionally I hit such a difficult problem in the middle of the required fifteen minutes and had to learn how to deal with it. Sometimes it simply required a little more thinking; sometimes it meant I would have to read something or talk to someone; sometimes it meant a lot more thinking. What I learned, though, was that I could deal with problems and didn't have to give up whenever I encountered them.

The second rule was that official increases in the amount of working time were limited to one fifteen-minute chunk at a time, with a break of any length available after every chunk. Fifteen minutes was the longest time I could guarantee being able to work solidly without fidgeting. I didn't want to make a rule about working twenty minutes straight, then twenty-five, and so on, because I was sure ahead of time that I wouldn't be able to do it. But I could imagine myself working four fifteen-minute chunks during the day. I was cautious: I disallowed increasing work by more than one chunk at a time because I wanted to make sure I was really comfortable at a given level before going on to another.

What is so special about fifteen minutes? I don't know if it was just a good amount for me, or if there is something about the thinking cycle of most people that makes for a reduction in concentration about every fifteen minutes. Now, I only use the fifteen-minute-chunk approach when I'm having particular difficulty working on something. The main virtue of fifteen minutes for me was that it was long enough for me to get something done and short enough to be sure I could get through it.

The third rule—in some ways the most important one for me—was to work every day. I do not think this rule is essential for everyone; it depends on one's personality. For example, when I quit smoking (in January 1970), I knew I could never smoke another cigarette for the rest of my life. That knowledge meant that I didn't have to make endless decisions about taking just one cigarette, or any other plan. I could never smoke again, period. Similarly, by having an inviolable rule that I must work every day I didn't have to play games with myself and wonder whether or not I would actually work that day. I knew I would, even if it would be at two in the morning. Therein lay some of the value of fifteen minutes. No matter how sleepy, or tired, or anything else I was, I could always work for fifteen minutes; no excuse could rule out fifteen minutes.

The fourth rule was to ignore thoughts about the end product and how the end product would be received. I could too easily find myself inhabiting a fantasy world in which my thesis led to fame and renown. Not only was this eventuality extremely unlikely, but it led me further away from, rather than closer to, my goal of discovering the pleasures of the process of work. I wanted to work not because of the supposed effect of my work on others, but for the gratifications, to me, of working. My fantasies made the reality of my barely begun thesis look so shabby I didn't want to have anything to do with it. At the beginning, then, I refused to dwell on actually finishing my work and concentrated instead on doing it.

That was it, as far as rules go. I told all my friends about my new program; everyone was interested, but no one with work problems was tempted to try it. It was too everyday, too gradually incremental. Others preferred to try to write their thesis in a sixteen-hour-a-day blitz of working until it got done. I understood. I had always preferred the hare to the tortoise myself. Now, though, it didn't seem attractive to me to be the hare, just self-destructive. In the course of following my program I learned how well the myth of the hare and the tortoise captured my ambivalence about competition, winning, and losing. I examined more deeply the role I wanted work to play in my life, and the role it did play in other people's lives. I also learned how not working had stunted my intellectual development.

FEARS AND FEELINGS. I approached work usually with two sorts of feelings. One was anger and resentment that I had to work; the other was a sense of competition as a life-or-death struggle—either I would kill others or they would kill me. Winning meant killing, losing meant being killed. Winning meant betraying the lives of those who were failures in the eyes of the world; it also meant that others would be jealous and envious of me, would want to destroy me. Losing meant that I was pathetic and unworthy. For most of my life my way of coping with that picture was neither to win nor to lose completely, to be smart and clever but to accomplish nothing. In other words, I could not renounce the picture, but I could embody the contradiction it evoked.

There were many reflections of my fears. For example, when I started my program, I preferred to work when J was around. I usually asked him to time me. His timing me served the function of sanctioning the act of working. I shared the responsibility of working with J, who was in effect telling me that it was all right to work, that nothing bad would happen to me, that he would still love me, that he would not be destroyed by my working.

Another example was my handicap fantasy, in which I imagined that I was handicapped, usually physically, and then was able to succeed. My being handicapped liberated me. After all, who could feel jealous of me if I became paralyzed from the neck down? I had two ways of implementing the fantasy in real life. One way, the "overwhelming odds syndrome," allows you to work if the deck is heavily (but not impossibly) stacked against you. What you have to feel is that for anyone else it would probably be impossible, but that you will just manage to get by. Thus, there was a magic amount of time before a deadline by which I could start to work. Not too soon or I would just waste time until I got close enough, and not too late or I would give up altogether. At just the right point I could feel that it would be a major achievement for me simply to get the assignment done; anything over and above that was a bonus.

The second implementation of the handicap fantasy was quite frightening to me, because it was completely unconscious and out of my willful control. It was a mental paralysis that prevented me from being able to think. Before analysis, the paralysis was an almost constant condition; afterward it came and went. I did not understand for some time that I was responsible for the paralysis, not just a victim of it. It occurred in the context of an argument—either an actual argument with someone else, or an implicit argument with the author of a book or paper. I wanted to win the argument so much that my aggression frightened me. In response to the aggression, I turned off my mind and refused to allow it combat. I gave myself the only handicap I could. I would lose, and feel miserable, but at least I didn't destroy anybody.

I had exaggerated feelings of both my own power and my own fragility, to which the mental paralysis contributed in interesting ways. I discovered, every time my mind failed and I lost an argument, that I could survive after all, that I was not as fragile as I thought; this left intact the notion that if my mind had worked, it would have been curtains for the other person. Once I started winning arguments I discovered that the other person in fact could walk away undamaged, that arguments were not as symbolic for others as they were for me, or that even if they were, others would not suffer any more than I did. Once I started losing arguments, not because of mental paralysis but because I was wrong, or didn't know enough, or think fast enough, I discovered that losing was not serious, either.

I am convinced that most academics have the same kill-or-be-killed attitude as I did, but they usually cope with it differently: they try to kill. The widespread presence of such behavior among academics makes it hard to view it as crazy. Can everybody be crazy? Yes. The pervasiveness of the kill-or-be-killed attitude also makes it difficult to discover viable alternatives. If they're really out to kill you, don't you have to kill back? No. When an argument is no longer viewed as a power struggle, when winning or losing no longer symbolizes killing or being killed, it doesn't matter whether you win or lose; what matters is what the argument allows you to understand that you did not understand before.

Most academics, of course, are men. I think the stereotype of men as destructively competitive is true. There are enough men who do not fit the stereotype (or who want to escape it) to make life bearable, but there are few people of either sex whose attitudes toward competition are worthy of emulation. The problem is not with competition and feeling competitive, but with the interpretation and generalization of winning and losing. Feeling good about winning is fine, as long as what you feel good about is limited to what you *did* and does not involve an estimation of your worth as a person. Feeling bad about losing is perhaps all right if you could have done better and your feeling bad is limited to that and, again, does not involve a judgment about your worth as a person.

Related to the fear of winning and losing was fear of having my own point of view. I had felt from childhood that I was separate from other people because I was different. While I prized my individuality, I also wanted to get rid of it. I wanted to be like other people so that they would accept me as one of them. Another reason, then, for not liking to argue with people was that it confirmed the idea that I was an oddball. The conflict between wanting to be myself and wanting to be like others also came out in how I viewed other's work. I often could not understand what other people were saying because I was afraid of losing myself and my own view in the process. If I were to figure out exactly what someone was saying, it was possible that I would not find anything wrong and would end up agreeing with them, abandoning my own former point of view, and by extension, myself. Work on my thesis helped reduce that fear. I did not get swallowed up by going deeply into someone's theory; when I had to modify my position, it was bearable.

For much of the time, however, I thought I had two choices. I could be myself or I could be like everybody else. It never occurred to me that I could be like others in some ways and unique in other ways. It also never occurred to me that others might prize the same aspects of my individuality that I did. Once I recognized that the conflict between being myself and being like others was largely of my own construction, it stopped being much of a problem.

I mentioned earlier that I had two feelings about work. In addition to feeling competitive, I felt resentful: work was an onerous obligation. When I approached the end of a project, I not only was afraid (as I will discuss later) that there would be nothing to take its place, but also feared the opposite: that the project I was about to complete was just one in a long series of endless tasks. Why should I finish this project when I'd just get another to take its place? I either saw my work as everything, so that to be without it was to be abandoned, or my work was simply an obligation, like working in a factory for somebody else, so that there was no point in fulfilling the obligation because another outrageous demand would appear in its place. To accept the idea that part of work is obligatory and part of it is personally important was the goal. This minor resentment was related to a larger one, namely, why is anything ever expected of me anyway? There is a pinch of rational objection here, which is that people's value as people should not be judged by the quality of their work. In particular, I don't want to earn others' love by a display of my professional abilities. Yet there is an irrational edge to the resentment, for the real problem was that emotionally I accepted that form of judgment and valued others less because their professional abilities were slight.

As a result, for much of the time that I worked on my thesis I was preoccupied with questions about my ability. How smart was I? How smart was I compared to so-and-so? How creative was I? How good was I at critical analysis? There was no end to these questions. They plagued me. They interfered with my work. I worried about whether I was smart enough to solve such-and-such a problem instead of getting on with trying to solve it. My preoccupation with my ability seemed to imply a need to be perfect, which is both a sign of arrogance and of weakness. It says, in effect, "I am so smart I can demand perfection of myself, something impossible for lesser mortals." But it also says, "I have so little confidence in my personal worth that professional imperfection is symbolic of personal unworthiness." The only escape from the two extremes is to put the question of ability in its proper place, which is, I think, no place at all. Ability is not important.

The important thing is how much you can come to understand, which of your abilities you can develop, how far you can grow. The priorities of our culture, however, are completely different. The culture decrees that you should do what you are good at rather than what you most like to do; that what you produce rather than what you get out of what you produce is what counts; that your ability, reflected in achievements, is what matters. Given cultural expectations, it is all too easy to equate personal and professional worth. Once the two are disentangled, work becomes less symbolic and therefore less problematic.

SOME CHARACTERISTICS OF SUCCESSFUL WORKERS. During my work program I decided that successful workers differed from me in three principal ways: their attitude toward their mistakes, their attitude toward finishing their work, and the nature of their commitment to it. I noticed, early in my program, that I hated to reread what I had written, because I was terrified of finding a mistake. In contrast, when I cooked I was eager to finish the dish and taste it, so I could see how it had turned out and enjoy it. The only importance of a failure in cooking was in terms of what I could learn from it. I did not expect, or even want, a limit on the number of mistakes I might make in cooking; I merely hoped my mistakes would be interesting ones that would teach me something. I looked forward to being a better and better cook, and assumed I would never be a perfect one. In my professional work, however, I did not think of my failures as useful to me or to others, but as a dead loss. Gradually I began to see that mistakes were a necessary part of learning and writing, that everybody (everybody!) made them, that they were to be exploited rather than ignored. One big difference between cooking and doing psychology was that I thought of cooking as woman's work, and I was sure I could succeed at any example of that. Another difference was that I didn't define myself as a cook, but as a psychologist; how good a cook I was didn't really matter.

Attitudes toward finishing work most distinguish successful from unsuccessful workers. I discovered that I resisted working my ideas out to the end. Many times I caught myself putting something away once the end was in sight. This was true both of writing papers and of doing more menial tasks. Sometimes, when I went back to a task, I would discover that I had as little as thirty minutes' work left. This resistance to the end product contrasts sharply with what I have seen of or read about successful workers, who always finish everything, even after they have lost interest in it. Successful workers are also always thinking about the next project, planning ahead, integrating their current work into a larger picture which is constantly being revised. I tended not to do this. One consequence of viewing work as a continuing process is that one wants to finish the present project to get on to the next. Although one could conceivably just go on to the next without finishing the present piece of work, important learning occurs in putting the finishing touches on a paper or project, learning that may govern the direction of the next work. One is gratified by the feeling of closure that comes with finishing a project, but aside from this feeling, the finishing touches to make what one has done present- able, to make sure the idea is expressed, puts the project in perspec- tive, aligns it with what one has done so far and what one is going to do next.

Unfinished projects also have a way of nagging at the back of the mind, even if one has decided that the enterprise was mistaken to begin with. In everything I have begun but not finished there was an idea that I thought was interesting and still think is interesting, even if its context was wrong, even if it itself was wrong. It's hard to lay those ideas to rest until they've been worked out and either found hopeless or given formal expression.

It also becomes depressing to be unsure from the very beginning whether or not you're actually going to do something with a new idea. If it's just going to end up in a drawer along with a bunch of other half- alive ideas, it's hard to get committed to it. Lack of commitment creates another problem; if you're going to be committed to an idea, you'll examine it very carefully at the outset to make sure it's worth spending time on. Thus, you are quicker to get rid of an idea that is only superficially appealing. The uncommitted person ends up neither developing worthwhile ideas nor getting rid of worthless ones soon enough.

To me, then, one of the striking differences between successful and unsuccessful workers is not necessarily how much time they spend working, or even how much they accomplish per unit of time, but how many half-written or almost-finished manuscripts they have lying around, how many interesting ideas for various projects that nothing much ever happened to.

I tried to analyze my own responses to finishing. Various emotions hit me when the end of a project was in sight: panic, boredom, fear. I almost never experienced impatience and eagerness to finish, unless there was a deadline. I may have wanted to finish magically, like waking up in the morning to find that I had finished the work in my sleep, but I didn't feel an urge to dispatch. This was invariably at odds with what I said. Although I said that I wished I were finished with project X, I didn't feel the corresponding emotions. Why not? If I were to finish something, then of course I wouldn't have it around anymore. I got panicky about finishing because I didn't know what I wanted to do next.

One way I coped with the fear of being bereft was to make projects infinitely long. Successful workers delimit what they're working on; when they get an ancillary idea in the course of a project, they keep it in mind to see if it will work in easily and naturally, or if it ought to be dropped temporarily and retrieved for consideration once the present project is finished. In contrast, I usually tried to incorporate that new idea no matter what; the result was that the project went all over the place and became impossible to finish. The panic mounted when this particular realization hit home, for then there seemed to be both nothing to do afterward (because hypothetically all problems would be solved once the project was finished) and nothing to do now (because the project had become impossible to finish).

In a way, work is like a love affair. It demands commitment, absorption, and care. The difference is that it is a love affair with oneself, or at least with one's creative abilities, and with an abstract world of ideas. For me there are two main rewards from working. One is the continual discovery within myself of new ideas; the other is deeper understanding of a problem. Before I started serious work on my thesis I had had flirtations with problems and ideas (to continue the love affair analogy), but no committed relationship. I was ignorant of others' work and ignorant of the process of finding and nurturing ideas. That double ignorance prevented me from developing my ideas and making something interesting of them. I neither knew how to develop an idea nor how to connect my ideas with those of others. I did not understand that it is necessary to know the literature of one's field well and to use that knowledge to give depth to one's own ideas. Since my ideas could not develop in a vacuum, they didn't develop at all. My ignorance was so complete that I did not understand that my inability to develop and sustain interesting ideas was not a reflection of my ability but of my ignorance and lack of training. I did not understand that ideas cannot come from nowhere and relate to nothing.

To work well you have to love, respect, and value yourself, as if you were another person. This is especially hard to do if there is no actual accomplishment to consider, if all you have to go on is potential. In my case, before I could begin my thesis, it was necessary to forget altogether about the world and about the final product. Only by writing for myself alone was I able to discover the intellectual qualities I liked about myself and those I didn't, independently of what the rest of the world valued. It was at first an act of faith. I didn't know who I was or what I could do but I finally felt strong enough to find out; also, I had finally recognized the need to understand what others thought.

THE ROLE OF WORK. Since becoming an assistant professor I have acquired the usual battery of professional responsibilities beyond research and writing. I rather enjoy these responsibilities, but they require enough of my energies so that I have had to reduce the number of purely selfish activities that I had time for when I was a graduate student and postdoctoral fellow. I have also, all too often, used professional obligations like seeing students as an excuse for not writing. I am glad that my year of thesis writing was free of outside responsibilities, because it allowed me to figure out what role I wanted work to play in my life and to live it at the same time. In the five years since then, I have not doubted the rightness, for me, of what I worked out, although I have not been able to live that life for several years.

I started thinking about the role of work in the middle of my thesis work program. I had set myself an interim goal of completing a certain amount of linguistic analysis by a certain date; I found I had to work ten to twelve hours a day to reach it. I discovered that I only felt I had worked enough when I had overworked, when I was physically exhausted by the end of the day. Work was still an obligation that I was fulfilling with a vengeance. Even the sternest evaluator would have agreed that I was working hard. The linguistic analysis was not as mentally taxing as actually writing, or it would have been impossible to do it for as long a stretch as I did. Furthermore, I was getting almost nothing of intellectual value from it—only a feeling of moral righteousness.

At this point I started thinking seriously about what I wanted the role of work in my life to be. I didn't want to work ten or more hours a day; moral righteousness was achieved at the cost of becoming a zombie. I asked myself what would I wish, fifty years from now, that I had done with my time. What would I most regret not having done? I had to distance myself from myself in this self-conscious way because I really didn't know what I wanted out of life, except that work and my relationship with J had to be part of it. What was the point of life? I asked myself. After a good deal of thought I decided that the point was to be happy. I consider this obvious to the point of triviality, except that I'm always running into people who can't believe I'm serious. I don't think it's a possible goal, given the political structure of the world, but it's possible for some to come close.

I decided that there were three main sources of happiness in my life: developing my various talents and interests; developing one talent deeply, namely my work; developing my relationships with other people in three ways—my intense involvement with J, my friendships, and my political interests. Before my work program, that is, before I was able to work, I didn't know how I spent my days, except that I never seemed to have enough time or energy to do things I wanted to do. By the end of a day, I would have accomplished nothing, have no idea where the time had gone, and then be very depressed. I felt so guilty about not working that I couldn't do anything else either, because I should have been spending that time working. But since I couldn't work when I "should," I often spent the allotted time doing nothing, literally nothing. One of the most self-destructive aspects of not working is that very little other activity or development takes place. When I started working I found I had a lot of time to do other things, as long as I wasn't working ten to twelve hours a day.

Once I began trying to fit work into the rest of my life, that is, once I began not just working but doing other things as well, I found that I had been denying myself many satisfactions. I had a number of interests and talents that had been lying fallow. I began to take up the piano again, to learn French, to learn about wines and wild mushrooms, to read more nonfiction for pleasure. I wanted to have more room in my life rather than less. This meant that I couldn't work eight to ten hours a day, but that was no longer a goal anyway.

Although work was not the sole important interest in my life, it was a major one. I wrestled with the problem of exactly how much time each day I should work. What was a reasonable amount? That way of putting it showed I still regarded work as punishment; for the most part it still was not something I freely chose to do. Now, I think that the right amount of time is whatever amount leaves room for the other important activities in my life and still allows me to make intellectual progress. There is no fixed right amount.

The short-term consequences of my work program were that I finished my thesis, and felt good about the part I had worked the hardest on, so good that I didn't even mind reading it over. My life seemed full for the first time, and happy. I began enjoying myself and my life without feeling so guilty about it. The enjoyable moments were not stolen from something else I was supposed to be doing; they were moments that I expected and planned for. I find it remarkable now that I had to convince myself that enjoyment and happiness were allowable for me. For a long time I didn't know what my attitude toward enjoyment was; I just assumed that of course I wanted to enjoy myself. Only when I started working and began to analyze my behavior with respect to work, did I realize that I didn't see a way to be happy unless that happiness was accompanied by guilt.

A footnote about the role of work in an individual's life is related to the analogy between work and love. In my experience, men's and women's work problems differ, reflecting a difference between men and women in how seriously they take themselves as workers. Men may have problems writing, particularly in finishing what they write, but they do not usually have trouble reading the work of others and discussing it. They appear to be full-fledged members of their field or profession, even where there is a lack of production. Women's alienation from their professional work, on the other hand, often seems more profound. For example, not only could I not write, but I could not read others' work or involve myself with the issues in my field at all. I always felt like an outsider, and could not take myself seriously as a thinker. The situation is undoubtedly related to our upbringing; boys are taught to take themselves seriously as workers and girls are not. In contrast, girls are taught to take themselves seriously as lovers and boys are not, which accounts for my observation that women have fewer problems than men in being committed in love.

THE PRESENT. It is hard to assess the long-term consequences of my program. On the plus side, I derive great pleasure from my work; I feel a part of my field; I have learned and am learning much; I have a realistically positive view of my abilities as a teacher, thinker, and researcher; I have written several good papers. On the minus side, I have not been as productive or made as much progress as I would like. In short, I am not my ego ideal, but at the same time, my work problem is no longer a *problem*. I know now the role I want work to play in my life, and the sorts of internal changes I need to make. Although I still have problems working, the problems do not devastate me or make me despair; I handle them well and expect to handle them better.

Whew. Finished.

Notes from an Extra in the American Moving Picture Show
Connie Young Yu

Connie Young Yu (center) interviews Carl Yue (left) on location for the film *Jung Sai* (Chinese Americans). Co-workers Freida Lee Mock and Chris Kobayashi at right.

IF SOMEONE had told me when I was a college student that I would not begin to write seriously until I was over thirty, I wouldn't have believed it. In my youth I had the romantic dream of being a *young* novelist, poet, or playwright. Now, at thirty-four, I have published a few historical essays for journals, several books reviews, one poem, and a set of activity cards for children on Chinese America, and I have produced some radio scripts for a community program. I am waiting for my latest work, a booklet on a people's Bicentennial quilt, to come off the press so that I can join my friends at the print shop in collating it. This is hardly what I had envisioned fifteen years ago as "making it," but my values have changed since then, and I feel successful now at what I really want to do.

Working with a group of women on the Bicentennial-quilt project was a major step in finding and expressing my identification with American culture, a focal point of previous writing. The quilt is composed of forty-five squares, each representing an event or phase of history commemorating the heroism, endurance, and struggle of the American people. When the completed "soft sculpture" was shown at a women's art exhibit, it moved some viewers to the point of tears. A friend of mine who spent three years of her childhood behind barbed wire in Arkansas during World War II stitched the Japanese relocation-camp square; an elderly black woman recreated her image of the Underground Railroad; a woman whose mother had been a child laborer did a square on children of the mills. My square showed the Chinese working on the transcontinental railroad which my great-grandfather helped to build. For ourselves, as well as for our compatriots, we wanted to portray the people making history, to counter the traditional imagery of the "men who made history."

In the words of artist Genny Guracar, the originator of the project, "Quilting bees were our grandmothers' consciousness-raising groups." This "women's work," this quilt project, gave us the chance to know each other, to discuss womanhood and our common, as well as different, heritages. We wanted to present not "textbook history," but our own history. Making the quilt was a symbolic effort to define and share our sense of American culture and to oppose the commercialization of the Bicentennial. My own job was to collect bits of information —memories, family anecdotes—from fellow workers, to research the historical background of each square, to describe some of our feelings about the historic events, and to compile everything into a booklet that would make what we had learned and what we had stitched available to others.[1]

Writing the booklet required careful research and, as writing doesn't come easily to me, struggle over every page. It was an emotional and liberating experience to discover the history I had never heard in any classroom. While my three children were at school (or running around the house with friends and animals), I moved in my book-littered room from world to world of labor uprising, feminist struggle, and racial conflict. As a whole different view of American history and culture was revealed to me, I began to define my own personal role in a people's culture movement, a movement that portrays Asian American history and culture as an integral part of the American story.

The learning and the awareness that came from doing the quilt booklet have been helpful in related work. As often happens, my other work involvements "connected." As a member of a California State educational committee appointed to evaluate public school textbooks for compliance with codes on racism and sexism, I read hundreds of newly published books. Rooting out these ancient prejudices sometimes seems like an uphill battle, given the assembly-line "Dick and Jane" books printed every year and the insensitivity of publishers to ethnic and feminist perspectives. I've learned a lot from others working on this committee and am becoming more skillful at pinpointing both omissions and stereotypes. As a result of my volunteer involvement in textbook evaluation, I have written articles on the subject, spoken for various groups and on the radio, and worked on a community television program. I am described as a "consultant" when hired by educational services and school districts to lecture and lead workshops on Asian America and other minorities as they are portrayed in textbooks. As these alternative means of expression opened up, my sense of my own work was no longer limited to writing.

Working on a film in 1974 was a definitive step for me. The film project combined all the elements important in my work—Chinese American history, writing, learning from my parents, interviews, and research. And for the first time, I was working closely with other Asian women. My present work is influenced not only by contemporary women, but by my mother and the spirit of my grandmothers. The film was a documentary on Chinese immigration; I worked first as a scriptwriter, then as the narrator-protagonist.

[1] *The People's Bicentennial Quilt: A Patchwork History* (East Palo Alto, California: Up Press, 1976).

People's Bicentennial Quilt (Courtesy University of Pennsylvania Press)

A scene shows my mother and me going to the immigration barracks on Angel Island. My mother, recalling how her mother was kept prisoner on the island for fifteen months, begins to cry. Her poised demeanor and composure dissolve as she switches from careful English to Cantonese. My mother had not been on this island for fifty years; yet the pain of an unjust and cruel situation was still sharp. The two directors, seizing the unexpected opportunity for capturing genuine emotion, scrambled about on the road in front of us, getting it all down in celluloid. Everyone who has seen the film has told me that the Angel Island sequence with my mother is the best part. It was certainly the most revealing and honest.

Only after my grandmother's death did I learn that she was on Angel Island, as were thousands of Asian immigrants to the United States. My mother's mother was a sharp-witted, brilliant woman, physically fragile and with bound feet. Before family banquets, one or two of her grandchildren would have to walk with her from her apartment on Powell Street in Chinatown, San Francisco, down to a restaurant on Grant Avenue—about a half-hour for those few blocks. I remember thinking how painful it must have been for her as a child to have her feet permanently stunted in that ancient, cruel Chinese practice. (Later I would learn of restraints and rituals for women in America that were just as crippling and useless.)

What my mother was remembering that morning of the Angel Island shoot was that her mother had been taken from her children, confined in those stark ugly barracks, faced with the threat of deportation. My mother, then fifteen years old, had to work in a sweatshop, sewing fine garments to be sold downtown, to support her brothers and sisters at home. Several times a week she would take a ferry to Angel Island; often she brought rice and salted eggs because the food served to the "aliens" was so bad. My mother's American-born father had died during the family's stay in China, and when her widowed mother decided to return to San Francisco with her five children in 1924, she was a victim of an exclusion law against Chinese immigrants designed to prevent women from coming to America. The American-born children were allowed to land while my grandmother suffered through the long months, awaiting the outcome of a court decision that finally secured her release. Soon after she was allowed to return to San Francisco, her second daughter—a lovely, intelligent teen-ager who wrote poetry—died of tuberculosis, a disease that took a heavy toll in Chinatown. My mother and another sister continued to work to support the family; their labors in the sewing factory lasted twelve years. (My mother never touched a sewing machine after that.)

All immigrants suffer hardship. But the Chinese have struggled against a particularly unique history of immigration exclusion and flagrant discriminatory legislation. My work cannot be separated from that struggle; in the documentary film I was able, in small measure and in one form, to memorialize it. I was the tour guide through Chinese America.

Making the film was the best work experience I've had. When we filmed in the gold country of California, the crew—except for one man, Terry Sanders, the excellent co-director and photographer—were Asian women. The people in the small towns through which we passed were startled to see Asian women carrying cameras and movie equipment. I felt proud to be working with such untraditional "sisters." We spent hours driving along dusty roads and, in motels, talking about our experiences and backgrounds. Two of the young women, Japanese Americans in their early twenties, had very different experiences and life-styles from mine. They had decided in their teens to get out on their own, to work in media. They were single, politically active, and concerned about the "colonization" of Third World women. When they found out that the crew grip—a Chinese immigrant who lugged equipment around—was paid far less than they (as technicians), they asked that her salary be raised; and it was. The co-director of the film, Freida Lee Mock, was a Chinese American of my generation; ten years earlier there had been little feeling of solidarity among our sex and race. As we discussed our changing attitudes, our awakened concern with ethnic history and culture, we purposely looked into our family backgrounds to find the history we wanted conveyed to America on film. Driving past historic California landmarks, we told each other stories about our lives, trying to put together the background of our people.

In some respects my family story is characteristically that of other Chinese Americans'. My parents were deeply affected by the depression and the limited opportunities for minorities at the time, but they worked hard, and my father managed, after working two jobs, to put himself through Stanford University. In San Jose's old Chinatown, his parents struggled to make ends meet in their general store, supplying an ever-diminishing number of Chinese farmers and laborers. Generous people, "grub-staking" those who couldn't pay, they never made a profit.

About six months before Pearl Harbor, I was born, second daughter to a struggling petroleum engineer and former seamstress, respectively second- and third-generation Chinese Americans. My father's parents moved in with us in a pleasant rented house in the then-small, quiet town of Whittier. My grandparents Young were at first very disappointed that I was another girl, and my mother cried, knowing how they felt. My father tried not to show any disappointment, and brought my mother a bunch of expensive gladiolas (which he couldn't afford) at the hospital. I am conscious of all this through oral history, a technique well mastered in our family. Somehow, I can even see my grandfather turning away and sighing as I was brought home.

Despite this beginning my early childhood was idyllic and happy. Though my first language was Chinese, and the neighborhood children were all blond and blue-eyed, I was unaware of prejudice or hostility. I remember my early years as sun-filled and free, surrounded by loving people. I had no idea until much later that my father was the sole Chinese engineer in his company and that he was given only a temporary position because of an all-white hiring policy.

My grandfather and grandmother indulged me, yet gave me discipline and guidance. My father's mother was the opposite of my maternal grandmother—illiterate, born of a peasant family in a Canton village, her feet unbound. She was a tough, hardy woman who lived to be ninety-six. My paternal grandfather had come to America as an eleven-year-old laborer in 1881, one year before the Chinese exclusion law. When he returned to China to get married at twenty-two, he told his mother he wanted a woman without bound feet because life in America was hard. His marriage was arranged, and fortunately, he and his wife were suited to each other. With a re-entry permit my grandfather came back to America to earn the money for Grandmother's passage. Times were never worse for Chinese laborers; no more of his class were allowed to immigrate. Year after year my grandfather saved, until he could afford to start a small general store, a branch of a Chinese company. Thus he was able to change his status to "merchant class," which allowed his wife eventually to come to America.

It took my grandfather sixteen years to be able to send for my grandmother; compared with all his "stranded bachelor" friends, he was considered lucky. I remember my grandmother yelling at him daily. She blamed him for everything—her wasted youth, the years of childless waiting. He took it all silently. He enjoyed being left alone to sit in the garden with a hand-rolled smoke, and sometimes asked me to pound his aching back. My grandmother, so kind to me, was harsh toward my mother, who endured being number two in the house and kitchen for twelve years. My grandmother considered my mother's work inferior; if my mother wanted to relax, she was thought indulgent and lazy. But then, who could work as hard as my grandmother?

She never wasted time; she got up early and cooked and cleaned. She grew a productive garden; she preserved vegetables and fruits and meats. She couldn't understand English, so she never spent time with the radio, newspapers, or magazines. Though she had been blinded in one eye by a splinter while chopping wood, she hardly missed a thing that was happening around her.

When my father went overseas for three years with the China-Burma-India division in the Second World War, my mother operated a small gift shop in downtown Whittier. Although she had had no business training, she took the initiative, borrowed money, and set up the shop. Her enterprise was good for the morale of the entire family and a real boon for my mother. Many years after the shop had closed, my mother showed me proudly her bank account with savings from her earnings.

My father returned a much-decorated army major, to the pride of his family and other Chinese Americans. Despite his abilities, the unchanged discriminatory hiring practices of the oil company that had employed him on a temporary basis meant there was little chance for advancement. In those days there were no affirmative action groups to challenge the all-white policies of major firms. After my brother was born, answering all prayers for a son, my father decided to go to San Francisco to become a partner in his brother-in-law's new business, manufacturing natural soy sauce.

I hated the small apartment in San Francisco's Chinatown. The windows faced the brick walls of a sewing factory; in bed at night I could hear the chatter of the women working and the roar of the machines. My sister (three years older), my baby brother, and I shared a room. It was in Chinatown that I became aware of prejudice and fear. My first-grade teacher, an irritable, imperious white woman, treated her all-Chinese class as dumb animals. She ridiculed a shy new immigrant girl who had an "accident" because she couldn't speak enough English to ask to go to the bathroom. I was so homesick for my grandparents and the cozy house in Whittier that I was a dazed and unresponsive pupil; my teacher concluded that I was retarded and told my mother so. Luckily, I didn't stay long at that school.

It wasn't easy to move out of Chinatown in 1949. With the help of my father's white army buddy, who bought our house for us, we became one of the first nonwhite families in the Richmond District (the "Avenues") of San Francisco. We were all glad to be out of the ghetto, lonely as the new neighborhood was in the beginning.

I had problems studying and paying attention in school. Even throughout college I was a daydreamer. My grades were uneven; I only enjoyed reading and writing, and failed in math courses. Consistently hard-working in everything, my sister was an enormously successful student, and each new teacher would ask me, "Are you as smart as your sister?" Unlike the stereotyped idea that many have of Asian girls, I was neither artistic nor neat. I constantly lost things and felt awkward. But by the time I was in the eighth grade I knew what I wanted to be: a creative writer. My daydreaming, wild imagination, and love of stories would be put to use. My teachers saw that I wrote well and encouraged me in this one talent.

My father was an ordinance officer at Oakland Army Base during the Korean War. He was glad to be called to serve his country. In the Red-baiting McCarthy years Chinese Americans felt compelled to show their patriotism, lest they suffer the fate of Japanese Americans during World War II. I loved seeing my father in uniform and, later, wearing the cap of the American Legion as commander of the "Cathay Post." He was involved in Chinatown's Republican Club and was an active supporter of Richard Nixon—also from Whittier—in his campaign against Helen Douglas. Later he volunteered his time to promote Chinatown festivals such as the New Year's parade, and year after year served as the Parade Marshal, organizing the floats and marching bands that attracted tourists to Chinatown. My mother was forever involved with the extended family; she helped relatives and more relatives, mediated, listened to their problems. She was more liberal than my father; never debating him on issues, she quietly voted differently. She was idealistic, concerned about world peace and the role of women in the world. She clipped newspaper and magazine articles—anything with "peace" or "women" in the headline. Eleanor Roosevelt was her heroine. She always encouraged me "to show what women can do." Because she had had to work in her youth, she had little formal education. When she was over forty, she began taking the streetcar to adult school, and one day she came home with a photograph of her graduation class. There she was, member of a proud group of older graduates, smiling, diploma in hand.

Because my parents were my "role models," I envisioned myself marrying someone like my father—a Republican engineer—and becoming a little like my mother's image of Eleanor Roosevelt, and a best-selling novelist as well.

The natural soy sauce was doing well, and my father invested in a new, fine Chinese restaurant—and then another one. He soon could afford to send all his children to good colleges. "Opportunity" was a word we children often heard. A month before entering Mills College I met my husband-to-be at a Chinese students' conference devoted to energetic Christian anticommunism. Later, when I told my friends in the film crew, we all had a good laugh at the irony of it. Kou-ping (John) Yu, born in Shanghai and educated in the Philippines, was an idealistic Stanford medical student. Most women of my generation saw the men in their lives as their destiny; they would make the decisions and take them away somewhere. I expected to be a helpmeet to John, to go wherever he went (preferably Asia) in his momentous adventures and tasks of healing. Yet underneath it all, I still aspired to be a great American writer. Mills fed my fantasies, and in the protected confines of the wooded campus above Oakland, I joined the United Nations Club, wrote for college publications, won a couple of prizes. My freshman short story won honorable mention in *Seventeen* magazine's fiction contest, and the short story became my favorite literary form. The summer after my sophomore year I attended the Middlebury Writers' Conference in Vermont to hear Robert Frost, John Ciardi, and others talk about writing. Practically everybody I met asked whether I was Japanese or Chinese. I returned to California with the impression that successful writers are white, male, and from New York. I was prepared to sign my manuscripts C. Young and have them mailed from the East Coast. So much for my ethnic awareness in that period of my life.

My memories of Mills have become less fond in the past few years; when I was an undergraduate, however, my friends and I endorsed the tradition that we were enjoying the "best"—the freest, most privileged, most attractive—years of our lives. "Remember who you are and what you represent" was the Mills motto. We were the elite, privileged class of women and represented the same. We ate in an elegant dormitory dining hall, served by uniformed fellow students who needed the money. Fresh flowers decorated every table, and I remember watching the blinking lights of San Francisco across the bay while we ate fine meals by candlelight on Wednesday nights, when nice dresses and high-heeled shoes were required. There were hardly any black or brown students at Mills then, and the closest thing to an ethnic course was Oriental Art I and II. I did, however, get a good background in English literature and writing; the faculty was excellent, classes were small, and all of us women were encouraged to speak up in class.

My graduation address as class representative that happy June '63 was full of gratitude. In those days, President Kennedy was often spoken of as a "Renaissance man"; the title of my address was "Swords, Plowshares, and the Renaissance Woman." My diamond engagement ring flashing in the sun, I delivered one worthwhile line:

"May we never be in such a state as to deserve the words of Kenneth Patchen: 'Hey, Fatty, don't look now but there's a revolution breathing down your neck.' "

The following year at San Francisco State College I first heard the rumblings of discontent as black students began to give amplified "raps" on the lawn at lunchtime. As a married graduate student studying creative writing while working part-time in the linens department at Macy's, I found the atmosphere of the "streetcar college" stimulating, but wrote crafted short stories totally unrelated to my own experiences—or to anyone else's for that matter. So it was no disappointment for me to drop my studies when my husband decided to take his third-year residency in a hospital in New York City. We packed everything we owned in a U-Haul, and drove cross-country. It was the first time I had lived away from my family in California; I was seven months pregnant.

Nothing in my English-major career prepared me for the realities of housekeeping and child-care. My trials in learning the basics of cooking, cleaning, and shopping were frustrating, and, in retrospect, comical. As a well-educated unskilled worker, I felt like the victim of a cruel joke. Yet there was newness and a sense of adventure in this early period of marriage and big-city living. After our first daughter was born, I would leave our tiny apartment and push the baby carriage for miles of fascinating city blocks on multiple errands. Seventeen months after the first baby, another daughter was born, and I had a double baby stroller. I was the typical "keeping-the-home-fires-burning" doctor's wife; my schedule was made up of nap times, feeding times, bath times, and errands. "Hectic" was the word I used a lot when people asked how I was doing. Our one year in New York extended to three as John accepted a fellowship in cancer research. Writing became an impossible task for me, not because my husband wasn't encouraging, or helpful with chores—he loved caring for our babies when he was home—but I could not concentrate for very long with two small children; I was fully occupied daily. Since I wanted a traditional family and loved being with my children, whose childhood seemed to me precious and fleeting, I decided I would just "wait" until they got older to "go back to work."

With much self-discipline, I managed to write one article on Chinese American history, an extension of a senior seminar paper inspired by a wonderful English professor. "Did you ever think of writing about Mark Twain and the Chinese?" he had asked provocatively, putting the new thought in my head. But for the most part, at this time in my life my concerns were far from academic; I felt a certain kinship with the heroines of *Up the Sandbox* and *Diary of a Mad Housewife*. I thought that society used, and then unjustly mocked, the woman who was "just a housewife." I was furious for days when a man who lived in our apartment building remarked on the "easy" life of housewives, or when another mumbled, when I was a few minutes late for an errand, "Just like a woman!"

At about this time I joined a discussion group made up of women of all different races in the community. We read current books and discussed the contemporary historical issues of Vietnam, racism, and poverty. Although we didn't discuss feminist issues directly, I felt a closer bond with other women. My "housewife" friends who cooked, cleaned, and cared for their children raised challenging questions about the direction the country was heading. Our discussions, though less intellectual than those in college, were more realistic. While they related to the particulars of our everyday lives, they also prepared me for the upheavals of the late sixties. My husband and I began to read together, saw Felix Green's movie on China, and talked endlessly about America's involvement in Asia. We began to realize what the revolution in China was about and that the same struggle was happening in Vietnam.

Moving back to California was another adjustment. Suburban living was as tricky as city life, and I had to learn the survival routines all over again. Only after my son was born (to my great joy, for I was influenced by family tradition to want a boy badly) did I feel settled enough to start writing again. I was encouraged by my parents to write about the pioneer Chinese. My mother had saved relevant books and articles for me; my father contributed oral history. I did what I could, not systematically or comprehensively perhaps, but adequately for a few articles for respectable publications. My writing on Chinese Americans presented interesting facts, but no broad perspective other than "pride" in one's heritage. I didn't deal with issues of racism and violence in America. Nonetheless, because it filled a need for information on Asian Americans, my writing was read by students and teachers. It was exciting to receive a few complimentary letters and inquiries. As a result of this public notice, I was asked in 1970 to be a trustee of my old alma mater.

The first meeting I attended (wearing a new suit made for the occasion) was a trustees' luncheon in an elegant San Francisco hotel. The press ran stories on the three new appointments to the Mills board: the first black trustee and the first two young trustees, a recent graduate of twenty-four and me, aged twenty-eight. This phenomenon —changing the establishment look of traditional bodies—was occurring all over the country; I mistook it as a revolutionary step. I chatted amicably with the college president and several captains of industry who were more or less permanent fixtures on the board. This was in 1970, after the invasion of Cambodia and the shootings at Kent State, and the college trustees were worried about alumnae sensitivities, fund raising, and the backlash caused by students agitating and striking. After some emotional (on my part) discussions with the old trustees on Vietnam, I realized that they didn't intend to relinquish power or even share it. Only appearances had changed; I was merely a token, part of a domestic pacification program.

Mills itself had changed, however. A large portion of the student body was now made up of "minorities." There were ethnic studies courses, and teachers and students professed concern for the world beyond the cloistered campus. Asked to speak at a senior dinner, I told the students that I had never been so proud of Mills as on the day the student body joined the strike to protest the invasion of Cambodia.

Two years later, when students were again talking about striking after the spring bombing of Hanoi and the mining of Haiphong Harbor, my brief term as trustee was coming to an end. A new young Asian American trustee was introduced at my last meeting; an even younger recent graduate would replace the first young trustee. As usual, the atmosphere was formal and intimidating. We were seated around a massive walnut table in the ensemble room adjacent to the concert hall. I mustered enough courage to make a quavery-voiced statement that went something like this: "Two years ago, when I became a trustee, there was a student strike because of the war in Indochina. Now, two years later, there is talk of another strike. This will continue unless all of you work to end United States involvement in Southeast Asia." So ended my career in the college establishment.

By this time I had become experienced in leaflet writing, demonstration organizing, guerrilla theater (I wore black pajamas and was pursued by Vietnam vets), speaking out at stockholder meetings of a munitions manufacturing company. Each incident radicalized me further. I made up for the years in which I did nothing but talk back to the six o'clock news. The fiction I once wanted to write seemed the wishful, individualistic thinking of the past. Now, instead, I wrote essays on the issues and edited the newsletter of the peace group to which I belonged. My girls were in school, and my cheerful little son often came with me to the speeches, marches, and many, many meetings. I felt that my work—futile as it often seemed—was necessary, even as each month I hoped it could end.

Several friends and I were involved in disrupting the Citizen-of-the-

Year-Award dinner in Palo Alto for David Packard, the former Deputy Secretary of Defense. We sat through the dinner (I shaking the whole time), then staged a walkout—or rather, after making our statements, we were firmly "escorted" out by numerous plainsclothesmen. My photograph appeared on the front page of the local paper. When my parents heard about my radical activity, they were stunned. What made me do such a terrible, rude thing? It was so unlike me, thought my worried, anxious mother. My parents had worked hard all their lives to see that their children would be safe and comfortable, and here I, who had so much, was involved in protest like an impetuous student. I was risking it all.

For me, however, there was no looking back. Still, it wasn't easy. I remember when, as the "MC" for a night rally against Vice-President Agnew that jammed El Camino Real for blocks, I hesitated for just a moment before mounting a sound truck, because I saw the sea of Viet Cong flags around me and "flashed back" to my anti-Communist past, the Chinese New Year parades, and the Kuomintang banners.

My husband and I talked nonstop during these days. Somehow our worries and fears, our misery over the unending war and the seemingly endless search for peace, brought us closer together. We were glad we had changed our political views together. He defended me when others expressed shock and dismay over my actions and, though constantly overworked at the hospital, he joined in my political activities when he could.

For the first time I began to make connections between past and present injustices in government policy toward Asians—and others. I began actively to support anti-war candidates and devoted a great deal of time and energy to the 1972 campaign as a McGovern delegate to the Democratic National Convention. Political activity gave me insight into American attitudes, and I gained skills and confidence for later work.

At this time too I became co-editor of a special Asian American issue of the *Bulletin of Concerned Asian Scholars*, and undertook the first academic writing I had done since college. I was excited to be involved in this work despite my diffidence because I was not a "scholar" while the other contributors were impressively credentialed writers. The publication turned out fine; the first definitive collection of Asian American essays, it soon became a sourcebook in ethnic-studies courses. Its success was reassuring and reaffirmed me in my decision not to go back to graduate school. I had become disillusioned with academic institutions, and I wanted to show that a "housewife" could do it on her own. Yet I was not really "on my own." For I learned a great deal from working on this project and similar ones with co-workers who became my friends.

My work acquired a new dimension as I became active in the media because of my knowledge of Asian America. As a member of a Chinese civil rights organization in San Francisco, I moderated several community programs on educational television and coordinated a weekly half-hour radio program. I had to manage with on-the-job training, and learned everything from friends and from my mistakes. On the radio show we produced poetry readings, satire, interviews, community news, and commentary; our theme was discrimination in American culture. Even though I was the oldest, the only one with a family and home in the suburbs, I felt a sense of common purpose working with fellow Asian Americans and relief at not having to explain where we all were coming from. (My comrades were students, writers, unemployed workers, and media people who had to hustle "gigs.") The management of the radio station, which became our chief enemy, practiced sexism and racism despite its liberal image. A member of a women's radio program, which supported us, said to me as she helped edit my tape, "You know how I learned all this? My old man's an engineer. No one here would take the time to show me how." The minority programs were given the worst time slots and production schedules. We were treated rudely, given no technical help, and yet continually criticized for our "poor sound quality." We were working with an "alternative" station, but found it just as bigoted and morally obtuse as the others; it differed only in that it was more disorganized and inconsistent.

Our program finally left the airwaves in protest when a Chinese language program was suddenly dropped. Surprisingly enough, some months later, our show was picked up by a slick, popular old-time rock-and-roll station. It wasn't easy at first. We had to negotiate several times with management about our language, "anti-white slurs," and so-called sectarian humor. But we gained listener support and became smoother and more innovative with each program. We became a collective, with Chinatown as "home base," and chose as our theme "the spirit of truth and defiance." We've all learned a great deal working on the show: sharing responsibility; communicating new ideas, history, and news. I learned to speak better, to write for immediate release, and to enjoy the feeling of accomplishment that comes from communicating instantly instead of waiting for publication. Ideally, "the airwaves belong to the people," in the words of one of our early leaflets. Still, given the control of the media by a very few, we have to fight to be heard.

*   *   *

People frequently ask me what I "do"—am I studying for my Ph.D. or am I teaching? I usually say that I am a writer. But I do not limit myself to just one form of communication. Right now I work on many projects. Eventually I will write that novel in the back of my mind. But I know now that I will never retreat from the moral and political concerns I have acquired. The time for my own work is limited because my children are still young, and my family is most important to me. Because I am a doctor's wife, I don't have to earn a wage. Sometimes, I feel guilty among my many friends who have to work at jobs they don't like so that they can do the work they really want to do, friends who often risk being fired from their necessary, burdensome jobs for their politics. Then I try to view my privileged situation as giving me valuable advantages that I must use to write honestly, what I want, both for my own pleasure and for the use of others.

Working on the film *Jung Sai—Chinese Americans* helped me to see many possibilities. Working with a crew of friends who had a shared purpose, being together and learning from each other, meant more than the product, more than the film itself. We have enabled each other to grow, to make longer, better films, to create more disciplined and committed writings and programs. During much of *Jung Sai* I am seen driving through California (with bluegrass music in the background yet) tracking down history, looking for my roots. I interview people, do research, and write. My roomy home is my place of work, my refuge; it includes a grassy corral we use to raise assorted fowl. At the end of the film I'm standing by our chicken coop, surrounded by husband and children and animals, looking inspired and happy. It's a nice story, and true, but acting in a movie, going through the motions, is only a rehearsal. The struggle remains to be enacted for myself and for many others who are working for change in this country. I feel ready for a greater commitment to being a minority voice in a majority culture, and the result has got to be more than a movie.

Connie Young Yu

Writing in the
Real World
Anne Lasoff

CAN YOU WRITE? No? Suppose you begin to see the world in a new dimension. Suppose that you no longer take your experiences and emotions in stride and absorb them as you go; instead, they fill your head like pieces in a jigsaw puzzle, waiting to be assembled. And the only way to assemble them is by writing.

Suppose you are a middle-aged woman. Your husband and your children and your friends have a fixed image of you as they think you are, but you know you are different. You need to write, to fit the pieces of the puzzle together. Do you say to your husband, "From now on I refuse to be a human appliance, existing only for your comfort, fitting my life around your needs"? Do you say to your children, "You are to be more independent. I have other things to do than pick up after you"? Do you say to your friends, "I won't be available for canasta in the afternoon"? Do you say to all of them, "I need to devote myself to my art"?

What will you do? Will you tell the world of this wondrous change? Will you write secretly until you gain the confidence to call yourself a writer? Will you keep your discovery to yourself for fear you will become the "oddball" in your group? Will you learn to protect yourself, to laugh before others laugh at you? Will you learn to silence your own voice that whispers over and over, "Who do you think you are to have artistic pretensions? You're too old to change, to break out of the mold. Don't be foolish; you are in a comfortable groove, you don't have to prove anything. Remember Papa's life."

My father. He was fondly known as "the mad inventor." His life was devoted to inventing items that just missed success because the timing was wrong. He invented a bell that would ring when the pan under the icebox was full. Refrigerators replaced iceboxes. He invented an improved window screen. Air conditioners came into use. He invented a new clothespin. Dryers replaced the clothesline. But he never gave up his dreams. The family was tolerant because he learned to laugh at himself, but I remember when the teasing became too much. I saw tears when my exasperated mother would scold, "When will you stop fooling around with these nuts and bolts?" He always expected his ship to come in. Whenever we asked *when,* he would sigh and say, "Unfortunately my ship is icebound in the North Pole, but when the ice thaws we'll all be rich."

I see my father in me. Will I give up my dreams or endure being the object of tolerant derision? I test myself. For a few days I pretend that the muse has never met me, I pretend it doesn't exist. A sadness envelops me. My days are formless, nothing matters. I look for a place where I can be at peace. Then I give up the pretense and hurry back to the warmth and excitement of my new-found creativity.

I am aware that buried in me is an unknown creature that is beginning to stir, to demand recognition. At first I think this is nonsense. Who can this creature be? Where has it been till now, when my life is more than half over? Who says I must create? But if I deny this living creature, I deny a part of myself. The creature must be acknowledged, must be nurtured. I am a willing captive of a new entity. Perhaps my father was also a captive of this creature.

I seek a haven, a milieu where I can be myself, where I can let my guard down. I seek a haven where the wonder of what has happened to me will be understood.

My life's story is the story of two lives. The incubation for my second life began ten years ago, when I was forty-two. During the next five years I underwent a transformation triggered by family crisis. My daughter hovered toward drug addiction.

Attempts to cope with her problems made me aware that I needed to order *my* life in a new way. I discovered that writing not only brought order but filled me with a sense of accomplishment I had never before experienced.

The change this produced in every sphere of myself has made my earlier life seem formless and blurred. I recall important events or turning points as if they happened not fifteen or twenty or thirty years ago, but in another lifetime and to someone else. Yet I know that one cannot dismiss the past, for it is the foundation of the present and the future. It must be considered in the quest for self-knowledge.

My parents came from Russia. They met in this country. My father had "wanderlust," as he called it. Before he knew my mother he traveled across the country as an itinerant bricklayer. He was a socialist, a follower of Norman Thomas.

World War I found him working in an army camp in Maryland. He complained to the camp commander that the laborers were being exploited by being made to work in freezing weather. The general was so impressed with my father's socialist rhetoric that they became friends and all my father had to do that cold winter was to light the gas lamps at dusk.

My father was born ahead of his time. His radical ideas of social security, labor unions, dignity for the worker, are now taken for granted, but at that time he was regarded as a revolutionary. If he were a young man today, he would have been a campus agitator, an activist in the peace movement, a champion for civil rights. When he married he put aside his wanderlust, but never his idealism.

My mother is a realist. She says she was never a child. She always had responsibility. My grandmother was sickly and my grandfather was in New York trying to establish a foothold in the "golden country" so that he could bring his family here. The care of the household fell on my mother's capable young shoulders.

She tells how she smuggled her two younger brothers hidden in a hay wagon across the *grenitz*—the Russian border—to escape their conscription into the Czar's dreaded army. Once her brothers were safe she returned home on a troop train. She pretended to have laryngitis so that the soldiers would not know she was Jewish and possibly assault her.

After my parents' marriage in 1921, they lived a few years on the Lower East Side until my father built a house in an undeveloped area of Brooklyn, East Flatbush. We only had a few years of country living with chickens and cow and water from a pump, because the neighborhood became a popular settling place for immigrants eager to escape the slums of the East Side. Streets were paved, lights installed, water came from the faucet. I was very young at the time of this transformation, but I still remember the smell of the barnyard, gathering eggs in my apron, my mother chasing our wandering cow.

I was eight years old, a chubby little girl trudging happily home from a school Christmas party. I was laden with books and Christmas candy and a cardboard Santa Claus I had made myself. My younger sister met me at the corner of our block. As I gave her some of my things to hold, she blurted,

"Papa had an accident and he's in the hospital and Mama is crying." I was frightened. Mama was crying. Mama never cried. I came quietly into the house and hid behind a door, but my mother spotted me.

"Annie, you're my big girl and you have to help me. Take care of the baby and your sister. I must go to the hospital to see Papa."

My father was proud of his work as a bricklayer because the results of his labor lasted a lifetime. He had worked on the Empire State Building, on the Hotel St. George in Brooklyn, and even on the high school I was to attend.

In those days workers did not wear helmets. My father was hit on the head by a wooden beam that fell off a scaffold. He was severely injured. The doctors did not think he would live. He survived, but the trauma wreaked havoc with his body and his mind. He was never able to work again.

Time passes slowly for a child. My father spent three months in the hospital. When he came home he was like a stranger in the house. I remember shyly watching him eat, my mother serving him as if he were a guest. Gradually the awkwardness passed and I had my father back again.

My father's left side was permanently weakened and numb. He forgot how to read and write. He forgot the names of objects. He could not remember the word for pen, but he knew it was used to write love letters. Amnesia wiped out the years before his accident. At the age of forty, my vigorous, hard-working father became a semi-invalid.

My mother taught him how to read and write Yiddish again. She spent hours each week reading the newspapers aloud until he gradually became able to pick out the words for himself. My father's intellectuality and his sense of humor were not impaired. If we did anything foolish he would say, "I was hit on the head, what's your excuse?"

My maternal grandfather was tyrannical in foisting religion onto his family. One reason my mother married my father was because he was a freethinker. He believed in God but didn't dwell on it. He ignored religious ritual. After the accident he seemed to undergo a conversion. Believing that the accident was God's punishment, he changed his attitude toward religion. He became observant, delighting in the ritual he had previously poked fun at. And he came to equate Judaism with socialism; each Saturday he would scour the outlying neighborhoods looking for rabbis who preached socialism. His efforts were not always successful. It became a family joke: "Papa is running out of rabbis."

Ironically, my father's accident, if it had to be, was well-timed. It 'was 1930, the early depression, and the twenty-five thousand dollars' compensation we received for the accident was considered a small fortune.

My mother opened a dry goods store to supplement the family income. She was a good businesswoman. The store prospered. My father took on the kitchen chores. He helped as much as he could at home with his limited capacities. My sister and I were supposed to share the household duties. I hated housework and she enjoyed it. We had an agreement—I did her homework and she did my housework.

In many ways my father was childlike. My mother seemed to be his mother too. He never asserted himself as the "man of the house" because he realized the burden my mother carried. Yet my home was peaceful. My parents respected each other. The only trouble I can remember is my mother's resentment of all the time my father spent on his seemingly farfetched inventions.

Today we worry about the generation gap, but our mothers never thought of it. They lived in one world. We, their daughters, lived in another. We coexisted companionably. Among my mother's peers it was understood that if one's husband had a job and the family was well, there was nothing to complain about. They never worried if their children were happy, only if they were well fed. They never thought about "fulfillment" or "finding oneself." Therapy for any and all problems was work and health.

I grew into timid maturity. I was an earnest, conscientious student; I still regret that I never had the courage to cut even one class in high school. I'd envy the flagrant girls who dared hang out on street corners or who went riding with boys or who smoked. I remember locking myself in the bathroom to practice how to use a cigarette. I was so clumsy at it I soon gave up and never tried again.

Though I excelled in English, I took a commercial course because I was afraid of the sciences. I realize now that I should have gone to college. Perhaps I would have begun writing earlier. Though I was always reading, no one seemed to connect my compulsive reading with higher education.

My mother would lend money to her brother, an impoverished rabbi with a large family. It was understood that his children had to have an education befitting a rabbi's offspring. A bricklayer's daughter could get by with just reading.

When it was time to marry, I married. I tell it casually because it happened that way. The year 1945, the war winding down. I was corresponding with a boy stationed in Belgium. Though he was from my neighborhood, we had never met. He was a friend of a friend. When he came back to the States, he came to see me. My letters had intrigued him. He never left my side again.

Two days before the war officially ended, Joe and I eloped to City Hall. I look back and wonder what was my hurry. It seemed the thing to do. Everyone was getting married.

Unlike the Vietnam veterans, the GI's of World War II were all heroes. If Joe appeared quiet, I attributed it to his war experiences. He was in the Battle of the Bulge. His truck was shelled. He was the only survivor.

I romanticized his shyness. I waited for the battle trauma to recede so we could really communicate. I knew he loved me. I thought I loved him.

Joe's formal education, like mine, ended with high school. His interest in words was mostly confined to the sports page. I was a romantic; I didn't think our intellectual differences would matter. When I was with Joe, I didn't read or discuss what I had read because I sensed he was not interested. If I persisted he would say, "That's all you have on your mind, you don't know anything about the real world."

But when I was alone, it was as if I had never married. I could still lose myself in a book.

Apartments were scarce. We moved in with my family. My mother could never break through Joe's shyness, but my father and he became good friends.

A year later our first child, Beverly, was born. Then we were able to get an apartment in my mother's building. This was the beginning of conflict with my mother which has continued over the years. We never openly quarreled, but I sensed her disappointment in how I managed my home and my family. My mother equated good housekeeping with virtue. She could not understand my negative attitude toward housekeeping. I did it because I had to. Unlike most of the other women I knew, I derived no pleasure or satisfaction from it.

My mother's theory was, "First finish all your household chores. Then read." But to me the task of cleaning was eternal. Whenever I finished, it would be time to begin all over again and so I interspersed my cleaning and cooking and laundry with my reading. Housework to me was like the mythological rock of Sisyphus. I would push it away, but it would only roll back again. Endlessly.

My mother felt it her duty to help me with my work. She would come into my house, see the dishes in the sink, and wash them before even taking her coat off. Before I was awake, she would knock at my door, eager to do my laundry or shop for me. I resented her help because it only served to delineate my shortcomings. But I could not hurt her feelings by telling her to let me manage alone.

If we had not lived so close, my mother's disapproval would not have mattered. But she was always on hand to point out my faults, always under the guise of "for your own good." Not until I began to write would I overcome the sense of inadequacy my mother instilled in me. I have even been able to develop a sense of humor about housekeeping, to poke fun at the ladies with the neat houses who seem to find an almost orgiastic pleasure in discussing housework.

When Beverly was two, I gave birth to Ellen. My father died soon afterward. I was so immersed in caring for my children I don't remember mourning for him then. The loss hit me a few months later. I felt I had lost a friend. I had always identified with him. We were both dreamers and impractical while my mother's head sat squarely on her shoulders. Now whenever I came across an interesting idea I would still say to myself, "I'll tell Papa about this," then realize he was gone, there was no one to tell.

The years passed quickly. I gave birth to a son, Steven. I do not remember being discontented or frustrated or feeling trapped in the role of mother and housewife. At that time having families was the "in" thing. The media played up family togetherness. The women's movement with its searching questions about motherhood was still to come.

The unknown creature slept soundly within. My life seemed to flow smoothly; there were no disturbing ripples. If Joe and I didn't have much to talk about besides the family and household affairs, it didn't matter. The children filled the empty spots. Joe's shyness and introversion extended to our daughters, but I was used to it by now. Our son was close to his father. He trailed him like a shadow, though Joe rarely showed him affection. I talked and gave affection for both of us. If something big was missing from our relationship, from my life, I didn't notice. Occasionally I would daydream about writing, but when I tried to write I had nothing to say.

These were my innocent years. I enjoyed caring for the children. I didn't learn the facts of life—that having children can be fraught with heartache—until they were teen-agers. During their childhood I rarely worried about their futures. I assumed that their lives would be like mine—school, work, marriage. They would just shift from one stage to another as the time came to do so.

This was the 1950s. There was no drug problem, at least not among middle-class kids. Drugs, we thought, were only used by the underprivileged. There was no student unrest, no burning of bras. The country was recuperating from the war. The civil rights movement was just beginning to stir. Vietnam was an obscure spot on the map.

Occasionally I would read about juvenile delinquency, but it had no meaning for me. If I thought about it at all, I blamed the parents for neglecting their children. I knew I was a good mother, my children would not cut out.

*   *   *

My first life ended and my second began when my oldest daughter entered high school. Until then Bev had never given us cause for serious concern. She had been a fair student, she had many friends. I assumed she was happy. She was rarely moody or sullen or rebellious. I took it for granted that to be a mother was pleasant and easy. Now I was to lose this grant.

Bev became restless; staying home was like being imprisoned. She cut classes, she lost interest in school. She dropped her old friends and found others who were as daring as she had become. Instead of going to school she would hang out on street corners. Bev did all the things I never dared to do as a teen-ager. She even looked like the girls I had envied—slim, pretty, and outgoing.

The drug culture, which was to envelop the middle class, was just beginning. Bev and her group experimented with drugs the way earlier generations experimented with tobacco and liquor. I did not know how to discipline her. I had never needed to before. I did what many parents did and do. I pretended that I didn't see what was going on. I told myself she was going through a difficult adolescence. She was becoming one of the delinquent children I used to see on the streets and mutter about self-righteously. I had been disdainful of parents who allowed their children to be so undisciplined. I had wondered where those kids' parents *were*. Now I knew. We were at home, hiding our heads like ostriches, hoping that if we didn't see what was happening, it would go away. Guilt set in. But what was I guilty of? Philosophers blame society, but mothers blame themselves.

In the midst of my concern about Bev I became pregnant again. At this time, 1964, abortions were still illegal. Although I could have had one for medical reasons and because of my age, Joe and I felt pregnancy was God's will. It never occurred to us even to consider an abortion.

This pregnancy was different from my others. I had no patience for the necessary contemplative preparation for another child. I was always depressed, torn between fretting about Bev and brooding about the future of the new baby. I was losing my confidence as a mother.

The first time Bev came home stoned I realized that she needed professional help. I could not turn my head away any longer. In my ninth month I took my unwilling daughter to a psychiatrist. He was a kind, elderly man who patted my hand and joked about my pregnancy. He said, "Don't worry so much about your daughter. She is suffering from a minor ailment called 'self-limiting immaturity.' " It would take ten years of our lives before she outgrew this ailment.

I came home feeling relieved, but the next day the high school dean called me in for a conference. He suggested I sign Bev out of school, with the implied threat that he would expel her if she didn't leave voluntarily. She had lost all interest in her studies. He felt that she would only get into one scrape after another if she stayed.

Perhaps I should have protested, asked for guidance or for time to think, but I was exhausted with the weight of the baby. I kept seeing myself trudging along the halls of the school obviously pregnant, with my reluctant daughter in tow. I had had enough. I wearily signed the papers.

A few weeks later I gave birth to a healthy, husky boy, Corey. The new baby brought with him new luck. After struggling for many years, Joe and his partner finally became successful in business, operating several lucrative gas stations. We moved into a new home, a few miles away from my mother. In spite of my worries about Bev, I was able to relax a bit, away from my mother's critical eyes.

For the first time since my marriage, I did not have to worry about money. Joe encouraged me to buy things for myself, for the house. He insisted I have household help. When he decided to buy an expensive car, I was uneasy. I said, "It would be nice, but can we afford it? The children always need—"

He interrupted me. "Listen to me. I've worked hard all my life. Now I've reached a point where I can live well. All you ever worry about is the children, the children. We are also entitled to pleasures. It's time you learned how to live."

Telling everyone it was a present for me, he bought the car.

By now most of my friends were returning to the business world. Their children were maturing, becoming independent. The women resumed their careers as bookkeepers and secretaries. They were entering a new phase while I seemed to be standing still—even moving backward. I had to stay home to take care of the new baby. I was so preoccupied with Bev's problems I tended Corey automatically. My love for him was tinged with self-pity.

Intellectually I understood that I was not the only one who had a child involved with drugs. Emotionally, however, I only thought of myself as Bev's mother—as if Bev were an extremity of mine, another arm, another leg, which I couldn't control. When she hurt I hurt.

If I attempted to talk to Joe about how badly I felt, he would say, impatiently, "The more you talk, the worse you make it."

I could not understand his objective attitude, his detachment. I would say, "But aren't you frantic also? She's your child too."

"I am worried about her. She needs help, but I have to make a living for the family. If I carry on like you, we'll all starve. You've got to take hold of yourself."

I knew he was right. I was grateful that at least one of us was strong, but I could neither put aside nor push under the gnawing pain and fear.

Because Bev presented a veneer of stability she was able to find office work easily. The jobs never lasted. After a few weeks she would come in late or not at all. She would always be high, as if the pressure of responsibility were too much to handle without the prop of pills. Each time she found a new job I would be optimistic. Each time she lost it I would panic.

I knew Bev needed regular counseling, but she would never cooperate, never keep appointments. We were told that it was a waste of time and money unless she herself wanted help. Finally one psychologist suggested that perhaps the whole family needed guidance. I did not think much of the idea. There was nothing wrong with our family, I thought. But I was desperate. Reluctantly, I made an appointment with an agency specializing in family therapy.

Casually I had met and married Joe. Casually too I met Dr. H., the man who was to play such an important part in my becoming a writer. I was not impressed at our first meeting. How could this slim young man, younger than I was, know the pain I felt? Dr. H. spoke softly with a Midwestern accent. Evidently he was a WASP. I thought of myself as a typical Jewish mother whose existence is vindicated solely through her children.

Dr. H. appeared so unassuming, with his horn-rimmed glasses over solemn brown eyes, that for the first few visits I could not remember his name or even what he looked like. Yet he was able not only to relieve my pain but to give legitimacy to the creature within. We were to have a Svengali-Trilby relationship. He was to tell me to write and I wrote.

At our first session Dr. H. introduced himself and invited us to find seats in the comfortable, softly lit office. I sat alone on one side of the room, Joe and the children on the other side.

Immediately I began to tell the doctor about Bev. Far from commiserating with me, he didn't seem particularly moved.

"Tell me about yourself. What kind of family life do you have?"

I became impatient. I felt he was asking the wrong questions.

"You don't understand, the problem is Bev, not us. How can we help her?"

For the first time Dr. H. raised his voice. "*You* don't seem to understand. Bev is only part of what's happening in your family. Unless you learn to cope with your daughter you will destroy yourself and the rest of the family. Nothing is gained by your hysteria, your overreacting to whatever Bev does. She must lead her own life. You can't live for her. Now tell me about yourself, not about your daughter."

The therapy was actually a course in learning about ourselves. I saw myself through the eyes of my family. I was surprised and hurt, but in the end I discovered who I really was and what I could be.

I had pictured myself as softhearted, maternal, ineffective—an unappreciated martyr. But Joe said, "Anne should never have married. Her head is always somewheres else. She is apart from the family even though she is always home. If we sit in the living room, she sits in the kitchen by herself, reading. Even now she sits away from us."

I expected my children to defend me, but they agreed with Joe. I could not understand why they were picking on me. We were here because of Bev.

I talk as easily as I breathe. Now I had so much to say in my defense I could have talked the whole session—I felt I could speak for everyone—and would have. But Dr. H., losing patience, finally said, in a casual, almost teasing way, "Why don't you write about how you feel so the others will have a chance to talk?"

"Why don't you write . . ." A few simple words and my life changed.

My first letters were full of self-pity. "No one understands me. If my daughters loved me, they would clean their room. I devote my life to my family and get nothing but criticism in return."

Gradually the letters became more reflective. "Perhaps Joe is right. I do stay apart from my family at times. It isn't because I don't love them. It's because I must keep part of my life for myself. They aren't interested in what interests me. Though I am surrounded by people, I am beginning to realize how lonely I am. I feel as if I live in two houses. In one I am huddled together with my family. In the other I am all alone, looking for someone to talk to."

Every few weeks I would write a letter. Each time I finished, no matter how depressed I may have been, I felt more peaceful, less lonely. Previously, I had absorbed experience and trauma like a sponge. Now I discovered that writing not only brought a sort of order to my life but gave me a sense of accomplishment I had never felt before. My shortcomings as a housekeeper and as a mother became unimportant. Creativity replaced the sponge.

The letters were becoming a carefully written journal. I slowly developed my own style. I would not be content unless I found the exact word, the exact phrase, to express myself. I would rewrite many times.

Whatever happened in my family, no matter how emotionally involved I was, part of me coolly stood aside, making mental notes. I was both the participant and the audience in the drama of my life. In the midst of anger or hurt or aggravation, I would be thinking of how to write about it.

I became so involved with the writing I stopped panicking about Bev; she became more relaxed because I didn't pick on her so much. There was still tension between us. She still had her problems. She could not hold a job, she still took pills. She drifted. But I was able to cope with her. The pain was lessening. Bev's adventures became ink for my pen. She once remarked, "If it wasn't for me, you would never have had anything to write about." I grudgingly agreed with her.

We continued family therapy for about a year. Then Joe, with Dr. H.'s approval, decided it was time to stand by ourselves. I had always complained that Joe could not express his feelings. Yet in therapy he spoke freely. I realized for the first time how concerned he had been about me, even more than he was about Bev. I did not realize how "neurotic" I had become.

Dr. H. was like a magician. Deftly, quietly—yes, magically—he brought our family closer. All of us benefitted from the therapy except Bev. Change in her would not come for several years, not until she was ready and independently willing to help herself. We could not do it for her. I finally understood that if I was to be able to help and support and accept my daughter, I had to help and support and accept myself first.

I continued to write to Dr. H. The following Christmas I received a card from him. Svengali writing to Trilby.

"I look forward to your letters. You are slowly finding yourself. You have a responsibility to develop your talents as a writer."

Me . . . a writer? I wrote back: "I only write to crystallize my life. I hoped you would find my letters worthwhile, but it didn't matter. Creating them was satisfaction enough. The more I write, the more compelled I am to write, as if an unknown force was prodding me."

Dr. H.'s encouragement was another turning point in my life.

I found myself comparing writing to painting. My need to write was my brush, the journal my box of paints. How was I to use them? It was time to stop doing only portraits of myself and my family. I wanted to broaden my vision, to include the landscape of my life. I had to learn how to transmute my experiences so that my work would have structure and dimension.

At the age of forty-seven I wanted to go back to school, but Joe's response to this idea was predictable.

"I can't see it, this foolishness. I could understand if you wanted to learn a skill like stenography or bookkeeping or even sewing. But writing? I work so hard for you, why can't you be content? What are you looking for?"

"Joe, I appreciate all you give me, but you do it for yourself as well. Sometimes I'm jealous because you enjoy your work. You have pride in yourself, in what you have accomplished. I have nothing except keeping house and raising the children. I've finally found work which makes me feel worthwhile too. Maybe it is foolishness but I want to try. If I don't try there will only be living through you and the children."

I spoke bravely, but in the back of my head I heard the voices of my mother and my mother-in-law. "If a man makes a good living and the family is well, then what are you complaining about?"

I wondered what would happen if Joe suddenly began to write, slyly taking notes, buying books and paper and typewriter ribbons, reading when he should be sleeping, wanting to go to school, having a life I could not share. Would I put my hands on my hips and say, "You must be crazy. How can you suddenly become a writer?"

It is unfair of women to expect immediate acceptance and tolerance from their men when they undergo a metamorphosis as I did. Joe felt bewildered and possibly threatened. He would say, shaking his head in puzzlement, "I didn't marry a writer, I married an ordinary girl."

I beat down guilt as one would beat down an igniting spark. I felt guilty toward my mother, my mother-in-law, my husband and my children. I felt guilty for writing at all, even more for writing about them as if I were exhibiting our lives. But the living creature was emerging. If I didn't fight for what it wanted, it would deteriorate into grayness.

We compromised. Instead of going to school, I enrolled in a correspondence course. I had taken the first step in nurturing that living creature.

For an assignment I wrote about an incident involving Bev and me when she had taken an overdose and was hospitalized. I sent the story to the *New York Times*. Instead of getting a rejection slip my story was accepted and published on the Op-Ed page of the newspaper. A few months later it was reprinted in the *Reader's Digest*. I made seven hundred dollars. I knew how hard it was for a beginner to break into print. It was as if I had won the lottery.

Receiving money was another turning point. I shall never forget the look on Joe's face when I showed him the checks. I saw a glimmer of respect for my work. If someone was willing to pay me for this "nonsense," then perhaps it wasn't nonsense after all. Others too seemed to assume that getting money made me a professional writer. I received offers from several publishers to write a book based on my story. I could not do it. There was too much about writing itself that I had yet to learn.

I knew now what I must do. A lonely correspondence course was not enough; I had to go to school—with or without Joe's consent. I wanted to learn the craft of writing.

I enrolled in courses at the New School and entered a new world. At home I thought of myself as an eccentric middle-aged woman wanting to write, when she should be content dwelling in the core of her family, basking in her husband's success. At school, however, I met many women like myself. I was not eccentric; I was only alone because I had no one at home who was like me, who shared my needs.

Critics of creative-writing courses say that good writing cannot be taught, that it is an innate talent. They may be right, but for me school took away my feeling of isolation. At home, if I talked about my writing problems to Joe or my friends, I sensed they were thinking, "Anne is involved in an unreal world while I'm involved in the real world because I work. I'll pretend to be interested."

Guiltily, I felt that writing and school were not an avocation but a private vice.

My life has become polarized since I've been going to school. I live on two levels. On one level I continue to be a housewife and mother, still scurrying in prosaic circles. I still worry about Bev. I still wish that Joe were tuned into me. I still wish I could run an efficient household. But on another level I am an explorer, an adventuress, mapping new courses for my life. I do not find it necessary to shut myself off from the world in order to write. My world generates my creativity; I carry "a room of my own" in my head.

I do not yet have the discipline to sit at my desk at an appointed hour each day. I do not know how to seek out my ideas. I must wait till my thoughts come to me. My mind is an uncharted sea. I am like a beachcomber waiting for the waves to wash up shells of ideas. The creativity works independently of what I would like it to do. I cannot force it. I must be patient.

Perhaps it is premature to call myself a writer. However, I cannot otherwise describe the sense of excitement, of anticipation, when I am at my typewriter. I even procrastinate before beginning to write because I enjoy the feeling of being pregnant with ideas and want to prolong it. When I have completed work to my satisfaction, when I've put on paper words that say what I feel, I am at peace with myself and with my family and with my world. For a few days my head is blissfully empty. Then gradually the waves roll in again and I must pick and choose from the glittering shells.

I don't know how other women juggle their lives to nurture family and muse. A man will find someone to wash his socks and prepare food and keep the children quiet, but women are conditioned to perform these time-consuming tasks for themselves—and for others. There was only one Alice B. Toklas.

How does a woman deal with the physical and emotional minutiae of her days and yet find time and energy to sit at a desk and spell out her visions? Perhaps I ponder foolishly. The strong compulsion to write, driven by the living creature, may overcome the obstacles.

I came to writing through Bev. As I began to get involved in that writing I found myself able to deal more rationally with my daughter and her problems. My life was no longer pinpointed on hers. My work occupied me now. I could give Bev space. She was released from the oppressive knowledge that I was affected by everything she did. She was freed by this psychological distance just as I gained leeway from my own mother when I moved away from her geographically.

Three years have passed since I made my commitment to writing, and it is also three years since my daughter finally made her own commitment to getting well. She awoke one morning acutely aware that she was wasting her life.

On the advice of her psychiatrist she signed herself into a psychiatric hospital. She was discharged six months later. Since then she has been on her own, supporting herself. Now she has a well-paying office job. She lives with a young man whom she plans to marry.

Bev is building a new life. At times it is a struggle not to fall back on the prop of pills, but as the days and weeks and months pass she gains strength. I share her triumphs.

My family looks back on the past ten years and feels that we were all on a voyage into unexplored territories. The knowledge we gained about ourselves made the turbulent trip worthwhile.

The realities of my life are no longer a cause of self-pity. I am slowly achieving a sense of objectivity, using the realities as a springboard to creativity. The truths that I am a desultory housekeeper, that my marriage was not heaven-made, that my child has given me pain, have become the jigsaw pieces to be assembled in my individual puzzle.

I no longer envy my friends who earn money while I am still on my husband's dole. If I had a nine-to-five job, I would not be able to devote as much time as I would like to my real work, writing. Unwittingly, my down-to-earth, practical, hardheaded husband has become a patron of the arts, subsidizing me so that I may pursue my new calling. The euphoria—that I am able to write at all—is subsiding as I contemplate the difficult road ahead. I will not turn back.

Anne Lasoff

Contradictions

Susan Harding

Marilyn Young

PERHAPS because I am a historian, the only way I can understand the contradictory and ambivalent relationship I have to the work I do (or even to work as such) is historically. As it happens with most people, my first idea of what work is came from my family. Work was hard, usually tedious, always ill-paid. It was what men did so that women and children could eat. My father worked. The first job I remember my father having was in the Railway Mail Service, a now defunct unit of the post office. When I was very young he worked "on the road," sorting mail as the train moved from New York to mythical places like Chicago, Washington, Buffalo. He would be away overnight and we'd get post cards. I only remember one: a picture of Niagara Falls labeled hot and cold with a message claiming that he'd had a fine shower there that morning. I can distinctly recall the sensation of believing and not believing simultaneously. His job was not without a certain romance and danger; when he came home he would talk about the split-second timing needed to hook the mailbag from the station as the train passed through barely slowing down. There were regular civil service tests that he studied for with an elaborate system of index cards and large egg cartons into which, chanting the names of the stations, he would toss the appropriate card. I don't know how many stations he had to memorize—thousands, it seemed—but my first sense of the power of words, any words, came from hearing his voice calling out the towns of America as I fell asleep. Later he worked in the office at Grand Central and Penn stations. It was, I suppose, a kind of promotion. But the work was routine and boring to a degree that seemed sometimes to strain his mind beyond bearing.

For a time my mother also had an outside job, but I remember little about it. I am told that my maternal grandmother took care of me when my mother was working—easy enough since we lived in the same building. But my grandfather objected, there was no alternative child-care, and she was forced to quit. From that point until I was about thirteen my mother "didn't work." Then, when my younger sister was six or seven, she passed the necessary exams and took a job as a school secretary. We got by through an elaborate system of juggled schedules—which became even more complex when my mother gave birth to yet another daughter—a system that involved my father working nights, my dropping the baby off at an aunt's house on the way to high school, my mother taking my middle sister to school with her, and so on.

Two peculiar characteristics were associated with my mother's working. First, as opposed to my father's having a job, her working was bad for us. It was "common wisdom" at the time that juvenile delinquents flowed from working mothers as the night the day. This notion had a significant impact on my younger sister and was mildly upsetting to me as well, though it was clear that neither of us was cut out for delinquency. Second, my mother's job was defined as interfering with her primary responsibilities to us and my father. Before she started on the job, all our family fights centered around money—or rather, the lack of it. These were terrible, bitter explosions, difficult to explain if you haven't experienced what a lack of money (which is not the same thing as poverty) can do to people in America. The foolish spending of some trifling amount provoked monumental, irrational fury. With my mother working for pay, the issue was different. Now there was much more money around. The problem was that she "brought her work home," that dinner might be late, or the laundry undone. "You owe them nothing," my father would shout. "It's just a job." Of course since she didn't get overtime, the office work she did after hours was indeed exploitative, and he was right to be angry. But there was something else involved too. It was as if the school work she did at home was on *his* time—and he wasn't paying her to do P.S. 183's final payroll, but to take care of us.

In a sense, I was raised with the hope that I wouldn't have to work, because I would become a professional—a doctor or a lawyer. The irony of this is that my father had the utmost contempt for the American medical and legal professions, a contempt I had no difficulty sharing, then or since. What marked such people was not only their high incomes, but the fact that what they did to earn them was not, in our sense, "work" at all. Work was what my father wrote to me about my first year away at college. His job, he said, was a prison. He went to it as one goes to death. He was doing time, a thirty-year sentence. Yet what was his crime? I would become enraged at the human waste explicit in those letters. The mindlessness of his job, the years and years of it stretching ahead of him, the viciousness of a world (later I would learn to call it a system, and name that system capitalism) that condemned people like my father to lives of nearly intolerable frustration made the experience of the elite woman's college I attended more than mildly contradictory.

How I got to Vassar College is a separate but related topic. Although all I knew of private high schools came from the back pages of the Sunday *Times* magazine section, my father—in pursuit of the medical or legal chimera—had often talked to me about private colleges. Vassar, he said, was where the children of Hollywood stars went. For scholarship, Barnard and Bryn Mawr were the best; there were, he told me, scholarship funds for good students, and if I also won a New York State Regents fellowship, it might be possible to swing Barnard. By my senior year in high school the discussion changed; now he said that Brooklyn College was "plenty good enough" and, in one furious battle, told me I should go to work and "give money into the house the way other children do." Part of the problem was the application fee each college required. This was a gamble in which the family stood to lose as much as fifty dollars if I failed to get admitted *and* receive scholarship funds. And we didn't fool around with fifty dollars. In any event, a high school guidance counselor put pressure on my parents to fill out the forms. I am certain they would have done so anyhow. My father wrote, in my name, truly touching appeals for financial aid. I went to a series of terrifying interviews—wearing, as per the guidance counselor's instructions, a small borrowed hat and a pair of gloves. The only catastrophe occurred when I looked down at my shoes in the full light of Saratoga Avenue's elevated subway stop and discovered I was wearing one brown and one blue suede pump. But it was too late to go home and change.

Vassar came through with enough money so that with the Regents fellowship and a five-hundred-dollar loan, I could attend. Given what it would have cost to commute from my neighborhood to Barnard, it almost seemed cheaper to live away from home. By my sophomore year a clerical error resulted in my receiving thirty-five dollars in cash over and above the scholarship. Summer work paid for clothes, books, vacation trips home. Clothes were a problem. That first year my mother took me to the College Shop at Abraham & Straus and also, if I remember correctly, Lord & Taylor—the latter an incredible journey beyond our accustomed turf. I got a polo coat (blue—which was, that year, quite the wrong color), several pairs of flannel Bermuda shorts, some shirts, a collar pin (again, an arrow—when small gold circles were proper), and, most disastrously, a pair of unspeakably collegiate plaid pajamas. On one of my first nights at college a knowledgeable freshman said with a laugh, "I bet you got those specially for college." I never wore them in public again.

The trouble was, I did not want to be a doctor. When, as a direct result of an inability to work a balance scale, I dropped freshman chemistry after two weeks, my family reluctantly agreed that there must be other ways to earn a living. At first I threatened to major in English literature, but I was deterred by my parents' depression-born conviction that that would prepare me to clerk in a shoe store and nothing else. (Were shoe stores specially staffed with English B.A.'s in the thirties? Or is it just Brooklyn folklore?) Later I majored in history, which for reasons still obscure, seemed to all three of us a more responsible choice.

College cut my world in half. At sixteen, I moved from a working-class Jewish neighborhood in Brooklyn, where you took a subway to look at the grass, to this residential park called Vassar College. And yet, despite an almost unnamable pleasure at what was happening to my mind, I related to college as *work*. Only one letter home survives from my freshman year; I can hardly believe a real person wrote it:

Dear Folks,
Today is a very busy day. I'm sitting in on Miss Nevins' class at 1:30. At 2:30 I get my first painting lesson from one of the talented freshmen here, who also teaches painting at Martha's Vineyard in the summer. Then I'll squeeze in some homework. At 4:30 the Davison baseball team gets out on the field for some practice. Tonight at 8:15 the Writers Club meets and I shall read my poetry . . . All this activity will just leave me time for my History and French homework, if that (both not due till Monday). Friday night there is a meeting of the Human Rights Committee. This means both Friday and Saturday nights will be occupied. My English paper will be worked on every waking hour in between then. Sandy Spatt got me a blind date (for several weeks hence). However I would much rather spend that weekend with you (hate blind dates anyhow). If you can't come up, I shall probably turn that date down anyhow since my 1500 w. English paper is due that week (but I shall finish it that weekend) and my 25 page History paper—with only 17 days to work on it— starts that weekend. At any rate, if you decide to come up great, I'll squeeze the work in somewhere. If not I shall have a wonderful week-end of research in the libe about some obscure 19th century topic. (I mean it about wonderful, I told you I love that sort of thing.)

The letter ends with a request for them to let me know if they want me to go to a seder with a Jewish family in town—this, to relieve anxieties aroused earlier in the year that I might convert out of a deep infatuation with the literary merits of the Gospel According to St. John.

Look at it. I want them to understand—no, *admit*—that I too am *working,* not playing. Only then could I bear the guilt. Here I was, really, doing nothing but pleasuring myself in the library. I knew they didn't think it was work; I didn't think so myself. So I had to transform it *into* work. That first year I reported every paper and course grade I got. I brought home final grades like salary checks. In high school we had all "worked for grades." What other medium of exchange was there? In Brooklyn we knew each other's grade-point average to the second decimal point; if those points were truly earned, and not the result of a teacher's favoritism, we respected the person the way the Chinese do "advanced producers" in agriculture and industry. For the first year I openly did the same at Vassar. There were embarrassments of course. Coming out of our first French test, I turned to Marcia Kennedy and asked her the classic Brooklyn high school question: "Whadja get?" To which she scornfully replied: "We don't do that here. This is a *college,* not a high school."

Gradually I was made to feel ashamed of the way I worked. I learned that one was not supposed to work for grades, or for anything other than the sheer pleasure of learning. We were not preparing ourselves for a world of work or wages. We were, it seemed, engaged in some other enterprise altogether, and if I was to belong there, I must discover what it was. I don't think I ever did. Instead, I tried to learn proper manners. Though burning to know, I rarely asked a fellow student her grades, and I disguised (to some degree) just how many hours I put in. But the more I accepted, however superficially, this ruling-class view of women's education, the more guilty I felt about what I had left behind at home. For how could I justify to myself what I was doing at college if it did not, in some measure, compare with the efforts my parents made, every day of their lives, to survive. Bad enough that I could experience quintessential springs at Vassar while my sisters mucked about in the dreariness of East Flatbush. Only some demonstration that I too toiled relieved me.

Summers were somewhat easier because they were less confused. Each June I would lie my way into a fairly well-paid secretarial job, swearing on all that was holy (and faking an occasional document) that I had no intention of going to college in the fall; and each fall I would sadly inform the boss that my family was "moving to Florida" and I would have to quit. (Once I suffered the acute embarrassment of being given a goodbye party and gifts from the other "girls" in my typing pool.) For those three months or so, I found myself in the familiar world of my parents. This was real work. I hated the job, the boss, the subway, the heat. That's what working was all about: a stubborn hatred, a reluctant resignation, and, somewhere in it too, pleasure in my typing skill, my friendships with co-workers, the way the thing ended at a certain hour, the weekend. Finally, I knew I didn't have an indeterminate sentence, merely a straight ninety days. Anyone can do ninety days.

By my junior year, my parents and I had made a not inconsiderable discovery. College professors, less munificently rewarded than doctors or lawyers, still seemed to be able to lead the good life without seriously working. This realization crystallized one weekend when my parents came to visit and we all had lunch with a favorite history teacher. He and his wife and two children lived in a substantial white house near the campus. They were clearly comfortably off, he loved what he was doing, his wife seemed content, and the kids had the run of the campus. What puzzles me now is whether my parents envisioned that I would be the professor or the wife? I had other models at college, but even to discuss them briefly with my parents led to terrible fights. I was much enamored, for example, of the life of another history professor. She was I suppose in her late fifties and shared a house with a woman colleague. She seemed to lead a life of enviable completeness, deeply involved in both her teaching and her research. In a word more commonly used in the fifties than it is now, my roommate and I thought of her as "fulfilled." My sense (and admiration) of this teacher enraged (and frightened) my parents, especially my mother. And what of marriage? And children? How could a little white-haired old maid seem anything but pathetic to me? This was most confusing; clearly I could never become the male history professor, but it seemed equally obvious that I *should* not become the female one. So, mouthing pieties about combining "marriage and career," I went to graduate school.

It is difficult to explain what graduate school was like in the late fifties, particularly at a place like Harvard. There was a sense of certainty about everything—at least among the people I knew. Few of us doubted the legitimacy of what we were doing, the splendors of the institution to which we were attached, the heady feeling of being at the heart of the heart of the matter. To my parents (and me), going to Harvard was like money in the bank; I'd never starve now. I was living according to my own schedule and, eventually, in my own apartment. I had picked a field on the basis of the generous financial support it offered, reasoning to myself that I was interested in history as such—whose history didn't really matter. I had no responsibilities beyond learning what I needed to know for the degree. And I no longer felt especially guilty. For this was clearly professional training —it was work and, in the form of fellowships, I was well paid.

Perhaps because I was in a small department, or because of the nature of the man who chaired it, I did not experience in graduate school the humiliation so many women of my generation suffered. John King Fairbank chose both "sons" and "daughters" from among his students. Fewer daughters, to be sure, but those singled out enjoyed the same privileges as their brothers. He ran a protective patriarchal establishment within which I was free to extend myself and to achieve. He pointed with pride to one of our predecessors who had successfully pursued a career while happily married to someone in the field. Few of us knew at the time the rather high price the woman had had to pay. We were not told of the compromises she had had to make in her work life, nor of her belated recognition.

The relative ease of those years was also a result of my experience at a women's college like Vassar. It never occurred to me not to speak in class, or indeed, to think of myself in terms of gender at all. I was a graduate student who happened to be female. True, I poured the tea at weekly department gatherings, but as this often saved me from tedious conversation, I did it gratefully.

Work on my thesis went slowly. I abandoned the careful system of note taking that the Vassar History Department considered one of its great contributions to academic scholarship. Instead, I used unwieldly looseleaf books, index cards of every size, and the back of an occasional paper bag. After a year of this, what would eventually become my completed dissertation was a mess of often unidentifiable scraps of paper. A persistent fantasy for months was of a long, say, five-year, sleep, from which I would awake with a finished thesis, a family, a job, a house—who knows, even a dog. Instead, within three years of my arrival at Harvard, I married a fellow graduate student, did not complete my thesis, lived in one of Cambridge's remaining cold-water flats, and did not even consider owning a pet.

Marriage did not change my relation to graduate school. Now, to be sure, I was a graduate student who happened to be a wife, but this *added* an identity. I learned to cook and liked it, not because I liked cooking but because I was a *wife* cooking. Partly, I had a sense of playing house (which may be the best way to do it). I got a heavy dose of the real thing when we left Cambridge for Tokyo in 1961. Ernie had accepted a two-year job there as a kind of private secretary to the ambassador and, despite the Bay of Pigs, we went. We lived well outside the American community, and our friends were mainly students—Japanese and American—of one kind or another. But for the first time Ernie and I lived in utterly separate worlds: his, a world of work, visible, paid, connected; mine, a world of make-work, invisible, unpaid, and hopelessly disconnected. I traveled some on my own, learned a fair amount of Japanese, tried to order my days. And yet I can remember whole weeks when it seems to me I did nothing but wait for him to get home from work.

By our second year in Japan I had more or less come to terms with my life there. I worked steadily on my thesis, completing the relatively minor research that remained to be done and banging out chapters at regular intervals. There was, to be sure, a fair amount of cognitive dissonance. Every couple of weeks or so I'd take a set of chapters to the Sanno Hotel, a downtown PX establishment. In my tailor-made maternity clothes, I would first mail the package and then, in the extravagantly air-conditioned lounge, order several drinks (paid for in scrip) while I waited for Ernie to finish work and drive us both home. Embassy and military wives ("dependents") would wander by, their hair identical with my own since we all had it set weekly at the Imperial. Some were fresh from class—flower arranging, *sumie*, tea ceremony—and carried the fruit of their labors with them, as I had just mailed mine to Cambridge. I was not them, but I wasn't not them either.

In the middle of our time in Japan, I gave birth to a daughter who dazzled us both. I nursed her publicly up and down the main islands of Japan—and in the ambassador's residence as well. At no time can I recall looking ahead to what it was going to be like once we returned to Cambridge. Subtly, I had become not a graduate-student-who-happened-to-be-a-wife, but a wife-and-mother-who-was-finishing-up-her-degree. Even now, I don't know quite why or how this happened. I think I let it happen gratefully; our life was now Ernie's responsibility. I would not have to grow up for a while yet. A pleasure.

Our return to Cambridge obscured this change for a time. For almost two years I dipped back into graduate school again, doing further research and revising the thesis for publication. I worked at night, and between three-thirty and five-thirty in the afternoon, when a succession of teen-agers came to sit for my daughter (whose mournful cries for me, I was told—but disbelieved out of guilt—stopped the instant I turned the corner on my bike). My feeling about my work was changing, however. Harvard looked less good to me, its standards and values not merely open to doubt, but shoddy, hypocritical, even murderous. It was one thing to argue about Vietnam with foreign service officers; it was quite another to discover indifference—or worse—among professors and fellow graduate students. I remember one argument in particular. It was 1963; in my professor's tidy living room, over the tea, which I no longer poured, a superstar graduate student told me that the United States must send a million men to Vietnam, occupy the place, and "reform" it. There were, I knew, Harvard men in the Justice Department who ignored what was happening to SNCC workers, and Harvard men in the State Department who lied about Vietnam; indeed, there was a Harvard man in the presidency.

We began to meet people whose engagement in and with the world was unlike anything we had known before—civil rights activists who worked in the South, or in support groups in the North, and who made that work an integral part of their lives through what they wrote, the groups they organized, the courses they taught. Through Howard and Roz Zinn, whom we had met before leaving for Japan, the focus of our lives gradually shifted. Our new friends were not all graduate students or faculty, and those who were, had, like Howie, made of their politics and their work a solid wholeness. I admired them tremendously, mingled with them as though proximity would induce transformation.

And yet, in the main, my life changed little. I had done it all more or less according to the rules. My book manuscript, while nodding to the new radical approaches to American history, didn't really incorporate them. Each thing I did felt like a debt I was paying off. The thesis paid off the fellowship support I'd received to write it; the book paid off the expectations of those who had accepted the thesis; and the whole shape of my life, somehow, paid off my parents. By the winter of 1965, Ernie had finished his thesis and accepted a job at Dartmouth. No, that is not accurate. *We* accepted the job. After years of graduate work he desperately needed to engage in something that would make it real. We talked, briefly, about the lack of employment possibilities for me at what was then not only an all-male institution, staff and students, but a decidedly misogynous one. Yet I needed some reality too. I could not be the male history professor, nor, any longer, the single woman professor. Well then, I would be the male history professor's wife. A faculty wife.

At Dartmouth, I gave birth to our second child. Appropriately, as my mother had flown to Tokyo to oversee the birth of my daughter, my father came to New Hampshire to usher in my son. My odd pride in having a son was too deep to articulate.

My book manuscript had been returned with requests for revision. I could not imagine touching it again; only fitfully alive for me when I'd worked on it first, it now seemed altogether dead. Its subject, American policy in China at the turn of the century, was clearly relevant to the current course of U.S. actions in Asia, and yet I had neither the imagination nor the energy to weave the connections. I put the manuscript in a drawer, bought second-hand ski equipment, worked resentfully as a $2/per hour research assistant to a history professor, enjoyed the seasons, tried to learn to entertain properly, participated (as confidante to other women) in the first wave of counter-culture pressure on established marriages, smoked pot, played squash, learned to dance, grew fat, dieted, grew fat again. I can remember walking by the tennis courts on some outrageously sunny, cheerful day and feeling so overwhelmed with self-hatred it made my skin crawl. In such a mood, I wrote in a journal bought especially for the purpose but never filled: "How confused I still am. How unlike what thirty sounds like. How ineffective. I shall live out the rest of my life as if it weren't really happening and then die surprised . . . I have no proper work, and for me that is hard. And I grow lazier, mentally, by the hour."

Much later, in a women's consciousness-raising group, I spoke the bitterness of those years. But I think it is important to understand that I wasn't angry *then*. On the whole, I was happy. For many of us, I think, the value of CR lies precisely in the way it reveals to us aspects of our accepted past and, retrospectively, withdraws that acceptance.

I'm not sure now how much longer that Dartmouth life could have continued. Had we stayed longer I would probably have had another child or gotten a divorce. Rather, given the experience of friends, I would have had another child *and* gotten a divorce. Instead, midway in Ernie's term there we had a year off—a summer in England, the bulk of the year in Taiwan, a final summer in Sydney. Somewhat earlier I had accepted an invitation to do an essay based essentially on my thesis topic for an anthology an old graduate school friend was editing. I accepted not because I wanted to do the thing so much as because it lent reality to my erstwhile—and still cherished—identity as a professional historian. (After all, had not one of the senior historians at Dartmouth once introduced me to a dinner party as a "person in my own right"?) That summer in London, while my fifteen-year-old sister gave my four-year-old daughter exhaustive tours of the city, while Ernie worked in the Public Record Office, and the baby napped, I wrote the essay. I was beginning, very cautiously, to make the logical links between American imperialism past and present. The piece hedges; I was not trained at Harvard for nothing. But it was a beginning.

Taiwan was even better. At the cost of exploiting not one but several other women (cook, baby amah, washwoman, seamstress), I started to work again for the first time since graduate school. My thesis chairman, determined not to let any publishable thesis go to waste, had hired an editor without my knowledge. Once informed, guilt and flattery combined to drive me steadily through the manuscript revision to final publication. In addition, I taught for the first time; my students were a curious group of California State College students on a junior year abroad. We met in the basement lunchroom of a Kuomintang party university, and there (hoping we'd be overheard and admonished) we praised Mao and the Chinese revolution together. There was no domestic help in Sydney, but it didn't matter. I spent the time walking the city with the children, reading novels, lying on the winter beach, writing letters—it was a vacation, and for the first time in years, one I felt I had earned.

Dartmouth was different when we got back. It was the fall of 1967 and the smell of Vietnam was everywhere. The Students for a Democratic Society (SDS) had a good strong campus chapter; there were meetings to go to and new politically active people (one or two anyhow) on the faculty. One of them, Jonathan Mirsky, invited me to teach a class with him—which I did gratefully. True, most of my life was lived in other people's coffee breaks. While my daughter was at school, my son and I would go to the snack bar at Hopkins Center, where he would consume his constant, if singular, diet of potato chips and orange drink while I sat in on lunches, study breaks, afternoon coffee. Somewhat spuriously, I felt connected with a larger world—a world, moreover, which because of its imminent crisis, held out the possibility of personal as well as political integration. The notion of pursuing some logical monographic extension of my book now struck me as absurd. I needed to write about what was starting to make a nightmare of our lives—the war, and how and why it happened. More than that, I needed to talk, to teach, to join others in talking, teaching, struggling against the one enormous fact: Vietnam. There was some opportunity to do so at Dartmouth; there would be more in the future.

Nineteen sixty-eight turned out to be our last year at Dartmouth. Ernie had accepted a job at the University of Michigan. Part of the deal was a half-time research fellowship for me. I was suddenly reluctant to leave. On a brief visit, Ann Arbor had seemed frighteningly far away from home (loosely defined as "the East"), alien, ugly. On the other hand, it was the place where both SDS and the teach-ins had started, I might get a teaching job there, it was *also* good for the kids, and it was a better job for Ernie.

I have come now so close to the present, I find it difficult to continue. Writing truth about one's current life is even more difficult than attempting to do so about the past. Some of the changes I put into words at an Association of Asian Scholars panel on Vietnam and the Academy four years ago. I like what I said then—it is still true:

> Vietnam and my academic life . . . Really it is Vietnam and my progress from relative youth (I was twenty-three when I became aware of what was going on in Vietnam) to early middle age (I will be thirty-five next month). Many things have happened to me—marriage and children and no job and a job and conferences and vacations and so on. Were there no war I think I would now be very much what

I was when I arrived at Harvard as a first-year graduate student, in 1957: a slightly edgy Jewish overachiever, aspiring to the cool world of WASP life-style and scholarship, an aspiration I knew I could never really fulfill but whose shining beacon would have led me on from first monograph to second monograph, from one straight course on American–East Asian relations to the next.

Vietnam and the black liberation struggle in America changed the shape of my moral world. Professors, no matter how loved, who could not understand the meaning of these events, who could not bring themselves to protest—loudly, boldly—I found such professors difficult to to listen to on any issue. Such men (and they *were* all men) began to seem crippled to me—morally lame, grotesquely blind to the real world . . .

Academically, the war in Vietnam has meant a shift in my attention from the detailed exploration of Sino-American relations in a supposed ideological vacuum (which of course was not a vacuum at all, but filled with well-concealed a priori assumptions) to a conscious search for the roots of American imperialism. The war taught me to use that word without quotation marks and to try to understand its meaning. And further, I was led from foreign policy as such to American history itself, particularly the history of the dead decade that had shaped me and my contemporaries—1950 to 1960.

What I needed to know—what I now need to know—is how my country could commit the acts that haunted my childhood in the shape of goose-stepping Nazi soldiers and wicked scientists who bled Jewish children for fun and profit. I needed to know what kind of fellow countryman it was who, perhaps sitting in his fiberglass boat peacefully fishing one Sunday, snapped his fingers and said, pounding the gunnels, "Just the thing for cluster bombs!" Who *is* it who keeps *improving* our weapons? And why doesn't he speak with a thick German accent? Why does he look like you?

And then I read Section VI of Robert Bly's great poem, "The Teeth-Mother Naked at Last." I was speaking in a sunlit New York hotel assembly room, before a collection of academics, some of whom had been my teachers. It was a kind of goodbye to all that.

Since 1969 I have been teaching at a curious unit of the University of Michigan called the Residential College. Founded in 1968 as a way of reducing the pains of the "multiversity," the College incorporated what its founding fathers (not a mother in the bunch) thought were the very latest in educational innovations. Its faculty would be drawn entirely from the "parent institution," so that no student would suffer from second-class instruction. University professors who had, apparently, been longing to work really closely with undergraduates would have the opportunity to do so. Students would benefit from a small college atmosphere at the same time that they might avail themselves of the facilities of a great research institution. There was a stiff core

curriculum, almost entirely required, which would see students
through their first two years. Composed of massive lectures and small
sections, this would save money even as it ensured the handing down
of the finest values of Western civilization to new generations of students.

It was a bad time for planning good things for students. Within a
year, the first entering class decided that the core curriculum was
nonsense and should be junked. Senior University professors, expecting grateful appreciation for their services, were exposed to rude students who called them by their first names, demanded class time to
announce protest demonstrations, and successfully closed down the
entire College for Vietnam moratoria and in support of the Black
Action Movement.

Increasingly the staff of the College was composed of "lecturers"—
extremely well-qualified faculty wives who had never had a chance to
teach, advanced graduate students whose feudal relationship with
their mentors had all but made them forget why they entered the
profession in the first place, younger faculty ready to risk departmental displeasure for the sake of teaching in a place where they
could offer precisely the courses they wanted to a group of students
more than ready to join them in learning. For a time, there was the
extraordinarily exhilarating sense that, even in America, even in a
corporate university, theory and praxis could become one. Instead of
teaching American–East Asian relations, I taught courses on American imperialism, comparative revolutionary movements, and varieties
of liberation from national to personal. Students and faculty shared a
world of concern. We were all going through Vietnam, we were all
trying to resolve the contradictions in our lives it revealed to us.

The disturbing thing about contradictions however, is how they
multiply. Resolve one and a dozen appear in its place. It was grand to
be running through the gas-filled streets of Washington on May Day,
waving to some of my students through the choking haze. I wanted
them to see me; I was proud so many of them were there. Yet when
we got back to Ann Arbor, what did it mean? The war went on, SDS
was cannibalizing itself, I still lived in considerable comfort (so did
the students), and our analyses of the crisis of capitalism became
more and more sophisticated in direct proportion to our inability to
achieve the changes we sought. Why were they in school anyhow?
And whom did my teaching serve?

Ironies abounded. Here was I, a first-generation member of the
middle class, instructing second- and third-generation middle-class
students in a radical political critique that sent many of them off to

discover and, if possible, join the working class. I was in a sense reversing the direction of the educational escalator. Students began dropping out at an alarming rate and congratulating me for having inspired them to do so. I feared becoming a Ms. Chips of the Left, or worse—a dealer in radical rhetoric. "Take Young's course for a quick hit; doesn't last long, but what a rush!" I had never been secure in my departure from the expectations of the intellectual establishment in which I was trained. Now the feeling of political futility made the very rewards I received from teaching almost intolerably suspect.

The women's movement, in fine dialectical fashion, worked to resolve some contradictions even as it raised others to an entirely new pitch. I realized, with something of a shock, that for years I had taught courses on the Chinese revolution without ever discussing the role women had played in it. Even more surprising, I had readily accepted notions of revolutionary "success" that avoided dealing with the continued oppression of women.

For the first time I began to see that conflicts about class and gender on a personal level had a larger systemic expression. The name of the system was not simply capitalism; it was patriarchy as well. Nor would it do just to assert that there was no *necessary* contradiction between feminism and socialism. What, precisely, did that mean in practice? Where should you put your political and intellectual energies? Can all levels of oppression be struggled against at once, or are there priorities, and if so what are they? Hardly the questions a degree in American–East Asian relations has prepared me to answer, but essential to confront before I can redefine the kind of scholarship I want to do.

More directly, I have begun to wonder whether it is only a personal problem that I continue to experience my job as somehow volunteer work, despite the fact that I am paid for it. Splitting household and child-care tasks right down the middle has been important in making my work seem objectively real. But subjectively I feel everything remains to be done. I now feel free "to do my own work." What has become difficult is determining what that work can be, and how I can connect with it more intimately than I have so far.

Marilyn B. Young

Naomi Thornton

MY AMBITION is driving me crazy.

*   *   *

When not on the stage, I am so used to presenting myself to others in ways I hope will please them that I distrust my own words. Am I telling the truth? Or do I want you to think of me as—good guy? committed artist? socially responsible? radical? pursuer of pure truth? sensitive? perceptive? and so on and so on.

What emerges is: "Yes, I do want you to think of me!"

*   *   *

Training:
"The training is so hard when you don't have to train . . . I enjoy it more when I'm making a comeback . . . Real strict. Real slim. I was real serious . . . You never know if you're going to get that chance or not, that chance to come back."
—Muhammad Ali
The New York Times Magazine, June 29, 1975
Every time I go on stage I'm making a comeback. And the rest of the time . . . He's right. It's real hard.

*   *   *

Normally I use other people's words.

*   *   *

Actors have to prove themselves all the time. They set impossible tests and standards.

*   *   *

Choices—too many. So much energy used up deciding how to spend a day.

What is the best thing to do in order to continue to do (and stay trained to do) the thing you must do, given too many choices, not many real options, and twenty-four hours?

Sometimes the best answer is "sleep" or "take a walk in the sun/ rain," but you never think of that.

"Do what you want to do," someone said to me recently. I like that.

*   *   *

If the practice of art is equal to the practice of love or sex, is it utopian to think they might occur simultaneously? In making love, you ought to be able to practice your art, and in practicing your art be able to make love. Among states of being these are of a very high order.

But however much I may insist that they are connected, can you be part of someone else and find/retain the singularity of your vision?

*   *   *

Commitment—impossible to perform without it, impossible even to audition. Yet the knowledge that performing today has no relation to a job tomorrow divides your attention between the glorious present and the awful future. As for auditions, there is no solution—it is best to think of them as a form of madness because one can't kill hope and one knows the percentages.

Actors who feel good about themselves and are very sure of themselves do best. This attitude has some relationship to their art.

*   *   *

Boys' Clubs—I have always felt that every theater I have worked for has been one or another kind of boys' club. Not bad for the training of boys—as are English public schools, military academies, or street gangs—but not good for women, who are then asked by the boys to play their mothers or their fantasy figures. I would not advocate girls' clubs as a vehicle for seeing/portraying real women. Simply theaters where power and competition cease to be the motivating force. My work with collectives has been as close to an aesthetic realization as I have ever come.

*   *   *

"They loved me!"

Is that the point? "They" will never love me. Am I to spend my life winning the love of un-lovers? To create that which is uniquely your own, in response to and in harmony with that which is around you, as an offering (call it gift), is the only justification of my existence I can conceive.

May I daily, hourly, minutely find the strength to live that.

* * *

There is no such thing as balance. How I long for that sense of repose after a good day's work. Does anyone have it?

Either the work I do to sell myself is so piecemeal as to have no central organization—chasing after a score of jobs, job possibilities, or work ideas (all unreal), through phone calls, letters, meetings, jottings, cursory readings (I am a walking anthology of plays to be produced under one rubric or another, possible theatrical seasons, women's roles, video ideas, material for revues, collages, songfests, readings aloud on radio, improvisations, street theater, etc.)—or the work of rehearsing and performing is so concentrated and demanding that I am left totaled, experiencing a momentary high before resting to meet the next day's challenge.

* * *

Making out the menu.

* * *

Bad temper while rehearsing.

I don't want to be bad-tempered, but I certainly am. I probably will be again.

* * *

It was said to me once that it's not the quantity of time you spend with your children that counts, but the quality. I would like to apply this (measure) to work.

* * *

T * I * M * E

*   *   *

Beauty is not skin-deep. Every actress knows it. Yet how much time must be spent learning to make that skin visible!

*   *   *

What counts? We can be very busy. I am so busy doing things that don't count in order to do the things that do count. A one-hour class becomes a ritual, a two-hour rehearsal a major religious event, a performance a brief miracle.

*   *   *

Note on day on which director who had cast me for a lead has called to say she's changed her mind:

Stay flexible. Go with the punches. You'll always lose more than you'll win. The only thing is to keep on trying.

Confidence, the belief that you can still do it, is such a fair-weather friend—flees at the slightest excuse. Guard yourself against that loss. Build walls, electrified fences against its escape.

Is it enough to know that one creature likes what you do and the way you do it and that that creature is your cat?

*   *   *

Stuck with me.

When I am not rehearsing and/or playing, I must continue to maintain my skills, hopefully improve them, but without the audience to play for, reach to, I center on myself for long periods of time. That can be depressing. It is too close to real depression, where you are literally incapable of getting outside yourself.

Also, there is too much time to think, "What am I going to do?" and therefore I overplan things to be done and my head whirls.

*   *   *

Making one's own artistic statement is particularly difficult for an actress. Having three guineas a week and a room of one's own is only a small fraction of the solution. Actors must work with other people and *for* other people and use this framework to define their individual truth while at the same time contributing to the realization of the group effort.

As a man will project an image onto a woman to suit his own needs (mother, wife, sex object, procreator–baby machine, etc., etc.), so a director, usually but not always male, projects an image onto an actress. Thus the actress is limited in exploring various aspects of herself, for she has to satisfy the director's image before and often to the exclusion of her own. Any method actress worth her salt would claim that once a role is hers (once she's hired) she can and will make it her own. Sometimes the fights are awful, but whatever the result the director still has the power.

A positive aspect of this situation is that a director can stretch an actress by suggesting images or roles that never occurred to her. I have an impulse to name four male directors whose compassion and love did just that for me. I have found, however, that I have had to move constantly from one director to another in order to explore different colors in my spectrum. Still, I must produce in an audition the image for which that director (male or female) is looking. Which usually is a one-dimensional female stereotype.

Recently I have been working for very open-minded women directors. The experience has created a whole range of new possibilities for me. While they are no less demanding or rigorous than other directors, their sensibility of what a woman could be in any given role is comparatively unlimited. With one director I have been exploring the possibilities of switching male and female roles. Can I play the tiger in Murray Schisgal's play, so named? Of course. The male actors with whom I work are finding this very exciting as well.

*   *   *

Note: The new danger is the stereotypes of liberation.

*   *   *

It is of the utmost importance for an actor to have a telephone—better if she has an answering service and an agent, all polite and speedy. Only three years ago did I change our family phone to my name and start to pay the bills. Why had I waited so long? To save my husband's pride? No. Slothfulness? No. Because everyone knew me through my husband? No. Because I wasn't important enough to have my own phone? Sounds right.

As I said, I paid the bills, but the phone company failed to change the listing. Only today, three years later, did I ask again to have the listing changed. I even asked that it be done free of charge as the failure to do so three years ago was theirs. I insisted. They called me "Ms." and agreed. Are they becoming afraid of militant women or did they think I was right?

In any case, I still feel a little funny having my husband's name erased. It will cost us ninety cents a month to keep him listed.

*   *   *

Today I am forty years old. The number does not bother me in the least, but what it signifies to others is of paramount importance for an actor. My advertised playing range is twenty-five to forty-five years old. On stage I look about thirty; in films and TV I look forty; in life I look about thirty-five or a hundred and two (depending on health and frame of mind). Now who will cast a forty-year-old to play a thirty-year-old on stage, or a woman looking thirty-five years old to play a forty-year-old on TV? Not many.

My grandmother used to say her last birthday was when she became sixteen. I thought she was being phony. Now I think she was smart for reasons not unlike my own. The minute a woman's age is known she is not seen for what she is—or for what her fantasies are—but quickly tagged by others with a certain mental set. She is pinioned by her years, able to go neither backward nor forward. Specific physical activities are ascribed and proscribed her, as well as socially acceptable sexual proclivities and abilities.

Can an actor survive this reputation? Why not? Regression and projection are her tools; flexibility is her training; she can play anything if given the chance. Still it might be safer to say my last birthday was my sixteenth.

*   *   *

Actresses aren't supposed to be athletic. It's too healthy.

I think I like swimming best which I do well, tennis next which I don't do well and have little opportunity for but love. This summer I climbed mountains for the first time. They were beautiful.

It's important to do something well besides act because often I don't think I'm doing that very well.

*   *   *

Actresses are so busy competing with each other, they don't have time to change their situation. Gotta change the rules of the game.

* * *

Sometimes I say actor and sometimes I say actress. That's because I really, truly believe all people who act are actors, and also because it is still harder to say "female actor" than it is to say "postperson," for example.

* * *

Waiting. Waiting backstage, waiting for the phone, waiting to create that moment of . . . waiting for the moment to create the moment, always ready and waiting.

* * *

Narcissism. I don't want to discuss it. A necessary element in any artistic process, only in the theater is it mistaken for the end result. Or vice versa.

* * *

I want to perform out of love, not anger.

* * *

Art has always been my politics.

Theater is by nature political. It presents human beings in various situations to which they react. The audience finds itself a participant through self-recognition. If this does not happen, then it is not theater but a lecture.

"Political theater," so called, tells people what to do and what to think. It is usually performed for the already politicized as reinforcement, giving them support as would a rally, or for the armchair liberal who by her/his attendance salves her/his conscience. It defuses most situations and rarely leads to action.

Actors have so little confidence in themselves and are so dependent on other people for script and set and directions that they distrust or cease to believe in the political value of art for art's sake. It feels too much like sheer narcissism. They cannot answer in simple language

"What do I want to say?" But they feel they must. And they search constantly for the socially significant act or vehicle. Yet they are the first to see the beauty in the work of another and cry over it. What could be more politicizing?

*   *   *

In touring a show on women's roles and identities—*Who's A Lady?*—I have discovered (once again) that I can enjoy it only if it succeeds artistically. I would like to portray with understanding as many different kinds of women as possible. Then I think the audience will not only have some understanding of women, they will, more importantly, have helped create a moment in which a human being's experience has become art. It is unusual still for more than a limited few kinds of women and a limited few kinds of female experience to be the subject of art.

For example, in a Tennessee Williams scene used in this show it is important for me to know why Amanda sends her daughter Laura to business school and then tries to get her married—not just for sociological or statistical reasons but because of how in your bones you worry about your children. And then I want to know: Who is the woman who says "working women are unfeminine" and why?

*   *   *

For lack of plays with a more existential approach to human problems in which women are the protagonists, many actresses have performed *Waiting for Godot*. I am now working on *The Dumb Waiter*, playing Ben as a woman opposite a male actor playing Gus (as a man). Pinter is hard. All plays are hard. It is surprising how just changing one given fact can make you get down to doing the real work and finding out what a play is about. I cannot play a stereotype gunperson. But I am not uncomfortable in the role. I have never minded competing with men (until they have minded competing with me), and I like hitting targets. I want to say I could not kill someone if I had to. Or is that an apology? Maybe it's not true. See the play.

*   *   *

Characters are not always written with such sympathy as the actor brings to them. The actor must choose when coming out as the bad guy has its own truth. Arthur Miller has successfully written about

Jim Harrison

"Playing Ben as a woman" (scene from *The Dumb Waiter*, by Harold Pinter)

very narcissistic, self-absorbed men, but in order to create them with sympathy he has made the women look like demons or half-wits.

Once, at some cost to my career, or so I was convinced at the time, I turned down a chance to stick my breast into a light socket in a protest play about Vietnam. It was not an act true to character but an hysterical outburst to hype up the play, which in other scenes was a rather acute satire. I felt it an insult to my politics and my art, not to my breast. I tried to think of it as an expression of frustration at political impotence—I wanted the part—but I couldn't make it.

*   *   *

Broadway? Movies? I'm not sure that's where it's at for me, or for anyone else either. You never know when or where it's going to happen. I love the audiences, and so sometimes the small ones I can hear breathing are the best.

*   *   *

Last year when I was artist-in-residence at a predominantly female college, we did *The Good Woman of Setzuan* as a collective. It was agreed that I would play Shen Te/Shui Ta, the Good Woman of the title, and that a woman student would play Yang Sun, Shen Te's lover, although there were four men in the group. She played him as a man. It is obvious that no actor *is* the character, and it is also true that every actor must make the other actors into what they are for her. I accepted the first of these truths, and for the first time in my acting life really had to face the challenge of the second—I couldn't fake it or be sloppy, but really had to do work. You must also accept what the other actor gives you. Had she been a male, would it have been easier? No. Had she been homosexual, would it have been easier? No. Had she been a less talented actor, would it have been harder? Yes. She was very committed. I learned a lot about my craft, and the scenes, which were really about suicide and survival, were a success.

Shen Te/Shui Ta was a fascinating exploration. When she has to deal realistically with people and make demands upon them, she takes on a male character (Shui Ta), and when she is totally giving, she wears her female garb (Shen Te). I found this an untrue and unfair nomenclature because I was always Shen Te inside the man's clothing. But I discovered that the softer I became and the more people took advantage of me (as Shen Te), the more I longed to be tough, rebel at the rape. And the harder and more demanding I became (as Shui Ta), the more I longed to love. It is a very good role for a woman.

* * *

Shafted twice in the same day. Is it because I am a woman or a dope?

* * *

My twelve-year-old daughter just came into the room. "I'm working," I said. "I know," said she and pressed on. "I mean it," I yelled. She retreated. She needed something. I called. "No," she said, "it's okay." Silence. And I knew she experienced for the first time the total awareness of being alone in the world, which I first experienced at that same age. Now she knows, and I can't turn the clock back. (Note: I made six typos in trying to type the first two lines of this entry.)

* * *

I know I am different from other actresses who have not birthed and cared for children, but I have always hoped that my experience outside the theater has enriched my work as much as their experience has enriched theirs.

* * *

On seeing *Equus* I was asked somewhat bitterly by my companion why there are no plays about women who have a low sperm count or can't stick it in, i.e., about female impotence. Because they haven't been written! But that's not entirely true. First of all they (the women) are rarely the protagonists of such plays, and if they were, would anyone go to see them, male or female? They are usually secondary characters—in a male world—and their expression of their impotence is seen with little sympathy—"harridan," "monster," "dyke" are but a few of the labels slapped on a suffering female. We like Martin Dysart, the psychiatrist, and we want him to find a way out. We also feel great empathy for the boy and his love for his personal god—as does Martin. I want a playwright to write a female version of Martin Dysart where I can be on her side, like her, cheer for her—and the same goes for the young boy. Is this possible? Or would such characters be contemptible or inaccessible to a large part of the theater-going public?

* * *

These notes were made randomly over the course of a summer, and yet only when I was clear about something. At this point I cannot put more energy into words, which coming from me I distrust, but must reserve the act of synthesizing, refining, and looking deeper for my work itself. Acting is the exploration to which I am committed, and my perceptions must wind up there. So for further elucidation, I ask you to see the play, hear it, smell it, feel it, taste it, and I shall help you toward that end as much as possible.

On rereading these notes in the autumn I am shocked to discover what I have left out of the deep satisfaction that work can give me—of the significant experiences in my life, which include a closing performance of *The Wax Museum,* a Sunday matinee of *Endgame* for an audience of fifteen attentive elderly ladies, a moment in a performance for my brother, and a host of other brief instants when I did not care whether or not the audience loved me but I knew the gift had been made.

October 1975

Naomi Weisstein

"How can a little girl like you
teach a great big class of men?"
the Chairman Said, and Other
Adventures of a Woman in Science

I AM an experimental psychologist. I do research in vision. The profession has for a long time considered this activity, on the part of one of my sex, to be an outrageous violation of the social order and against all the laws of nature. Yet at the time I entered graduate school in the early sixties, I was unaware of this. I was remarkably naive. Stupid, you might say. Anybody can be president, no? So, anybody can be a scientist. Weisstein in Wonderland. I had to discover that what I wanted to do constituted unseemly social deviance. It was a discovery I was not prepared for: Weisstein is dragged, kicking and screaming, out of Wonderland and into Plunderland. Or Blunderland, at the very least.

What made me want to become a scientist in the first place? The trouble may have started with *Microbe Hunters*,[1] de Kruif's book about the early bacteriologists. I remember reading about Leeuwenhoek's discovery of organisms too small to be seen with the naked eye. When he told the Royal Society about this, most of them thought he was crazy. He told them he wasn't. The "wretched beasties" were there, he insisted; one could see them unmistakably through the lenses he had so carefully made. It was very important to me that he could reply that he had his evidence: evidence became a hero of mine.

It may have been then that I decided that *I* was going to become a scientist, too. I was going to explore the world and discover its wonders. I was going to understand the brain in a better and more complete way than it had been understood before. If anyone questioned me, I would have my evidence. Evidence and reason: my heroes and my guides. I might add that my sense of ecstatic exploration when reading *Microbe Hunters* has never left me through all the years I have struggled to be a scientist.

As I mentioned, I was not prepared for the discovery that women were not welcome in science, primarily because nobody had told me. In fact, I was supported in thinking—even encouraged to think—that my aspirations were perfectly legitimate. I graduated from the Bronx High School of Science in New York City where gender did not enter very much into intellectual pursuits; the place was a nightmare for everybody. We were all, boys and girls alike, equal contestants; all of us were competing for that thousandth of a percentage point in our

[1] Paul de Kruif, *Microbe Hunters* (New York: Harcourt, Brace & World, 1926).

grade average that would allow entry into one of those high-class out-of-town schools, where we could go, get smart, and lose our New York accents.

I ended up at Wellesley, and this further retarded my discovery that women were supposed to be stupid and incompetent: the women faculty at Wellesley were brilliant. (I learned later on that they were at Wellesley because the schools that had graduated them,—the "very best" schools where you were taught to do the very best research— couldn't, or didn't care to, place them in similar schools, where they could continue their research.) So they are our brilliant unknowns, unable to do research because they labor under enormous teaching loads, unable to obtain the minimal support necessary for scholarship —graduate students, facilities, communication with colleagues. Whereas I was ignorant then about the lot of women in the academy, others at Wellesley knew what it was like. Deans from an earlier, more conscious feminist era would tell me that I was lucky to be at a women's college where I could discover what I was good at and do it. They told me that women in a man's world were in for a rough time. They told me to watch out when I went on to graduate school. They said that men would not like my competing with them. I did not listen to the deans, however; or, when I did listen, I thought what they were telling me might have been true in the nineteenth century, but not then, in the late fifties.

So my discovery that women were not welcome in psychology began when I got to Harvard, on the first day of class. That day, the entering graduate students had been invited to lunch with one of the star professors in the department. After lunch, he leaned back in his chair, lit his pipe, began to puff, and announced: "Women don't belong in graduate school.

The male graduate students, as if by prearranged signal, then leaned back in their chairs, puffed on their newly bought pipes, nodded, and assented: "Yeah."

"Yeah," said the male graduate students. "No man is going to want you. No man wants a woman who is more intelligent than he is. Of course, that's not a real possibility, but just in case. You are out of your *natural* roles; you are no longer feminine."

My mouth dropped open, and my big blue eyes (they have since changed back to brown) went wide as saucers. An initiation ceremony, I thought. Very funny. Tomorrow, for sure, the male graduate students will get it.

But the male graduate students never were told that they didn't belong. They rapidly became trusted junior partners in the great research firms at Harvard. They were carefully nurtured, groomed, and run. Before long, they would take up the white man's burden and expand the empire. But for me and for the other women in my class, it was different. We were shut out of these plans; we were *shown* we didn't belong. For instance, even though I was first in my class, when I wanted to do my dissertation research, I couldn't get access to the necessary equipment. The excuse was that I might break the equipment. This was certainly true. The equipment was eminently breakable. The male graduate students working with it broke it every week; I didn't expect to be any different.

I was determined to collect my data. I had to see how the experiment I proposed would turn out. If Harvard wouldn't let me use its equipment, maybe Yale would. I moved to New Haven, collected my data at Yale, returned to Harvard, and was awarded my Ph.D. in 1964, and afterward could not get an academic job. I had graduated Phi Beta Kappa from Wellesley, had obtained my Ph.D. in psychology at Harvard in two and one half years, ranked first in my graduate class, and I couldn't get a job. Yet most universities were expanding in 1964, and jobs were everywhere. But at the places where I was being considered for jobs they were asking me questions like—

"How can a little girl like you teach a great big class of men?" At that time, still unaware of how serious the situation was, I replied, "Beats me. I guess I must have a talent."

and

"Who did your research for you?" This last was from a famous faculty liberal at another school, who then put what I assume was a fatherly hand on my knee and said in a tone of deep concern, "You ought to get married."

Meanwhile, I was hanging on by means of a National Science Foundation postdoctoral fellowship in mathematical biology, at the University of Chicago, and attempting to do some research. Prior to my second postdoctoral year, the University of Chicago began negotiations with me for something like a real job: an instructorship jointly in the undergraduate college and the psychology department. The negotiations appeared to be proceeding in good faith, so I wrote to Washington and informed them that I would not be taking my second postdoctoral year. Then, ten days before classes began, when that option as well as any others I might have taken had been closed, the person responsible for the negotiations called to tell me that, because of a nepotism rule—my husband taught history at the University of Chicago—I would not be hired as a regular faculty member. If I wanted to, I could be appointed lecturer, teaching general education courses in the college; there was no possibility of an appointment in psychology. The lectureship paid very little for a lot of work, and I would be teaching material unconnected with my research. Furthermore, a university rule stipulated that lecturers (because their position in the university was so insecure) could not apply for research grants. He concluded by asking me whether I was willing to take the job; ten days before the beginning of classes, he asked me whether I was willing to take the only option still available to me.

I took the job, and "sat in," so to speak, in the office of another dean, until he waived the restriction on applying for research grants. Acknowledging my presence, he told a colleague: "This is Naomi Weisstein. She hates men."

I had simply been telling him that women are considered unproductive precisely because universities do their best to keep women unproductive through such procedures as the selective application of the nepotism rule. I had also asked this dean whether I could read through the provisions of the rule. He replied that the nepotism rule was informal, not a written statute—flexibility being necessary in its application. Later, a nepotism committee set up partly in response to my protest agreed that the rule should stay precisely as it was: that it was a good idea, should not be written out, and should be applied selectively.

Lecturers at major universities are generally women. They are generally married to men who teach at these major universities. And they generally labor under conditions which seem almost designed to show them that they don't belong. In many places, they are not granted faculty library privileges; in my case, I had to get a note from the secretary each time I wanted to take a book out for an extended period. Lecturers' classrooms are continually changed; at least once a month, I would go to my assigned classroom only to find a note pinned to the door instructing me and my class to go elsewhere: down the hall, across the campus, out to Gary, Indiana.

In the winter of my first year, notices were distributed to all those teaching the courses I was teaching, announcing a meeting to discuss the next year's syllabus. I didn't receive the notice. As I was to learn shortly, this is the customary way a profession that prides itself on its civility and genteel traditions indicates to lecturers and other "nuisance personnel" that they're fired: they simply don't inform them about what's going on. I inquired further. Yes, my research and teaching had been "evaluated" (after five months: surely enough time), and they had decided to "let me go" (a brilliant euphemism). Of course, the decision had nothing to do with my questioning the nepotism rules and explaining to deans why women are thought unproductive.

I convinced them to "let me stay" another year. I don't know to this day why they changed their minds. Perhaps they changed their minds because it looked like I was going to receive the research grant for which I had applied, bringing in money not only for me, but for the university as well. A little while later, Loyola University in Chicago offered me a job.

So I left the University of Chicago. I was awarded the research grant and found the Psychology Department at Loyola at first very supportive. The chairman, Ron Walker, was especially helpful and especially enlightened about women at a time when few academic men were. I was on my way, right? Not exactly. There is a big difference between a place like Loyola and a place with a heavy commitment to research—any large state university, for example—a difference that no amount of good will on the part of an individual chairman could cancel out. The Psychology Department was one of the few active departments at Loyola. The other kinds of support one needs to do experimental psychology—machine and electrical shops, physics and electrical engineering departments, technicians, a large computer—were either not available or were available at that time only in primitive form.

When you are a woman at an "unknown" place, you are considered out of the running. It was hard for me to keep my career from "shriveling like a raisin" (as an erstwhile colleague predicted it would). I was completely isolated. I did not have access to the normal channels of communication, debate, and exchange in the profession—those informal networks where you get the news, the comment and the criticism, the latest reports of what is going on. I sent my manuscripts to various people for comment and criticism before sending them off to journals; few replied. I asked others working in my field to send me their prepublication drafts; even fewer responded. Nobody outside Loyola informed me about special meetings in my area of psychology, and few inside Loyola knew about them. Given the snobbery rife in academic circles (which has eased lately since jobs are much harder to find and thus even "outstanding" young male graduates from the "best" schools may now be found at places formerly beneath their condescension), my being at Loyola almost automatically disqualified me from the serious attention of professional colleagues.

The "inner reaches" of the profession, from which I had been exiled, are not just metaphorical and intangible. For instance, I am aware of two secret societies of experimental psychologists in which fifty or so of the "really excellent" young scientists get together regularly to make themselves better scientists. The ostensible purpose of these societies is to allow these "best and brightest" young psychologists to get together to discuss and criticize each other's work; they also function, of course, to define who is excellent and who is not, and to help those defined as excellent to remain so, by providing them with information to which "outsiders" in the profession will not have access until much later (if at all).

But the intangibles are there as well. Women are treated in ways men hardly ever experience. Let me give you one stunning example. I wrote up an experiment I thought was really good and its results, which were fascinating, and sent the paper to a journal editor whose interests I knew to be close to what was reported in my paper. The editor replied that there were some control conditions that should be run, and some methodological loose ends, so they couldn't publish the paper. Fair enough. He went on to say that they had much better equipment over there, and they would like to test my ideas themselves. Would I mind? I wrote them back, told them I thought it was a bit unusual, asked if they were suggesting a collaboration, and concluded by saying that I would be most happy to visit with them and collaborate on my experiment. The editor replied with a nasty letter explaining to me that by suggesting that they test my ideas themselves, they had merely been trying to help me. If I didn't want their help in this way, they certainly didn't want mine, that is, they had had no intention of suggesting a collaboration.

In other words, what they meant by "did I mind" was: Did I mind if they took my idea and did the experiment themselves? As we know, instances of taking someone else's idea and pretending it's your own are not at all uncommon in science. The striking thing about this exchange, however, was that the editor was arrogant enough, and assumed that I would be submissive enough, so that he could openly ask me whether I would agree to this arrangement. Would I mind? No, of course not. Women are joyful altruists. We are happy to give of ourselves. After all, how many good ideas do you get in your lifetime? One? Two? Why not give them away?

Generally, the justification for treating women in such disgraceful ways is simply that they are women. Let me give another spectacular example. I was promised the use of a small digital laboratory computer, which was to be purchased on a grant. The funds from the grant would become available if a certain job position entailing administration of this grant could be filled. I was part of the group which considered the candidates and which recommended appointing a particular individual. During the discussions of future directions of this individual's work, it was agreed that he would of course share the computer with me. He was hired, bought the computer, and refused me access to it. I offered to put in money for peripherals which would make the system faster and easier for both of us to work with, but this didn't sway him. As justification for his conduct, the man confessed to the chairman that he simply couldn't share the computer with me: he has difficulty working with women. To back this up, he indicated that he'd been "burned twice." Although the chairman had previously been very helpful and not bothered in the least about women, he accepted that statement as an explanation. Difficulty in working with women was not a problem this man should work out. It was *my* problem. Colleagues thought no worse of him for this problem; it might even have raised him in their estimation. He obtained tenure quickly, and retains an influential voice in the department. Yet if a woman comes to *any* chairman of *any* department and confesses that she has difficulty working with men, she is thought pathological.

What this meant for me at the time was that my research was in jeopardy. There were experimental conditions I needed to run that simply could not be done without a computer. So there I was, doing research with stone-age equipment, trying to get by with wonder-woman reflexes and a flashlight, while a few floors below, my colleague was happily operating "his" computer. It's as if we women are in a totally rigged race. A lot of men are driving souped-up, low-slung racing cars, and we're running as fast as we can in tennis shoes we managed to salvage from a local garage sale.

Perhaps the most painful of the appalling working conditions for women in science is the peculiar kind of social-sexual assault women sustain. Let me illustrate with a letter to *Chemical and Engineering News* from a research chemist named McGauley:

> There are differences between men and women . . . just one of these differences is a decided gap in leadership potential and ability . . . this is no reflection upon intelligence, experience, or sincerity. Evolution made it that way. . . . Then consider the problems that can arise if the potential employee, Dr. Y (a woman) [*sic*: he could at least get his chromosomes straight] will be expected to take an occasional business trip with Dr. X. . . . Could it be that the guys in shipping and receiving will not take too kindly to the lone Miss Y?[2]

Now what is being said here, very simply, and to paraphrase the Bible, is that women are trouble. And by trouble, McGauley means

[2] T. J. McGauley, letter to *Chemical and Engineering News*, December 7, 1970, pp. 8–9.

sexual trouble. Moreover, somehow, someway, it is our fault. *We* are provoking the guys in shipping and receiving. Women are universally assigned by men, first—no matter who the women are or what they have in mind—to sexual categories. Then, we are accused by men of taking their minds away from work. When feminists say that women are treated as sex objects, we are compressing into a single, perhaps rhetorical phrase, an enormous area of discomfort, pain, harassment, and humiliation.

This harassment is especially clear at conventions. Scientific meetings, conferences, and conventions are harassing and humiliating for women because women, by and large, cannot have male colleagues. Conversations, social relations, invitations to lunch, and the like are generally viewed as sexual, not professional, encounters if a woman participates in them. It does not cross many men's minds that a woman's motivation may be entirely professional.

I have been at too many professional meetings where the "joke" slide was a woman's body, dressed or undressed. A woman in a bikini is a favorite with past and perhaps present presidents of psychological associations. Hake showed such a slide in his presidential address to the Midwestern Psychological Association, and Harlow, past president of the American Psychological Association, has a whole set of such slides, which he shows at the various colloquia to which he is invited. This business of making jokes at women's bodies constitutes a primary social-sexual assault. The ensuing raucous laughter expresses the shared understanding of what is assumed to be women's primary function—to which we can always be reduced. Showing pictures of nude and sexy women insults us: it puts us in our place. You may think you are a scientist, it is saying, but what you really are is an object for our pleasure and amusement. Don't forget it.

I could continue recounting the horrors, as could almost any woman who is in science or who has ever been in science, but I want to stop now and ask: What conclusions can we draw from my experience? What does it all add up to?

Perhaps we should conclude that persistence will finally win out. Or that life is hard, but cheerful struggle and a "sense of humor" may make it bearable. Or perhaps we should search back through my family, and find my domineering mother and passive father or my domineering father and passive mother, to explain my persistence. Perhaps, but all these conclusions are beside the point. The point is that none of us should have to face this kind of offense. The point is that we must change this man's world and this man's science.

How will other women do better? One of the dangers of this kind of narrative is that it may validate the punishment as it singles out the few survivors. The lesson appears to be that those (and only those) with extraordinary strength will survive. This is not the way I see it. Many have had extraordinary strength and have *not* survived.

Much of the explanation for my professional survival has to do with the emergence and growth of the women's movement. I am an experimental psychologist, a scientist. I am also a feminist. I am a feminist because I have seen my life and the lives of women I know harassed, dismissed, damaged, destroyed. I am a feminist because without others I can do little to stop the outrage. Without a political and social movement of which I am a part—without feminism—my determination and persistence, my clever retorts, my hours of patient explanation, my years of exhortation amount to little. If the scientific world has changed since I entered it, it is not because I managed to become an established psychologist within it. Rather, it is because a women's movement came along to change its character. It is true that as a member of that movement, I have acted to change the character of the scientific world. But without the movement, none of my actions would have brought about change. And now, as the strength of the women's movement ebbs, the old horrors are returning. This must not happen.

Science, knowledge, the search for fundamental understanding is part of our humanity. It is an endeavor that seems to give us some glimpse of what we might be and what we might do in a better world. To deny us the right to do science is to deny us our humanity. We shall not have our humanity denied.

Naomi Weisstein

What Counts as Work?
Cynthia Lovelace Sears

Cynthia Sears (right) with writing partner, Karen Grassle

WHEN I WAS ASKED to contribute to a book of essays treating women and work, I was thrilled to be taken seriously, to be thought able to make a meaningful contribution. But from that immediate rush of pleasure the pendulum swung toward apprehension. What was there for me to say? What, in fact, *was* the "work that I do?"

I have, since the birth of my first child, thought of my work primarily as parenting—even though raising a family had not been my original ambition or even, at the time, a conscious decision. When I first learned I was pregnant, I had mixed emotions. Chief among them was a sense of pure relief. I remember thinking, "Now I won't have to get a job." It was not a thought I wished to share with anyone, nor one I cared to admit to myself. There was too much guilt attendant upon it, and shame. I was, after all, copping out—on my training, my education, my talents, the "such-great-promise!" others had seen in me. It even seemed a betrayal of my own strong if ill-defined ambitions to be a writer, a teacher, a critic—something that would allow me to work with words. Rather than face the outside world, put my abilities on the counters of the retail market, I was in retreat. The baby was my free pass to safety; no more examinations to pass, deadlines to meet, outside authorities to please. (I was wrong about that, as you will see, but I did not know it then.)

As it happened, the actual *business* (or profession or career) of being a mother—first to one daughter and then, almost three years later, to a second—was an experience of intense pleasure and gratification, despite the overly compulsive way I went about it. Deep inside me I knew, with quiet certainty, that nothing had ever given me greater personal satisfaction and pride. Nevertheless I floundered before the questions of outsiders—those of concerned friends as well as of critical observers: Was "just raising children" really enough? How could I stand it, being with only my babies day after day? Didn't I feel trapped? Weren't there other things I wished I might be doing? Much as I wanted, needed, to believe that I was entirely content, an unwelcome pin of awareness pricked me with the knowledge that I did have areas of dissatisfaction in my life, together with ambitions that I did not have the courage to pursue. It never occurred to me that this was a general condition of life, familiar to almost everyone, no matter what his or her line of work. I only knew that I dared not admit there was anything amiss in my particular world. So I responded to the questions with the conviction of a fanatic: Being a full-time mother was the most challenging, rewarding, exciting, fulfilling, significant career any woman could have. This pathetically arrogant generalization, born of defensiveness, is one I no longer find it necessary to make. Although it had turned out to be mostly true for *me,* it served also to screen my occasional uneasiness, my private daydreams. Even during the most demanding periods of parenting, when my girls were very small, I had frequent Walter Mitty fantasies that were not about great works created or performed by my children, but rather about *my* personal and

separate triumphs. Still, for a very long time—in fact, until my marriage ended seven years ago at the time I took my first job—I kept
very quiet about all of this.

Now my children are thirteen and eleven, growing swiftly into
strong and independent young women. While they need me still as a
given in their lives, a loving presence they can count upon and turn to
for support and counsel, as well as for sharing their own successes and
defeats, I realize that in terms of actual physical presence and care my
participation in their world is over. They and I are sustained by our
reciprocal family love, but the activity of parenting no longer keeps
me occupied full-time. So now the radar of my mind, my private
ambition, keeps scanning the professional horizon. What is that over
there? Is it something I can do? Is it for me, for me, for me . . . ?

I am thirty-nine years old, and in the past seven years have held
many positions. While there is no linear logic to this sequence of jobs,
there has been an internal consistency: they have all involved working
with words. To a great extent my part has been reactive rather than
active; the words are those of others, not my own. I have been the
listener, the reader, the recorder, the editor, the audience. Perhaps this
is partially why I view the events of my hopscotch careering from one
job to another as more suitable for dinner party anecdotes than for
serious consideration. But I think the tendency to downgrade my jobs
comes from a different source. I think it results more from the conflict
between my concerns and values and those that bombard me in messages from the world outside.

These messages tell me that I should turn my efforts toward the
pursuit of a single worthwhile career—a steady job with a reliable
salary—instead of frittering them away on minor enterprises like
those of the past which have paid me little if anything. When I am
feeling really good about myself, I can believe that the series of small
satisfactions, derived from various aspects of my work and scattered
through the fabric of my everyday life, is worth more to me than any
potential pride in holding a position I do not care about but which the
world judges as meaningful. That, as I say, is what I can believe when
my self-esteem is high. It usually does not last for very long. I am
susceptible to the outside voices which proclaim that one kind of work
really "counts" whereas another doesn't, and which announce the
credits following from that assessment. This is where my confusion
and conflicts have their roots.

To whom do these voices belong? Who decides what kind of work
has value and what kind does not, and on what basis is that decision
made? How can a person develop or maintain a sense of work-pride

without receiving signs of worldly approval? (The notion that the simple act of putting effort into a project and deriving gratification from completing it should be enough in itself, and that no further recognition from society—in the form of status or monetary rewards —is necessary, must come from someone who either knows people of greater emotional independence than I can even imagine, or from someone who hasn't visited our world recently.) Money, clearly, is our surest index of accomplishment. A person may talk about having a horribly dull and meaningless job and yet, because of the magic addendum, "but it pays well," we do not advocate quitting. High pay, ipso facto, means social recognition (if not social significance). At the other extreme, a job performed as a volunteer may be entirely fulfilling to the one who does it, but it is viewed with condescension by most men (who see it as one step above the bridge luncheon), and with concern and often anger by feminist groups. Consequently, when one mentions one's volunteer activities, it is invariably with a defensive attitude, and usually with a torrent of explanations about unseen or future benefits. The whole issue of volunteerism is so loaded at the moment that I would avoid it altogether—except that it pertains in a major way to what I have done and am now doing.[1]

The same sort of ambivalence about the importance of worldly acknowledgment arises when I consider the years I spent as a full-time mother. Feminist literature I have been reading (and I consider myself a feminist) seems to be telling me that a woman no longer has to make a choice between "motherhood" and "a career." Implicit in such a statement is the idea that raising children is *not* a career—not even a restricted one, limited to a fairly definite number of years, as ballet, gymnastics, and certain sports are. I find myself resenting that attitude, less because I believe that "homemaking is the greatest unpaid profession" (although I *do* agree with that) than because the honor and dignity and status one might hope to be accorded by other women, at least, seem now to be rescinded by them, and another set of values and priorities imposed with the same absolute authority that once went with the phrase, "A woman's place is in the home." This is not Women's Liberation; it is Women's Alternative Enslavement, and it is

[1] Groups such as NOW maintain that volunteerism is counter-productive to desirable social change; that it makes it easier for governmental or social agencies to avoid obligations to provide needed services by offering free labor; that it further takes paying jobs away from women who need to make a living; and that it encourages exploitation of women in stereotyped sex-roles by assigning them to tasks that amount to nothing more than housework for a public clientele. I question some of NOW's points and agree totally with others. Fortunately, all of my volunteer work happened to fall within the "acceptable" categories of extending myself as a person as well as extending my vocation as an interviewer and writer.

not, I believe, what the truly thoughtful feminists had or have in mind. It was heartening, therefore, to come upon a few recent articles by professional women who discuss parenting not as a kind of extracurricular activity to be engaged in only when it is convenient, and never when it might impinge upon The Career, but as an art and a positive option.

However much one believes in the inherent rightness of a choice, it still is important to receive confirmation and support from an outside, public source. My own reasons, some fourteen years ago, for focusing all of my energies and attention upon my children were not particularly sound ones. I recognize now that I was operating less from choice than from a sense of necessity. Having been brought up by a Nana, I was adamant on the subject of surrogate mothers. I wanted to be sure that my children would never feel I might prefer to hire someone to care for them (meaning, in my mind, to love them) rather than tend to them myself (unless I had to take a job for financial reasons). In addition, having been raised to believe that you had to *earn* your loving—it did not come as part of your birthright—I approached everything I did, from social behavior to schoolwork, with a determination to be perfect at it and thus, perhaps, to win love. Consequently, when I had children, overriding my sense of miracle that I had given birth to two lovely, unflawed, joyous girls was the drive (or obsession) to be a perfect mother. The concept of "being kind to yourself" was entirely foreign to me; and, had it been suggested, I would have summarily rejected it as a form of unacceptable selfishness. It did not occur to me until much later that there was a cost and a danger in maintaining this attitude. At the time, my children's response to my constant presence and unflagging attention seemed reward enough. And since their father did not return from work until close to their bedtime, they did not feel any diminution of care when I shifted from being Mother to being Wife.

Based on our assumptions about how others expected a "happily married couple" to act, both my husband and I lived out our marriage according to the dictates of appearance. We were completely innocent of the possibilities of a relationship. Marriage was something that you *did,* like a long term paper, and if you did it well, everything would work out fine. To accomplish this, however, traditional role-playing was essential; it provided the only guidelines either of us had. And for me the traditional role became hateful.

I loathed housework and was poor at it, save for the creative or decorative aspects like sewing curtains, painting a cabinet, arranging furniture or flowers. I found no value (symbolic or other) in scrubbing and waxing floors. Washing dishes was an experience similar to solitary confinement—lonely, unpleasant, bleak. I enjoyed a clean and orderly house but disliked the process of making it so. Because we could afford to, I wanted to hire a cleaning woman, a part-time housekeeper. My husband refused; no, it was a necessary part of my role, it was *my job*. My thought-response, "Then why do you have a secretary to do your typing, why isn't that part of *your job*?" remained unspoken. It would have been pointless in any case. This was not a logical issue but an emotional one. He didn't want a housekeeper around because his own childhood (with two professional, absentee parents) had been full of them. I could understand that since I too was operating in reaction to painful early experiences. What was destructive about our non-interaction, our refusal to argue out these problems, was that I really *believed* that my silent deference to all his decisions and demands was a virtue. It showed my thoughtfulness, my concern, my essential *goodness*. However miserable I might be, a part of me felt smug. I was certainly better than those slipshod wives who either had lots of help or henpecked their husbands into doing their work for them. (I really thought like that a thousand years ago.) The long view escaped me altogether. Not only was I building up resentment toward my husband, but I was also helping him to develop clumsiness in the simplest domestic chore. Just as later, when I announced to friends with a certain pride (disguised as exasperation) that he had never changed one diaper, never got up with a sick child at night, never given the girls a meal, I didn't see that my "tolerance" had actually deprived him of a real sense of participation in raising our children. The only thing I could see was the immediate benefit of avoiding any criticism or complaints. This shortsighted, inappropriate view of what was best pervaded our entire marriage.

And gradually I was becoming depleted. Any agar must have something put back into it if it is to remain a fertile culture that will continue to support growth. I had not structured my life to allow for this. I had no daytime friends to talk to or to visit, except on occasions centered around our children. As a result of an early automobile accident, I didn't drive; I did all marketing and errands with first one and then two children in the stroller. These were my outings. My husband would then arrive home exhausted from encounters with students and colleagues, and the last thing he wanted was a conversation with someone who was relying upon him to supply her entire social and intellectual stimulus. These became our television years: evenings of silence unless the set was on. Occasionally we would entertain his professional associates, but soon I was so full of doubts about my worth or interest as a person (save as a mother) that I concentrated solely upon creating elaborate meals, believing that that was the only offering I could make to the evening.

My husband, who had a younger sister, once told me (laughing) how an older sibling maintained a position of dominance. The catechism was as follows: "If the younger one has something that you want, first take it. If you can't get it, then try to break it. If you can't do that, then denigrate it." I had grown up with an older sister and so this strategy, from the receiving end, seemed familiar—almost comfortable—to me. (And I echoed his laugh.) I was used to it, and when it appeared in various ways during our marriage, I may have obliquely expressed dismay, but I never tried to change it. I became a co-conspirator in my own subjugation and my ever-diminishing sense of self-esteem. And no amount of unqualified love from a three- or five- or seven-year-old child can finally offset that.

When I was thirty-one, I went into therapy. By that time I was feeling resentment as a physical sensation—a constriction of the chest and a pounding of the blood. I had stored up so much frustration and rage and anguish that I was afraid of what might happen if my self-control ever slipped. I was suffering what Judy Sullivan tellingly describes (in *Mama Doesn't Live Here Anymore*) as "that unnamed disease, the housewife's breakdown." For a while during my sessions I simply unloaded complaints. Then, after listing the myriad reasons why change was impossible, I began to think about change. How could I alter the situation that I had helped to create, and that was now binding me intolerably? I spoke about writing, an ambition I had (secretly, uncertainly) held after some heady instances of success in high school and college. And I recalled the one time I had tried to get back into writing at home. It was a peaceful afternoon; my two-year-old was having a nap; I had an idea for a poem. Soon the dining room table was covered with page after page of false starts, single lines, abandoned images. I took time out to feed my daughter her early supper and then went back to my efforts as she triked around the living room. When my husband got home, the customary martini was not waiting on the coffee table; there was no dinner on the stove. I was sitting in a welter of yellow paper. I do not know what might have happened if he had criticized me for forgetting my responsibility as a wife always to have drinks and dinner waiting. (Probably nothing much different.) But what he attacked was my immaturity, my "attempt to escape back to college," my ridiculous efforts to live in and off of the past: "*Poetry!* for God's sake!" When was I going to give up that schoolgirl nonsense and begin to live like an adult in the present?

I couldn't say anything. I collected all the papers, stowed them away, and did not try to write again during the remainder of my marriage.

One must wonder (as my therapist made me question then and many times afterward) why a single negative response—fair or unfair —would have such potency. It was, of course, because it confirmed what I had come to suspect (at the very least) about myself. And it came from someone upon whom I had developed a profound negative dependency. I did not look to my husband for praise or support so much as I awaited his criticism. And because he was a man, a professional who worked in the "real" world and received both money and acclaim for his work, he was an authority. His judgment had the weight of an absolute decree.

It took a long time and a lot of letting go of inculcated resistance before I could consider and eventually believe what we were talking about in both individual and group therapy. The essence of it was this: When I said I had no ability or talent and so did not want to try anything new because I was afraid I might fail, I was lying. My fear— like that of most neurotic people—was of success. Success makes you visible, makes others not only notice you but perhaps come to count on you for further accomplishment. And until you feel strong enough within yourself to accept and welcome this visibility, all it does is increase your fears that eventually you will be exposed as the fraud you believe yourself to be. Each success intensifies the horror you anticipate in that final, inevitable unmasking. It is easier, therefore, not to take the risk, not ever to try. Furthermore, if you dare—and succeed—people may resent your success, try to put you down, or— worst of all—not *like* you. No one dislikes a loser. A loser poses no threat, offers no competition. A winner, on the other hand, may endanger another's sense of his own ability and even become a potential rival.

After a year of talking and thinking about this, I took my first cautious step into the world outside that of home-to-market-to-therapist. A friend involved in a local educational radio station asked me to join her on the air in interviewing a poet/photographer. My immediate terror at the prospect faded somewhat when she explained that the listener-supported station was conducting a marathon to raise funds and that *anything* was better than a straight sales pitch. So I went on the air with her and her guest, asked more questions than I had expected to, and left Studio One with a heady feeling of triumph. I was so intoxicated by this single small achievement that when I met the program director I asked him why the station had no programs on modern literature, with interviews and readings by current writers. He said that no one had volunteered to produce such a program—or, rather, that no one had followed through on the offer to do so. If I wanted to give it a try, he continued, why didn't I borrow a tape machine, record something along the lines I had in mind, and submit the result as an audition tape? That sounded unintimidating. I found someone to run the tape recorder for me and got in touch with two young poets I admired, who had given readings at nearby colleges and who agreed to participate in my project. A piece of cake! I had only to ask one question somewhere in the middle of the session; they did the rest. The day I turned in the tape the program director who had encouraged me was fired; but, he assured me, *someone* would listen to the recording.

A month later, at a fund-raising dinner for the station, it was announced that I had a show of my own—two hours every Thursday afternoon. I felt temporary elation—they had liked the tape! [tape!—] —followed by alarm when I learned that no one had listened to even a portion of it. The fact that I had actually *done* something had been enough. Then panic set in. How was I going to fill those Thursday afternoons? The first one was settled—my audition tape, with some additional conversation between the poets and myself. I entered the studio without much concern—and immediately encountered the greatest difficulty I was ever to have. I could not, literally *could* not, say "I am Cynthia Sears and this is . . ." or any permutation of that introduction. I could risk "going public." I could risk presenting something I had done (with maximum assistance) to an audience. I could *not* verbally take responsibility for my work.

This problem remained with me as time and programs passed. It was not simple stage-fright—I could appear on someone else's show with only a tremor and could talk without undue self-consciousness. It was only when I had to stand up and be counted, when I had to identify the work as my own, that I was rendered speechless. Even when I had the full text written out, and had rehearsed my statements repeatedly, I could barely get those words out; and when I did, it was in a voice from a sepulcher. The programs (especially as I learned to edit them) became increasingly professional. I got worse. No one at the station mentioned this because it was a kind of point of honor not to listen to any program but your own. And letters didn't pour in asking, "Who is that apparently dead-or-dying person?" because, with a few exceptions, the only people who listened to a program on contemporary literature (especially modern poetry) were invalids or other house-bounds. They simply turned on the station in the morning and kept it on until bedtime, paying attention chiefly to news or music programs and treating the rest as simple background noise, like elevator music.

Out of this experience three things happened. First, I became (of necessity) an experienced tape editor. I could pare down my programs so that the quavery questions were deleted from the "interviews" and a sort of autobiographical narrative by the writer remained. My part on the air consisted of a minimal intro and outro which I prerecorded, rerecorded, and edited until it sounded like a human voice speaking. Sleight of hand can disguise slight of nerve.

Second, I met many of my heroes in literature (at least those in California and New York), all of whom agreed willingly to offer their time without remuneration, simply as a contribution to education. Among them were writers as diverse as Isaac Bashevis Singer, Kenneth Millar (Ross MacDonald), John Cheever, N. Scott Momaday, Henry Miller, (and through Miller) Lawrence Durrell. All of this was immensely gratifying. My world was expanding and I was able to talk with people whom I admired and whose concerns I shared—concern for art and literature, and for the degree to which a writer might effect social change by affecting public consciousness, by making people think about issues they had not previously considered.

The third outcome was that my marriage came to an end. It is pointless to speculate upon what aspect of my changed life made the emptiness of our relationship inescapable and termination of it essential. Part of it, I know, had to do with my having an independent existence that gave me the courage to confront my husband directly and express what I was feeling. Therapy had brought about the insight and understanding; but having a sense of an active and separate self allowed me to do something about it. A part also stemmed from a curious sort of competition that resulted from my entering a professional area. I did not in any way feel myself to be a rival to my husband, but I believe that I was perceived by him as one. In any case he refused, from the outset, to listen to any of my programs. This was "my thing," he claimed; to bring him into it in any way was a reflection of my neurotic need for his sanction. That sounded awfully plausible, for a while. I did not, for some time, get around to comparing this attitude to his desire that I share in his work, read his papers, listen to his theories or his proposed experiments. I am not saying that going to work (even as a volunteer) broke down my marriage; that had happened silently, inexorably, over the years. It simply made the breakdown too obvious to ignore, and the maintenance of a meaningless outward form too painful to continue.

Now I became a woman on my own and in need of establishing a new structure for my life. Concern for my children and for the impact on their lives of my separation from their father (however preferable it might ultimately be to the alternative) created a feeling of intense guilt. I still had my program; but once I was not a wife-and-mother but "just a mother," a volunteer job no longer "counted." If I was to spend time away from my children, I had to have a "real job"—that is, one that earned money. This reasoning was not dictated by financial necessity. I was fortunate enough to have an independent income that would allow us to live without alimony or more than minimal child support. It was social pressure I was feeling. I knuckled under and took a staff position at the station as Co-director of Drama and Literature. Although I wasn't happy with the position, which was chiefly administrative and secretarial, I received immediate acclaim from friends and relatives. I was, in their eyes, *really* working now. And I needed that kind of support and approval.

Then I learned that as long as I held a paying position on the staff, every program I produced was the station's property, to do with as they wished. And they were selling the programs to listeners. This would have seemed entirely appropriate to me, had any of the profits gone to the writers who generously contributed their time and efforts. But the station management would not agree to that, and I realized that I was betraying the writers: they could not, for profit, now do a reading of material already read on programs being marketed by the station. I quit my job and returned to the position of independent programmer, dreaming someday of selling the tapes and paying the writers on a royalty basis. It was just a dream; I had neither the facilities nor the capital necessary to bring off such a venture. And my status fell accordingly. When was I going to get a *real* job?

I had left the station late in 1972. In the fall of 1974 I was offered a position that seemed almost too good to be true. For some time I had been doing piecemeal work as a reader of books and scripts for a studio, writing synopses of the plots and evaluating their chances of being turned into successful films. It was a lot of work for very little pay, but it led me to my "big break." A well-known young producer asked me to be a reader for a major star. The salary was good, the hours flexible. I had an office—if I wished to use it—but I could also work out of my home. The trade papers carried an announcement of my appointment: I had been "inked in" as the executive head of a new production company, assigned to secure properties to be developed into feature films for the star. Private and public applause was deafening. I was ecstatic and delirious with pride. But as the months went by, and I could never seem to get in touch with either the producer or the star, my frustration began to mount. No one seemed to want to read the stories I had found interesting and was prepared to defend. And then, at the end of six months (when my salary for the project was to be renegotiated) I was informed that the star had abandoned the idea and my job was over. That was a disappointment—but these things happen. The real blow came shortly afterward when I learned (from friends in the business and articles in the national press) that there never had been a job in the sense that I had understood it. I was the window dressing for the star's negotiations with the network that carried his series. He had wanted an increase in pay and his threat was that, without it, he was starting an independent production facility for feature films. I was his evidence: the company existed; I was a salaried employee of it; he had even allowed me to go to New York to investigate works-in-progress by writers living there. In the face of this clear proof of serious intent, the network agreed to his demands. The issue was settled, and I was no longer needed.

When I consider these two jobs in retrospect, I see the source of my confusion about work. On the one hand, I held a volunteer position that had many internal rewards and compensations, to be sure, but no commercial value or real significance in the eyes of the world. On the other, the "real job" that had brought public status and a good salary turned out to be a fake from start to finish and left me feeling exploited and ashamed of my naiveté. It is obviously rhetorical to ask which of the two should be considered meaningful work, but the issue points up the problem of defining work in a satisfactory way. And it doesn't help to realize that the second position would carry much more weight on a job application form than the first, since "volunteer activities" have about as much clout as "hobbies." The concept of "work pride" is very important to me. But I also live in society as a single woman and need to have some external confirmation that what I do is significant and valuable to others.

Between leaving the radio station in 1972 and the "window dressing" job in 1974 I had a third kind of work experience. Gay Talese was in California collecting material for a book about the sexual revolution in the sixties. He needed someone to research the background material and also to assist him in interviewing individuals whose first-person accounts were to form a portion of the book. I was hired for the job of recording our interviews, transcribing the tapes, and editing them in the sense of ordering the related events and experiences more or less chronologically and translating the question/answer interview format into personal narrative. During the six months of this project I learned more about the techniques of interviewing and reporting than I might ever have anticipated.

Another aspect of the association with Gay surprised me even more. Never having employed an assistant, he asked me (in our initial discussions about the job) to suggest a salary I thought appropriate. The amount I suggested seemed fair to him. Later, however, he said that while it might be fair in the abstract, after thinking it over he did not feel it was enough in my particular case. I had neither a housekeeper nor live-in help, and carried the full responsibility for raising young children. This would be disrupted somewhat by the project. (Until this time I had been able to work entirely at home, producing my radio programs on recording equipment kept in the living room.) Furthermore, we would be doing the interviews in the late afternoons and evenings, which would take me away from the girls during mealtime and "family time," when they were used to my being home. Because of these things, Gay felt he should offer further remuneration. He would pay for all sitters, for all meals out or movies for the girls—in fact, for anything that might compensate them for my being taken away from my existing primary profession of motherhood. I found—and still find—this attitude remarkable. It was the first time in my experience that any man had given more than lip service to the idea that raising children could be a serious occupation, to be taken into account in a parent's consideration and negotiation of an outside job. His understanding and support strengthened my own sense of parenting as a legitimate career.

Now I am involved in a wholly new venture, writing screenplays and teleplays with first one and then another woman as a writing partner. My initial collaboration resulted from good luck and fortunate timing more than anything else. Alison Herzig, a close friend from college with whom I had lost touch over the years visited Los Angeles with her family in 1974. Allie and I rapidly renewed our old friendship, talking for hours in my elegant studio office (which I did not yet know was part of the set for my fradulent job with the star). Our decision to collaborate evolved out of the suggestive coincidence of three facts. First, Allie had just completed a children's book and was looking around for a new project; second, I had grown weary of reading endless scripts and screen treatments and was thinking about trying to write something of my own; and third, a friend of mine, Karen Grassle, who was co-starring in the new TV series, "Little House on the Prairie," described to us at length one day the elements she missed both in her own role as Caroline Ingalls and in the program's portrayal of women in general. Impatient with playing the part of a woman who was forever "good" and knew the solution to any problem, Karen felt that, instead of depicting only human strengths and romanticizing frontier life, the program should say something about human frailties—especially the irritation, anger, anxiety, loneliness, and frustration—brought about by the harsh realities of life as a pioneer woman. Moreover, she said, the importance of women's interrelatedness had never been fully explored in the program. Maybe, for example, given the limitations of commercial television, "Ma" herself couldn't be allowed to falter or break down; but an emotional collapse *might* be permissible in a woman she knew and the conflicts of pioneer women thus examined as Caroline Ingalls goes to help her friend. This became the theme of our story.

Allie went back to New York and set a date to return to California in the spring. In the meantime we both plunged in to do research about the Midwest in the 1870s. By the time she flew back for the ten days during which we would "write the screenplay," my initial optimism had eroded into terror at the prospect of having actually to begin. I stalled, insisted on talking out ideas, tried every delaying tactic I knew to avoid putting words on paper. Finally Allie, who shared my fears but refused to be swamped by them, took matters in hand. She sat down and recklessly whipped off twenty lines of dialogue. It worked. Reading over what she had written, I protested, "You can't have that man say 'down the road a piece.' It's hokey!" She replied, "What then?" And we were off. She would write part of a scene while I jotted down ideas for another. I would read her work— correct, alter, expand, extend it—then hand it back. She did the same for whatever I had written. Our writing, like our ideas, proceeded contrapuntally. This is not to say we always agreed. There were frequent, heated arguments; and some of them we could not sort out. At these times, however, we had access to more experienced writers who could suggest alternatives to the scene or bit of dialogue that was causing us difficulty. Each of us went through periods of discouragement, dissatisfaction, and depression—but fortunately they were never simultaneous. We had a kind of hydraulic interaction going: when one of us was down the other could lift with the buoyancy of confidence; when one flagged the other could propel by force of enthusiasm and excitement. It was a heady, chaotic, and exhausting period, fraught with interruptions by children (mine in person and hers via telephone), family crises, extraneous obligations. But, once we started, we completed the first draft in five days.

When we showed the results of our efforts to Karen and a friend (a professional screenwriter), they were extravagant in their praise and encouragement. Only as they began to suggest the structural changes necessary to make the work suitable for an hour-long segment on television did we realize how full of holes this first draft was—how very drafty! The four of us devised an outline for the next stage of the script before Allie returned to New York. We planned to work independently on the scenes needed to flesh out the story, and to get together later to dash off the final version. But our independent work did not prosper. We needed one another as catalysts. Apart, we lost our adrenalized momentum, slowed to a near standstill, began to doubt whether we would ever finish.

At this point Karen stepped in. She believed in the story and in the characters we had created. She said she felt it was time for her to "put her money where her mouth was"; and she volunteered to pay the air fare for one of us to meet the other, and to cover the expenses of our work in completing the script. This was "worldly confirmation," and then some. Our work was being taken seriously not merely by a sympathetic friend to bolster our egos, but by a professional actress who wanted to finance the project in order that it might be produced—who wanted, further, to *act* in it. This made all the difference. It was a form of approval neither of us could discount. We saw our writing in a new light.

Once again Allie flew to California, partly because leaving home was slightly more difficult for me than for her; partly because we needed access to Karen, and to other friends who were experienced writers, for help in learning how to put together a shooting script. In plan and in theory this work period was to be more sane. We would not, as before, stay up all night and subsist on coffee and cigarettes and deli sandwiches. We would pace ourselves, alternating writing sessions with periods of rest and quiet talk. My children would be away the first week, while we completed the bulk of the script. They would be home the second week while we did the final polishing— surely an easy task to accomplish during the hours they would be in school.

In fact none of these things happened as we had hoped and expected. There was far more to be done in this second stage than we had anticipated, and ideas did not come on demand. Scenes necessary to carry the dramatic line or establish a transition did not flow naturally; they seemed to us obligatory and we tried to force them into existence before their rationale was clear. Meanwhile time was passing and our mutual tension growing. Karen's sponsorship began to acquire the weight of an obligation, a burden. We *had* to finish the script during this trip in order to justify her faith. We couldn't let her down. As this self-induced sense of pressure mounted, we completely forgot Karen's originally stated intention—that she wanted to assist in the completion of this story, not as a one-shot proposition, but as the first step of an active writing collaboration. While she hoped that we might eventually sell the script, she was not counting on that; realistically, its chances were slim. But she wanted to see us finish it if only to encourage us to go on and write others. When we finally met to talk with her, all of this was reiterated, and remembered. But for a while, her own work schedule was such that it was impossible to get together, discuss our problems, decide what to do. So panic took us firmly by the scruff of the neck.

And then my children came home. They expected to find us with the main portion of our writing over, ready to take time off for and with them. When instead they found us both spent and under strain, responding to their appearance as to intrusion, to their presence as distraction, they were stung to near-mutiny. Their previous tolerance of our need for uninterrupted work periods, for makeshift meals followed by hasty good-nights, had worn thin. Their personal support of our project and good will toward our goal of completion were used up. It wasn't fair—we had promised!

We explained the necessity for breaking promises sometimes. They understood what we were saying, but were not about to accept the idea gracefully or to make the best of it. I could see Allie stifle her criticism. Her own girls—the same ages as mine—had been raised to deal with difficult or unpleasant realities without voicing defiance or protest. If it had to be, then it had to be, period. My children had never learned that kind of discipline or control. They felt betrayed and angry and let us know it. I felt guilty toward them and guilty toward Allie. I was aware of her unspoken reaction and of her thoughts (also unspoken) about her own children—also deprived of their mother's presence. I knew she would not say anything to me, because she realized as I did that the surest way to jeopardize a friendship or a working partnership is to criticize the friend-partner's children. But, as we tried to smooth over the problem and go on working, we were treading on an emotional mine-field, and we each moved with heart in mouth.

The explosion came about 3:00 A.M. one night when we were too exhausted to consider another line of dialogue, or to continue our pretense that all was well. We raged at each other for a time, then wept, and finally subsided with the relief of a crisis passed, and understanding gained. Two days later the script was ready for the typist and Allie returned to New York.

The eventual fate of the screenplay was less important than the collaboration that produced it. The producer/star of the series turned it down on the basis of the "inappropriate" subject material. Although we had known from the outset that our story would meet a lot of resistance, the rejection was still a blow. Nevertheless we had accomplished our first objective: Karen had loved the script and had worked hard to have it approved. In addition, others in the industry who read the work praised it; and they all had assumed we were experienced, professional writers. We had demonstrated that we *could* do it.

So we drew up plans for further collaborative efforts. We would write other teleplays, other screenplays—perhaps even a book about women, with Karen as a third participant. Our ambitions were boundless. Allie and I, with both our families, met again during the summer in Vermont, to have a vacation and to outline future projects and work schedules. But this time our expectations outstripped our circumstances. Each night, by the time the household was quiet and we were free of family responsibilities, neither of us could summon the mental energy for the brainstorming we had planned. And without a specific topic to stimulate our thinking, engage our curiosity, the notion of setting a date for a blitzkrieg work period was clearly unreasonable. We parted, still optimistic about our collaboration, but worn out by the experience of having attempted too much, and discouraged by our complete lack of progress. Once back at home, on opposite coasts, the very fact of distance created a circular bind. Neither of us could commit herself to another extended trip that would again disrupt our households unless we had a really absorbing project to justify the effort. At the same time we needed to be together in order to find and develop ideas for just such a project. Our hopeful intentions were not enough; temporarily at least, our partnership was unable to span the three thousand miles that separated us.

Several months after the Vermont trip, I accompanied Karen to the "Salute to Everywoman" presented by the American Civil Liberties Union. We were moved and disturbed by the topics discussed during the evening, and drove home brimming with ideas for possible stories. A journalist friend of Karen's sent her a series of articles on one of the issues raised at the ACLU dinner: the problem of wife-battering. The material in Katie Brown's articles was extraordinarily powerful and compelling. Karen and I immediately agreed that we wanted to explore the possibilities of dramatizing this "single most unreported crime in the country," not as a documentary but as a drama for prime time television. Karen had only two months before resuming work on the *Little House* series, so time was short. We began at once, and have just completed an extended screen treatment.

The work, which went well, was not easy for either of us. Dealing with highly charged emotional material requires a steady perspective and an objectivity that must constantly be watched, tended, and guarded. Mindful of this, we staked out a firm work schedule of three to four hours each weekday, with nights and weekends left free. We trusted that this regimen would help us maintain the distance, order, and rhythm necessary to allow us to absorb the material without being overwhelmed by it. In addition, we built flexibility into our regimen. Each of us was free to choose where and when we would work each day, and to adjust her schedule to accommodate everyday concerns: other appointments, professional obligations, or family crises such as a child home with the flu. These arrangements permitted us to continue our day-to-day lives along with our writing, without conflict on a strictly practical level and without losing our creative momentum.

The combination of steady routine plus variable rhythm proved essential to us both. Some of our best writing was accomplished when neither felt like doing it, when our minds shied away from the subject itself. Because we had made a mutual commitment to a specific block of writing time, we would stick with it, acknowledging our problems or resistances and at the same time trying to focus on neutral aspects of the story until we were once again emotionally capable of returning to the more demanding parts. The knowledge that these writing periods were finite not only encouraged concentration, but also promised relief: in two more hours we would be able to leave the lives of these characters we had created on multicolored index cards and return to our own familiar lives with family and friends. The principle was sound and it worked. Still, we had frequent nightmares.

In my collaboration with Karen, as with Allie, our differences complement one another. My instinct to sketch out a scene or describe a character in words is balanced by Karen's talent and experience in rendering a point dramatically. Our similarities have proved equally valuable; accustomed to introspection and self-examination, both of us can thread our way back into the fabric of earlier experience to summon details of an incident or personality in order to strengthen the credibility of our story. But perhaps the most important feature of our collaboration—and I suspect it is true of most working partnerships—is instant feedback. Some of my most tentative ideas, which on my own I might dismiss or ignore, are grasped at once: "Yes! Right! And then she would— Yes! It works." Or the reverse occurs: I quickly discover that what seems enormously significant to me has only private, not universal, meaning, and thus do not waste time or energy trying to make a point that is unidentifiable to a general audience.

For many reasons I enjoy writing in partnership with a friend more than on my own. Whatever I continue to do independently, working with someone else will remain an increasingly important part of my life as a writer. The experience of collaborative effort is fascinating in and of itself. Furthermore, in what other situation can you be assured that at least *one* other person is as interested in your work as you are? (Collaboration also benefits family and friends, who therefore are spared a detailed daily progress report.) Of course, the need for social or "worldly" recognition and validation remains. However much satisfaction Karen and I find writing together, neither of us considers the job finished until we see our work accepted and produced. But that is as it should be. When you care about your work, when *you* feel that it counts, how can you believe it would be any the worse for a little recognition?

Cynthia L. Sears

Coming of Age
the Long Way Around
Nanette Vonnegut Mengel

WHEN I WAS SUPPOSED to be coming of age at twenty-one, I felt more as though my life were terminating than commencing. One of the madly comic inventions of Rube Goldberg's Professor Lucifer Butts

The dissertation section of Nanette Mengel's essay, "Coming of Age the Long Way Round," will appear in an expanded and modified form as part of a longer essay, "A Dissertation on Dissertations," to be published by the Montaigne Press at the Wright Institute in Berkeley in a collection of essays on the graduate school experience.

nicely cartoons the course of my life, in retrospect, from the black confusion I felt at twenty-one as a new graduate to my present sense at forty-one of being somehow at home. On a night when he was dimmed by gin, Goldberg's hero conceived a perfect way to get his car into his garage though the door of that building was closed and he was not able to get out of the car. When we see him, his delicately coordinated system of incongruously selected agents promises to bring him safely to port.

Precisely, he has contrived to drive his auto bumper (A) against a mallet (B) that pushes the bumper down and explodes a cap (C). The cap in turn frightens a rabbit (D), who runs toward his burrow (E), pulling a string (F), which discharges a pistol (G). The bullet penetrates a can (H) from which the water drips into an aquarium (I). As the tide rises in the aquarium, it elevates a floating cork (J), which pushes up the end of a seesaw (K), causing a flea (L) to lose its balance and fall on a gedunk hound's tail (M). The hound wakes up and chases his tail round and round, causing a platform (N) to spin and turn on a faucet (O). Water runs through a hose (P), which starts a revolving lawn sprinkler (Q) on which a rope (R) winds itself, opening the garage door. By inching forward, Butts has ingeniously set in motion a series of small explosions, frights, leakages, reflex actions, and compulsive activities that will accomplish his simple wish with marvelous indirection.

The history of my own course has had little of the professor's ingenious planning, though it began in 1956 with what was perhaps equivalent to the overdose of gin that created both Dr. Butts's problem and his imagined solution: my realization that I had no clearly defined long-term goals, no idea of what I could do after college, and no confidence that I would find my way, despite hours of consultation with my academic adviser and the college career counselor.

The summer after graduation I came very near nervous collapse. I spent July and August "therapeutically" making silver jewelry in the Tennessee mountains at the Pi Beta Phi Craft School among other novice artisans, most of whom were women from the South. I was at least as conscious daily of mental conflict about what I should do in the fall as I was of designing, sawing, and soldering. Should I try to teach history to Appalachian students at Hindman Folk School in Kentucky where I had interviewed for a job? Or should I go to Harvard, where I had been accepted in the masters program in the School of Education? Should I withdraw to the rural South—after all, I had grown up in Knoxville—or should I plunge into the intense social and intellectual atmosphere of Cambridge?

This conflict was heightened by the question my friends in the craft school posed: What was the use of my liberal education if I was unprepared for work and discouraged about love? Most of the women with whom I was living and working that summer had been home economics majors in college; some were engaged, and all of them, it seemed, were happily planning to marry in the next year or so and to use their artistic talents in the service of their homes. I, who had just finished a thesis on eighteenth-century English social history, had neither boyfriend nor anything but a negative interest in domestic life. With college over I felt futureless. My advertisement in the spring issues of the *Saturday Review* was symptomatic of my situation: "Vassar graduate, willing to go anywhere and do anything." It was really a desperate cry for help: "Somebody tell me what to do and I will do it!"

Only now, twenty years later, have I found my way to a clearer perspective. If one's self-realization can be compared to the full three-dimensional field of binocular vision, I can claim finally that the focus of one lens at least, the vocational one, is clear, although the other, the intimate lens, is still blurred. I teach English literature and composition in the University of North Carolina Evening College in Chapel Hill, help students of public administration with their writing, lead a senior seminar on vocation in the American Studies Program, and direct a literature course for residents in the Department of Psychiatry. I also teach a peer-therapy class in Reevaluation Counseling and occasionally mat and frame pictures. In a way I have said "yes" both to the nearly rural South and a life that includes handwork, and also to the intellectual excitement that attracted me to Harvard. I have not denied my concern with the problems of vocations or with the possibilities of self-help and psychological insight. At last I have committed myself to a particular field and institution, a second profession, and a kind of craft. It is as though, finally, I have come into that unobstructed sweep of serenely infinite sea that Emerson talks about in his "Spiritual Laws": by answering the call of our talents, we are like a ship in a river that runs against obstructions on every side but one. And that one shows us a direction in which all space seems to open and invite us to endless exertion.

What broke the Harvard-Hindman impasse? A thousand hours of depression were smashed by one painful conversation that summer in Tennessee with a man on a "first date." He had taught Child Study at Vassar, though I had not known him there, and was now teaching at the University of Tennessee. Since I took it for granted that he was a fellow academic, that he would see things as I did—that he would value the goals of Emerson and the eighteenth-century *Gentleman's Magazine* more than the lessons of home economics—he shocked me early in the evening when he said, critically, that Vassar didn't prepare women for their "feminine role." I had never consciously heard that term before, but I felt instinctively that he had tested me out as a woman and found me wanting. At the end of the evening I was deeply morose. The only hope for my condition, he challenged me, was psychiatric help—but he gave me no better than 50-50 odds that I would get the help I needed.

That bet was what I needed. The next day I made a list of the "real" advantages of Hindman and the "real" attractions of Harvard. The chance for therapy and romance tilted the balance toward the latter. I knew I wouldn't find either in the Kentucky mountains.

I made the right choice. The year at Harvard gave me a way to go forward. I saw a psychiatrist; by practice-teaching I found that I *could* do some worthwhile work; and I got "involved," though not very happily, with a divinity student. I found a foothold, in other words, on the edge of a future. But in retrospect I can see that the most important development that year happened by accident. My adviser in the School of Education offered me a job practice-teaching in a kindergarten in Newton. I remember thinking as he described it that it should give me a great deal of physical contact with the children and that I somehow wanted this. I said "yes" at once. I know I accepted because I wanted my work to give me intimacy; I wanted to be close to "my children," and I imagined this would be a chance to continue teaching children recreational crafts such as papier-mâché and collage —work in which I was experienced and felt comfortable.

I can see now that this work allowed me to do exactly what I needed to do for the next two years. I discovered that I could rely on myself to earn my own way, and I developed some confidence in the mothering side of myself. The things I remember above all from those days are the beauty of a stylized, colored-chalk fish one of the children made, the way that same little boy sometimes stepped on my feet in his eagerness to tell me something—we wore the same size shoes—and the excitement of a kindergarten production of *Hansel and Gretel*. But kindergarten also took so much of my energy that I had little left for my own, adult, life. Newton was a ten-mile commute from where I lived in Cambridge, and I felt increasingly the need to return to "the center."

I decided not to teach a third year. To support myself, I worked half-time at one dollar an hour in the Harvard Coop's Text Book Annex. That was a terrible year. A dollar an hour on a part-time basis left me so little margin that I thought hard before I invested ten cents in a phone call. Like the poor everywhere I spent much of my energy worrying about money. I also bitterly resented my lack of position. Emotionally I was living very close to zero. To make matters bleaker, that was the year both the United States and Russia stepped up their atmospheric atomic testing. The previous summer I had picketed and leafleted with the Fellowship of Reconciliation at Cape Canaveral to ban the bomb. With the testing now resumed, hope of retarding the arms race was feeble everywhere. From the perspective of 1974, it sounds pretentious to claim personal depression resulting from a fact that most of us live with unthinkingly now. But then, I was one of those people whom Robert J. Lifton describes as chronically anxious because they are cut off from the hope of a future. Perhaps at the heart of this fear of futurelessness were my private, personal anxieties, but public stimulation made them worse. In December 1959 I started psychoanalysis.

Although my memories of that year are mostly dark ones, in looking back I can see that the move to Cambridge was the beginning of a kind of centering and that psychoanalytic therapy meant having a steady supporter. It was also the year of a happy, Buttsian accident. One afternoon that spring, H. Stuart Hughes came to the American Friends Service Committee (where I worked as a volunteer) to discuss his part in a panel on arms control. I overheard the switchboard operator in the next room say that she would give anything if she could take the job as his secretary. Her exclamation was like the flea that fell on the gedunk hound's tail. Prompted by my analyst, I was taking a secretarial course in Boston and would be ready to work in the fall. Did Stuart Hughes know how much I wanted the job? I don't know, but I got it.

The next four years were in many ways a bootstrap operation for me. Being at Harvard, working for the chairman of a well-established honors program in a small office—a safe fold in the larger field of the university—was like being in a psychological halfway house for me. It was the perfect place for someone filled with self-doubt, who needed both the constant tangible evidence that all was well in a small universe and the responsibility to do her part to keep it that way. Yet, in a psychological sense, I was like a polio victim with atrophied muscles; only by gathering the courage to admit my mistakes and to ask for help when I didn't know what to do did I gradually gain the wherewithal to become a good secretary. I doubt that anyone in the office had the slightest idea how much courage those early phone calls, questions, and minuscule initiatives required. Learning to handle the daily

details of responsibility made me know that I could count on myself—
and others could too—and that I deserved my place in the program.

My work then, like picture framing, was to make certain relationships possible. It meant creating conditions in which people could get
together. I was the one who scheduled appointments and who encouraged shy students to ask for special permission to do what they
wanted to do. After my first year, I was the one who pressed the Head
Tutor to answer difficult correspondence and who made tea for our
casual staff and student gatherings in the afternoons.

The "gravy," the unbargained-for rewards, were many in my job.
To be a secretary in the history and literature office meant taking a
personal interest in the national news, rubbing elbows with the powerful. My work had a certain glamor; more important, it made sense to
me in human terms and gave me a feeling of balance. For a time,
being a secretary meant living and working in that mythical kingdom
where all servants can be good servants because their masters are
good. In Stuart Hughes I had a resident hero who was a model of
effectiveness. His manuscripts—on the politics of peace, modern
European history, history as art and as science—seemed to me important and often courageous. In 1962, when Hughes decided to run for
the Senate from Massachusetts as an Independent and a peace candidate against Ted Kennedy and George Lodge, I worked in his
campaign as well as in his university office. Here was someone advocating the admission of Red China to the United Nations and a ban on
nuclear testing, who could handle William Buckley in debate, and
who attracted supporters like Dr. Spock and Thomas Merton. In
many ways it was a time of hope and I felt secure in my relationship to
the forces of progress.

Two aspects of the job as a secretary, however, made me uneasy—
two worrisome flaws that were to widen into fissures. The first was a
flickering, utterly unreasonable resentment toward some of the
women tutors, who, though they were as natural with me as the men
were, aroused this hostility in me. Who did they think they were anyway? And why did I feel inferior to them? I had no intellectual ambitions then—certainly no interest in graduate work—so I simply tried
to suppress those ugly feelings. I needed this job too much to sabotage
it with ambivalence. I would have rejected outright the suggestion that
secretarial work was degrading, and although these other women's
jobs gave them more range than mine gave me, I couldn't rationalize
my jealousy.

The other problem was time. The tutors in History and Literature
had mapped out careers as a pathway to the future; they moved on

with time, while I stood still. After a certain set period they finished their dissertations or their books and left to teach a new generation of students in other universities. What would I be doing in years to come if I stayed on? My old anxieties returned.

By the spring of 1964, I knew I had to do something about them. President Kennedy had been assassinated, Hughes's tenure as chairman of History and Literature was almost up and the prospects of anything more than boring repetition in the job looked poor. As my thirtieth birthday approached, I decided to make a significant "move" of some sort. The only one I could think of was geographical. I would go to California, where I had a number of good friends.

I arrived in Palo Alto one week before the beginning of the fall semester and there was only one opening at Stanford, where I definitely wanted to work—an office job in the medical anthropology program. Never mind that it meant tedious hours and boring filing. It was on the campus and I liked the professor who interviewed me. I could have done much worse. But from the outset I knew that my identity as a worker, my sense of my own worth, depended too heavily on others at work; since my own work was unoriginal, to say the least, I needed to live through the work going on around me. I missed Harvard, the intimate camaraderie I had come to feel in History and Literature. These Stanford students proved to be social scientists with a highly developed sense of social and vocational fraternity. Though still students they already called themselves "anthropologists"; they spent most of their spare time drinking beer together; and they had very little concern for political action. They had cast their lot with the peasant populations of the world, in Micronesia, Guatemala, and Ghana, where they did their fieldwork, so that Europe and the East Coast of the United States hardly figured in their mental landscapes. Their interests were elemental; no more endless discussions of subjects like Yeats's psychic experience. They analyzed feces in Guatemala for parasites, or investigated the quality of health care for Indian patients at the Palo Alto Hospital. What they did was closer, in some ways, to life and death, but it lacked two dimensions that were important to me: political concern and an aesthetic ideal. These anthropologists were not out organizing speakers' bureaus to protest the Vietnam war as their counterparts in the English Department were doing; and their love of the written word was limited to compulsive patronage of the newly installed Xerox machine, where I must have spent hours having routine departmental memos copied.

I was unsympathetic to those around me, no doubt about it. Our differences in values and style were unbridgeable. As it turned out, however, my work experience with them sharpened my sense of priorities and forced me to realize that eventually—soon!—I would have to take responsibility for my own work. The experience depleted my tolerance for secretarial work and paved the way for a crucial decision. For the entire two years I held the Stanford job, I continually fretted about my future. "If not this, then what should I be doing?" I asked myself that question day and night. If only I could think of the right questions to ask, I used to say to myself, I could get some answers. At the same time, I tried practical probes. I registered at the university employment office, I visited a friend who taught at the Stanford nursery school, I trained as a hospital volunteer, and again I taught crafts, this time at the Stanford Children's Hospital. And I talked. Endlessly, like a broken record, I talked with my friends, with anyone who was interested; about what I should do. Every path seemed closed. Graduate school was out: I did not want any part of the anxiety I had watched others suffer. But nothing else seemed possible. Each time I thought of something, like opening a restaurant in Marin County, for example, I almost immediately excluded it as too narrow a prospect.

One day, while I was transcribing a tape, I experienced a moment of intense anger at my boss and a chance insight into something else. The interviewer on the tape had obviously not been paying attention to the interviewee, someone in acute emotional pain, for he repeated questions at the end of his session that he had asked at the beginning. He was being careless with her feelings and with my time. We were worth more than that! I had a very sharp, quick fantasy of taking the long rectangular sheet of ventilation glass out of the window frame by my desk and shattering it over his head. The effect was stunning: I suddenly saw that I had done as much of what we would later come to call "shit work" as I was willing to do.

I forget now whether that moment of insight came before or after I enrolled in one of the free courses available to Stanford staff, whether the ventilator fantasy was cause or effect. The course on the novel in which I had enrolled was canceled at the last minute, so I took Shakespeare instead. Like Lucifer Butts, I pulled a string that discharged a pistol, and by sheer luck found myself inspired by a genuine teacher and reading what I most needed to read. I am thinking in particular of Hotspur in *Henry IV, Part One*; I cared more for that fiery rebel and his tragedy than I had cared about anything for a long time.

After Hotspur, Desdemona and Hamlet meant just as much to me. "How can you feel so much for people who have never lived?" my best friend in anthropology quizzed me over the file cabinet one day. I didn't answer very well, but I knew quite surely that graduate school, that erstwhile unthinkable possibility for me, was just what I wanted. My vocational logjam was broken, and if nearby Berkeley, whose admissions had not yet closed, would accept me, I was on my way.

After Berkeley said yes, I never again had serious doubts about the work I wanted to do. Not that I glided along in graduate school. Far from it. Many times I felt like a dreamer in a nightmare, pursued by terror while my feet were deep in quicksand. I felt that fear, for example when—unsure of what a critique was, unsure of what the poem said—I wrote my first critique of a poem, Donne's "Twicknam Garden." And I blocked so badly on a Renaissance final that I would have failed if half of it had not been a take-home exam that I could work on all night. Doubt that I would make it constantly hummed in my brain through the M.A.; yet I never looked back. Reading Tennyson's *In Memoriam*, feeling the heartsickness of the poet as he worked out his grief for the death of his friend, or awakening to Dickens' animation of objects in *Our Mutual Friend*, assured me that I was where I belonged, lonely as I often felt.

The period between the M.A. and the dissertation was psychologically the easiest part of graduate school. I had a university scholarship by then and prepared for the orals regularly with a small group of friends. So strong was our fellowship that I dreamed before my exam that John, one of my best friends, helped me over a stile (style) on a hill I was climbing, that he pointed out the three snakes (examiners) that were waiting below, and that he provoked one of them to bite him to save me. The next day we both passed into the last phase of our graduate careers.

The hardest part of graduate school was the dissertation. Yet, it was only here that the pieces of the work puzzle fell into place and that I gradually came to find myself in my work.

I remember many images of emotional hardship in dreams and fantasies during the three and a half years that I struggled to write my thesis, to find ways to "see" Dickens' novels whole and my own relationship to them clearly. The most persistent image—the one that best describes my fears as I worked—was of Svi Kanar, a student of Marcel Marceau, performing a pantomime called "The Ball."

It was May 1968; the thesis I was hatching on Dickens' comic technique in *Pickwick Papers*, a subject I had chosen because I thought I could live with it happily for months, was something I was not often proud of. It seemed a kind of comic luxury in a world that was everywhere in trouble. President Johnson had recently announced that he would not run for a second term and the black-student movement had just struck the campus with disturbing force. My Ph.D. orals were postponed because tear gas filled the English building. Who wouldn't have doubted, daily, the value of scholarship such as mine? But I always came back to my thesis. At the age of thirty-four I had gone too far in my graduate work to turn back.

It was 1968, and Kanar's mime gave symbolic shape to my anxieties about myself as an academic. As his act began, Kanar, alone on the stage, playfully bounced an imaginary basketball, tossed it in the air, and dribbled rhythmically at varying speeds. Suddenly the imaginary ball asserted a life of its own; it began to expand at a frightening rate so that his pleasure, and ours as well, turned to panic—it seemed unlikely that he could regain control of the ball. It was a relief to see him stop the ball by main force from expanding, and then to watch him, with enormous exertion, force it back toward its original size until, finally, he had a basketball again. True, he handled the ball more warily now, but it was once again manageable. The game could go on.

The next time the ball asserted its mysterious growing-power, Kanar was not so successful. He strained valiantly to contain it, but it became so large that his arms could barely support it. He ended the act in the posture of Atlas, one knee on the floor, the ball weighing on his shoulders and the back of his neck. I remember that I clapped very hard for Kanar's performance and that my hands were cold. There was something familiar in it that frightened me. In retrospect, his act seems to have prefigured the life that lay ahead of me as I tried to control my thesis, to keep it within bounds.

I do not remember that Kanar acted out the opposite problem— shrinkage, the fear that the ball would diminish to the size of a jawbreaker and slip between the boards—but I retain that image of him as clearly in my mind's eye as if he had. What if my ideas came to nothing? What if my dissertation went the other way and vanished? These two fantasies of myself as Atlas and anti-Atlas were especially strong as my topic slowly evolved. I was dismayed at the accumulation of my earlier drafts and papers. Although it was painfully clear that I could not use most of them, I was determined to do something with those excruciatingly hard-won bits of work. Stubbornly, I filed them for later use, and at the same time loaded my dissertation for a while with a pointless accumulation of pages—until it reminded me of the children's book *Every Haystack Doesn't Have a Needle.*

Weeding lines from draft after draft as my adviser returned them, trying to glean whatever was salvageable, endlessly, gratefully, unquestioningly, I retyped the phrases he liked. If he made the smallest positive sign in the margin, I would not let that sentence go. Those phrases asserted a claim to immortality even stronger than the mortification I felt each time I redid them. On the one side, then, I was forever discarding, and on the other, I was forever preserving, as I swung between the polar fears symbolized in Kanar's mime: the fear that my work was trivial and liable to evaporate, and the fear that it was so enormous it would immobilize me.

My problems were only incidentally intellectual. At the deepest level they were moral and psychological. What difference did this thesis make? What *difference* did it make? I hoped bleakly for some kind of a breakthrough, but I was too worried about breakdown to make something positive happen. At times I cheered myself wanly that the way would open if only I suffered enough. But beneath the self-accusations, the self-doubt, I also knew that something larger was wrong, and my anger was part of what paralyzed me. It was not because we were intellectually feeble that our lives were nightmarish as my friends and I struggled with our independent projects. By and large, we simply had no shared way to express the full force of our feelings therapeutically—either our fears or the pleasure we felt in our work.

Luckily, at this point in 1969, I found the only real help I was capable of using during this period of lowest ebb: the help of a friend, a graduate student in history. Listening carefully one night, with full attention, he jotted down things I told him about Dickens and about my despair. He recorded my ideas and my feelings about my material and played them back to me. What I really cared about, I heard from him, was not comic form, or Dickens' debt to Cervantes and the eighteenth-century novelists, but the way Dickens' novels objectified his struggle for identity, the way he used them to explore and express his conflicts and to celebrate his psychic triumphs. For me, the "living Dickens" was the distressed child surviving in a grown writer whose imaginative world burst with life. I admired him because he was able to create his vocation as he wrote, and because his fiction played out and integrated the multiple versions of parent and child that filled his psyche. It became clear to me that the kernel of Dickens' novels, the germinating force, was his own childhood conflict. That idea was a thesis, a statement that I was prepared to argue.

At last I had broken through the stone wall of my anxieties. As I "discovered" my subject, it seemed that my subject discovered me.

For a while the sensation of freedom was exhilarating. I felt in charge, somehow human again. Looked at through a psychoanalytic lens, however, my new thesis raised a disturbing question: What was I avoiding in my own life that attracted me to this particular novel by Dickens?

At about this time, as I was marching grimly along Telegraph Avenue to the library one morning, I had another Buttsian experience. Noticing my feet buttoned up in rain shoes—never mind that it was a beautiful day; it might rain later—a hippie hurt my feelings and brought me close to the answer. "Up-tight lady," he murmured indolently as I passed. Not long after this, a professor who had read one of my drafts expressed his annoyance at the number of times I neutered my pronouns and began my sentences with "it." What were these outsiders seeing in me that I didn't recognize?

I had not intended to face *myself* in my work, yet here I had come up against the personal fears that inhibited me most. If I was going to pursue the genuine source of my interest in Dickens, I could count on the emotional energy that his novels released in me. But the pursuit would require me to face the fact that certain aspects of these novels matched my own fears. Dickens and I were both distressed about the need for closeness, both dubious about the possibilities of meaningful work. We both tried to deal with these problems at the same time that we energetically distracted ourselves and other people from seeing them. I wanted to affirm these facts about Dickens just as I wanted to recognize and validate them in myself. I needed to accept the continuity beneath the surface of my own experience.

Now that I had a thesis and a method of analysis, I had begun to regain control of the ball. I had only to endure the classic long-distance loneliness of writing. But in September 1971 I temporarily set my thesis aside for other work. I had turned up a two-year instructorship at the University of North Carolina. There, mercifully for me, I had authority over students, forty of whom wrote "long, argumentative papers," as the freshman English syllabus specified; this appointment gave me analytical practice as well as the chance to cheer someone else along for a change. As a teacher I had responsibility. For the first time since beginning graduate school, I had a sense that I was coming into my own in a way that the world recognized.

When I picked up my own thesis again in the summer of 1972, however, anxiety still thwarted my progress. But at this point in my work my fears paralyzed me for shorter and shorter periods; I "bounced back" more quickly. This growth in self-confidence stemmed in part from my experience as an instructor. But I had discovered something else in Chapel Hill that promised to be as important for my future as the degree would be: Re-evaluation Counseling, an emotional support group. In spring 1972, worried about finishing my thesis during the summer vacation, I had signed up for a weekend workshop with twenty people of all ages who wanted to work together on a variety of individual problems. My goal was to complete that thesis that summer; I brought my concern about whether or not I could accomplish this to the group and they helped me accordingly. The group became friends to whom I could turn with every inadmissible feeling—my angers, my fears, my doubts, and my excitement. They, in turn, taught me a great deal about other kinds of adult conflict as they worked on their distresses about aging, divorce, or relations with colleagues.

The dissertation I finally wrote was something between Svi Kanar's back-breaking globe and my image of a vanishing jawbreaker. It is no longer my sole universe, claiming all my attention, defining who I am. In surviving our association I discovered my own deepest fears, a serviceable grit, and the power of friendship.

In what sense can I say that my life, in all its patchwork, is of a piece? What clear threads of identity run through Cambridge and Stanford, Berkeley and Chapel Hill? Why were those Buttsian accidents important? And what does it mean to be, or rather to feel, whole? The simplest answer has something to do with the university, with my need to live somehow at that center and to do it without losing touch with children or the child in me, to satisfy social and intellectual calls at the same time that I affirm my sense of myself as a woman. Perhaps feeling safely "at home" now means having said no to other voices that would keep me in a subordinate role and to the desire in myself to remain, somehow, fixed. It also means having said yes to currents of intuition. My work now frees me from old obstructions, offers a wide space to sail. It is a long time since commencing looked like terminating.

Nanette V. Mengel

Notes from a Conversation on Art, Feminism, and Work

Miriam Schapiro

I

I WAS RAISED in a patriarchal home—as we all were. I watched both my parents work their whole lives. To me, work has always been a natural thing to do; leisure has little attraction. I early identified with my father, an artist. Although today I admire my mother for striving to exceed her limitations, as a child I was acutely conscious of them. My mother's view of the world was not a "world" view; she lived "inside," at home, and in fact felt considerable anxiety about venturing outside. My father shared his art with me and taught me to love all art. My mother was a dreamer and a constant reader. I chose to see her dreaming and her reading, her having a "world of her own" as a validation of my own inner life.

My mother was also a splendid housekeeper. About her domestic gifts I was, and am, ambivalent. When I talk of work, I mean "outside" work. My own attitude toward householding is to do as little of it as possible. My mother's floors were always shined, her linens always clean. Even as I describe this, I realize that in the development of my own attitudes toward nesting, her kind of caring was important. Yet, like everyone else in this society, I still have difficulty assigning reality or meaning to the work-at-home to which many women have devoted their entire lives. Although my mother gave me many important examples of caring and working, it was only when I joined the women's movement, only when I provided a context of femaleness for myself, that I could absorb and appreciate my mother's experience. Yet, I have lived out an experience parallel to hers all through the years; I too have been a homemaker, a nester, and a mother.

During the depression, my mother took a job in a department store. Once she had "real" work—"worldly" work—I began to assign her a space I had previously reserved for my father; however, I still believed that to be out in the world, making your mark on it, you had to be a man. Once my mother took that job she appeared more forceful, more concentrated, more economical in her use of time—as we would say now, "more together." But even this didn't prove to me that a woman, my mother, could do real work in the world. Somehow my conditioning rigidly reinforced a perverse sense of the world as being a place where only a man could work.

As a child, as an adolescent, as a college student, I was remarkably single-minded. I cared most about being an artist, about making my art. The first complication in my life was marriage to another artist, whom I met when we were graduate students together at the University of Iowa. Our love seemed predestined then: I "fell" in love, married for love. Looking back twenty-nine years later, I realize the brilliance of my choice. I not only married for love, I married for an education—and Paul Brach and I have educated each other, artistically, intellectually, politically. Of course, as two artists, workers in the same field, we had problems of competition—problems we talked out. We were fortunate to be living in a psychological age, and in our talks with each other we benefitted from psychology as thoughtful people can.

Only once did marriage and work seem at odds—when Paul took a job at the University of Missouri and, jobless, I went with him. I was not happy. The transition between graduate school and the world hadn't worked for me. When we married, we had made an unspoken pact to preserve *his* ego and career. I didn't realize what it would cost me. Nor did he. After two years, I prevailed upon him to move to New York.

New York was a small art world then and we plunged immediately into it. We found companionship among artists for the first time. Abstract expressionism was the prevailing, vigorous style of the period —I began making abstract expressionist paintings. I was also conducting my own postgraduate education in painting. I was tapped for the work I did and invited to show my paintings. I became "visible."

As I neared the age of thirty-two, I wanted to have a child. I felt as if it were "now or never." Paul was doubtful about combining art with parenthood, but felt it was my *right* to have a child. I was living in the realm of WISH and fantasized that I could do *everything*—take care of my child, do my art, enjoy my friends.

From the time I was pregnant, I entered the world of mothers. I belatedly realized that inside I had suffered from the gossip and gaze of people who maligned women who stepped out into the world to make a place for themselves in it. Now I felt womanly, I was womanly, and the whole world could see it. I painted paintings of pregnant women. I wanted to glorify my condition. I felt the glory. I lived it out.

When the baby was born, people congratulated me as if I had done something very special. The other women artists we knew did not have children, and they cast me in a heroic light. The dramatic side of me lived it to the hilt, but the painter was suddenly confronted with the problem of TIME. Although my husband "helped" with the baby, he limited the time he would spend and put professional needs first. I was left with total responsibility.

Fortunately, I had two unbelievable mothers on call—my own, Fannie Schapiro, and my husband's, Molly Brach. They gave me the impression that they had waited all their lives to take care of my baby. Both of them accepted my ambitions and my art completely. Of course their old-fashioned ways produced no small amount of guilt in me. (My mother had a certain way of looking in the refrigerator and saying, "My *God*, there's no milk," as if the holocaust had come.) But this effect was so unintended, so unrecognized by them, that the guilt became my problem.

Despite their help, I still felt I never had enough time. I seemed to be forever making *arrangements* for the baby and the household, even when I wasn't caring for them. I insisted to my husband that we must have help. But we were very poor, my husband and I. I did not have a job that brought in a weekly paycheck. Sales were as sales are. They come when they come. You can't count on them. Paul said, "If you want help, *pay* for it. I can only pay for what we have now." The income from his paintings and teaching was supporting all three of us, and he felt that if I required more money it was my responsibility to earn it. I have always been grateful to my husband for taking a very specific and clear stand on this. He was not against me, not my enemy, at any level; at the same time he knew his own mind.

I got my first teaching job at Parsons School of Design. In teaching I was challenged by a whole new world. I put myself into the hands of Marvin Israel, an artist who also taught at Parsons. He bequeathed me everything he knew.

Teaching became my second work. It is interesting to reflect on how we decide what counts as work. (How do you decide whether this interview is your work or taking time from your work?) When I say that my principal work problem now is to clear my calendar in order to make time for my work, how do I "decide" that political engagements and encounters with other artists, or with other women like you, aren't work? Although teaching opened up a new world for me, and although I am a very good teacher, I consider teaching second to painting. As my teaching expanded and flourished, as demands became greater in this sphere of work, it seemed I could give less and less to my "real" work, to my painting. I have recently returned to New York and severed, at least temporarily, all ties with institutions. I am reconsidering the place teaching should have in my life now that I can earn sufficient money from my paintings, lecturing, and writing.

When I was younger, my decision to teach was of paramount importance. I remember, before the women's movement, young women coming to me for advice. "How did you manage?" they would ask.

"How were you able to have a child, sustain a marriage, and pursue a career at the same time?" I would tell them the story of *my* decision to get help with child care and with the household—to earn the necessary money for it—to have help when my husband and I couldn't afford help. I have always cited this decision as one of the most important in my life. With it I established my freedom for four hours a day, hours exclusively devoted to solitary work in the studio.

II

I realize now that although I loved New York, was comfortable painting in the dominant abstract expressionist style, had splendid companionship with men and women co-artists, I was nonetheless unhappy and fearful. I was fearful despite the fact that I had work in which I was quite single-minded and successful, work that my husband encouraged and the community recognized. Nonetheless, I kept saying, "I'm not sure I can do this, I'm not sure I *should* do this. I am a woman." I was a "token" woman in the male world. There was some slight satisfaction in that. I enjoyed taking part in shows with the best male painters—even though my work, the only work by a woman, seemed so different as to be peripheral. Whatever the satisfactions of tokenism, however, the pains were greater.

There was something about me—as an artist, as a woman, or as a personality, I don't know—that made male painters shrink from me. Men like de Kooning, Pollock, and Kline were much more comfortable with a woman who presented herself as a woman first. Ideas or paintings could be discussed once sexual identity was established.

There were several interested and dedicated women artists in New York, but with them I had only "girl talk." The men would get together in studios to talk about their work. The women really didn't respect each other deeply. I don't think that another woman, at that time, really cared about my opinion of her work. She wanted a man's opinion. We are emerging from these attitudes now; we tend to forget how it was. But women didn't care about each other's opinions of their work in the fifties and early sixties—and frankly, many of them don't even now. We used to party a lot together—arrange champagne and steak picnics on the beach in East Hampton. We talked about our love lives, shared each other's romances. But I can assure you we never came together over painting. Once the women's movement was underway, we came together again. Then most of us could connect on a new plane.

I was not only unhappy among my co-artists, men and women, I was also unhappy in the social world that surrounds artists. When I socialized in that larger group of collectors, artists, writers, and museum people, I was seen as Mrs. Paul Brach. These people also knew me as Miriam Schapiro, but for social convenience they dealt with me as Mrs. Paul Brach. In their presence, I myself was confused, unsure of who I was.

Because of my loneliness and confusion in the social and art worlds, because of my sense that others could not see and respond to the woman Miriam Schapiro as a whole person, I felt increasing pressure alone in my studio. I needed, more than ever, to be a special, different, original artist, to have my art represent me in a clear and unmistakable way, so that I wouldn't have to bother with social identity. My art alone would reveal me to the world and to myself.

But I had less time for my art than ever. I had to accommodate myself to my husband, my mother, my mother-in-law, my son, and my maid, not to mention my father, my father-in-law, my students, and my dear friends. I was taking little bits out of my whole self and giving them out here and there all over. The stories of Rembrandt we read as children presented an idealized version of the artist's life. Rembrandt was allowed to go into the studio at nine o'clock in the morning and stay there until nine o'clock at night. He was totally protected by a Mrs. Rembrandt, who took care of him. That was my ideal. Who does not have this ideal? For whom would it not work? Yet the reality of my life was just the opposite.

I tried to affirm *myself* in the place where, despite the fragmentation and the complexity of my life, I continued to make images; but when I got to my studio, those few hours a day, I found myself with a "work problem." I felt enormous guilt about leaving the baby. I felt I didn't deserve my good fortunes, didn't deserve the decisions I had managed to make in my own interest. At some point the pressures of fragmentation, the division between my private and social selves, my sense of unworthiness, my doubts about my condition as a woman—all these came to a head. I lost the *ability* to work. I experienced the severity of this as not knowing *how* to make a painting—it was as if everything I had ever learned had washed out of my brains.

Fortunately, the decision to take a job, to earn a steady income, also allowed me to go into therapy. Luckily too, I found a therapist who was a follower of Karen Horney. He completely identified with me, aided me in all sorts of ways principally related to issues of work and career, and never suggested that I question the validity of my ambition or my art.

"A painted image based on a new self-image." *Shrine: Homage to M.L.*, 1962, magna and graphite

I soon developed a ritual that allowed me to start work again. I talked to myself as if I were reborn, totally new on this earth. "You have to have turpentine. You have to have your paints laid out. You dip the brush in the turpentine. You mix the color you want. You start to draw." I repeated this litany, followed my own instructions. I began to work again.

A totally new image surfaced in this period of renewal, a painted image based on a new self-image. I finally came out of the jungle of abstract expressionism. The new image was vertical, almost my size. Narrow like a person. It was compartmentalized. The top compartment was gold, a symbol of aspiration. The next compartment was a fragment "quoted" from the history of art, such as a rendering of part

Frank J. Thomas

"Large painting with the aid of a computer." *Iris*, 1971, acrylic spray
(Collection Amstar Corporation, New York City)

of a Cézanne or a Da Vinci painting. Beneath that was an egg—the woman, the creative person, I, myself. At the bottom was the mirror where I looked into myself, where I would find my images for the future. These four compartments became my hallmark. I worked on the series for about three years.

These paintings, "the Shrines" as they are called, established for me a self. But my doubts continued. Do you know the image of the creative person with an angel on her shoulder? The fantasy that it is not you who produces, but the angel directing your hand? Whatever the origin of this image, in the circumstances of my unhappiness and insecurity I adopted it. I took responsibility for my work, but I couldn't believe that I was actually *able* to do it. Sometimes, my old fears would rise up. Work belonged to men; could *I*, could a woman, be an artist? Moreover, I was unclear, I realized that I had always been unclear, about whom I worked or painted *for*.

Let me give an anecdote to illustrate my confusion. When I was growing up, my parents took a place in the country so that we could leave New York City during the summer. My mother and I were left alone there all week to amuse ourselves as we wanted to; my father came for the weekends. It was established, when I was about six, that I was to draw regularly during the week and show my father my work at the end of each week. Some weeks, though, I didn't want to work. When my father joined us for the weekend, we would fight. My mother would say that she'd tried to get me to do some drawings, but that I refused. My father would scold me because I wouldn't do anything. I wondered: Who am I working for? My father? My mother? Myself? Whom did I make these drawings for? I loved doing the drawings, but I didn't like to be told to do them. Later on in my life, I had to try to clarify this "audience" problem. Was I painting for myself alone? For the art world? For an anonymous, faceless public? It wasn't until the women's movement that I clearly saw that I wasn't working only for myself, but for a very specific audience of women. Although I was indoctrinated early into the ways of work, no one had been able to tell me before why to work or for whom.

III

The first feminist book I read was *The Second Sex*, but I had no one with whom to discuss it, learn from it. It was Doris Lessing's *The Golden Notebook* that seemed to change my life. I read it at forty-three. I identified with the artist, whose struggles resembled my own. I seemed to myself very weak—and Anna seemed to me weak, except in being an artist. I was overwhelmed by the idea that Lessing might have taken her life as a source and transformed it in her writing. Reading Lessing did not move me toward the women's movement, then in its embryonic stage, but it enabled me, for the first time, to identify with another woman artist. It was a private identification, which nonetheless was the foundation for a more public commitment, which came a few years later when we moved to California.

When in California, I made a series of large paintings with the aid of a computer. They were constructions of strange architectural visions in space. The paintings reflect a specific masculine tradition, one in which I made my place and felt at home; however, I now realize that these paintings are also connected in an elementary way to my female past.

The paintings are about exotic space. My grandmother lived in Russia, in a *shtetl*. Her space was confined. Her activities were limited to the kitchen, the bedroom, the small garden where she hung her clothes to dry—except once, when she took her entire brood of children alone, and crossed the Atlantic Ocean to come to this country to join her husband. She had two spatial experiences: one limited, confined in the extreme; the other an expansive voyaging out. Growing up, I listened to my mother and her sister talk about the world—my grandmother's world and their own. I felt the spatial limits of their lives. I saw my own future in terms of spatial expansion. I wanted to "move out." Women's world seemed limited to the tribe, the clan, the family. The women never talked of moving, of traveling. A visit to relatives was an occasion that called for months of anxiety and preparation.

As an adult woman, as a painter, I wanted to acknowledge and to share their experience; just as strongly, I felt the need to escape it. The computer paintings are visually expressive of my desire to separate myself from my grandmother in the *shtetl* and at the same time to include myself with her in her voyage from the old country to a new world.

In California in 1970 I met Judy Chicago, a woman fifteen years younger than I, who stressed consciousness raising and autobiography in the training of women artists. She invited me to come to Fresno University, where she taught, to give a public lecture. After the lecture, I was invited to the off-campus studio where Judy and the women made their art. The first "work" they had made was a wall which they built in the studio to improve the space. It was an impressive piece of carpentry, occupying a major part of the vast barn/studio.

Michael Arthur

"Vaginal iconography." *OX*, 1968, acrylic (Collection La Jolla Museum of Contemporary Art, California)

Proudly, they showed it to me and I responded immediately, understanding that it represented their strength in using skills normally assigned to men and also their sense of territoriality, which preceded assigning themselves the task of "making art."

Judy had prepared the women for my coming. In one part of the barn they had a modified kitchen and they had each cooked a special dish for me. I was impressed by their sense of themselves and by what they wore: hiking boots, shirts hanging out, slacks or long skirts, woolen caps pulled over their ears (there wasn't much heat). It was far from my usual experience with women in college. They were my first female audience and they appreciated me and my work in a way that presaged the public appreciation which was to come for women artists in the seventies.

My experience with these California women, and with Judy in particular, inspired a deep, fruitful look at myself. I learned to call feelings by their names. I began to understand (as many other women were also realizing about themselves) that I had been living a double life. We professional women might have been living out the lives we had chosen for ourselves, but we had sealed ourselves off from our feelings about being women. To assert oneself as a creative woman in the fifties was to ask to be called names: such as hard, aggressive, tough. That hurt, but we couldn't afford to admit the pain. Better to turn away from one's own needs, to cry alone, without admitting why.

Judy and I began to collaborate on several projects. We traveled together to visit women artists on the West Coast. The trip was a revelation to me. I was used to big lofts, naked light bulbs; and to "dedicated" New York artists, spending all their money on material, every moment on their art. In California I found serious women artists who worked in the most invisible, most anonymous way. What they made was usually very personal and very small—they didn't have money for good paper or for canvas. They made their art on dining room tables, worried about getting jobs, compared notes about raising their children. They were unlike any woman artist I had known—or imagined.

Judy and I collaborated on a monograph on vaginal iconography. My work on this project grew out of a painting entitled *OX* that I had made in 1967. I had needed to symbolize the self then, and the symbol I used was a centered hexagonal image which I have since learned is a classic, tantric symbol for the vagina.

We also collaborated on Womanhouse, a project that Judy and I co-sponsored as teachers in the newly formed Feminist Art Program at the California Institute of the Arts in Valencia. I began teaching in the Art School there in 1970. A year later Judy was invited to join the faculty. Together we formed the special program for the training of women as artists. Twenty-one women students from our program found a wrecked, abandoned mansion in Hollywood. Directed by Judy and me, they worked on it, putting in glass windows, rebuilding walls, peeling off wallpaper, putting up new wallpaper, working with their hands, working physically, learning all sorts of new skills— feeling their own power to construct and to build. When the building was in shape, we asked the students to create a house in those empty rooms out of their own experiences and fantasies. We used "consciousness-raising" discussions to provoke new images. We promised immunity from intrusive male criticism. No spectator-critics, no faculty, would come around, peering into the room, advising, directing the artist's space, telling her the way her room should be done. Unexpectedly, this project became an enormously successful exhibit, and was visited by thousands, and filmed and screened extensively.

For fourteen months, while active in the women's movement in California, I didn't paint. I did make, in collaboration with another

Debora Dyer

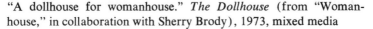

"A dollhouse for womanhouse." *The Dollhouse* (from "Womanhouse," in collaboration with Sherry Brody), 1973, mixed media

"The new work was different from anything I had done before."
Nightsong, 1973, acrylic/collage

younger woman, Sherry Brody, a dollhouse for Womanhouse. It had six rooms: a nursery, a kitchen, a parlor, a seraglio, an artist's studio, and a star's bedroom. When the dollhouse was finished, I realized that it was a pivotal expression in my life. I returned to my studio, and the work just poured out of me.

The new work was different from anything I had done before. I worked on canvas, using fabric. I wanted to explore and express a part of my life which I had always dismissed—my homemaking, my nesting. I wanted to validate the traditional activities of women, to connect myself to the unknown women artists who made quilts, who had done the invisible "women's work" of civilization. I wanted to acknowledge them, to honor them. The collagists who came before me were men, who lived in cities, and often roamed the streets at night scavenging, collecting material, their junk, from urban spaces. My world, my mother's and grandmother's world, was a different one. The fabrics I used would be beautiful if sewed into clothes or draped

against windows, made into pillows, or slipped over chairs. My "junk," my fabrics, allude to a particular universe, which I wish to make real, to represent.

In 1973, after my collaboration with Judy ended, I began to re-shape my feminism so that it suited my ambitions, my life. First, I made it one of my principal concerns to correct art history, to see to it that women artists are included in the formal story and teaching texts of art. The authoritative book on art history, Janson's *History of Art*,[1] the book most widely used in and outside the classroom, does not include one woman artist; yet we know of women who have, through the ages, made art. Janson is culturally blind. It may be unseemly to say so, but he is blind and his blindness infuriates me. I want to publish as many women artists as I can, including living women artists. I will collaborate with others to put back into the culture a heritage denied us, and to build our own tradition for the future.

[1] H. W. Janson, *History of Art* (New York: Prentice-Hall, 1969).

I am repeatedly questioned about the conflict between the requirement of excellence, the demand to maintain "standards," and the
feminist requirement that we be supportive and open to each other. I
answer that I do respect, I insist on, excellence in art. But I find no
conflict of excellence with openness and mutual support. We women
are in a transitional period. When a book comes out or a painting is
made, we measure it against the standards we know—which are male
standards. But we, the transitional women, are in the process of developing new standards. We don't yet know what they will be. We
must not make war on each other while, in our vulnerability, we try to
create something new. I do not insist that whatever a woman makes
now will, in the future, be seen to meet the standards we develop. I do
say that if a woman's work is *authentic*, if—whatever the pain, anxiety, repetition, and tentativeness—she tries to make a statement of
her own, unmindful of the awards of establishment critics, she will
help to create the standards by which we may *then* judge her work. I
have sat in consciousness-raising groups and been bored to tears with
what I was hearing. But I always remind myself that what I am listening to has never been spoken before.

I realize that there is an apparent contradiction here. On the one
hand, I speak of the art, the good art, that women have done, art that
has been unjustly overlooked. By "good," I refer to the standards that
are male, but also mine since I was educated in this culture. So when I
say Janson is blind—simply wrong—I mean that he is wrong by those
standards. On the other hand, I seem to be advocating that we forget
our customary conceptions of "good" and "bad," that we await and
attend to the emergence of new standards, and ask only that works be
authentic, fresh. There is no practical incompatibility between these
attitudes. The future Janson will include both the "good" art done by
women in the past and also quite new art which we cannot yet describe because we women are doing it for the first time.

Let me describe a personal feminist experience that illustrates—as
it has inspired—my attitude toward criticism. I once sat for ten hours
in a darkened room with other women watching slides of paintings
and sculpture done by women in the room. Some of those women, like
me, were well known. Most of them had been invisible as artists; many
were trained in universities, but they hadn't exhibited their art. Ten
hours I sat there. Do you know what I discovered? As each slide was
shown there was a flutter of applause, an acknowledgment that this
woman had made this statement. But for some women there was more
applause. After ten hours, I was shocked to realize that the good work
had surfaced. There was a natural consensus among the range of

"My fabrics allude to a universe which I wish to make real, to represent."

individual artists in that room about what was good. I learned that you must show everything; the especially good work *will* surface. Everyone will be acknowledged. No one need be put down. The good will surface and we will learn to understand it.

Art—good art—occurs when there is some agreement that good art, in fact, exists. When women artists seriously decide to assume responsibility for making history—for making whatever they agree good art is, instead of waiting to be recognized for their achievements —then and only then will they assure themselves of inclusion in recorded art history.

In reshaping my feminism I realized that my painting itself has a political dimension. Merely to speak out, to describe the daily ways of your life, turns out to be political. To say that you make a bed, cook a meal, live with someone you love, care for a child, that you cover windows and clothe your family—to say these things is to redress the trivialization of women's experience.

In my painting—and less directly in my lecturing, teaching, organizing, and publishing—I try to acknowledge and to underscore the realities of women's lives. In a new series of collages, I have glued in a painting by Mary Cassatt. I collaborate with women out of the past, as I do with the women I actually work with, to bring women's experience to the world.

Sitting with other women, in a barn, in a studio, in a darkened room, changed my life. Feminism came to me simply from being in a room with other women. You don't have to get more complicated than that. I learned in that room, among those women, that my sense of my life, of my conflicts, of my work as mine alone, was a false view of my own history. I learned that all women had experienced some version of problems I had taken to be unique. Yet in all the years of my unhappiness, I had never connected with another woman in search of relief.

I take feminism to provide *the* place, the space where we can connect with each other as we connect with our own feelings and our own past. I sit on the board of the College Art Association in a room with Janson and other men like him. I watch these wise old owls, so impervious to women's lives and art, so apparently invulnerable, so armored against experience and change. I go back to a room full of women and I am in a different world. I am outside the defensive system of social gatherings and collegial meetings in which contact and "mutuality" are a matter of giving and receiving credit cards. I take a deep breath. I can be foolish. I can be vulnerable, I can be human.

eeva-inkeri

"I wish to collaborate with women out of the past." *Collaboration Series: Mary Cassatt and Me*, 1976, collage/watercolor (Collection Dorothy Seiberling)

When I talk to you about my ambivalence, my fears, my guilts, I too am trying to help us make new connections. I too was "victimized" by this culture. It took a movement of women to equal, to balance, in my head, my father's image. Until I was struck by the mass, the weight, of women's works, I could only live with my fears, not overcome them. Women made me understand that I could join them, that we could join together, that I could proclaim myself a woman and do my work. Things seemed to snap into place; my work became joy. I had been in the fog for many years. I had been clear about being an artist, but not about much else.

A woman today who decides to be an artist has an easier time of it. She need not be burdened by a patriarchal history. She can take comfort in a world of critics (many female) who are rewriting that history, a new generation of women not overwhelmed by a patriarchal past. If she addresses herself to the world of women, she has a world on her side. Every woman wants her to succeed because every woman wants every other woman's success.

You interrupt, you say that I am too idealistic, however pleasant my nonsense sounds to the ear—that women are at least as competitive with each other as they are with men, that we are at best ambivalent about each other's success, that the rifts are wide and deep both in the women's movement and among women with various degrees of connection or hostility to feminism. But I reply: You are taking the short view of history, and a dim and partial view of the present. Of course women are human. Of course we are subject to human failures. As individuals we are weak—competitive, envious, petty, shortsighted. We *kvetch*, we complain—not to the person who can do something about it, but to everyone. We whine, talk, make noise, waste time, cry, and quarrel. Nothing seems constructive, no progress is in sight. O.K. We live with this. We are not perfect. Whoever said we were? We may have special virtues, but we have also been especially hindered in mind and spirit.

This weakness does not account for our whole selves. A part of us *is* perfect. And that small part of us wholeheartedly wishes that every woman succeed. We want to go to the bookstore and find many books by many Susan Brownmillers. We want to buy ten of them, not one. We want to see thousands of women painters, women poets, expressing *our* anger, realizing *our* hopes, confirming *our* lives. We want to be proud of all the women in the bookstores, the museums, the concert halls of the future. That perfect side of us is on the side of every young woman artist. We will do more than wish her well; we will join with her to help discover and create the communities in which she and her art can prosper.

IV

I have talked of many fears today, fears pertaining to my life as a woman. I have largely overcome these fears; however, there are other fears, pertaining to the human condition, to which, if I allowed myself, I would still be subject.

Visualize a room where I am solitary with my work. Alone in that room, I have to confront myself. Normally we do not allow ourselves to be in touch with our fears, although we assign them names—fear of success, fear of failure, fear of completion, fear of loss, fear of God-knows-what. My own conviction is that when we are alone, our fundamental fear is the fear of death, although we can neither recognize it nor name it.

We arrange our days to avoid thinking about death. Each day is a space we must fill, to avoid the empty hour, the experience of being alone with difficult thoughts. When I go into the studio, that white-walled room, I am alone. I have made the decision that I will confront my devil's thoughts. I must listen to the voices within, stop confusing life with mere activity.

When I look back on the years of excessive self-doubt, I wonder how I was able to make my paintings. In part, I managed to paint because I had a desire, as strong as the desire for food or sex, to push through, to make an image that signified.

The fear of death is the other side of that desire, the other side of creativity. We are afraid that we won't have time, that we won't be able to create, that death will end our creating—which of course it will someday. The relation between creativity and death takes on complicated nonliteral meanings. We not only want to do our work before we die; we want our work to be significant. We don't just want to make pretty pictures. Then, doubting ourselves, we almost wish for death. At the same time we know that death is *always* around the corner, that we have gone into the studio to create life. It is as if on one shoulder stands the creative angel, while on the other is the angel of death. I don't want to be mystical. I do want to stress—however elusive the words—the interconnectedness, the experienced duality, of death and creation.

The principal artists in the fifties were men; and almost every other one drank himself to death. Why? It wasn't just the fear of success. It had to do with something deeper: responsibility for one's work and doubts about fulfilling that responsibility alone in the studio. It had to do with facing death, alone, while trying to create life. An individual overcomes the fear of death by working. As long as I work I maintain life, ward off death. After death, work will "stand in" for my being.

When a woman decides to be a painter—a decision for which, until the past few years, there has been no precedent—she assumes the primary responsibility for her life. She becomes responsible for her perceptual, emotional, and intellectual experience. The responsibility is overwhelming. Every coffee cup she places on every table, every table on every rug, in relation to every floor, has meaning for her. Everything in her life becomes a part of her perceptual encyclopedia. She goes into a studio that is empty, bare. Here she must act on the decision she has made; here her responsibility is tested. Nothing could be more painful. However talented, however gifted she is, it is very painful.

I have been talking about the underlying drama that is continuously played out when I, a woman, go into my studio. Now I want to talk about the process by which I actually get to work. I have lived with a man, an artist, for twenty-nine years. He works in an entirely different way from mine, and from his discrete vantage point has described to me what I do. Frankly, if I hadn't lived with him, I might not be aware of my own way of working.

I am serious about the images I make. That is a given. I never waver from my ambition—indeed, my compulsion—to do something significant. Yet I cannot just walk into my studio and "do something significant." I have had to develop a way of getting down to work that is probably best thought of as a way of playing.

When I make up my mind to start work on a new painting, I go through what I call a "blood bath." I get out all my papers, all my paints. I play with them in every way I can imagine; I smear around on paper to get the feeling of paint on my hands. I leave my ordinary world and literally go into another house, a house of painting.

Then I may wash my hands at the sink and start making images on paper, freely, mindlessly, without a thought in my head. At the end of the day, I may have twenty-five "works" all over the floor. My husband stands at the door aghast. He always asks the same question: How can you so deprofessionalize yourself? How can you allow yourself to make something even a child, a beginner, could make? My answer is always the same: It is both easy and necessary. I am "getting somewhere," "being constructive." It just doesn't look that way.

I go on like this for several days. Sometimes I move in the opposite direction. I do tight little drawings. Perhaps I copy from a book or I make detailed renderings of an object, say a bowl of flowers. These drawings are minutely detailed, totally obsessive. When that day's work is done, I may have finished that particular kind of play-exercise.

I continue to invent ways of play-painting, moving from one style or one process to another. I will not "do something" with this work. No one will see it. I try to recapture my early childhood—not those days when I had been told to draw for my father, but those times when I made art because I loved to do it. I was quiet. I didn't bother my mother. I was in a world of my own. I was happy. There were the seeds of my talent. I try to recover them. It is instinctive. I didn't *plan* to work in this way. It began to happen many years ago. It keeps on happening.

After several days of playing around, I am disgusted. It is as if I have been coughing and am now able to breathe again. Then I lay out my palette, get my brushes together, get my equipment, my tapes, my fabrics. I make my canvas ready and begin to paint. There is inside me always, a fragile, unarmored creature, timid, and self-doubting. As my painting grows, I watch this creature, this child-woman change. She becomes stronger, more assertive, alive, happier and freer in her movements.

You ask me to suppose a young woman coming to me for advice. She is tempted to give up the struggle to find, to learn to do, her work; she will continue to paint in her "free," "extra," "spare" time, but her painting, her work, will no longer be at the center of her life. She asks me what she will lose if she gives up. She gives up her dreams. She gives up struggle, harassment, disappointment, exhaustion, rejection. She gives up the song of angels, the creative angel and the angel of death. She gives up the magic of making, the miracle of being alive. What does she give up? The capacity to turn dreams into reality, the joy of accomplishment, the pleasure of sharing herself with the world, the fun of pretending, the chance to be part of a new breed of women who are creating *themselves*. She gives up adulthood, she gives up playing, she gives up hours alone in her studio, becoming once more a child. She relinquishes her time, her moment, when she can change, can amend history. What does she give up? Nothing, if she has to ask.

Miriam Schapiro

The Sacred Fire
Celia Gilbert

I

IN A STUDIO in the woods a woman sits alone. Outside, the forest goes about its work; a bird repeats a note. Above the flames in the fireplace a plaque reads: "Dedicated to the artist and to the artist's need for solitude." This woman has been married for twenty years and this is her first time away from husband and children. This place is the first place that has ever been hers alone. The silence collects: a healing; she feels herself coming together.

In the evening she eats with strangers, loving them because they know nothing about her, except that she is a woman and a poet. Bliss and uneasiness are part of the life of impostors. But she is who she seems to be, only she is other people as well: father's daughter, husband's wife, mother of her children, child of her mother. Later, during her two months' stay at a retreat for artists, composers, writers, people will come to know these things about her; some will be indifferent, some will envy her, others will have shared the same experiences; but she will always miss those first weeks of being a stranger among strangers.

What never fades are the marvels of her life here: not having to think about the food, the housekeeping, the needs of her fellows; not having to justify or explain her work; rising and going to sleep at the bidding of *her* internal clock. She is a secular nun released from the bonds of an implacable domestic liturgy.

In May the lady's-slippers appear in the woods. She contemplates their delicate puffed female-maleness. Why did it take her so long to dare to reach for what she wanted? She tries to forgive herself, recalling Rilke's words to a young poet, "Live the questions now. Perhaps you will then gradually without noticing it live along some distant day into the answers."

II

The first questions put to us have always looked like answers: mother and father. My father worked, my mother mothered. My parents' marriage was out of the nineteenth century. Mother played Jane to father's Thomas Carlyle. Or, call it "Life with Father," father the exuberant zestful autocratic writer; mother no less an upper-case character.

My father supported us—my mother, my two brothers, and myself —by his writing. His was a life of deadlines, pressure, competition, unrelenting hard work; it was also a life of absorbing fulfillment as he fought for the principles he believed in, earning the admiration of his readers and his own self-respect.

Father and his work were one, and to that one we were all of secondary importance. When father napped, we tiptoed; when he was hungry, we ate; when he needed an outing we were packed into the car (we children, carsick; mother, exhausted from the preparations) and driven off for long hot rides to the beach accompanied by his cheery calls to the back seat, "Isn't this fun, kids?" If he wanted to sleep at nine o'clock, mother was corralled upstairs; if he wanted to practice the piano, the dinner guests were assembled to listen; if the teacup wasn't filled to the brim, he raged as though he had uncovered a plot to destroy him. I felt at home reading memoirs about Louis XIV.

Father was *le roi soleil*. Mother was the minister and mistress every regent dreams of. She counseled, but always obliquely; governed, but only the Interior. What the daughter resented on her behalf she made light of, excusing father's outbursts of anger as necessary outlets for the tensions of his work. She applauded and admired his unwavering commitment to his principles and his writing; but she had her own order of priorities: personal loyalties, love of family, friends, her daily relationship with the people around her. To me she was the mirror image of father: he could only be happy satisfying himself; she, others. There are women like that—Virginia Woolf called them "The Angel in the House."

The daughter of the angel was confused and superficially rebellious. Why, why, why? Why is mother not permitted to speak her thoughts directly, why can father do as he pleases? I thought my mother loved me, but why was she always insisting that it was I who had to give way to my father and brothers, teaching me that men are small children, irrational, fragile, needing constant praise and reassurance. No matter what my feelings were I had to give and give without the expectation of being given to.

In the world of the daughter there were no women married with children, working at something they loved. There was my father's only sister, independent and energetic, well-satisfied with her bachelor-girl life. "Poor thing," said my mother, "she's all *alone*." Of the women who talked politics with my father, the majority were homely, which depressed him, or opinionated, which unsexed them.

But I, I was different. He could see that I was "just like him." I was going to be the writer, not my brothers. I was encouraged to speak up and be as direct as I pleased, with others. Only sometimes, for a joke, when I was going out on a date father would say, "Now for God's sake, act dumb." A joke, of course, but wasn't mother serious when she would whisper triumphantly, "He's going to do exactly what I suggested last night, but of course he thinks it's his idea."

My mother might claim covertly that the domestic world took precedence over the public one, but from the time I was very little, listening to my parents discuss the books their friends were writing, I knew that writing was the important endeavor in life. Perhaps that's why I remember so clearly my visit, at the age of seven, to Miss Schmidt, dreaded Miss Schmidt, the principal of P.S. 95, who dressed always in black. Trembling, I handed her a composition written in my first-grader's large hand. It was entitled, "A Dress of Moonbeams." My teacher had sent me to Miss Schmidt's office; I wasn't sure why. What if I had done something wrong? Miss Schmidt read it, then said, "This is poe-eh-tree. Can you pronounce that? Perhaps someday you will be a poet." And a second memory stands out: my father, giving me, when I was ten, some Robinson Jeffers to read, saying, "To be a great poet is the greatest thing in the world."

But I didn't write as a child. I didn't begin to write poetry until I was fifteen and fell in love. At nineteen I won the annual poetry competition at Smith. At twenty-one I married and ceased abruptly to write poetry for the next ten years.

III

Diaries of the college years bear witness to my fantasies and terrors about writing. I was going to be a "great writer," but I avoided all writing courses. I wrote poetry constantly but sent it only to the college literary magazine. Entering the poetry competition was the depersonalized act of handing a large brown manila envelope to a secretary in a dean's office. I protected myself from the effort of craft, from real competition and criticism. Poetry was a dream work, college was a dream time, a span between the girlhood of being a daughter and what I accepted as the inevitable reality, the womanhood of being a wife and mother.

I married a man as unlike my father as I was unlike my mother, and yet, insofar as I could bring it about, our marriage was made to resemble that of my parents. It was I who insisted on forms my husband never demanded. He didn't believe in marriage as an institution; neither was it important to him to become a father. He would have accepted as perfectly natural my claiming for myself the right to work at anything that pleased me. However, I was bent on a marriage that would signify my becoming as much like my mother as possible. I would be the "good" woman, raising a family, encouraging my husband in his work. How could a writer and the good woman exist in one body?

Entering the world of marriage, I left behind my family's world, where writing had, after all, been the keystone of existence. The new world of my husband, whose career in best fifties tradition was to be *ours*, was the world of science. He was the priest of a very male magic: theoretical physics. In Cambridge, England, where we spent the first two years of our marriage, science was the subject of interest; everything else was reserved for polite conversation—along with the weather. Finishing his doctorate on fellowships, my husband was taken very seriously. I pretended halfheartedly to write fiction, but in fact I was spending most of my energy coping with the system I had set up as I spun myself into the cocoon of marriage.

Some of my confusions were those of the college-bred female. At a women's college the ambiguities were many. On the one hand, the women in them, in the fifties, tended to be self-deprecating; on the other hand, the women who wanted to excel were being taken more seriously than they would have been at a co-ed institution. In a sense, one could profit from the extra four years of attention and support, but perhaps at the cost of being (eventually) more disconcerted by the dominating maleness of the "real" world.

Then, too, nothing had prepared me for the chores of domesticity. At home I had never been asked to help beyond doing dishes on the maid's night off. I knew my mother took no special pride in running a house, but she never complained or discussed it, either. I was better prepared to re-enact my mother's feelings as a wife than as a house-keeper. It was easy to take pride in my husband's achievements, ad-mire his knowledge, his patience, his devotion to *his* work.

After three years of marriage, children; I had three in five years, just as my mother had. For the next seven years I knew both the joy of their growth and the inadmissible tensions of total motherhood. Today I might remember that time as a whisper—*You were utterly happy*—but my journals are shards that record other truths. Who was it who wrote that after six years of marriage she couldn't make a move without consulting her husband; that her love for her first child had become a way of extinguishing everything else? Who wrote that only by trying to write again could she save a part of herself that was withering from neglect? And was it the same person who wrote, that same year, at twenty-seven, "I am reading Wallace Stevens with great pleasure. It has been such a long time since I read poetry. Perhaps I will write again but I am afraid. I think only some dreadful tragedy could make that happen." How convinced I was that self-expression for me could only be bought at the price of destruction to those I loved. Wasn't that why, over coffee with my best friend, also a would-be writer, we told each other so often that, really, it was much more creative to have babies than to write?

Ten years of marriage. Our youngest was a year and a half when the first in a series of wonderful *au pair* girls arrived. With my degree of domestic incompetence, the nonstop entertaining we did, and the children, all preschoolers, always coming down with colds, it seemed to take all the two of us could do to keep things running smoothly. In addition to the responsibility of the children, my husband's career had moments of indecision and doubt, leaving me a worried and helpless spectator. The children were growing, but my husband was too busy to give them anything but distant affection. Yet this life seemed acceptable because it was so much a repetition of my parents' household; in fact, I began to think of having a fourth child.

Then there were revelations. Although I think I believed that I could not be separated physically from my children and continue to exist—my mother had never left us as children—a summer came when I went to a conference in Italy with my husband. Going over on the plane, I felt as though I were being torn apart; later, at the conference, conversation with other wives and observation of older children made me realize that inevitably, no matter how many children one has, the day comes when they grow up.

It was the summer of 1964; I read Betty Friedan's just-published *The Feminine Mystique*, and for the first time thought about the similarity between myself and other women my age whom she described as discontented and frustrated. I began to think of getting a job. Then, as abruptly as it had stopped, poetry returned to my life, perhaps because I was beginning to let myself listen to what I had been feeling. I can remember standing at a window, holding a child in my arms, the lines coming in my head, like a piece of music overheard.

The crazy, chaotic household with its ministering Swedish angel had stabilized just enough so that for two hours a week I managed to get out to write. I was sick more often than I was well in those years; most of my poetry was written while I was recovering from the colds I caught from the children. I used to apologize to friends for being sick so often; now I recognize that being sick was my way of "mothering" myself, of trying to replenish psychic and physical energies that I gave to everyone but myself.

But I was very far from being able to mother myself in more profound ways. As long as I was exclusively a wife and mother I knew I had my mother's full approval; to deviate from that path would threaten me with the loss of her love. I can remember my feeling of frustration as I told her over the phone about a poem I'd been working on, only to hear her say quickly, "That's good . . . but how are the *children*?" I felt betrayed again as I had when a child, as though her love was bestowed only when I took care of others; I couldn't understand then her terrible lack of self-confidence projected onto me, her daughter.

To give myself permission and approval to do what I was doing took a long time; in the beginning I couldn't do that by myself. Happily, there was an approving mother for me—my mother's sister, who had been writing poetry for years and who understood as my mother couldn't what poetry meant to me. At the beginning, poetry was my secret; I showed my poems only to my aunt and in the years which followed it was she especially who gave the loving support that nourished me. Without her encouragement I would never have dared, that first year, to send poems out and find to my astonishment that editors would actually comment on my work.

A year later I showed some poems to my best friend's sister, a published poet a few years older than I, with a husband and three children, with books and prizes. I can remember the heat of that July day when we talked about my work. Despite her thinking I wasn't yet ready, I submitted my work to Robert Lowell for his class at Harvard. To my amazement I was permitted to attend. I would have tried to diminish that pleasure by saying that the class was, after all, only for undergraduates, except that graduate students and junior faculty too vied for places as auditors. At thirty-four I began to move out, self-conscious about my age and my ignorance.

I didn't realize then that what I was most ignorant of was not poetry, but work. I was unfamiliar with the process: the need for persistence, and encouragement, the small achievements that lead to greater confidence, the courage to try, the courage to fail. I was setting out on a natural path, and would make my way along it by effort and luck, but each step was going to feel like a random leap rather than the natural laws that govern work.

Of course, much of what I brought from my other life was a handicap. I was completely unused to viewing my actions as important. Raising a family and running a house is work accorded a perfunctory approval. There was the timidity arising from years of living invisibly; the habitual denial of one's own impulses. Again and again in workshops I would question my legitimacy, my right to be there, to benefit, to take up room, to speak out. There was my age, sign of past inadequacies and omen of failure each time I met women poets my own age or younger with families *and* books of poetry. There was my double set of standards: a sense of inferiority masquerading as modesty. What I accomplished I made light of; what others did was "real." Dovetailing with my hesitancies there were always the exigencies of the family.

Lowell's class was a first step away from the house, my first view of a world I had not dared to approach. Lit by Lowell's presence, it was a very exciting place. His reputation, already secure in the literary world, was beginning to reach the general public as well. To hear him read one's own words in his deep voice, inimitably blending Eastern aristocrat and Southern drawl, words intoned through a mask at times weary, puckish, or mad, was a bit of instant Olympus. His comments, with their sting of truth, were always tactfully sugarcoated.

"Ah think that's almost perfect . . . of its *kind*," he would breathe, leaving us to brood over what that "kind" might be. He would go over the poems word by word, line by line. "You've got to *load* the line," he would murmur, pushing his palms outward with graceful emphasis. With a grimace over a poem too blatant, he would advise, "Murk it up." In general he was mellow and tolerant; we were very little fish. He entertained us with stories of the "Greats": Eliot, Pound, Frost; spoke with self-conscious deference of Marianne Moore and Elizabeth Bishop, with friendly approval of Adrienne Rich. It was 1965 and Plath's *Ariel* had not yet burst upon the scene. West Coast poets, Black Mountain poets were not discussed; students would bring them up from time to time, but Lowell's response was one of good-natured dismissal.

If Lowell viewed us with benevolent disinterest, the ambitious graduate students and already published poets who attended his open office hours afforded a different perspective. Those Tuesday mornings from nine to twelve gave me a first glimpse of the competition and cabals of the literary world. The atmosphere, as heavy with intrigue and animosity as a Jacobean drama, was frightening for me and the undergraduates who ventured in. "But I don't even know how to *talk* about a poem," I wailed to my husband. "They learned," he said. "You'll learn." Everyone vied for Lowell's approval; no one ever publicly questioned his judgment. Such were the scars those sessions left that the first time I read before an audience I calmed my stage fright by reminding myself that, after all, it was in no way as hostile as the poet pack of the office hours. I learned that I could survive; that I could read a poem, take the criticism, and return; that disapproval was not disaster.

But what about Lowell's comment, repeated to me by a friend, that it was odd how almost all *good* women poets were either divorced or lesbian? A remark that so confirmed my fears both of failing and of succeeding as a poet left me unable to reflect that undoubtedly the same might be said of male poets. I thrust it from me. *I* was not a woman poet, I was only a woman writing poetry.

The daughter in me was still proving to her mother that she was a good wife and mother before all else. In my poetry the feeling of being without control over my own life translated itself into themes of passivity and dependency, into images of a captive and paralyzed self. Yet slowly I was making progress. At the close of another Harvard workshop, with Robert Fitzgerald, he encouraged me by suggesting that I was ready to publish. Three poems were accepted by magazines. Despite my uneasiness, time was showing me that writing—the demand of a long-neglected need to grow—was natural and imperative.

But then I couldn't write at all for two years. The illness and loss of a child left us devastated. My husband took a year's leave and we went abroad to try to reknit our family. When we returned and I started to write again, work was more important than ever. Old attitudes about being a wife and a mother had changed. My extended protected childhood with its simple faith in my husband as a powerful parent was over. Death had broken the old covenant by which I had lived, practicing the magic of my mother and generations of women before her: belief that a single-minded preoccupation would be recompensed by the survival of my children, the barter of a life for a life, renouncing mine for theirs. I saw that one reason I had so feared to work was that work affirmed the separateness that *good* mothers are taught to deny; to value my work meant valuing myself as a person.

How does one slough off the invisibility that cloaks the woman with only a domestic existence? Poetry was a private pursuit; writing at home, unheard and unacknowledged, did not appear to be work to my family; for me, too, a sense of writing as work could only come from a public experience. The answer in my case—to go back to school as a formal student—was one I wouldn't have thought of on my own, one which in fact frightened me. However, I realized that I had outgrown the Harvard classes; there I was too much of a non-person, grateful, like a charity case, for any crumb of attention. A friend informed me that Boston University gave an M.A. in Creative Writing. "They'll take you seriously if you enroll in the program," she said, when I, fearful of a commitment, thought of attending as a special student. Her argument told; I wanted desperately to be taken seriously.

The two years I spent at BU were my first work experience. At thirty-eight I was a graduate student, judged only on the basis of my work. I was forced to survive the pressures of exams, term papers, deadlines, classes, and my anxieties about running the house and taking care of the family. But what I really wanted I had; I was forced to take responsibility for myself. There was no time now for all the things that had become burdensome since our return from abroad: the domestic rituals of a decade, the elaborate dinner parties that took endless hours of preparation, the unnecessary, unreal mothering that turns mothers into nags and drudges for lack of something else to do. The children, eleven and thirteen, learned to help take care of themselves and the house. My husband and I struggled over the new demands I was making, demands that seemed irrational to him, such as my refusal to make his breakfast unless he got up when I was making it for myself. For years he had gotten up hours later than I, and I had always stopped what I was doing to attend to him. He couldn't understand the overwhelming anxiety I had to fight off before I could even *think* about writing. Now that I had decided to try to write in the mornings, when I was least distracted by household pressures, the knowledge that I would have to break my concentration and fix his breakfast in the middle of the morning blocked my impulse to work. This made no sense to him. I was fighting for the first time to give my work precedence over family duties, to have my work needs considered as important as his. He felt love was being withheld from him; I felt love was being equated with service. To him, as a non-writer, writing was something that could be done anytime. To him, as a man with only the vaguest notion of how the household was run, I had all the time in the world. It was much easier to effect changes between us in the new situation that school imposed, a situation he understood and respected.

What people who work take for granted was a constant delight to me those years. I had a place to be other than my house. I had friends of my own, with a common bond of poetry. They were mostly younger than I, and at first I felt strange, closer in age to their mothers than to them; but this wore off and I ceased to judge myself as I had a few years before. What mattered was the poem, not the age of the poet. Too, in many ways I felt myself younger than they—I who had never lived on my own, or supported myself. All the while, the enforced discipline and dailiness of school was like a patterning system that helped me to live out a stage of development I had skipped. A year after I started school, I was offered a part-time job as poetry editor of a large Boston weekly; I took it on the strength of the confidence I had acquired at BU. On the paper, I had a chance to write reviews, news and features, as well as edit, and I learned another kind of writing. The work was new, but being on a newspaper staff had a delightful familiarity. Childhood memories of trips to my father's office came back as I listened to newspaper talk, wrote to inches, met deadlines, and rushed out to buy a paper with my byline in it. I could talk shop with my father about "leads" and "typos"—"worse than fascism!" he exclaimed sympathetically when the paper produced a typo in 48-point bold in an article of mine. In a small way I now got a sense of my father's life and work from the inside; I could love more the part of me that was like him. How many daughters have disowned half of themselves as I had for fear of being "unwomaned"?

Although I had been blocked in the past by the decrees of a gender-crazed culture, it would have been disastrous for me to disavow that I was a woman; to deny that source of my poetry would have been to repeat earlier denials of other parts of myself. I was very lucky that the time was 1971 and that at BU I had Anne Sexton as a teacher. No one could have been more unlike the authority figure of Robert Lowell. Anne—she was always Anne to her students—had never been to college. She had a wide public following, but nothing like the assured critical success of Lowell. Anne, by contrast, was a loner—a natural, almost a sport—cut off from literary coteries and criticized, sometimes viciously, for being "popular." She wore her laurels with a certain diffidence and a touch of defiance. Her workshops reflected those attitudes as well as her natural modesty. Anne's opinions never intimidated her students from expressing their own because she listened very seriously to them. She played down competition; she liked the thought that all poems were really part of one great poem, an attitude that eased students' self-consciousness. People in her workshops became friends and met independently outside of class. Every so often, however, when students wilted under the slightest criticism or grew despondent over the sharp comments of unfeeling editors, Anne would have a sudden attack of conscience. "There should be a bastard in every class," she would growl in her husky voice, her green eyes blazing. "The editors and critics out there—they're bastards, and poets have got to learn to be tough and ignore them."

She gave her unlisted number to students so we could call her anytime to talk about a poem, or a depression. Once, in a panic before giving a reading, I telephoned her. "Just eat mothering foods," she advised, "you know, something soft like scrambled eggs and cocoa . . . and take three slugs of whiskey right before you go on stage."

For a woman like myself, trying to write out of years of an exclusively domestic life, Anne was a source of support and encouragement. She, too, had been "just a housewife." She, too, had found her way to poetry late, through the modest door of an adult education class. While she lived, poetry was the gift she had to share, and her astonishing productivity, her unflagging enthusiasm for "the poem," made poetry a reality for her students. For me it was crucial to have as a teacher someone who understood the experiences from which I, as a woman, was writing.

During those years from 1971 to 1973, the women's movement was seeding consciousness-raising groups everywhere, and many women were beginning to talk openly about things they had felt and experienced but always repressed. I can't imagine what it would have been like to begin to grow in my poetry before Sexton and Plath and the women's movement. In the past many women poets had to invent devious and denying ways to talk about what most concerned them. I remember the shock of one of my male professors at BU, one who liked my work and encouraged me, but who could not stomach a poem I had written about a young girl's menstruation that spoke of "blood" and "the curse," words he advised me to remove.

Had I been writing seriously earlier, I might have believed in the androgyny of art and ignored the hegemony of male editors, publishers, and attitudes; but even though I had been published, and the editors were all men, I was beginning to play the countdown game every time I picked up a poetry magazine, counting down the table of contents to see how many women had made the issue—always a tiny fraction. Could it really be that women poets, as the numbers suggested, were less gifted than men?

In 1971, for a woman's day demonstration, two other women and I brought out a pamphlet of women's poems. We thought of it as a one-time effort, but the pleasure of doing it, combined with the obvious need for such a venture, kept it alive, and our fourth issue has just appeared with support from the Co-ordinating Council of Literary Magazines. Small, local, ongoing publishing like *Women/Poems* helps establish a community of women and an audience that takes some of the curse from the woman writing in isolation. For us, this experience demystified what had seemed an unknowable process—the emergence of the private poem into the public world. Always, before, that emergence had depended on the validation of someone else; now we discovered that we could constitute ourselves authorities. On another level, we learned the pleasures of being makers, as the actual publication came into being: typed, pasted up, printed, collated, bound, and presented to the booksellers. Doing these things is a way of asserting one's presence publicly. It mitigates the writer's terror of the judgment of others, and dispels much of the helpless feeling that stems from the ignorance of a process.

In part, this experience was similar to the one I had been living at BU, one that had been taking me, step by step, away from isolation into a community that gave encouragement and support.

My two months' stay at MacDowell in 1974 established a public, professional sense of myself which was one more natural outcome of the years at BU. Applicants to MacDowell must submit samples of their work and have three recommendations from people in their field, a routine procedure for graduate students. Yet it came as a surprise to me, nonetheless, that by being at BU I had provided myself with people who knew my work and me. It was a giant step to have come that far. When I was accepted in the fall of '73 for the following spring, I had months to get myself and my family used to the idea that I would be away for two months. The children were casual and reassuring; it was my husband who was more shaken. And yet I knew I had his approval to do what was necessary for my work.

At MacDowell I found what I had needed—not the solitude, but the separateness I had craved but never been able to name. How could I have named what I had never had: a sense of myself unrelated to the needs of others? Even a house from which the family is absent all day is charged with its presence and, for me, with my old anxieties about work. When I returned I knew that it was essential for me to have a room of my own, out of the house, a space that would be only mine. I now rent a tiny room in a rooming house not far from our home; a miraculous sense of wholeness never fails to come when I unlock the door and walk in.

What is the nature of the conflict for women like me? Looking back, I see how many values I accepted unquestioningly without daring to assert my deepest sense of my own needs. I took responsibility for others and feared to take it for myself. To some extent I still do. I felt that I had to choose between self and others, between home and work. Women will continue to be caught in this crossfire until attitudes and social conditions undergo a dramatic change in our society. Women will continue to put themselves into marriage and motherhood, as I did, without understanding why, or what it will be like for them as they grow older to discover that they are unprepared to live as independent beings. I had to do my growing within the context of a marriage, but I believe that it is better for women to try to establish their independence in some measure before marriage. Women's issues today are kept alive not so much by the women's movement as by the growing number of divorced women of all ages who have found that marriage is neither an answer nor a refuge.

For me, there had been a taboo on work as powerful as the proscription against incest. To give myself to my work—to admit that I loved it as much as husband and children, needed it as much, perhaps

more, was the most terrifying admission I could make. Only after
many years have I come to realize that the challenge of work is in
daring to use my whole self in the struggle for growth. Without that
growth, I would be living an "unlived life."

The myth of Prometheus is well known. We should have a feminist
version of that myth. Women, defying their fear of punishment, wrest
from men that jealously guarded fire, the sacred right to a work. No
longer will we agree to protect the hearth at the price of extinguishing
the fire within ourselves.

On Refusing Your Invitation to Come to Dinner

Country I've lived in, I know what I'll find,
your table,
where we will fish our reflections
from pools of polished wood;
surprise ourselves, gross
in the depths of silver spoons.

It is circumstance, not you,
the Circe I fear.
I know how the women will flicker
beautiful as candelabra
and twisted.
I know our eyes
staring nowhere
and our hands plucking idly at the heavy linen.
I know this terrain.

But I am forgetting the language,
sitting has become difficult,
and the speaking, intolerable,
to say, "how interesting"
makes me weep.
I can no longer bear to hear
the men around the table laugh,
argue, agree,
then pause, politely
while we speak,
their breath held in, exhaled
when we've finished,
politely,

they turn to the real conversation,
the unspoken expectation of applause.

Once I knew their language cold.
For years I spoke it better than my own, but,
I've been away so long now, I've
grown rusty. I
stammer
take forever
to tell a story, and then
no one understands anything, except,
I'm a foreigner.

And I might go berserk
after dinner, having to confront
that phalanx, wedged over brandy,
massed, to conceal the emptiness
which seeps through their ranks . . .
those strange ones, my dear,
those Ghosts-In-The-Bush
who never bleed.

Birthday Poem

Alone now, and most certainly.
Alone,
In a room.

Shadows spiral
in the
updraft.

The acrid sex of the tomato.
Moist pulp
swollen.

Milkweed pods still green.
Inside the seed
packed tight and wet.

Over the autumn stubble
the cow crops
in peace.

Stalks topple,
the wasp's children
eat.

She leaves him.
He leaves her.
"Used, used," they cry.

The marigolds persist,
rank suns
uneclipsed by cold.

The self I hid
so many years
alone, now, most certainly.

Little Devil

Only the Pope says Satan still walks the earth,
but I have a devil, small and still,
named Leave-The-Bills-To-Me,
named Don't-Move-I'll-Do-It,
named Close-Your-Eyes-And-Let-Me-Stroke-You,
named Sleep-With-Contentment.
He is as bitter as earwax, and keeps out the noise,
He is as constant as an icecream cone can
never be licked down.
He is a house cat as big as an owl
with asthma.
He is a pair of silver hands.

In the morning picking roses
no thorns can hurt me.
At night I pluck my lute
effortlessly.
The devil nodding in my lap
I search for lice
and snap them with my clever fingers.

But there is being tired of devils,
yet no doctor prescribes.
There is being wearied of devils
but no mother understands.
There is wanting to get rid of the devil—
but this makes a father very angry.
There is looking around for ways to drown the devil,
to shoot the devil,

to go mad so the devil will leave because
he doesn't want to be locked up with other devils.

There is the last, worst way:
coming to love the devil,
to lie in a bed, in a room
where the shades are drawn tighter than eyelids
and the body is pulled up
like a baby's fist.
Then the devil comes with his spacecraft.
He is the dearest one, he is the voice, he is control,
the unbroken cord that lets me float off
in that downstream of black,
tied, to the mother ship.

Celia Gilbert

One Out of Twelve: Women Who Are Writers in Our Century

(A Talk to College Teachers of Literature, 1971)

Tillie Olsen at the MacDowell Colony

Tillie Olsen

IT IS THE WOMEN'S MOVEMENT, part of the other movements of our time for a fully human life, that has brought this forum into being; kindling a renewed, in most instances a first-time, interest in the writings and writers of our sex.

This essay was originally a talk, spoken from notes, at the 1971 MLA Forum on Women Writers in the Twentieth Century. Its tone is distinctly of that year of cumulative discovery.

Linked with the old, resurrected classics on women, this movement in three years has accumulated a vast new mass of testimony, of new comprehensions as to what it is to be female. Inequities, restrictions, penalties, denials, leechings have been painstakingly and painfully documented; damaging differences in circumstances and treatment from that of males attested to; and limitations, harms, a sense of wrong, voiced.

It is in the light and dark of this testimony that I examine my subject today: the lives and work of writers, women, in our century (though I speak primarily of those writing in the English language in prose).

Compared to the countless centuries of the silence of women, compared to the century preceding ours—the first in which women wrote in any noticeable numbers—ours has been a favorable one.

The road was cut many years ago, as Virginia Woolf reminds us,

> by Fanny Burney, by Aphra Behn, by Harriet Martineau, by Jane Austen, by George Eliot, many famous women and many more unknown and forgotten. . . . Thus, when I came to write . . . writing was a reputable and harmless occupation.

Predecessors, ancestors, a body of literature, an acceptance of the right to write: each in themselves an advantage.

In this second century we have access to areas of work and of life experience previously denied: higher education; longer, stronger lives; for the first time in human history, freedom from compulsory childbearing; freer bodies and attitudes toward sexuality; and—of the greatest importance to those like myself who come from generations of illiterate women—increasing literacy, and higher degrees of it. Each one of these a vast gain.

And the results?

Productivity: books of all manner and kind. My own crude sampling, having to be made without benefit of research assistants, secretary, studies (nobody's made them), or computer (to feed *Books in Print* into, for instance) indicates that four to five books are written by men to every one by a woman.

Comparative earnings: ("equal pay for equal work"): no figures available.

Achievement, as gauged by what supposedly designates it: appearance in twentieth-century literature courses, required reading lists, textbooks; in quality anthologies; the year's best, the decade's best, the fifty years' best; consideration by critics or in current reviews; *one woman writer for every twelve men.* For a week or two, make your own survey whenever you pick up an anthology, course bibliography, quality magazine or quarterly, book review section, book of criticism.[1]

One woman writer of achievement for every twelve men writers so ranked. Is this proof again—and in this so much more favorable century—of women's innately inferior capacity for creative achievement?

Only a few months ago (June 1971), during a Radcliffe-sponsored panel on "Women's Liberation, Myth or Reality," Diana Trilling, asking why it is that women

> have not made even a fraction of the intellectual, scientific or artistic-cultural contributions which men have made

came again to the considered conclusion that

> it is not enough to blame women's place in culture or culture itself, because that leaves certain fundamental questions unanswered . . . necessarily raises the question of the biological aspects of the problem.

Biology: that difference. But what of the centuries of prehistory during which biology did not deny equal contribution; and the other determining difference we are only beginning to know and understand —not biology—between male and female in the centuries after; the past of women that should be part of every human consciousness, certainly every woman's consciousness (in the same way that the four hundred years of bondage, colonialism, the slave passage are to black humans).

Work first:

> Within our bodies we bore the race. Through us it was shaped, fed and clothed. . . . Labour more toilsome and unending than that of man was ours. . . . No work was too hard, no labor too strenuous to exclude us.[2]

True for most women in most of the world still.

Unclean; taboo. The Devil's Gateway. The three steps behind; the girl babies drowned in the river; the baby strapped to the back. Buried alive with the lord, burned alive on the funeral pyre, burned as a witch

---

[1] What weights my figures so heavily towards the one-out-of-twelve ratio is course offerings and writers considered in serious critical estimates. Otherwise my figures would have been closer to one out of seven. But it would not matter if the ratio were one out of six, or five. Any figure but one to one insists on query: Why? What, not true for men, but only for women, makes this difference?

[2] Olive Schreiner, *Women and Labour*, 9th ed.

at the stake. Stoned to death for adultery. Beaten, raped. Bartered. Bought and sold. Concubinage, prostitution, white slavery. The hunt, the sexual prey, "I am a lost creature, o the poor Clarissa." Purdah, the veil of Islam, domestic confinement. Illiterate. Excluded, excluded, excluded from council, ritual, activity, language, when there was neither biological nor economic reason to be excluded.

Religion, when all believed. In sorrow shalt thou bring forth children. May thy wife's womb never cease from bearing. Neither was the man created for the woman but the woman for the man. Let the woman learn in silence and in all subjection. (Contrary to biological birth fact) Adam's rib. The Jewish male morning prayer: thank God I was not born a woman. Silence in holy places, seated apart, or not permitted entrance at all; castration of boys because women too profane to sing in church.

And for the comparative handful of women born into the privileged class: being, not doing; man does, woman is; to you the world says work, to us it says seem. "God is thy law, thou mine." Isolated. Cabin'd, cribb'd, confin'd, the private sphere. Bound feet: corseted, cosseted, bedecked; denied one's body. Powerlessness. Fear of rape, male strength. Fear of aging. Subject to. Fear of expressing capacities. Soft attractive graces; the mirror to magnify man. Marriage as property arrangement. "The vices of slaves"[3]—dissembling, flattering, manipulating, appeasing. Bolstering. Vicarious living, infantilization, trivialization. Parasitism, individualism, madness. Shut up, you're only a girl. O Elizabeth, why couldn't you have been born a boy? Roles, discontinuities, part self, part time; "a man can give full energy to his profession, a woman cannot" (twentieth-century woman).

> *How is it that women have not made a fraction of the*
> *intellectual, scientific, or artistic-cultural contributions*
> *that men have made?*

Only in the context of this punitive difference in circumstance, in history, between the sexes; this past, hidden or evident, that though objectively obsolete (yes, even the toil and the compulsory childbearing obsolete) continues so terribly, so determiningly to live on; can the question be answered or my subject here today—the woman writer in our century: one out of twelve—be understood.

How much it takes to become a writer. Bent (far more common than we assume), circumstances, time, development of craft—but beyond that: how much conviction as to the importance of what one

---

[3] Elizabeth Barrett Browning's phrase.

has to say, one's right to say it. And the will, the measureless store of belief in oneself to be able to come to, cleave to, find the form for one's own life comprehensions. Difficult for any male not born into a class that breeds such confidence. Almost impossible for a girl, a woman.

The leeching of belief, of will, the damaging of capacity, begin so early. Sparse indeed is the literature on the way of denial to small girl children of the development of their endowment as born human: active, vigorous bodies; exercise of the power to do, to make, to investigate, to invent, to conquer obstacles, to resist violations of the self; to think, create, choose; to attain community, confidence in self. Little has been written on the harms of instilling constant concern with appearance, the need to please, to support, the training in acceptance, deferring. Little has been added in our century to George Eliot's *Mill on the Floss* on the effect of the differing treatment—"climate of expectation"—for boys and for girls.

But it is there if one knows how to read for it, and indelibly there in the damage. One—out of twelve.

In the vulnerable girl years, unlike their sisters in the previous century, women writers go to college.[4] The kind of experience it may be for them is stunningly documented in Elaine Showalter's "Women and the Literary Curriculum."[5] Freshman texts in which women have little place, if at all; language itself, all achievement, anything to do with the human in male terms; *Man in Crisis; The Individual and His World*. Three hundred thirteen male writers taught; seventeen women writers. That classic of adolescent rebellion, *Portrait of the Artist as a Young Man*, and sagas (male) of the quest for identity (but then Erikson, the father of the concept, propounds that identity concerns girls only insofar as making themselves into attractive beings for the right kind of man). Most, not all, of the predominantly male literature studied, written by men whose understandings are not universal, but restrictively male; and in our time as Mary Ellmann, Kate Millett, and Dolores Schmidt have pointed out, more and more surface, hostile, and stereotypic in portraying women.

In a writer's young years, susceptibility to the vision and style of the great is extreme. Add the aspiration-denying implication, consciously felt or not, that (as Woolf noted years ago) women writers, women's experience, and literature written by women are by definition minor.

---

[4] True almost without exception among the writers who are women in *Twentieth Century Authors* and *Contemporary Authors*.

[5] *College English*, May 1971.

(Mailer will not grant even the minor: "the one thing a writer has to have is balls.") No wonder that Showalter observes:

> Women [students] are estranged from their own experience and unable to perceive its shape and authenticity, in part because they do not see it mirrored and given resonance in literature. . . . They have no faith in the validity of their own perceptions and experiences, rarely seeing them confirmed in literature, or accepted in criticism. . . . [They] notoriously lack the happy confidence, the exuberant sense of the value of their individual observations which enables young men to risk making fools of themselves for the sake of an idea.

Harms difficult to work through. Nevertheless, some young women (others are already lost) maintain their ardent intention to write—fed indeed by the very glories of some of this literature that puts them down.

But other invisible worms are finding out the bed of crimson joy. Self-doubt; seriousness questioned by the hours agonizing over appearance; concentration shredded into attracting, being attractive; the absorbing real need and love for working with words felt as hypocritical self-delusion, for what seems to be (and is) esteemed is whether or not the phone rings for you, and how often. High aim, and accomplishment towards it discounted by the prevalent attitude that, as girls will probably marry (attitudes not applied to boys who will probably marry), writing is no more than an attainment of a dowry to be spent later according to the needs and circumstances within the true vocation: husband and family. The growing conviction that going on will threaten other needs; that "a woman has to sacrifice all claims to femininity and family to be a writer."[6]

And the agony—peculiarly mid-century, escaped by their sisters of pre-Freudian, pre-Jungian times—that "creation and femininity are incompatible." Anais Nin's words:

> The aggressive act of creation; the guilt for creating. I did not want to rival man; to steal man's creation, his thunder. I must protect them, not outshine them.

The acceptance—against one's experienced reality—of the sexist notion that the act of creation is not as inherently natural to a woman as to a man, but rooted instead in unnatural competition, or envy, or imitation, or thwarted sexuality.

And in all the usual college teaching—the English, history, psychology, sociology courses—little to help that young woman under-

---

[6] Sylvia Plath, letter when a graduate student.

stand the source or nature of this inexplicable draining unsureness, self-doubt, loss of aspiration, of confidence.[7]

It is all there in the extreme in Plath's *Bell Jar*—that portrait of the artist as a young woman (significantly, one of the few that we have) —from the precarious sense of vocation to the paralyzing conviction that (in a sense different than she wrote years later)

> Perfection is terrible, it cannot have children.
> . . . it tamps the womb

And indeed, in our century as in the last, until very recently almost all distinguished achievement has come from childless women: Willa Cather, Ellen Glasgow, Gertrude Stein, Edith Wharton, Virginia Woolf, Elizabeth Bowen, Katherine Mansfield, Isak Dinesen, Katherine Anne Porter, Dorothy Richardson, Henry Handel Richardson, Susan Glaspell, Dorothy Parker, Lillian Hellman, Eudora Welty, Djuna Barnes, Anais Nin, Ivy Compton-Burnett, Elizabeth Madox Roberts, Christina Stead, Carson McCullers, Flannery O'Connor, Jean Stafford, May Sarton, Josephine Herbst, Jessamyn West, Janet Frame, Lillian Smith, Zora Neale Hurston, Iris Murdoch, Joyce Carol Oates, Lorraine Hansberry.

Most never questioned, or at least accepted (a few sanctified), this different condition for achievement, not imposed on men writers. Few asked the fundamental human-equality question regarding it that Elizabeth Mann Borghese, Thomas Mann's daughter, asked when she was eighteen and sent to a psychiatrist for help in getting over an unhappy love affair (revealing also an unrealistic working ambition to become a great musician although "women cannot be great musi-

---

[7] It is here that another significant turn to silencing takes place. What was needed to confirm and vivify has been meager—and occasional, accidental. The compound of what denies, vitiates, actively discourages, has been powerful—and continuous, institutionalized. The young unhelped "sexless bound in sex" being is now in

> . . . the glade
> Wherein Fate sprung Love's ambuscade
> To flush me in this sensuous strife . . .
> Of that which makes the sexual feud
> And clogs the aspirant life.*

How many in the one-to-twelve ratio foundered here?

With more than is recognized, it is not a leaving of literature, but an attempt at solution, a keeping and using of it within the precedented woman ways—for others. So is born the enabler, the encourager, the "inspirer beloved"; the wife, the helper— where there is economic imperative (that mammoth silencer only indicated in this talk), the teacher or editor. And still the want to write does not die; it waits, unsleeping.

* Herman Melville, "After the Pleasure Party," *Collected Poems.*

cians"). "You must choose between your art and fulfillment as a woman," the analyst told her, "between music and family life." "Why?" she asked, "Why must I choose? No one said to Toscanini or to Bach or my father, that they must choose between their art and fulfillment as a man, family life. . . . Injustice everywhere." Not unjust if it were truly free choice. But where it is forced because of the circumstances for the sex into which one is born—a choice men of the same class do not have to make in order to do their work—that is not *choice*, but a working of sexist injustice. (How much of the one-to-twelve ratio is accounted for by those lost here?)

What possible difference, you may ask, does it make to literature whether or not a woman writer remains childless—free choice or not—especially in view of the marvels these childless women have created.

Might there not have been other marvels as well, or other dimensions to these marvels? Might there not have been present profound aspects and understandings of human life—as yet largely absent in literature?

More and more women writers in our century, primarily in the last two decades, are assuming as their right, too, fullness of work *and* family life.[8] Their emergence is evidence of changing circumstances making possible for them what (with rarest exception) was not possible in the generations of women before. But the fundamental situation remains unchanged. Unlike men writers who embarked on the same course, they do not have the societal equivalent of wives—nor (in a society hostile to growing life) anyone but themselves to mother their children. Even those who can afford help, good schools, summer camps, may suffer what seventy years ago W. E. B. Du Bois called The Damnation of Women: "that only at the sacrifice of the chance to do their best work can women bear and rear children."

---

8 Among those with children: Harriette Arnow, Mary Lavin, Mary McCarthy, Elizabeth Janeway, Tess Slesinger, Storm Jameson, Janet Lewis, Jean Rhys, Kay Boyle, Dorothy Canfield Fisher, Pearl Buck, Josephine Johnson, Ann Petry, Caroline Gordon, Nancy Hale, Shirley Jackson, Eleanor Clark; and a sampling in the unparalleled last two decades: Hortense Calisher, Margaret Walker, Grace Paley, Doris Lessing, Edna O'Brien, Margaret Drabble, Cynthia Ozick, Pauli Murray, Joanne Greenberg (Hannah Green), Joan Didion, Penelope Mortimer, Alison Lurie, Doris Betts, Nadine Gordimer, Muriel Spark, Lael Wertenbaker, Maxine Kumin, Lore Segal, Alice Walker, Mary Gray Hughes, Sallie Bingham, Maureen Howard, Norma Rosen, Diane Johnston, Alta, Susan Griffin, Helen Yglesias. Some wrote before children, some only in the middle or late years afterward. Not many, so far, have used the material open to them out of motherhood as a central source for their writing.

Substantial creative achievement demands time . . . and with rare exceptions only full-time workers have created it.⁹

I am quoting myself from "Silences,"¹⁰ a talk nine years ago. In motherhood, as it is structured,

> circumstances for sustained creation are almost impossible. Not because the capacities to create no longer exist, or the need (though for a while as in any fullness of life the need may be obscured), but . . . the need cannot be first. It can have at best only part self, part time. . . . Motherhood means being instantly interruptible, responsive, responsible. Children need one *now* (and remember, in our society, the family must often try to be the center for love and health the outside world is not). The very fact that these are needs of love, not duty, that one feels them as one's self; that there is no one else to be responsible for these needs, gives them primacy. It is distraction, not meditation, that becomes habitual; interruption, not continuity; spasmodic, not constant, toil. Work interrupted, deferred, postponed makes blockage—at best, lesser accomplishment. Unused capacities atrophy, cease to be.

There are other vulnerabilities to loss, diminishment. Rare is the woman writer who has not had bred into her what Virginia Woolf called "The Angel in the House," who "must charm, sympathize, conciliate . . . be extremely sensitive to the needs and moods and wishes of others before her own . . . excel in the difficult arts of family life."

> It was she who used to come between me and my paper . . . who bothered me and wasted my time and so tormented me that at last I killed her . . . or she would have plucked out my heart as a writer.¹¹

There is another angel, so lowly as to be invisible, although without her no art, or any human endeavor, could be carried on for even one day—the essential angel, with whom Virginia Woolf (and most women writers, still in the privileged class) did not have to contend—

---

⁹ This does not mean those full-time writers were hermetic or denied themselves social or personal life (think of James, Turgenev, Tolstoy, Balzac, Joyce). Nor did they, except perhaps at the flood, put in as many hours daily as those doing more usual kinds of work. Four hours daily has been the norm (Henry James: "the quiet, patient, generous mornings will bring it"). Zola and Trollope are famous last-century examples of the four-hours; the *Paris Review* interviews with writers disclose many others. Full-timeness is not in the actual number of hours at one's desk but in writing being one's major profession, practiced habitually in protected, undistracted time as needed, when it is needed.

¹⁰ Reprinted in *Harper's*, October 1965.

¹¹ "Professions for Women," *Collected Essays*.

the angel who must assume the physical responsibilities for daily living, for the maintenance of life.

Almost always in one form or another (usually in the wife, two-angel form) she has dwelt in the house of men. She it was who made it possible for Joseph Conrad to "wrestle with the Lord for his creation":

> Mind and will and conscience engaged to the full, hour after hour, day after day . . . never aware of the even flow of daily life made easy and noiseless for me by a silent, watchful, tireless affection.

The angel who was "essential" to Rilke's "great task":

> like a sister who would run the house like a friendly climate, there or not there as one wished . . . and would ask for nothing except just to be there working and warding at the frontiers of the invisible.

Men (even part-time writers who must carry on work other than writing[12]) have had and have this inestimable advantage towards productivity. I cannot help but notice how curiously absent both of these angels, these watchers and warders at the frontiers of the invisible, are from the actual contents of most men's books, except perhaps on the dedication page:

> *To my wife, without whom . . .*

Mailer made clear that as a writer he was not so much a prisoner of sex as of service—supportive, secretarial, household.

I digress, and yet I do not; the disregard for the essential angel, the large absence of any sense of her in literature or elsewhere, has not only cost literature great contributions from those so occupied or partially occupied, but by failing to help create an arousing awareness (as literature has done in other realms) has contributed to the agonizingly slow elimination of this technologically and socially obsolete, human-wasting drudgery. Recall Virginia Woolf's dream of a long-since possible

> economical, powerful and efficient future when houses will be cleaned by a puff of hot wind.

Sometimes the essential angel is present in women's books,[13] though still "heroines are in white dresses that never need washing"

---

[12] As do many women writers.

[13] Among them: Harriette Arnow, Willa Cather, Dorothy Canfield Fisher, H. H. Richardson (of *Ultima Thule*), Ruth Suckow, Elizabeth Madox Roberts, Sarah Wright, Agnes Smedley (of *Daughter of Earth*), Emily Dickinson, Sylvia Plath. Sometimes Christina Stead, Mary Gray Hughes, Doris Lessing. (I would now add Edith Summers Kelley [*Weeds* and *The Devil's Hand*], the Marge Piercy of *Small Changes*, and my own fiction.)

(Rebecca Harding Davis's phrase of one hundred years ago). Some poets admit her as occasional domestic image; a few preen her as femininity; Sylvia Plath could escape her only by suicide:

> ... flying ...
> Over the engine that killed her—
> The mausoleum, the wax house.

For the first time in literary history, a woman writer of stature, accustomed through years to the habits of creation, began to live the life of most of her sex, the honey drudgers: the winged unmiraculous two-angel, whirled mother-maintenance life that most women, not privileged, know. A situation without help or husband and with twenty-four hours' responsibility for two small human lives whom she adored and at their most fascinating and demanding. The world was blood hot and personal. Creation's needs at its height. She had to get up at

> four in the morning, that still blue almost eternal hour before the baby's cry

to write at all. After the long expending day, tending, eating, cleaning, enjoying, laundering, feeding, marketing, delighting, outing, being

> a very efficient tool or weapon, used and in demand from moment to moment . . . Nights (were) no good (for writing). I'm so flat by then that all I can cope with is music and brandy and water.

The smog of cooking, the smog of hell floated her head. The smile of the icebox annihilated. There was stink of fat and baby crap; vicious-ness in the kitchen! And the blood-jet poetry (for which there was never time and self except in that still blue hour before the baby's cry), there was no stopping it.[14]

> It is not a question in these last weeks of the conflict in a woman's life between the claims of the feminine and the agonized work of art.

—Elizabeth Hardwick, a woman, can say of Sylvia Plath's suicide—

> Every artist is either a man or woman and the struggle is pretty much the same for both.

Comments as insensible of the two-angel realities ("so lowly as to be invisible") as are the oblivious masculine assumptions either that the suicide was because of Daddy's death twenty-three years before, re-vived by her husband's desertion; or else a real-life Story of O, that elegant pornography, sacramental culmination of being used up by ecstasy (poetry in place of sex this time):

---

[14] Phrases, lines, quoted throughout from Plath's poetry, letters, or talks.

the pride of an utter and ultimate surrender like the pride of O naked and chained in her owl mask as she asks Sir Stephen for death.[15]

If in such an examined extremity, the profound realities of woman's situation are ignored, how much less likely are they—particularly the subtler ones—to be seen, comprehended, taken into account, as they affect lesser-known women writers in more usual circumstances.

In younger years, confidence and vision leeched, aspiration reduced. In adult years, sporadic effort and unfinished work; women made "mediocre caretakers" of their talent: that is, writing is not first. The angel in the house situation; probably also the essential angel, maintenance-of-life one; increasingly in our century, the need to earn one's living at a paid job; and for more and more women writers the whirled expending motherhood years. Is it so difficult to account for the many occasional-fine-story or one-book writers; the distinguished but limited production of others (Janet Lewis, Ann Petry, for example); the slowly increasing numbers of women who when in their forties, fifties, sixties, publish for the first time (Dorothy Richardson; Hortense Calisher; Theodora Kroeber; Linda Hoyer, Updike's mother; Laura Ingalls Wilder; Elizabeth Madox Roberts); the women who start modestly with children's, girls' books (Maxine Kumin); some like Cid Ricketts Sumner (the Tammy books) seldom or never getting to adult fiction that would encompass their wisdom; and most of all the unsatisfactory quality of book after book that evidences the marks of part-time; part-self authorship, and to whose authors Sarah Orne Jewett's words to the part-time, part-self (because of a job) young Willa Cather still apply seventy years after:

> If you don't keep and mature your force and above all have time and quiet to perfect your work, you will be writing things not much better than you did five years ago. . . . Otherwise, what might be strength is only crudeness, and what might be insight is only observation. You will write about life, but never life itself.

Yes, the loss in quality, the minor work, the hidden silences are there in woman after woman writer in our century. We will never have the body of work that we were capable of producing. Blight, said Blake, never does good to a tree:

> And if a blight kill not a tree but it still bear fruit, say not the fruit was in consequence of the blight, but in spite of it.

[15] Richard Howard, in Charles Newman, ed., *The Art of Sylvia Plath.*

As for myself, who did not publish a book until I was fifty, who raised children without household help or the help of the "technological sublime" (the atom bomb was in manufacture before the first automatic washing machine); who worked outside the house on everyday jobs as well (as nearly half of all women do now, though a woman with a paid job, except as a maid, is rarest of any in literature); who could not kill the essential angel (there was no one else to do her work); would not—if I could—have killed the caring part of the Woolf angels—as distant from the world of literature most of my life as literature is distant (in content too) from my world.

The years when I should have been writing, my hands and being were at other (inescapable) tasks. Now, lightened as they are, when I must do those tasks into which most of my life went (like the old mother, grandmother in my *Tell Me a Riddle* who could not make herself touch a baby), I pay a psychic cost: "the sweat beads, the long shudder begins." The habits of a lifetime when everything else had to come before writing are not easily broken, even when circumstances now often make it possible for the writing to be first; habits of years: response to others, distractibility, responsibility for daily matters, stay with you, mark you, become you. The cost of "discontinuity" (that pattern still imposed on women) is such a weight of things unsaid, an accumulation of material so great, that everything starts up something else in me; what should take weeks, takes me sometimes months to write; what should take months, takes years.

I speak of myself to bring here the sense of those others to whom this is in the process of happening (unnecessarily happening, for it need not, must not continue to be) and to remind us of those (I so nearly was one) who never come to writing at all.

We cannot speak of women writers in our century (as we cannot speak of women in any area of human achievement) without speaking also of the invisible, the as innately capable: the born to the wrong circumstances, the diminished, the excluded, the lost, the silenced.

We who write are survivors, "onlys."[16] *One—out of twelve.*

---

[16] For myself, "survivor" contains its other meaning: one who must bear witness to those who foundered; tell how and why it was that they, also worthy of life, did not also survive. "Onlys" is an expression out of the 1950s Civil Rights time. The young Ralph Abernathy, reporting to his Birmingham church congregation on his trip up North for support: "I go to Seattle and they tell me, 'Brother, you've got to meet so and so, why, he's the only Negro federal circuit judge in the Northwest'; I go to Chicago and they tell me, 'Brother, you've got to meet so and so, he's the only black full professor of sociology there is'; I go to Albany and they say, 'You've got to meet so and so, he's the only black senator in the state legislature' . . . WE DON'T WANT NO ONLYS."

I must go very fast now, telescope and omit (there has already been so much telescoping and omitting), move to work, professional circumstances.

Devaluation: Still in our century, women's books of great worth suffer the death of being unknown, or at best a peculiar eclipsing, far outnumbering the similar fate of the few such books by men. I think of Kate Chopin, Mary Austin, Dorothy Richardson, Henry Handel Richardson (*Ultima Thule*), Jean Rhys, Storm Jameson, Christina Stead, Elizabeth Madox Roberts (*The Time of Man*), Janet Lewis, May Sarton, Harriette Arnow (*The Dollmaker*), Agnes Smedley (*Daughter of Earth*), Djuna Barnes (*Nightwood*), Kay Boyle—every one of whom is rewarding, and some with the stamp of enduring.[17] Considering their stature, how comparatively unread, untaught are Glasgow, Glaspell, Bowen, Parker, Stein, Mansfield—even Cather and Porter.

Critical attitudes: Two centuries after, still what Cynthia Ozick calls "the perpetual dancing dog phenomena,"[18] the injurious reacting to a book not for its quality or content, but on the basis of its having been written by a woman, with consequent misreading, mistreatment. Read Mary Ellmann's inimitable *Thinking About Women*.

One addition to the "she writes like a man," "with masculine power" kind of "praise." Power is not recognized as the power it is at all if the subject matter is considered women's: it is minor, moving, evocative, instinctive, delicate. "As delicate as a surgeon's scalpel," says Katherine Anne Porter of such a falsifying description for Katherine Mansfield's art. Instinctive?

> I judge her work to have been to a great degree a matter of intelligent use of her faculties, a conscious practice of a hard-won craftsmanship, a triumph of discipline. . . .[19]

Climate in literary circles for those who move in them:[20] writers know the importance of respect for one's vision and integrity; of the comradeship of other writers; of being dealt with as a writer on the basis of one's work and not for other reasons; how chancy is recogni-

---

[17] This was 1971. At least some of these writers are now coming out of eclipse. But Glaspell and H. H. Richardson are still out of print. So is most of Christina Stead.
I would now add to this list Edith Summers Kelley and Cora Sandel (the incomparable *Alberta* trilogy), writers unknown to me then. And Anzia Yezierska, whose books I have lent, taught, tried to get republished. Her *The Bread Giver* is now again in print.
[18] "Women and Creativity," *Motive*, April 1969.
[19] "The Art of Katherine Mansfield," *Collected Essays and Occasional Writings*.
[20] Read Carolyn Kizer's "Pro-Femina" in her *Knock upon Silence*.

tion and getting published. There is no time to speak of this today; but nearly all writers who are women are at a disadvantage here.

Restriction: For all our freer life in this century—our significantly greater access to work, education, travel, varied experience—there is still limitation of circumstances for scope, subject, social context, the kind of comprehensions which come only in situations beyond the private. What Charlotte Brontë felt so keenly 125 years ago as a denial of "facilities for observation . . . a knowledge of the world," which gives other writers, "Thackeray, Dickens . . . an importance, variety, depth greatly beyond what I can offer."[21] "Trespass vision" cannot substitute.

Constriction: not always recognized as constriction. The age-old coercion of women towards one dimension continues to be "terribly, determiningly" present. Women writers are still suspect as unnatural if they concern themselves with aspects of their experience, interests, being, beyond the traditionally defined women's sphere. Hortense Calisher is troubled that women writers

> straining toward a world sensibility, or one equivalent to the roaming conscience of the men . . . or dispens[ing] with whatever was clearly female in their sensibility or experience . . . flee from the image society projects on her.[22]

But consciences and world sensibility are as natural to women as to men; men have been freer to develop and exercise them, that is all. Indeed, one of the most characteristic strains in literature written by women (however dropped out of sight, or derided) *is* conscience, concern with wrongs to human beings in their time—from the first novel in our language by a woman, Aphra Behn's *Oroonoko*, that first by anyone against slavery, through Harriet Martineau, Elizabeth Gaskell, George Sand, Harriet Beecher Stowe, Elizabeth Barrett Browning, Rebecca Harding Davis, Helen Hunt Jackson, Olive Schreiner, Charlotte Perkins Gilman, Ethel Voynich, to our own century's Gabriela Mistral, Nelly Sachs, Anna Seghers, Rachel Carson, Lillian Hellman, Lorraine Hansberry, Theodora Kroeber (*Ishi*), Agnes Smedley, Harriette Arnow, Doris Lessing, Nadine Gordimer, Sylvia Ashton-Warner.

In contradiction to the compass of her own distinguished fiction, Calisher defines the "basic female experience from puberty on through childbed" as women's natural subject:

---

[21] Letter to her publisher, W. S. Williams, 1849.
[22] "No Important Woman Writer . . . ," *Mademoiselle*, February 1970. My excerpts and exceptions do not indicate what a superb essay this is, well worth reading and teaching.

For myself the feminism that comes straight from the belly, from the bed, and from childbed. A sensibility trusting itself for what it is, as the *other* half of basic life.

The stereotypic biological woman (breeder, sex-partner) sphere. False to reality. Not only leaving out (what men writers usually leave out) ongoing motherhood, maintenance of life, and the angel in the house so determiningly the basic experience of most women once they get out of bed and up from childbed, but other common female realities as well.[23]

And it leaves out the rest of women's biological endowment as born human (including the creative capacity out of which women and men write). It was the denial of this capacity to live the whole of human life, the confinement of woman to a sphere, that brought the women's rights movement into being in the last century—feminism born of humanism—and that prevented our Calishers from writing throughout centuries.

The acceptance of these age-old coercive, restrictive definitions of woman at a time when it is less true than ever to the realities of most women's lives—and need not be true at all—remains a complex problem for women writing in our time. Mary Wollstonecraft defined it as "the consciousness of being always woman which degrades our sex."

So Anaïs Nin: accepting the constriction to a "feminine sensibility that would not threaten man." Dwelling in the private, the inner: endless vibrations of mood; writing what was muted, exquisite, sensuous, subterranean. That is, in her fiction. In her *Journals* (along with the narcissistic), the public, the social; power of characterization, penetrating observation, hard intellect, range of experience and relationship, different beauties. Qualities and complexities not present in her fiction—to its impoverishment.

"The Bold New Women," to use another example (this from the title of a recent anthology), are the old old women, allowing themselves to be confined within the literary, bed-partner, biological-woman ghetto; mistaking themselves as new because the sex is explicit (current male genre); the style and conception of female sexuality, Lawrentian or Milleresque. "Whole areas of me are made by the kind

---

[23] Among them: what goes on in jobs; penalties for aging; children and the having to raise them in a world in which they are "no miracles at all"; what it is to live as a single woman having to raise children alone; causes, besides the accepted psychiatric ones, of breakdown in women; the cost of vicarious living; ways in which human capacities (organization, art, intellect, invention, resistance to harm, community), denied development and scope, still manifest themselves. The list goes on and on.

of experience women haven't had before," reminds Doris Lessing. "Liberty is the right not to lie," says Camus.

These pressures towards censorship, self-censorship—towards accepting, abiding by dominant attitudes, thus falsifying one's own reality, range, vision, truth, voice—are extreme for woman writers. (Indeed, they have much to do with the fear, the sense of powerlessness that pervades certain of our books; the "above all, amuse, clown, be entertaining" tone of others.) Not to be able to come to one's truth[24] or not to use it in one's writing, even when telling the truth having to "tell it slant," robs one of drive, of conviction; limits potential stature; results in loss to literature and the comprehensions we seek in it.

My time is up.

You who teach, read writers who are women. There is a whole literature to be re-estimated, re-valued. Some works will prove to be, like the lives of their human authors, mortal—speaking only to their time. Others now forgotten, obscured, ignored, will live again for us.

Read, listen to, living women writers; our new as well as our established, often neglected ones. Not to have audience is a kind of death.

Read the compass of women writers in our infinite variety. Not only those who tell us of ourselves as "the other half," but also those who write of the other human dimensions, realms.

Teach women's lives through the lives of the women who wrote the books, as well as through their books; and through autobiography, biography, journals, letters. Because most literature concerns itself with the lives of the few, know and teach the few books closer to most female lives. It should not be that Harriette Arnow's *The Dollmaker*, Elizabeth Madox Roberts's *The Time of Man*, Grace Paley's *Little Disturbances* are out of paperback print; that a Zora Neale Hurston is reprinted for the first time; that Agnes Smedley's classic *Daughter of Earth* has been out of print, unread, unknown, for forty years (a book of the greatest meaning, too, for those many students who are the first generation of their families to come into college).[25]

Be critical. Women have the right to say: This is surface, this falsifies reality, this degrades.

---

[24] Compounding the difficulty, experiences and comprehensions not previously admitted into literature—especially when at variance with the canon—are exceedingly hard to come to, validate, establish as legitimate material for literature—let alone shape for art.

[25] Now, in 1977, these are all back in print.

Help create writers, perhaps among them yourselves. There is so much unwritten that needs to be written. There are more than the other eleven, silent, who could write, bringing into literature what is not there now. That first generation in the colleges who come from my world, which in Camus's words gives "emotion without measure," are a special hope for literature. It does not matter if in its beginning it is not great, or even always good, writing.

> Whether that is literature, or whether that is not literature, I will not presume to say,

wrote Virginia Woolf in her preface to *Memoirs of the Working Women's Guild,*

> but that it explains much and tells much, that is certain.

The greatness of literature is not only in the great writers, the good writers; it is also in that which explains much and tells much; the soil from which greater writers burgeon. Hopefully, before the end of our second writing century, we will begin to have writers who are women in numbers equal to our innate capacity—at least twelve for every one woman writer able to come to recognized achievement now.[26]

Tillie Olsen

---

[26] And for every twelve, remember the countless others, silenced by the other age-old silencers of humanity, class (economic circumstance) and/or color.

About the Contributors

Pamela Daniels was born in 1937, the first child of parents who, with their country, were making their way out of the depression. Her father, born near Buffalo, New York, was commissioned as an army lieutenant to supervise a CCC camp on Long Island in the 1930s, and remained "on active duty" in the army until his retirement in 1957; he then taught high school physics for thirteen years—work that was closer to his heart. Her mother, born in Illinois, taught high school English and Latin in the Middle West until she married at the age of thirty, whereupon she devoted herself to her marriage and family, including a stint of "single parenting" in a wartime matriarchal community in California; she resumed full-time teaching in the 1950s, and taught until her death in 1960.

Formally educated in four elementary schools, one junior high school, four high schools, one college, and one graduate school, Pamela Daniels was prepared to become a college teacher. As a result of the transformations described in her essay, this career orientation was supplanted by motherhood, an unconventional apprenticeship in the psychoanalytic study of lives, an interim of professional "support work" as an editor, and lately research in the psychology of adult development. This research includes the first phase of a longitudinal study of the lives of men and women who were her students in the 1960s.

She is a research associate at the Center for Research on Women at Wellesley College, where she is currently collaborating in a field study of family and career timing patterns in three generations of adult women and their husbands living in the Boston metropolitan area. She lives with her family in Boston.

Celia Gilbert was born in 1932 in Philadelphia, Pennsylvania, the birthplace of her parents. Her mother is a wife-and-mother, her father a journalist.

She was married in 1953, and graduated from Smith College in 1954. In 1973, she received an M.A. in Creative Writing from Boston University. From 1972 to 1975, she was the poetry editor of *The Boston Phoenix*. In 1974, she won a Discovery Award for her poetry. She was a fellow at the MacDowell Colony in 1974 and 1975. She is co-editor and co-publisher of *Women/Poems*, a magazine of poetry. A collection of her poems, *Queen of Darkness*, will be published by Viking in the spring of 1977.

She lives in Cambridge, Massachusetts, with her husband, a professor of molecular biology at Harvard University, and their two children, a son, eighteen, and a daughter, sixteen.

Joann Green was born in Philadelphia in 1938. She is the only child of Dr. Louis A. Soloff, who was born in Paris while his mother was en route from Russia to meet her husband in America, and of Mathilde Robin Soloff, whose sister Clara played the role of Nell in the Camden, New Jersey, production of *He Ain't Done Right by Nell.*

Joann Green attended Friends' Select School in Philadelphia, Wellesley College, and Radcliffe College. She worked at a boarding house and then as an apprentice in summer stock during high school. At Wellesley, she became director of the student theater. After college, she married and mothered. She did volunteer political work and avoided the theater, until the women's movement and her secret longings grew too strong to ignore.

She is now the artistic director of The Cambridge Ensemble, which she helped found in Cambridge, Massachusetts. There, she has directed several American premieres, including works of Peter Handke and Gertrude Stein, and several original adaptations, among them *Gulliver's Travels.* Her production of *Tales of Chelm,* for children, is presented free in hospitals.

The Cambridge Ensemble is supported in part by grants from the National Endowment for the Arts and the Massachusetts Council on the Arts and Humanities. The theater is the recipient of the Association for Performing Arts 1975 and 1976 awards for excellence in theater.

Joann Green lives in Cambridge with her two children, Shoshanna, twelve, and Jonas, eleven.

Kay Keeshan Hamod, a historian, was born in Omaha, Nebraska, in 1936.

"My mother, a teacher, and my father, an attorney, were both born in small Nebraska towns. Mother's family—in the sense of extended family—was very much aware of its pioneer background. Our forebears had come from Norway; Great-grandmother and her siblings were the first white children born in the "Shell Creek" area in Nebraska, lived in a sod house, confronted prairie fires, traded with Indians. Even now there is a family historian, and all the descendants assemble periodically for family picnics. My father's family was primarily Irish Catholic, except that Grandpa left the church after some obscure quarrel. Grandmother was a farm wife with six children, but she wrote poetry and steered her daughters toward professional work; one of my aunts was in charge of the American press staff at the Nuremberg trials."

She was raised in a small Nebraska town and attended St. Olaf College in Northfield, Minnesota. She received a B.A. in English Literature from Northwestern University in 1958; her M.A. in Liberal Studies from Valparaiso University in Indiana in 1965; and after a period of study at Oxford, her Ph.D. in Modern European Intellectual History from the University of Iowa in 1976. Her son, David, is a freshman at the University of Iowa. Her fourteen-year-old daughter, Laura, lives with Kay.

Evelyn Fox Keller is Associate Professor of Mathematics at SUNY at Purchase. She has published numerous articles in molecular biology, theoretical physics, and mathematical biology. She is currently writing on the ways in which science is shaped by its commitment to masculinity.

The youngest of three children, she was born in 1936 to Russian-Jewish immigrant parents who, following a long tradition, had sought to make their lives in New York City. Opportunities were not plentiful in the mid- and post-depression years, and her father eked out a living in a series of never-quite-successful ventures in the world of delicatessens. He worked round the clock, with grim determination, as long as his health permitted. Her mother, sorely challenged by the difficulties of raising three children alone, remained home.

"Education provided the only visible means of progress, and all three of us children pursued success in our studies, ultimately shaping our lives around academic careers. Before their lives were out, my parents had the pleasure of seeing us all succeed, beyond both their dreams and their comprehension. Even their own lives had begun to acquire comfort, as my father's lifelong efforts began to pay off in the affluence of the fifties and early sixties.

"Once again, I live in New York, now with my children, Jeffrey and Sarah. Their father, from whom I am recently separated, lives close by."

Anne Lasoff, the oldest of three children of Russian immigrants, was born in Brooklyn in 1922 and has lived there all her life. "My father, who died in 1952, was a radical, an ardent socialist born before his time. He worked as a brick-layer; at the age of forty he was permanently disabled by an accident on the job. My mother, a practical, hard-headed woman, says she was never young, that she always had responsibility, even as a young child in Russia. In order to support the family after my father's accident, she opened a small retail store in which she worked until her reluctant retirement at the age of seventy-six."

For most of her life Anne Lasoff considered herself a typical high-school-educated, middle-class housewife and mother. Her only aspiration was to raise a happy family. She and her husband have four children ranging in age from twelve to twenty-eight.

About ten years ago, because of the family crisis she describes, she underwent a metamorphosis. She discovered a latent ability to write and a need to use it. She eventually returned to school to take writing and literature courses at the New School for Social Research in New York. Her essay, "Saturday's Mother," which discusses the impact of today's changing social mores on traditional family structure, was published in *The Indignant Years*, a collection of essays from the *New York Times*. Anne Lasoff says, "I'm both a participant and a journalist in the drama of family life."

alice atkinson lyndon was born in 1935 in Indiana to Charles and Elizabeth Hall Atkinson. Her mother has always been a housewife. Her father (son of farmers) has been principally a contractor, also a farmer, milkman, gas station owner, and real estate agent. Both have worked all their lives. "My mother's aunt wanted her to be a newspaperwoman, but my mother opted for marriage and Charles Atkinson, to my great-aunt's dismay."

alice lyndon is a product of three public schools: Eagle Township (Indiana) Schools, Indiana University, and the University of California at Berkeley. She also studied sculpture and architectural history in France and Denmark. She has taught at the University of California at Berkeley, the University of Oregon, and Wellesley College. She has traveled and learned a good deal outside of schools, and considers herself basically self-taught in sculpture and photography.

"My life today includes a lot of sculpture, an increasing number of negatives, one husband, Donlyn, three children, Andrew, Audrey, and Laura-Kate, studio and darkroom at home in a house in Newton, Massachusetts, one guitar, and a present passion for paper making and Kodalith high-contrast prints."

Nanette Vonnegut Mengel teaches English at the University of North Carolina and re-evaluation counseling, or peer co-counseling, in the larger community in Chapel Hill. Her main professional interest is in writing as inter- and intra-personal relationship—the relationships between a text, its author, and its reader, and the uses of writing for self-discovery. She is currently teaching composition to students in the Evening College, literature to residents in the Department of Psychiatry, and writing to graduate students of public administration.

The younger of two children, she was born in 1934 and grew up in Knoxville, Tennessee, where her father had moved from Louisville, as a young man, to manufacture foreign and domestic veneers. Her mother took care of the family in a town that, especially during the depression, seemed very far away from the large, close network of relatives in which she had grown up in Indianapolis and Louisville.

"Three years in boarding school in Chatham, Virginia, were the warm beginning of independence and pointed the way north to Vassar and the inevitable confrontation with serious questions about work, questions which also set this essay in motion."

Nanette Mengel lives in her own house in Chapel Hill.

Diana Michener was born in 1940 in Boston, Massachusetts. From the age of four she lived in Ross, California. Her father was a lawyer, her mother an active participant in Democratic politics.

She was educated in fine arts at Barnard and, at the same time, took courses in painting and sculpture. She became fascinated by photography four years ago and has published a photographic essay in *Ms.* Magazine. She lives in New York with her husband, Charles Michener, and her two daughters, Natalie and Nancy Geary.

Tillie Olsen was born in Nebraska in 1913 to political refugees from the Czarist repression of 1905. Her origin, identification, and life are primarily working-class. Her father was a farmer, packing-house worker, house painter, and jack-of-all-trades. Her mother was a needle-trades and factory worker; later, she laundered, sewed, took care of children for others—did what women who have to stay home with children do when it is necessary to bring in money.

A depression high school dropout, Tillie Olsen has lived most of her life in San Francisco, where she raised four daughters and worked on everyday paid jobs—in earlier years, in service and factory work; in the fifties, in offices, mostly as a transcriber. "My great colleges were the worlds of work, mother-hood, struggle, and literature." For many years she was unable to write: "The simplest circumstances for creation did not exist." She began to try to write again in her mid-forties when her youngest child entered school.

Tillie Olsen is the author of *Tell Me A Riddle*, the title story of which won the O. Henry Award for the best story of 1961; *Yonnondio: From The Thirties*; a long afterword for Rebecca Harding Davis's *Life in the Iron Mills*; and *Requa*. She has won numerous awards for her writing. She writes, "The real awards and true honors were not from foundations or institutions—except for the fellowship from the Radcliffe Institute. There, for the first time in my adult life I had thinking, reading-freely time—true circumstance—and the company of women able to, enabled to, come to intellectual and artistic flowering."

She has taught at Amherst College, Stanford University, MIT, and the University of Massachusetts (Boston). She is a long-time feminist and activist.

Adrienne Rich was born in Baltimore in 1929. "My mother had trained from an early age as a concert pianist and a composer; she gave up her professional career at the behest of my father, a research pathologist, finally professor of pathology at Johns Hopkins Medical School. My childhood heroines were the Brontë sisters, Emily Dickinson, Elizabeth Barrett. As a student at Radcliffe College, however, I rarely heard of a woman writer, let alone a woman scientist, mystic, or activist. I married in full flight from the conflict and confusion of being a woman artist (my first book of poems had been published when I was twenty-one). I had three children in four years, finally left the marriage, found myself a head of household upon my husband's subsequent death. Beginning with involvement in the SEEK program at City College, where I began to understand and analyze the political power concealed in language, and with the antiwar movement, which I entered more as a mother than as an artist or intellectual, I became radicalized into feminism, though I had been reading Wollstonecraft, Mill, and de Beauvoir in the mid-fifties. I am a lesbian/feminist/socialist; I am currently teaching at Douglass College and I live in New York City."

Amelie Oksenberg Rorty was born in 1932 in Belgium of Polish parents. She is now Professor of Philosophy at Livingston College, Rutgers University. General editor of the Anchor *Modern Studies in Philosophy*, she has also edited a book on pragmatic philosophy and an anthology of papers on personal identity. *The Identities of Persons*. She contributes to philosophical journals, occasionally publishes poetry, and is an active participant in the American Philosophical Association. Interested in educational policy, she was on the committee that originated and planned the program and curriculum for Livingston College, from the time when it was just a gleam in a dean's eye until it rose in cinderblock and mortar and opened in 1969. She is currently working on a book, *From Self-Interest to the General Will: Moral Psychology From Hobbes to Rousseau.*

Sara Ruddick was born in Toledo, Ohio, in 1935. Her mother, born in 1908, took primary responsibility for the home, three children, and the extended family, and engaged in ever more responsible and time-consuming volunteer work in the community; when her children were older, she attended various classes, for example in painting, ancient Greek, Biblical studies, and Shakespeare. Her father, born in 1907, rejected an apparently promising future as a professional golfer in order to study law. He worked long hours at work he was said to "love," and eventually came to head the law firm he had entered as a young man.

"My parents took an active interest in my education. When I was young, they paid for schools they could not easily afford. Some twenty years later, they continued to finance, with no strings attached, an education that aggravated political and philosophical differences between us. Only since I have been a parent have I appreciated their support and restraint."

Sara Ruddick teaches philosophy, literature, and biography at the New School for Social Research. She lives in Manhattan with her husband, William Ruddick, and their two children, Hal and Lizza.

Miriam Schapiro was born in 1923, the only child of parents who were hopeful and ambitious for her. Her father, an artist and industrial designer, directed the Rand School of Social Science and was a frequent candidate for office on the Socialist party ticket. Her mother never worked outside the home until the depression, when, in her forties, she took a job in a department store.

Miriam Schapiro grew up in New York and was educated at the University of Iowa. She has shown her work in group exhibitions all over the world. Her recent one-woman shows have taken place in the A.R.C. Gallery in Chicago, where she exchanged her work for service and goods rather than money, and in California, where her retrospective exhibition, entitled "The Shrine, The Computer, and the Dollhouse," was shown in several galleries. Her ninth solo exhibition at the Andre Emmerich Gallery in New York took place September 1976. Her work is owned by the Museum of Modern Art and the Whitney Museum in New York City, by the Hirshhorn Museum in Washington, D.C., and by many other institutions.

As a teacher, she collaborated with her students on two books presenting the biographies, art, and critical writings of living women artists: *Anonymous Was a Woman* (1974), and *Art: A Woman's Sensibility* (1974). She lives and works in the Soho district of New York City. "My work has flourished in a domestic atmosphere. The love of my husband, an artist, of my twenty-one-year-old son, a poet and writer, and the continued support of my parents sustain me. Without these people, I feel lost. I do not cultivate loss, I cultivate connections. Where there are connections—preferably connections of love—there is strength for work."

Cynthia Lovelace Sears, a writer, was born in Los Angeles, California, in 1937. "My birth took place on the coldest day in L.A.'s recorded history, and I have been looking for a place in the sun ever since." Her father, born in Brewton, Alabama, is now retired from the investment management firm he founded; her mother, from Charlevoix, Michigan, is what used to be referred to as "just a housewife."

Cynthia Sears graduated in 1959 from Bryn Mawr College, where she majored in English literature and minored in Latin. After college she taught for two years at a private elementary school in New York City, then moved back to California, and was married to a faculty member at UCLA until they separated in 1970. She now resides in West Los Angeles. "My household includes my two daughters, Juliet (age thirteen) and Olivia (age eleven), a Welsh pony (stabled at a neighbor's house), a dwarf bunny, five cats, and four guinea pigs."

May Stevens, a painter, was born in Boston, Massachusetts, in 1924, the daughter of Alice Dick (born in 1895 in New Brunswick, Canada, of Irish Catholic parents) and Ralph Stevens (1897–1968, born in Boston of Yankee stock).

She grew up in Quincy, Massachusetts, and studied art in Boston, New York, and Paris.

Her exhibitions include: "Recent Acquisitions," Whitney Museum of American Art, 1970; "American Woman Artist Show," Kunsthaus, Hamburg, 1972; "May Stevens," Herbert F. Johnson Museum, Cornell University, 1973; "Selections *Big Daddy 1967–75*," Lerner-Heller Gallery, New York City, 1975; "Three American Realists: Alice Neel, Sylvia Sleigh, May Stevens," Everson Museum, Syracuse, 1976.

Catharine R. Stimpson was born in 1936 in Bellingham, Washington. Her father, who is dead, was a general practitioner; her mother, who is "still very much alive," was a housewife engaged in lots of civic activities.

Catharine Stimpson was educated at Bryn Mawr, Cambridge, and Columbia. A writer of fiction and nonfiction, she teaches at Barnard College and is the editor of *Signs: Journal of Women in Culture and Society*. She formally resides in New York City.

Naomi Thornton was born in York, Maine, in 1935. Her father was an attorney, practicing mostly in Boston but also throughout the state of Maine, even as far north as Houlton, where he was born and where he maintained a small interest in timber. Her mother, born in Dayton, Ohio, was a housewife with five children. She lived to be forty.

Naomi Thornton was formally educated at Bryn Mawr College in philosophy and at Paul Mann Actors Workshop in theater, and less formally by a dozen or more private teachers and workshops and by her colleagues. She is an actress by profession as well as professionally—that is, she belongs to a number of unions. In 1963, she founded and was the producer for the Theatre Company of Boston.

She is married and has two children. As well as acting full time in everything from street theater to movies she teaches at the YWCA and MIT.

Virginia Valian was born in Detroit in 1942. Her parents both worked: one of her earliest daily memories is of her father arriving home first and making the salad for dinner. Her mother is now an executive secretary and her father a successful businessman.

Virginia Valian is Assistant Professor of Psychology at the Graduate Center of the City University of New York. Her professional interests are in psycholinguistics and cognitive psychology.

Alice Walker was born in Georgia in 1944. She attended Spelman and Sarah Lawrence colleges, and has lived and worked in Mississippi, New England, and New York. She has published two collections of poems, *Once* and *Revolutionary Petunias*, the latter nominated for a National Book Award in 1973, as well as a biography, *Langston Hughes, American Poet*; two novels, *The Third Life of Grange Copeland* and *Meridian*; and a collection of short stories, *In Love and Trouble*.

Alice Walker's father was born in Georgia and most of his life worked on farms. In her essay, she writes about her mother, Minnie Tallulah Walker, who was born in 1912, one of twelve children. Minnie Walker married at seventeen and by her thirty-second birthday had eight children. "During the 'working' day, she labored beside—not behind"—her husband on the farms. She also worked in her church and taught Sunday school. "My mother never lost faith. No matter how desolate things looked, she never lost her belief that they would turn out right if *you* were right. Her faith was not in "the future," but in her children and in her way of raising them. Because she had faith in herself and in us she was quite willing to let us go our surprising and diverse ways. As I remember it, we were really not allowed to be discouraged. Discouragement couldn't hold out against her faith."

Alice Walker lives in New York with her daughter; Minnie Walker, of whom she writes, lives in Eatonton, Georgia.

Naomi Weisstein, Professor of Psychology at SUNY at Buffalo, does research in vision, perception, and cognition. Her work has been published in *Science, Journal of the Optical Society of America, Journal of Experimental Psychology, Psychological Review*, and other scientific journals. She is a consulting editor for *Journal of Experimental Psychology* and *Cognitive Psychology*. During the 1960s she was active in CORE (1963) and formed women's caucuses in SDS (1966) and the New University Conference (1968). In the early women's liberation movement she participated in the Chicago West Side Group (1967) and was a founding member of the Chicago Women's Liberation Union (1968). She has been active in building and defining an insurgent feminist culture, as organizer and pianist for the Chicago Women's Liberation Rock Band (1970–73), writer and critic (her article "Psychology Constructs the Female" has been widely reprinted), and currently, as feminist comedienne.

Passionate anti-authoritarianism is a family tradition. Her mother, Mary Menk Weisstein, a former concert pianist and now a psychoanalyst, got it from *her* mother, who thought that Grandpa, a carpenter and socialist, was much too far to the right. Her father, Samuel Weisstein, is a lawyer. Naomi was born October 16, 1939, in New York City. She is married to Jesse Lemisch, a historian.

Marilyn Young was born in 1937 in Brooklyn, New York. Her father, born in 1915 on the Lower East Side of New York, was a postal clerk until his retirement three years ago. Her mother, born in 1917 in New Haven, Connecticut, is a school secretary at Canarsie High School in Brooklyn.

Marilyn Young is Associate Professor of History at Residential College, the University of Michigan. She is the author of *The Rhetoric of Empire*, as well as numerous reviews and articles, and editor of *Women in China: Studies in Social Change and Feminism*. She has two children, Lauren, age thirteen, and Michael Jacob, age eleven.

Connie Young Yu was born in 1941 in Los Angeles, and grew up in San Francisco. Her mother was born in San Francisco, her father in San Jose, California. Her father received a B.A. and M.A. in engineering at Stanford University; he is a soy sauce manufacturer in San Francisco. Her mother is a house spouse with the hobbies of Chinese brush painting and tai chi.

Connie Young Yu is married to Dr. Kouping Yu, an internist and cancer specialist. They live with their three children, Jennifer, Jessica, and Martin, in California. She has recently compiled and edited *The People's Bicentennial Quilt: A Patchwork History*, published in 1976 by UP Press in California.